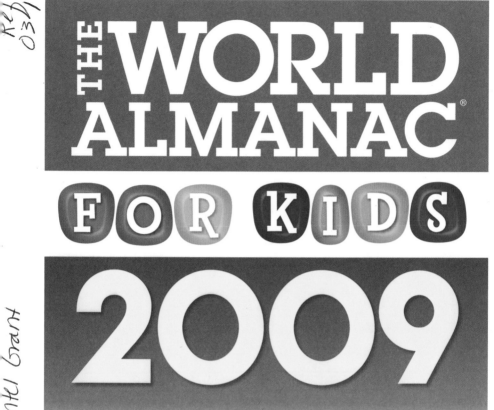

THE WORLD ALMANAC
ALMANAC
FOR KIDS
2009

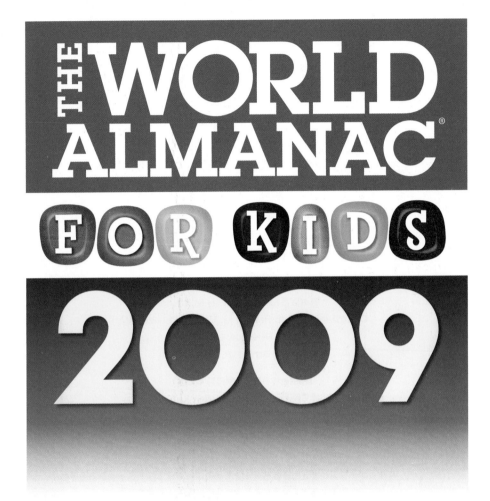

THE WORLD ALMANAC

FOR KIDS

2009

WORLD ALMANAC FOR KIDS
Published by World Almanac Education Group, Inc.
A Weekly Reader Company

THE WORLD ALMANAC
ALMANAC®
FOR KIDS
2009

Managing Editor: Phyllis Rosner
Contributors: Ann Petroni McMullen, Rebecca Motil
Creative Director: Lisa Donovan
Editorial Director: Keith Garton

Design: BILL SMITH GROUP
Chief Creative Officer: Brian Kobberger
Project Director: David Borkman, Shaunna Coon
Design: Ron Leighton, Jennifer Basilio, Tamara English
Photo: Scott B. Rosen, Timothy Herzog
Production: Eric Murray, Kevin English, Bob Horvath

WORLD ALMANAC EDUCATION GROUP
A Weekly Reader Company

President: Neal Goff
Publisher: Paul Gullickson

The World Almanac For Kids 2009
Copyright © 2009 by World Almanac Education Group, Inc.
The World Almanac and The World Almanac for Kids are registered trademarks of World Almanac
Education Group, Inc. Distributed by World Almanac Education, 1-800-321-1147.

Hardcover ISBN: 978-1-60057-102-2
Smyth-sewn ISBN: 978-1-60057-110-7

Printed in the United States of America

WORLD ALMANAC FOR KIDS
Published by Weekly Reader Corporation
1 Reader's Digest Road
Pleasantville, NY 10570

CONTENTS

ELECTION

How old do you have to be to vote? ➡ page 17

Meet the Winners!

After a wild and crazy primary season and then long, rough days on the campaign trail — we finally had a winner! Barack Obama will become the 44th President of the United States on January 20, 2009. His Vice President is Joe Biden.

President Barack Obama

Barack Obama attended Columbia University. He became a community organizer for a Chicago church, helping poor South Side residents cope with a wave of unemployment. He then attended Harvard Law School, and in 1990 became the first African-American editor of the Harvard Law Review. After graduating and passing the bar, he chose to practice civil-rights law back in Chicago. He represented victims of housing and employment discrimination and worked on voting-rights legislation. In 2004, Obama was elected to the U.S. Senate as a Democrat, representing Illinois, and gained national attention by giving a rousing and well-received keynote speech at the Democratic National Convention in Boston.

He and his wife, Michelle, have two children.

Vice President Joe Biden

Joe Biden was born in 1942, in Scranton, Pennsylvania. He is a lawyer by profession. However since 1972, his main job has been representing the state of Delaware in the U.S. Senate. As a senator, he served on the Committee on the Judiciary, and for three decades, on the Foreign Relations Committee becoming its chairman in 2007.

He and his wife, Jill, have three children.

What Does the President Do?

According to the U.S. Constitution, the president is the chief executive, or head, of the executive branch of the government. The president has a role in all parts of government. Following are some of the president's jobs:

★ Suggest laws to Congress;

★ Send Congress a budget which recommends how the government should raise and spend money;

★ Approve or veto (reject) bills passed by Congress;

★ Is commander-in-chief of the U.S. armed forces;

★ Make treaties, or agreements, with other countries;

★ Appoint justices to the Supreme Court and judges to other federal courts.

The president must share power with the other two branches of government. They are the legislative branch, or Congress, and the judicial branch, headed by the U.S. Supreme Court.

The U.S. Constitution tells how each of the three branches of government checks, or limits, the powers of the other two. This system of checks and balances is intended to prevent any branch from becoming too powerful.

★ ★ ★ ★ ★

What Does the Vice President Do?

John Adams, the first vice president, found the job very frustrating. He described it as "the most insignificant office that ever the invention of man contrived or his imagination conceived." But the vice president is just a heartbeat away from the presidency.

According to our Constitution, the vice president has two major duties. First, the vice president must be ready to become president if the president dies, resigns, or is removed from office. Second, the vice president presides over the Senate and casts the deciding vote in case of a tie.

Popular and Electoral Votes*

	John McCain		Barack Obama	
	Popular Votes	Electoral Votes	Popular Votes	Electoral Votes
Alabama	1,264,879	9	811,764	
Alaska	136,348	3	80,340	
Arizona	1,118,312	10	937,400	
Arkansas	632,672	6	418,049	
California	4,075,470		6,679,106	55
Colorado	1,020,135		1,216,793	9
Connecticut	614,584		973,302	7
Delaware	152,356		255,394	3
District of Columbia	14,821		210,403	3
Florida	3,939,380		4,143,957	27
Georgia	2,044,870	15	1,838,281	
Hawaii	110,848		298,621	4
Idaho	400,989	4	235,219	
Illinois	1,975,801		3,293,340	21
Indiana	1,341,667		1,367,503	11
Iowa	677,508		818,240	7
Kansas	685,541	6	499,979	
Kentucky	1,050,599	8	751,515	
Louisiana	1,147,603	9	780,981	
Maine	296,195	1	421,484	3
Maryland	899,372		1,481,303	10
Massachusetts	1,104,284		1,891,083	12
Michigan	2,044,405		2,867,680	17
Minnesota	1,275,399		1,573,322	10
Mississippi	687,266	6	520,864	
Missouri	1,442,673	11	1,436,814	

* Popular and Electoral vote counts are as of 11/10/08

	John McCain		Barack Obama	
	Popular Votes	Electoral Votes	Popular Votes	Electoral Votes
Montana	241,816	3	229,725	
Nebraska	446,039	4	324,352	1
Nevada	411,988		531,884	5
New Hampshire	316,937		384,591	4
New Jersey	1,545,495		2,085,051	15
New Mexico	343,768		464,322	5
New York	2,576,360		4,363,386	31
North Carolina	2,109,402		2,123,395	15
North Dakota	168,523	3	141,113	
Ohio	2,502,218		2,708,988	20
Oklahoma	959,645	7	502,286	
Oregon	699,673		978,605	7
Pennsylvania	2,586,496		3,192,316	21
Rhode Island	157,317		281,209	4
South Carolina	1,034,500	8	862,042	
South Dakota	203,019	3	170,886	
Tennessee	1,487,564	11	1,093,213	
Texas	4,467,748	34	3,521,164	
Utah	555,497	5	301,771	
Vermont	96,458		203,952	3
Virginia	1,726,053		1,958,370	13
Washington	1,097,176		1,534,632	11
West Virginia	394,278	5	301,438	
Wisconsin	1,258,181		1,670,474	10
Wyoming	160,639	3	80,496	
TOTALS	**57,700,767**	**174**	**65,812,398**	**364**

How Candidates are Chosen

Democratic candidates for president held their first debate in April 2007.

The contest for the presidency of the United States starts much earlier than the summer or fall of an election year. Some candidates for president announce their intention to run a year or more before Election Day. Candidates in each of the major political parties – the Democratic Party and the Republican Party – face one another in a series of primaries and caucuses. A primary gives a state's voters a chance to help choose their party's candidate. In a caucus, party members and leaders meet in small groups to vote for a candidate.

The primary season begins in January of the election year and ends in June. During that time, every state holds either a primary or a caucus. Some hold both! In 2008 the first caucus, traditionally held in Iowa, took place on January 3. The first primary, always held in New Hampshire, was on January 8.

All the candidates took part in many television debates. They traveled from state to state to campaign. Most of the candidates began to drop out of the race early in 2008 because they had done poorly in the primaries and caucuses. Lack of money made it hard for those candidates to continue running.

By March, John McCain had won enough votes to be certain that he would become the Republican **nominee**, or official candidate. The race between Democrats Hillary Clinton and Barack Obama was very tight. But by early June, Obama had enough votes to win the Democratic nomination.

The nominees of the Democratic and Republican parties are officially chosen at each party's **national convention**. The people who vote at conventions are called **delegates**.

The candidates of the Democratic and Republican parties are not the only ones running for president. Several so-called third parties also have presidential candidates. Third-party candidates usually suggest different solutions to problems than the Republican and Democratic party candidates.

Republican presidential candidates held their first debate in May 2007.

Who Can Be President?

The qualifications for being president are set by the U.S. Constitution. To become president a person must:
▶ be a native-born citizen of the United States
▶ be at least 35 years old, and
▶ have been a resident of the United States for at least 14 years.

The Road to the White House

Pennsylvania Avenue may look flat, but the road candidates take to the White House is anything but smooth! Presidential hopefuls campaign for up to two years, facing off in debates and meeting with voters. Here's a look at key steps in the process.

January–June 2008

1

Primaries/Caucuses
Candidates in a party compete in **primaries** and **caucuses**. In a typical primary, party members cast ballots for a candidate. In a typical caucus, party members and leaders meet to choose a candidate. For each state a candidate wins, he or she secures **delegates**, or representatives.

Aug. 25–28 (Democrats) Sept. 1–4 (Republicans)

2

Nominating Conventions
Delegates vote on a party **platform**, which says how the party wants to solve the nation's problems. Then delegates select the official presidential and vice presidential nominees. Delegates tend to vote based on their states' primary or caucus results.

3

Election Day
Election Day is the first Tuesday after the first Monday in November. Every four years on that day, Americans head to the polls to vote for the next president. Voters don't choose the president directly. Their votes go toward **electors**, special delegates who make up the Electoral College.

Nov. 4, 2008

4

Electoral College Vote
The Electoral College is made up of electors from every state. The candidate who wins the most votes in a state on Election Day almost always receives that state's electoral votes. A candidate must win at least 270 electoral votes to become the president.

Dec. 15, 2008

5

Congress Declares Winner
Members of Congress officially count the electoral votes. The president of the Senate, a position held by the vice president, announces the results.

Jan. 6, 2009

6

Inauguration Day
The new president takes the oath of office and gives an inaugural address outlining his or her goals. Later, the president celebrates at festive parties called **inaugural balls** in Washington, D.C.

Jan. 20, 2009

NATIONAL CONVENTIONS

Presidential candidates are officially chosen at each political party's national convention. From the beginning, Republican and Democratic conventions have been colorful and noisy. Although a convention may seem like a party, it is an important event. It is attended by delegates from every state, Washington, D.C., and U.S. territories.

One of the first jobs of the delegates is to meet and discuss their party's platform. The **platform** says what the party wants to do about issues facing the nation. The parts of the platform are called its planks. The platform committee meets ahead of time and writes a series of planks. Then the delegates vote on each plank.

Next comes the nominating process. Through most of their history, the conventions were truly contests. No one knew for sure who would win the nominations for president and vice president. In recent years, though, conventions have declined in importance. One candidate usually has gone to each party's convention with enough delegates from primaries and caucuses to be the agreed–upon nominee.

Even if the outcome is known, the conventions still follow the same process. Party leaders make a nominating speech and several seconding speeches for each

candidate. Then the delegates vote. The convention secretary calls the name of each state in alphabetical order. The head of the state delegation announces the breakdown of votes from that state. The nominee who gets the required number of votes becomes the party's official presidential candidate. The newly nominated presidential candidate then chooses the candidate for vice president. This person must also be voted on by the delegates.

On the last two days of the convention, the nominees for president and vice president make their acceptance speeches. They tell the party—and the nation—what to expect during the campaign and what to expect if they are elected. The goal of acceptance speeches is to try to get voters excited about the nominees' ideas for running the country. After the convention, party members who supported different candidates usually work together to help their party's nominee win the presidential election.

Democratic Convention

The high-profile Democratic National Convention took place in Denver, Colorado at the Pepsi Center from August 25-28, 2008. This is 100 years after the city hosted its first and only other national party convention. On August 28, the convention moved to INVESCO Field at Mile High Stadium so that more Americans could be a part of the fourth night of the convention as Barack Obama accepted the Democratic nomination. It was estimated that more than 75,000 were at INVESCO Field to hear Obama's acceptance speech.

More than 35,000 delegates, journalists, volunteers and others visited the city as part of the convention. Business leaders estimated the potential economic impact on the city of Denver and the state of Colorado to be more than $160 million.

ON THE ISSUES

War in Iraq

- Opposes the war in Iraq.
- Wants a timeline for the withdrawal of U.S. troops from Iraq.
- Supports a major diplomatic effort with Iraq and its neighbors to bring about stability in Iraq and the Middle East.
- Believes the United States has a responsibility to provide financial aid for the reconstruction of Iraq and to improve the lives of its people.

Immigration

- Wants to protect the security of American borders.
- Believes the United States must fix its broken immigration system and increase the number of legal immigrants to keep families together and meet the demand for jobs that employers cannot fill.
- Supports a system that allows undocumented immigrants, who are in good standing, pay a fine, learn English, and go to the back of the line for the opportunity to become citizens.

Health Care

- Wants to make health insurance available to all Americans by eliminating tax cuts for the wealthy to pay for it.
- Believes that all employers, except for small businesses, should be required to provide health insurance for workers or contribute to the cost of health insurance.
- Wants to provide subsidies for low-income people to purchase health insurance.

Economy

- Supports a tax cut for working families.
- Wants a trade policy that opens up foreign markets to provide good American jobs at home.
- Wants to ensure that homebuyers have complete and honest information about their mortgage choices.

13

Republican Convention

The Republican National Convention was held from September 1 through 4 at the Xcel Energy Center located in downtown Saint Paul, Minnesota. However, the Republicans actually lost one whole evening of their convention when Monday, September 1 was cancelled because of the threat of hurricane Gustav on the Gulf of Mexico coast.

ON THE ISSUES

War in Iraq

- Supports the war in Iraq.
- Believes U.S. troops must remain in Iraq as long as it takes to establish a stable and secure democratic nation.
- Supports speeding up training and equipping of the Iraqi armed forces and police so they can play a larger role in making Iraq safe for its people.
- Wants other countries to apply pressure to Iran and Syria to end their interference in Iraq.

Immigration

- Believes that a secure border is an essential part of national security.
- Supports building strong, allies in Mexico and Latin America that will provide economic opportunities for their citizens.
- Believes the U.S. education system must provide skilled American workers and provide retraining programs for workers who lose their jobs.

Economy

- Supports making the Bush tax cuts permanent.
- Opposes raising taxes on small businesses.
- Wants to reduce government spending.

Health Care

- Believes that bringing costs under control is the only way to stop the rising costs of health insurance.
- Wants to lower costs by encouraging insurance company competition.
- Believes the tax code should be reformed to provide all individuals and families with refundable tax credits for health insurance.

Who Can Vote?

Voting rules vary from state to state. However, rules in each state must agree with the Constitution, its amendments, and federal laws. States allow voters who must be away or who are serving in the military on Election Day to vote by mail using an absentee ballot. A growing number of states allow anyone to vote before Election Day.

Some states require voters to have an I.D. that was issued by the state, such as a driver's license. In some states, people convicted of a felony lose the right to vote for the rest of their lives.

These are the qualifications for voting in the United States:

- ☑ U.S. citizenship
- ☑ At least 18 years old
- ☑ Registration: citizens must register, or sign up, before voting *(required except in North Dakota)*

Who Does Vote?

Everyone has heard the statement, "Every vote counts." Well, it's true. A remarkably small number of votes can be the margin between victory and defeat. In 2000, for example, George W. Bush defeated Al Gore in Florida by only 537 votes and became president!

The hard fought 2008 primaries, especially for the Democrats, had some of the highest voter turnouts in history. Many people believe that the percentage of voters registered to vote on Election Day 2008 may be the highest ever.

About the Electoral College

What is the Electoral College?

It's a group called electors who meet in December in their state capitals to vote for president.

But I thought Election Day was on November 4?

It is, but on Election Day, voters aren't directly voting for president. Instead, they vote for a group of presidential electors who have pledged to support whichever candidate wins that state's popular vote.

What's the total number of electoral votes?

There are 538 total votes. A presidential candidate must win at least 270 of those.

What if there's a tie?

Then the election is in the hands of the U.S. House of Representatives. That's what happened in 1800, when Thomas Jefferson and Aaron Burr each received 73 electoral votes. Because there were fewer states and Congress was smaller then, there weren't as many electoral votes. The House voted to make Jefferson president.

Electoral College MAP

WA 11
MT 3
ND 3
MN 10
ME 4
VT 3
NH 4
OR 7
ID 4
WY 3
SD 3
WI 10
MI 17
NY 31
MA 12
RI 4
CT 7
NV 5
UT 5
CO 9
NE 5
IA 7
IL 21
IN 11
OH 20
PA 21
NJ 15
DE 3
MD 10
DC 3
CA 55
AZ 10
NM 5
KS 6
MO 11
KY 8
WV 5
VA 13
NC 15
OK 7
AR 6
TN 11
SC 8
HI 4
TX 34
LA 9
MS 6
AL 9
GA 15
FL 27
AK 3

KEY
3–9 VOTES   10–19 VOTES   20 or more VOTES

Source: Federal Election Commission

Elections

▶ George Washington was the only president to win every single electoral vote cast for president. James Monroe was one vote short of winning them all in 1820.

▶ In 1912, Theodore Roosevelt was shot in the chest by a would-be assassin right before he gave a campaign speech. He survived the bullet, but lost the election.

▶ The *Chicago Tribune* printed in its Nov. 4, 1948, morning edition that Thomas Dewey had defeated President Harry Truman. Early returns showed Dewey in the lead, but when all the votes were counted, Truman won. The newspaper was printed with the incorrect headline, "Dewey Defeats Truman." Today, original copies of that edition are collectors' items.

▶ In the 2000 election, Al Gore won the popular vote by about 500,000 votes, but lost the election by 5 electoral votes to George W. Bush.

2008 Election
- Won by McCain
- Won by Obama

The **Electoral College** *State by State*

This map shows the Electoral College votes that candidates Barack Obama and John McCain received in the 2008 election. The Electoral College is not really a college, but a group of people chosen in each state who in turn vote for president. The writers of the Constitution did not agree on how a president should be selected. Some did not trust ordinary people to make a good choice. So they compromised and agreed to have the Electoral College do it.

The number of electors for each state is equal to the number of senators (2), plus the U.S. House members each state has in Congress. In addition, the District of Columbia has 3 electoral votes. When a citizen votes for a candidate of a particular party, they are actually choosing electors from that party. These electors have agreed to vote for their party's candidate, and except in very rare cases this is what they do.

The electors chosen in November meet in state capitals in December. In almost all states, the party that gets the most votes in November wins ALL the electoral votes for the state. In January, the electors' votes are officially opened during a special session of Congress. If no presidential candidate wins a majority of these votes, the House of Representatives chooses the president. This happened in 1800, 1824, and 1877.

Can a candidate who didn't win the most popular votes still win a majority of electoral votes? Yes. That's what happened in 1876, 1888, and again in 2000, when George W. Bush was elected to a first term.

★★ Inauguration ★★
Scramble Speech

Scrambled Speech

"I do _____ swear (or affirm) that
    lmnloyse

I will faithfully _____ the Office
    teuceex

of _____ of the United States,
    snetpidre

and will to the best of my _____,
    iyliatb

_____, protect and _____
pevreers   *nedfed*

the Constitution of the United States."

Word Bank

ability *(noun):* skill or power

defend *(verb):* to guard or stand up for

execute *(verb):* to carry out or perform

preserve *(verb):* to care for or maintain

president *(noun):* chief elected official of a republic

solemnly *(adverb):* thoughtfully or seriously

★ ★ ★

After taking the oath, the new president gives an inaugural address. The speech explains how the president plans to solve the country's problems.

★ ★ ★

Trivia About Inaugurations

1793 ▶ George Washington's was the shortest inaugural address at 135 words.

1801 ▶ Thomas Jefferson was the only president to walk to and from his inaugural. He was also the first to be inaugurated at the Capitol.

1809 ▶ The first inaugural ball was held for James Madison.

1825 ▶ John Quincy Adams was the first president sworn in wearing long trousers.

1841 ▶ William H. Harrison's was the longest inaugural address at 8,445 words. Despite a snowstorm, Harrison did not wear an overcoat, hat, or gloves during his nearly two-hour Inaugural Address. He died of pneumonia one month later.

1857 ▶ The first inauguration to be photographed was James Buchanan's.

1865 ▶ Abraham Lincoln was the first to include African-Americans in his parade.

1897 ▶ William McKinley's inauguration was the first ceremony to be recorded by a motion picture camera.

1909 ▶ William Taft's wife was the first one to accompany her husband in the procession from the Capitol to the White House.

1917 ▶ Women were included for the first time in Woodrow Wilson's second inaugural parade.

1921 ▶ Warren G. Harding was the first president to ride to and from his inaugural in an automobile.

1925 ▶ Calvin Coolidge's oath was the first inaugural address broadcast on the radio.

1949 ▶ Harry Truman's was the first to be televised.

1963 ▶ Lyndon Johnson was the first (and so far) only president to be sworn in by a woman, U.S. District Judge Sarah T. Hughes.

1977 ▶ Jimmy Carter's inaugural parade featured solar heat for the reviewing stand and handicap-accessible viewing.

1985 ▶ Ronald Reagan's second inaugural had to compete with Super Bowl Sunday.

1997 ▶ The first ceremony broadcast on the Internet was Bill Clinton's second inauguration.

TELEVISION

WIZARDLY WONDER

Actress Selena Gomez played Alex Russo, a teenager from Manhattan struggling with the magical powers of her wizardly heritage, in the sitcom *Wizards of Waverly Place*.

GIRL'S BLOG

Serena (Blake Lively), Nate (Chace Crawford), and friends returned for a second season of love, loss, and drama in *Gossip Girl*.

FAMILY FOLLIES

Family Guy Peter Griffin did his best to take care of his wacky family as the show headed into its seventh season.

FAMILY GUY

PATRIOT ALE

PAIR OF STARS

Figure skater Kristi Yamaguchi choreographed a victory with Mark Ballas to claim the mirror-ball trophy on *Dancing With the Stars*.

ROLE MODEL

Supermodel Tyra Banks searched for *America's Next Top Model* while also chatting with guests on *The Tyra Banks Show*.

21

MOVIES

LAST MAN STANDING

In *I Am Legend*, scientist Robert Neville (Will Smith) tried to reverse the effects of a terrible plague using his own immune blood.

THE ADVENTURE CONTINUES

In *The Chronicles of Narnia: Prince Caspian*, the Pevensie siblings headed back to the magical land of Narnia to aid the rightful heir to the throne.

MOVIES

DANCING IN THE STREETS

In *Step Up 2: The Streets*, two dance students from different backgrounds found romance—and displayed some incredible street dancing.

DYNAMIC DUO

Shia LaBoeuf teamed up with everyone's favorite archeologist in *Indiana Jones and the Kingdom of the Crystal Skull.*

SUPER SLAPSTICK

After being bitten by a radioactive dragonfly, Drake Bell developed super powers in the slapstick comedy *Superhero Movie.*

TAXI FARE

MUSIC

HAPPY HANNAH

Miley Cyrus landed her second No. 1 album on the Billboard 200 with *Breakout* selling 371,000 copies in the first week.

PLATINUM BLONDE

Taylor Swift's debut album went triple platinum, selling more than 3 million copies.

BURNIN' UP

The Jonas Brothers — Kevin, Joe, and Nick — burned up the charts with hit singles from their second album.

FOREVER CHRIS

At the end of 2007, R&B vocalist Chris Brown released his second album *Exclusive*, which featured a No. 1 pop single.

SPORTS

ELI GETS HIS RING

Superbowl MVP quarterback Eli Manning led the New York Giants to a 17-14 upset over the New England Patriots in Super Bowl XLII, just one year after big brother Peyton led his own team to a Superbowl win.

PHE-NOMINAL

Michael Phelps won a record-breaking eight gold medals at the 2008 Summer Olympics in Beijing.

GRAND SLAMMING AWAY

Swiss tennis star Roger Federer is the only active tennis player with 12 career Grand Slam singles championships. At the 2008 Summer Olympics, Federer won the Men's Doubles gold medal for Switzerland, partnered by Stanislas Wawrinka.

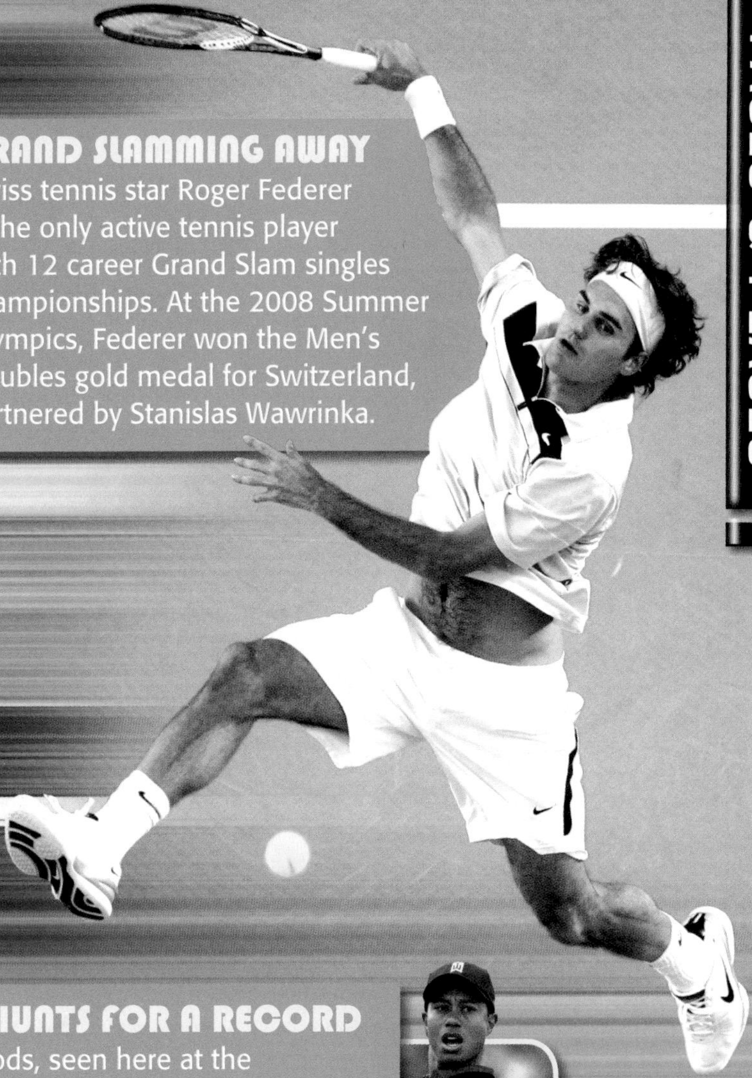

TIGER HUNTS FOR A RECORD

Tiger Woods, seen here at the Buick Invitational, has won 14 career "majors," second only to Jack Nicklaus's record of 18 wins.

SPORTS

MOST VALUABLE LAKER

Lakers' guard Kobe Bryant received NBA's Most Valuable Player award. Later in the year, he led the USA "Redeem Team" to a victory at the Olympics, taking back the gold lost in 2004.

GOING FOR GOLD

The U.S. women's soccer team successfully defended their gold medal at the 2008 Olympics, beating Brazil 1-0.

REIGNING CHAMP

Triple H reclaimed the WWE championship belt for the seventh time in April 2008. He now shares the record with The Rock for most WWE championship reigns.

DOUBLE TROUBLE

At the 2008 Olympics, USA's Nastia Liukin edged teammate Shawn Johnson for the All-Around gold in gymnastics, by six-tenths of a point. Two months before, Johnson beat Liukin at the U.S. Championships in Boston.

ANIMALS

What happens if a cat's whiskers are cut? ➡ page 38

Furry or scaly, creepy or crawly, schoolbus-sized or microscopic—animals fascinate people of all stripes. Here are some facts about the Animal Kingdom.

WEIRD ANIMAL FACTS

DEEP-SEA ANGLERFISH

Deep-sea life is full of pressure! Creatures that inhabit the ocean waters one-half to two miles below the surface must resist the pressure of all that water weighing down upon them. Their environment is only a few degrees Fahrenheit above freezing and dark because little of the sun's light can reach that far.

Not many animals can survive at such depths. The ones who do, have evolved in unique ways. Deep-sea anglerfish are one common species in this harsh environment. They sprout a growth from their heads that they use like a fishing rod. They make the end of it glow using **bioluminescence**. Bioluminescence is the ability of some animals to create light. Deep-sea anglerfish use this glow to lure prey so they don't waste energy swimming around looking for food.

ANTS AND APHIDS

Species within an ecosystem depend on one another for survival. Sometimes, however, odd couples can be found. When animals of different species form a relationship that benefits all involved, it's called mutualism. Ants and aphids have this kind of relationship.

Aphids are insects that feed on plants. As part of digestion, they produce a sugary waste called honeydew. Ants will protect and take care of aphids in return for honeydew, which they eat. They will even carry aphids into their nest so they will survive through the winter.

LIFE ON EARTH

This time line shows how life developed on Earth. The earliest life forms are at the bottom of the chart. The most recent are at the top of the chart.

Years Ago		Animal Life on Earth
Cenozoic	**10,000 to present**	Human civilization develops.
	1.8 million to 10,000	Large mammals like mammoths, saber-toothed cats, and giant ground sloths develop. Modern human beings evolve. This era ends with an ice age.
	65 to 1.8 million	Ancestors of modern-day horses, zebras, rhinos, sheep, goats, camels, pigs, cows, deer, giraffes, elephants, cats, dogs, and primates begin to develop.
Mesozoic	**144 to 65 million**	In the Cretaceous period, new dinosaurs appear. Many insect groups, modern mammal and bird groups also develop. A global extinction of most dinosaurs occurs at the end of this period.
	206 to 144 million	The Jurassic is dominated by giant dinosaurs. In the late Jurassic, birds evolve.
	248 to 206 million	In the Triassic period, marine life develops again. Reptiles also move into the water. Reptiles begin to dominate the land areas. Dinosaurs and mammals develop.
Paleozoic	**290 to 248 million**	A mass extinction wipes out 95% of all marine life.
	354 to 290 million	Reptiles develop. Much of the land is covered by swamps.
	417 to 354 million	The first trees and forests appear. The first land-living vertebrates, amphibians, and wingless insects appear. Many new sea creatures also appear.
	443 to 417 million	Coral reefs form. Other animals, such as the first known freshwater fish, develop. Relatives of spiders and centipedes develop.
	542 to 443 million	Animals with shells (called trilobites) and some mollusks form. Primitive fish and corals develop. Evidence of the first primitive land plants.
Precambrian	**3.8 billion to 542 million**	First evidence of life on Earth. All life is in water. Early single-celled bacteria and achaea appear, followed by multi-celled organisms, including early animals.
	4.6 billion	Formation of the Earth.

ANIMAL KINGDOM

The world has so many animals that scientists looked for a way to organize them into groups. A Swedish scientist named Carolus Linnaeus (1707-1778) worked out a system for classifying both animals and plants. We still use it today.

The Animal Kingdom is separated into two large groups—animals with backbones, called **vertebrates**, and animals without backbones, called **invertebrates**.

These large groups are divided into smaller groups called **phyla**. And phyla are divided into even smaller groups called **classes**. The animals in each group are classified together when their bodies are similar in certain ways.

Vertebrates
Animals with Backbones

FISH	Swordfish, tuna, salmon, trout, halibut, goldfish
AMPHIBIANS	Frogs, toads, mud puppies
REPTILES	Turtles, alligators, crocodiles, lizards
BIRDS	Sparrows, owls, turkeys, hawks
MAMMALS	Kangaroos, opossums, dogs, cats, bears, seals, rats, squirrels, rabbits, chipmunks, porcupines, horses, pigs, cows, deer, bats, whales, dolphins, monkeys, apes, humans

Invertebrates
Animals without Backbones

PROTOZOA	The simplest form of animals
COELENTERATES	Jellyfish, hydra, sea anemones, coral
MOLLUSKS	Clams, snails, squid, oysters
ANNELIDS	Earthworms
ARTHROPODS	
Crustaceans	Lobsters, crayfish
Centipedes and Millipedes	
Arachnids	Spiders, scorpions
Insects	Butterflies, grasshoppers, bees, termites, cockroaches
ECHINODERMS	Starfish, sea urchins, sea cucumbers

Homework Tip

How can you remember the animal classifications from most general to most specific? Try this sentence:

King **P**hilip **C**ame **O**ver **F**rom **G**reat **S**pain.

K = Kingdom; **P** = Phylum; **C** = Class; **O** = Order; **F** = Family; **G** = Genus; **S** = Species

WHAT IS BIODIVERSITY?

The Earth is shared by millions of species of living things. The wide variety of life on Earth, as shown by the many species, is called "biodiversity" (bio means "life" and diversity means "variety"). Human beings of all colors, races, and nationalities make up just one species, *Homo sapiens*.

Species, Species Everywhere

Here is just a sampling of how diverse life on Earth is. The numbers are only estimates, and more species are being discovered all the time!

ARTHROPODS (1.1 million species)
- insects: 1,000,000 species
- moths & butterflies: 175,000 species
- flies: about 122,000 species
- cockroaches: about 4,000 species
- crustaceans: 40,000 species
- spiders: 35,000 species

FISH (24,500 species)
- bony fish: 21,000 species
- skates & rays: 450 species
- sharks: 350 species
- seahorses: 32 species

BIRDS (10,000 species)
- perching birds: 5,200-5,500 species
- parrots: 353 species
- pigeons: 309 species
- raptors (eagles, hawks, etc.): 307 species
- penguins: 17 species
- ostrich: 1 species

MAMMALS (9,000 species)
- rodents: 2,000 species
- bats: 1,000 species
- monkeys: 242 species
- whales & dolphins: 83 species
- cats: 37 species
- apes: 21 species
- pigs: 16 species
- bears: 8 species

REPTILES (6,000 species)
- lizards: 4,500 species
- snakes: 2,900 species
- tortoises & turtles: about 294 species
- crocodiles & alligators: 23 species

AMPHIBIANS (4,500 species)
- frogs & toads: +4,000 species
- newts & salamanders: 470 species

PLANTS (260,000 species)
- flowering plants: 250,000 species
- bamboo: about 1,000 species
- evergreens: 550 species

Biodiversity Q&A

What percentage of all known living species are vertebrates (with backbones)?
About 5%. Although they all have backbones, vertebrates can differ greatly in form, size, and habitat. They range from blue whales in the ocean to birds and of course humans.

True or false? Snakes aren't found naturally in the wild in Ireland. True. According to legend, St. Patrick banished snakes from Ireland. More likely, ancient snakes never migrated to the Emerald Isle, which doesn't have much biodiversity. Snakes are also not found in the wild in Iceland, Greenland, and Antarctica. Not only is the ground frozen year-round in these places, they're completely surrounded by water, like Ireland.

Why is biodiversity important? Forms of life are interlinked. If one species of plant or animal becomes extinct it affects other life forms. Studies have shown that biomes, or environments, with wider varieties of life forms can better survive difficult conditions, such as drought.

BIGGEST, SMALLEST, FASTEST

IN THE WORLD

WORLD'S BIGGEST ANIMALS

Marine mammal: Blue whale (100 feet long, 200 tons)

Heaviest land mammal: African bush elephant (12 feet high, 4-7 tons)
Tallest land mammal: Giraffe (18 feet tall)

Reptile: Saltwater crocodile (20-23 feet long, 1,150 pounds)

Heaviest snake: Green anaconda (16-30 feet, 550 pounds)
Longest snake: Reticulated python (26-32 feet long)

Fish: Whale shark (40-60 feet long, 10-20 tons)

Bird: Ostrich (9 feet tall, 345 pounds)

Insect: Stick insect (15 inches long)

WORLD'S FASTEST ANIMALS

Marine mammal: Killer whale and Dall's porpoise (35 miles per hour)

Land mammal: Cheetah (70 miles per hour)

Fish: Sailfish (68 miles per hour, leaping)

Bird: Peregrine falcon (200 miles per hour)

Insect: Dragonfly (35 miles per hour)

Snake: Black mamba (14 miles per hour)

WORLD'S SMALLEST ANIMALS

Mammal: Bumblebee bat (1.1-1.3 inches)

Fish: *Paedocypris progenetica* or stout infantfish (0.31-0.33 inches)

Bird: Bee hummingbird (1-2 inches)

Snake: Thread snake and brahminy blind snake (4.25 inches)

Lizard: Jaragua sphaero and Virgin Islands dwarf sphaero (0.63 inch)

Insect: Fairyfly (0.01 inch)

HOW FAST DO ANIMALS RUN?

This table shows how fast some animals can go on land. A snail can take more than 30 hours just to go 1 mile. But humans at their fastest are still slower than many animals. The human record for fastest speed for a recognized race distance is held by Usain Bolt, who won the 2008 Olympic 200-meter dash in 19.30 seconds, for an average speed of about 23 miles per hour.

MILES PER HOUR	
Cheetah	70
Pronghorn antelope	60
Elk	45
Ostrich	40
Rabbit	35
Giraffe	32
Grizzly bear	30
Elephant	25
Wild turkey	15
Crocodile	10
Tiger beetle	5.5
Snail	0.03

HOW LONG DO ANIMALS LIVE?

Most animals do not live as long as humans do. A monkey that's 14 years old is thought to be old, while a person at that age is still considered young. The average life spans of some animals in the wild are shown here. An average 10-year-old boy in the U.S. can expect to live to be about 75.

Galapagos tortoise .... 100+ years
Box turtle............. 100 years
Blue whale .... 80 years
Alligator .... 50 years
Chimpanzee........... 50 years
Macaw............... 50 years
African elephant ...... 35 years
Bottlenose dolphin..... 30 years
Gorilla................ 30 years
Horse .... 20 years
Periodical cicada....... 17 years
Tiger .... 16 years
Lion................. 15 years
Lobster............... 15 years
Cat (domestic) .... 15 years
Cow .... 15 years
Tarantula .... 15 years
Dog (domestic)........ 13 years
Camel (bactrian)....... 12 years
Moose .... 12 years
Pig................... 10 years
Squirrel .... 10 years
Deer (white-tailed)....... 8 years
Goat .... 8 years
Kangaroo.............. 7 years
Chipmunk.............. 6 years
Beaver .... 5 years
Rabbit (domestic)....... 5 years
Guinea pig............ 4 years
Mouse .... 3 years
Opossum .... 1 year
Worker bee........... 6 weeks
Adult housefly........ 1-3 weeks

ANIMAL WORDS

Animal	Male	Female	Young
bear	boar	sow	cub
cat	tom	queen	kitten
cattle, elephant, moose, whale	bull	cow	calf
deer	buck, stag	doe	fawn
donkey	jack	jenny	foal
ferret	hob	jill	kit
fox	reynard	vixen	kit, cub, pup
goat	buck, billy	nanny, doe	kid
goose	gander	goose	gosling
gorilla	male	female	infant
hawk	tiercel	hen	eyas
horse	stallion	mare	foal, filly (female), colt (male)
kangaroo	buck	doe	joey
lion	lion	lioness	cub
pig	boar	sow	piglet
rabbit	buck	doe	kit, bunny
swan	cob	pen	cygnet
turkey	gobbler, tom	hen	chick, poult

WHAT ARE GROUPS OF ANIMALS CALLED?

Here are some (often odd) names for animal groups:

BEARS: *sleuth* of bears

CATS: *clowder* of cats

CATTLE: *drove* of cattle

CROCODILES: *bask* of crocodiles

CROWS: *murder* of crows

FISH: *school* or *shoal* of fish

FLIES: *swarm* or *cloud* of flies

FOXES: *skulk* of foxes

GIRAFFES: *tower* of giraffes

HARES: *down* of hares

HAWKS: *cast* of hawks

HYENAS: *cackle* of hyenas

JELLYFISH: *smack* of jellyfish

KITTENS: *kindle* or *kendle* of kittens

LEOPARDS: *leap* of leopards

MONKEYS: *troop* of monkeys

MULES: *span* of mules

NIGHTINGALES: *watch* of nightingales

OWLS: *parliament* of owls

OYSTERS: *bed* of oysters

PEACOCKS: *muster* of peacocks

RAVENS: *unkindness* of ravens

SHARKS: *shiver* of sharks

SQUIRRELS: *dray* or *scurry* of squirrels

TURTLES: *bale* of turtles

WHALES: *pod* of whales

PETS AT THE TOP

Here are some of the most popular pets in the United States and the approximate number of each pet in 2008:

1. Freshwater fish	142,000,000	5. Birds	16,000,000
2. Cats	88,300,000	6. Reptiles	13,400,000
3. Dogs	74,800,000	7. Saltwater fish	9,600,000
4. Small animals	18,200,000		

Source: American Pet Products Manufacturers Association's 2007/2008 National Pet Owners Survey

PETS Q&A

What happens if a cat's whiskers are cut? **Cats rely on their whiskers as part of their senses. Cats easily move about in the dark because their whiskers detect changes in the air caused by obstacles in their path. Cats also use their whiskers to judge the size of openings.**

True or false? Dogs and cats are color-blind. **False. Despite the myth, dogs and cats can see in color, though not all the colors humans can see. For example, dogs can see blues but not greens.**

What breed of dog was the most popular in the U.S. in 2007? **The Labrador Retriever. According to the American Kennel Club, the Labrador retriever has been the most popular breed of dog in the U.S. for many years.**

URBAN WILDLIFE

Opportunistic Species/Urban Wildlife are animal species that have taken the opportunity of their closeness to humans to increase their chances of survival. A species can be native to one area but opportunistic as it spreads to another.

Pigeons are the typical urban bird. Almost everyone recognizes this wild neighbor. The pigeon's diet consists primarily of seeds and grains, as well as insects and some greens. They are not picky and are known to accept human food scraps and leftovers when they are offered. Pigeons live in groups called flocks, and are comfortable in human-built structures.

Canadian Geese are associated with lakes and ponds, however they also spend time on land and will nest some distance from water if the site seems safe. Artificial ponds and lakes and good grazing places like those found in parks, corporate and school campuses, and golf courses are ideal habitats for geese. This is the main reason they have settled in to year-round residency and have grown in numbers in suburban and urban areas.

Adult **American Black Bear** range from five to six feet long and between 250 and 330 pounds. For such large animals, they can run fairly quickly—up to 25 miles per hour—and are skillful tree climbers. A common assumption is that bears are exclusively meat eaters, however ripening fruits, berries, and nuts make up the bulk of their diet. Animal material eaten by bears includes insects, carrion, and occasional small prey, such as deer fawns. Around homes and in passing through suburban neighborhoods, bears may stop to sample the fare in gardens, compost bins, trash cans, birdfeeders, beehives, and outdoor barbecues.

ENDANGERED

When a species becomes extinct, it reduces the variety of life on Earth. In the world today, 7,725 known species of animals (and even more plant species) are threatened with extinction, according to the World Conservation Union. Humans have been able to save some endangered animals and are working to save more.

Some Endangered Animals

Western Lowland Gorilla Western lowland gorillas live in regions of Africa near the equator, specifically Angola, Cameroon, Central African Republic, Congo, Equatorial Guinea, Gabon, and Nigeria. Gorillas get around on all four limbs, placing their weight on the knuckles of their hands and their feet. Following chimpanzees, gorillas are the second closest relatives of humans.

Reasons for population decline:
- Disease caused by Ebola virus
- Chopping down of trees in their habitat has made it easier for people to illegally hunt these gorillas for food.

Wellington's Solitary Coral The Wellington's Solitary Coral is found in Galápagos Archipelago in Ecuador. There has been a decline of more than 90% in the population since the 1982 El Niño—an unusual weather/ocean event that occurs every few years. The rapid decline in the numbers of Wellington's Solitary Coral following the 1982 El Niño leads scientists to believe the coral are very sensitive to temperature changes.

Reasons for population decline:
- El Niño
- Global warming
- Pollution

Yangtze River Dolphin The Yangtze River dolphin, also know as the Baiji, lived in the Yangtze River, in China. The Yangtze River dolphin is probably the world's most endangered aquatic mammal. The last documented sighting of a Yangtze river dolphin was in 2002. Since then, scientists have been unable to find proof the dolphins are still around. It is possibly extinct.

Reasons for population decline:
- Fishing methods, including use of nets and hooks, that indirectly harmed dolphins
- Loss of habitat due to increased development
- Collisions with large ships
- Pollution

SPECIES

Townsend's Shearwater The Townsend's shearwater is a rare seabird of the tropics. They are found on the Revillagigedo Islands in Mexico. Efforts are being made to remove introduced species from these islands.

Reasons for population decline:
- Decline in quality of habitat due to overgrazing by sheep, which were introduced to Socorro and Claríon islands
- Preyed upon by cats, which were introduced to Socorro Island
- Destruction of nests by pigs and rabbits, which were introduced to Claríon Island
- Volcanic eruption on San Benedicto Island

Kakapo They live on Anchor Island and Codfish Island, New Zealand. Scientists transferred all remaining known kakapo to these two sanctuaries because of the threat of invasive predators on other New Zealand islands. As of March 2008 the remaining population of kakapo was 91. The kakapo, which cannot fly, is the world's largest parrot. It can weigh up to 13 pounds.

Reasons for population decline:
- Habitat loss
- Hunting by humans
- Preyed upon by introduced predators, including cats, dogs, weasels, and rats
- Competition from possums, deer, which feed on similar items
- Low rate of reproduction

Panamanian Golden Frog The Panamanian golden frog is from Panama. The remaining population in the wild is not known. There are about 1,000 of these frogs in zoos. Since amphibians—including frogs, toads, and salamanders—absorb water through their skin, they are especially vulnerable to changes in the environment. Scientists estimate about one-third of all known amphibian species are threatened or endangered.

Reasons for population decline:
- Disease caused by a fungus
- Habitat loss and decline in habitat quality because of deforestation
- Pollution, exposure to chemicals such as those in fertilizers
- Over-collection to sell as pets

FACTORS THAT CAN MAKE A SPECIES ENDANGERED:

HABITAT DESTRUCTION. As human populations grow, they need places to live and work. People build houses and factories in areas where plants and animals live. Filling in wetlands and clearing forests (**deforestation**) are examples of this threat.

OVERHARVESTING. People may catch a kind of fish or hunt an animal until its numbers are too low to reproduce fast enough. Bison, or buffalo, once roamed the entire Great Plains until they were almost hunted into extinction in the 19th century. They are now protected by law, and their numbers are increasing.

ALIEN SPECIES are plants and animals that have been moved by humans into areas where they are not naturally found. They may have no natural enemies there and can push out native species. Red fire ants and zebra mussels are examples of alien species in the U.S.

POLLUTION in the air, water, and land can harm plants and animals. It can poison them or make it hard for them to grow or reproduce. Factories are not the only source of pollution. Oil, salt, and other substances dumped on roads can wash into streams, rivers, and lakes. Acid rain damages and kills trees, especially in the mountains where trees are often surrounded by acidic clouds and fog.

GET BUGGED

What's a really heavy insect? The African goliath beetle only gets to be about 4 to 5 inches long compared to the stick insect, which can grow up to 15 inches long. But the goliath can weigh nearly a quarter of a pound.

What characteristics do all insects share? Insects do not have backbones. They have three pairs of walking legs. (Spiders, which have eight legs, are arachnids, not insects.) Also, insects' bodies can be divided into a head, thorax, and abdomen. Another thing they lack is lungs. Instead, insects breathe through tubes that open directly onto the surface of their bodies.

True or false? Malaria, a disease transmitted through mosquito bites, kills more than one million people each year. True. You could say the mosquito is one of the most dangerous creatures in the world. Malaria can be prevented and cured, but over one million people still die from it each year. Most of the victims are younger children in Africa, where people often lack the resources to prevent the spread of the disease.

How fast can a cockroach move? 4 miles per hour. Cockroaches are one of the fastest insects on land. At their top speed, over short distances, they run only on their two hind legs. That's because those legs are longer than their front legs.

ANT COLONY

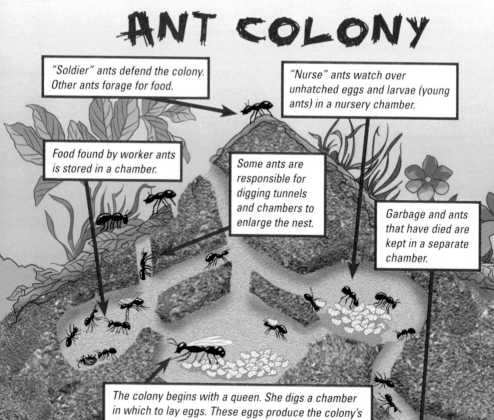

"Soldier" ants defend the colony. Other ants forage for food.

"Nurse" ants watch over unhatched eggs and larvae (young ants) in a nursery chamber.

Food found by worker ants is stored in a chamber.

Some ants are responsible for digging tunnels and chambers to enlarge the nest.

Garbage and ants that have died are kept in a separate chamber.

The colony begins with a queen. She digs a chamber in which to lay eggs. These eggs produce the colony's first ants. (Practically all the ants in a colony are female. Male ants survive only long enough to mate.)

THE **WORLD ALMANAC** FOR KIDS ON THE JOB: **VETERINARIAN**

A veterinarian, often shortened to vet, is a physician for animals.

What do you do as a veterinarian?

There are more than 62,000 veterinarians in the United States. Most care for small animals, especially pets. Others care for large animals like cattle, horses, and sheep. Vets also do research for companies that make medicine for animals. Pet food makers use vets to help make their products better. The U.S. government hires vets as food inspectors. They help make sure that the meat and poultry we eat are safe and clean. In addition, vets work in zoos, animal parks, and circuses.

Could you be a veterinarian?

If you are considering being a veterinarian, ask yourself these questions:
1. Do you love animals and want to help them?
2. Do you like working with people too?
3. Are you interested in science?
4. Are you calm and patient?
5. Do you pay attention to details and like solving problems?

If your answer to these questions is "yes," a career as a veterinarian would be for you!

How can you become a veterinarian?

It takes a long time be become a Doctor of Veterinary Medicine (DVM). First comes four years of college. Veterinary school is four years more. Three of these years are spent learning about animals, diseases, and medicines. One year is spent working with vets in an animal hospital or clinic.

Some vets go on to become specialists in one area. It may be animal cancer, eye treatment, or blood diseases. This takes two to five more years of study. Vets must continue to learn as long as they work. They take classes, read studies on new medicines and treatments, and attend conventions.

How can you work with animals now?

If you think you might want to be a vet, you can start working now. Vets say you can start by caring for your own pets. Read about them and learn about their habits and how to train them. Next, care for other people's pets. You might walk your neighbor's dog or feed a friend's cat or bird when they are away on vacation. Volunteering at a pet store, a zoo, or an animal shelter is also a great idea.

From "Cool Careers: Veterinarian," published by Gareth Stevens Inc.

ART

What color complements red? ➡ page 46

ART Q&A

HOW OLD IS ART?
Art goes back to our earliest records of human life. See the cave paintings on the next page for an example.

IS ARTISTIC TALENT SOMETHING YOU ARE BORN WITH OR SOMETHING YOU CAN LEARN?
Learning to draw is a skill like writing or playing a sport. Some people are naturally more talented, but anyone can learn to draw. Even people with severe physical disabilities can make masterpieces.

WHEN I SEE A PAINTING IN A MUSEUM, WHAT MIGHT I SAY ABOUT IT?

Look at the painting without thinking too hard about it. How does it make you feel? Happy, sad, confused, silly? Study the painting and try to discover the colors, shapes, and textures that create those feelings in you.

Look at the information card next to the work of art. Usually, it will tell you who painted it, when it was made, and what media (materials) were used. You can compare it to other works of art by the same artist, from the same time, or in the same medium.

WHAT IS ART?
The answer is up for debate. People who study this question are studying aesthetics (ess-THET-ics), which is a kind of philosophy. Usually art is something that an artist interprets for an audience. Art reveals something that you can see, that then makes you think and feel.

DIFFERENT KINDS OF ART

Throughout history, artists have painted pictures of nature (called landscapes), pictures of people (called portraits), and pictures of flowers in vases, food, and other objects (known as still lifes). Today many artists create pictures that do not look like anything in the real world. These are examples of abstract art.

▶ Photography, too, is a form of art. Photos record both the commonplace and the exotic and help us look at events in new ways.

▶ Sculpture is a three-dimensional form made from clay, stone, metal, or other material. Sculptures can be large, like the Statue of Liberty. Some are realistic. Others have no form you can recognize.

▶ Contemporary artists today often use computers and video screens to create art. Some video art uses 20 or 30 video screens that show different colors or images to create one big work of art.

ART ALL-STARS

Check out these famous works of art.

Lascaux (13,000-15,000 B.C.)

Lascaux is a cave in France. It contains some of the earliest known cave art. The cave was discovered in 1940 by four teenagers. The images found on the cave walls consist of handprints and animals such as bison, deer, horses, and cattle. It is believed that the paintings may have been part of a ritual to help make a successful hunt.

VINCENT VAN GOGH (1853–1890)
Starry Night (1889)

Van Gogh was a Dutch-born painter who lived in France for many years. With his masterpiece *Starry Night*, the Expressionist movement was born. Expressionism stresses the emotion and inner vision of the artist, instead of depicting the subject matter as it appears. This is done through distorted lines and shapes and the use of intense color. *Starry Night* shows a night sky filled with exploding stars.

GEORGIA O'KEEFE (1887–1986)
Poppy (1927)

O'Keefe is considered one of the great American artists of the 20th century. Her paintings and drawings of her beloved New Mexico show the stark beauty of its mesas and sun-drenched landscape. But she is perhaps best known for her lush still lifes of flowers. In *Poppy*, a single bloom fills the canvas, so that the viewer sees both a flower and the abstract colors which form its parts.

AUGUSTE RODIN (1840-1917)
The Thinker (1902)

Rodin modeled his sculptures in clay and often casted them in bronze. *The Thinker* is a sculpture of a seated man with his head propped on his fist. He appears deep in thought. *The Thinker* is believed to be based on the Italian poet Dante. It has become a symbol for philosophy and intellectual activity. As a result of its fame, the sculpture has been used as the basis for a joke many times. This began in Rodin's lifetime.

COLOR WHEEL

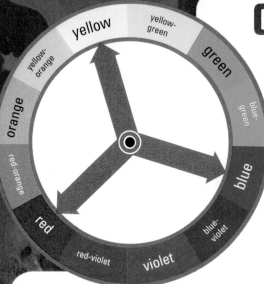

This color wheel shows how colors are related to each other.

Primary colors The most basic colors are **RED**, **YELLOW**, and **BLUE**. They're called primary because you can't get them by mixing any other colors. In fact, the other colors are made by mixing red, blue, or yellow. Arrows on this wheel show the primary colors.

Secondary colors ORANGE, **GREEN**, and **VIOLET** are the secondary colors. They are made by mixing two primary colors. You make orange by mixing yellow and red, or green by mixing yellow and blue. On the color wheel, **GREEN** appears between **BLUE** and **YELLOW**.

Tertiary colors When you mix a primary and a secondary color, you get a tertiary, or intermediate, color. **BLUE-GREEN** and **YELLOW-GREEN** are intermediate colors.

More Color Terms

VALUES The lightness or darkness of a color is its value. Tints are light values made by mixing a color with white. **PINK** is a tint of **RED**. Shades are dark values made by mixing a color with black. **MAROON** is a shade of **RED**.

COMPLEMENTARY COLORS

are contrasting colors that please the eye when used together. These colors appear opposite each other on the wheel and don't have any colors in common. **RED** is a complement to **GREEN**, which is made by mixing **YELLOW** and **BLUE**.

ANALOGOUS COLORS

The colors next to each other on the wheel are from the same "family." **BLUE**, **BLUE-GREEN**, and **GREEN** all have **BLUE** in them and are analogous colors.

COOL COLORS

are mostly **GREEN**, **BLUE**, and **PURPLE**. They make you think of cool things like water and can even make you feel cooler.

WARM COLORS

are mostly **RED**, **ORANGE**, and **YELLOW**. They suggest heat and can actually make you feel warmer.

ART: PASS-AROUND PICTURE
PROJECT

This artistic game was invented by a group called the Surrealists in 1925 and is often called Exquisite Corpse. Three artists take turns drawing on a sheet of paper, folding it to conceal their work, and then passing it to the next player for a further contribution.

Materials: *Paper and crayons, colored pencils, or markers*

Step 1: Fold the paper into thirds.

Fold a blank sheet of paper into thirds, as shown at right, then unfold it.

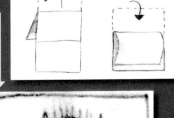

Step 2: Set up the order of artists.

Find two friends and assign numbers to yourselves: 1, 2, and 3. Artist #1 will draw in the top section of the paper, Artist #2 will draw in the middle section, and Artist #3 will draw in the bottom section. Each artist will draw different parts of a body:

  Top section (Artist #1) - Head, neck, and shoulders
  Middle section (Artist #2) - Body and arms
  Bottom section (Artist #3) - Legs and feet

You can draw any kind of creature you want, as long as you draw your assigned body parts. It can be real or unreal, plant, human, monster, or animal.

Step 3: Pass around the drawing.

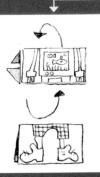

Each artist should sit with his or her back to the other artists while drawing. Artist #1 begins by drawing the creature's head, neck, and shoulders in the top section of the paper. Then Artist #1 folds the top section back so that only the middle and bottom sections are visible, and passes the paper to Artist #2. After Artist #2 draws in the middle section of the paper, he or she folds the middle section back so that only the bottom section is visible, then passes the paper to Artist #3. Artist #3 finishes the picture by drawing the creature's legs and feet in the bottom section.

Step 4: Color in the drawing.

Unfold the paper and look at your drawing. Pass your paper from artist to artist and color the section that you have drawn with colored pencils, crayons, or markers. Hang your art on the wall and enjoy!

47

BIRTHDAYS

What is the birthstone for August? ➡ page 50

Martin Luther King, Jr.

JANUARY
Birthstone: Garnet

1 J.D. Salinger, author, 1919
2 Kate Bosworth, actress, 1983
3 Eli Manning, football player, 1981
4 Isaac Newton, physicist/ mathematician, 1643
5 Alvin Ailey, choreographer, 1931
6 Early Wynn, baseball player, 1920
7 Liam Aiken, actor, 1990
8 Stephen Hawking, physicist, 1942
9 Dave Matthews, musician, 1967
10 Jake Delhomme, football player, 1975
11 Amanda Peet, actress, 1972
12 Christiane Amanpour, journalist, 1958
13 Orlando Bloom, actor, 1977
14 Dave Grohl, musician, 1969
15 Rev. Martin Luther King Jr., civil rights leader, 1929
16 Sade, singer, 1959
17 Jim Carrey, actor, 1962
18 Mark Messier, hockey player, 1961
19 Edgar Allan Poe, writer, 1809
20 Buzz Aldrin, astronaut, 1930
21 Geena Davis, actress, 1956
22 Sir Francis Bacon, philosopher, 1561
23 John Hancock, revolutionary leader, 1737
24 Mischa Barton, actress, 1986
25 Alicia Keys, singer, 1981
26 Wayne Gretsky, hockey player, 1961
27 Wolfgang Amadeus Mozart, composer, 1756
28 Elijah Wood, actor, 1981
29 Heather Graham, actress, 1970
30 Christian Bale, actor, 1974
31 Justin Timberlake, singer, 1981

FEBRUARY
Birthstone: Amethyst

1 Langston Hughes, poet, 1902
2 Bob Marley, singer, 1945
3 Elizabeth Blackwell, first woman physician, 1821
4 Rosa Parks, civil rights activist, 1913
5 Sara Evans, singer, 1971
6 Ronald Reagan, 40th president, 1911
7 Frederick Douglass, abolitionist, 1817
8 Ted Koppel, journalist, 1940
9 Travis Tritt, singer, 1963
10 Emma Roberts, actress, 1991
11 Jennifer Aniston, actress, 1969
12 Abraham Lincoln, U.S. President, 1809
13 Grant Wood, artist, 1891
14 Drew Bledsoe, football player, 1972
15 Matt Groening, cartoonist, 1954
16 Jerome Bettis, football player, 1972
17 Chaim Potok, novelist, 1929
18 Molly Ringwald, actress, 1968
19 Haylie Duff, singer/actress, 1985
20 Ansel Adams, photographer, 1902
21 Jennifer Love Hewitt, actress, 1979
22 Edna St. Vincent Millay, poet, 1892
23 Dakota Fanning, actress, 1994
24 Steve Jobs, computer innovator, 1955
25 Sean Astin, actor, 1971
26 Marshall Faulk, football player, 1973
27 Josh Groban, singer, 1981
28 Lemony Snicket (Daniel Handler), author, 1970
29 Ja Rule, rapper, 1976

Dakota Fanning

Cesar Chavez

MARCH
Birthstone: Aquamarine

1 Frederic Chopin, composer, 1810
2 Dr. Seuss, author, 1904
3 Jessica Biel, actress, 1982
4 Landon Donovan, soccer player, 1982
5 Jake Lloyd, actor, 1989
6 D.L. Hughley, actor/comedian, 1964
7 Laura Prepon, actress, 1980
8 Marcia Newby, gymnast, 1988
9 Bow Wow, actor/rapper, 1987
10 Carrie Underwood, singer, 1983
11 Benji and Joel Madden, musicians, 1979
12 Edward Albee, playwright, 1928
13 Percival Lowell, astronomer, 1855
14 Albert Einstein, physicist/ Nobel laureate, 1879
15 Ruth Bader Ginsburg, U.S. Supreme Court justice, 1933
16 Lauren Graham, actress, 1967
17 Mia Hamm, soccer player, 1972
18 Queen Latifah, rapper, actress, 1970
19 Jason LaRue, baseball player, 1974
20 Spike Lee, filmmaker, 1957
21 Matthew Broderick, actor, 1962
22 Reese Witherspoon, actress, 1976
23 Jason Kidd, basketball player, 1973
24 Peyton Manning, football player, 1976
25 Sheryl Swoopes, basketball player, 1971
26 Keira Knightley, actress, 1985
27 Mariah Carey, singer, 1970
28 Vince Vaughn, actor, 1970
29 Sam Walton, Wal-Mart founder, 1918
30 Vincent Van Gogh, artist, 1853
31 Cesar Chavez, labor leader, 1927

APRIL
Birthstone: Diamond

1 Phil Niekro, baseball player, 1939
2 Hans Christian Andersen, author, 1805
3 Amanda Bynes, actress, 1986
4 Heath Ledger, actor, 1979
5 Booker T. Washington, educator, 1856
6 Zach Braff, actor, 1975
7 Jackie Chan, actor, 1954
8 Kirsten Storms, actress, 1984
9 Jesse McCartney, actor/singer, 1987
10 John Madden, sportscaster, 1936
11 Jason Varitek, baseball player, 1972
12 Beverly Cleary, author, 1916
13 Thomas Jefferson, 3rd president, 1743
14 Abigail Breslin, actress, 1996
15 Emma Watson, actress, 1990
16 Kareem Abdul-Jabbar, basketball player, 1947
17 Jennifer Garner, actress, 1972
18 Alia Shawkat, actress, 1989
19 Kate Hudson, actress, 1979
20 Tito Puente, musician, 1923
21 Queen Elizabeth II, British monarch, 1926
22 Robert J. Oppenheimer, physicist, 1904
23 Andruw Jones, baseball player, 1977
24 Kelly Clarkson, singer, 1982
25 Jason Lee, actor, 1970
26 Kane, WWE wrestler, 1967
27 Samuel Morse, inventor, 1791
28 Harper Lee, author, 1926
29 Uma Thurman, actress, 1970
30 Kirsten Dunst, actress, 1982

Sally Ride

MAY
Birthstone: Emerald

1 Tim McGraw, musician, 1967
2 Dwayne "The Rock" Johnson, actor/wrestler, 1972
3 Sugar Ray Robinson, boxer, 1921
4 Dawn Staley, basketball player, 1970
5 Brian Williams, journalist, 1959
6 Martin Brodeur, hockey player, 1972
7 Johannes Brahms, composer, 1833
8 Enrique Iglesias, singer, 1975
9 Rosario Dawson, actress, 1979
10 Bono, musician/activist, 1960
11 Salvador Dali, artist, 1904
12 Tony Hawk, skateboarder, 1968
13 Stevie Wonder, singer, 1950
14 Miranda Cosgrove, actress, 1993
15 L. Frank Baum, author, 1856
16 Janet Jackson, singer, 1966
17 Sugar Ray Leonard, boxer, 1956
18 Tina Fey, actress/comedian, 1970
19 Malcolm X, militant civil rights activist, 1925
20 Stan Mikita, hockey player, 1940
21 John Muir, naturalist, 1838
22 Sir Arthur Conan Doyle, author, 1859
23 Margaret Wise Brown, author, 1910
24 Tracy McGrady, basketball player, 1979
25 Mike Myers, actor, 1963
26 Sally Ride, astronaut, 1951
27 André 3000, musician, 1975
28 Jim Thorpe, Olympic champion, 1888
29 Andre Agassi, tennis champion, 1970
30 Manny Ramirez, baseball player, 1972
31 Walt Whitman, poet, 1819

JUNE
Birthstone: Pearl

1 Justine Henin-Hardenne, tennis player, 1982
2 Freddy Adu, soccer player, 1989
3 Carl Everett, baseball player, 1971
4 Angelina Jolie, actress, 1975
5 Richard Scarry, author/illustrator, 1919
6 Cynthia Rylant, author, 1954
7 Michael Cera, actor, 1988
8 Kanye West, musician, 1977
9 Natalie Portman, actress, 1981
10 Maurice Sendak, author/illustrator, 1928
11 Diana Taurasi, basketball player, 1982
12 Anne Frank, diary writer, 1929
13 William Butler Yeats, poet, 1865
14 Harriet Beecher Stowe, author, 1811
15 Neil Patrick Harris, actor, 1973
16 Kerry Wood, baseball player, 1977
17 Venus Williams, tennis player, 1980
18 Sir Paul McCartney, musician, 1942
19 Paula Abdul, singer/TV personality, 1962
20 Nicole Kidman, actress, 1967
21 Prince William of Great Britain, 1982
22 Donald Faison, actor, 1974
23 Clarence Thomas, U.S. Supreme Court justice, 1948
24 Solange Knowles, singer/actress, 1986
25 Carlos Delgado, baseball player, 1972
26 Babe Didrikson Zaharias, Olympic champion, 1914
27 Tobey Maguire, actor, 1975
28 John Elway, football player, 1960
29 Theo Fleury, hockey player, 1968
30 Michael Phelps, Olympic champion, 1985

Carlos Delgado

Booker T. Washington

Charlie Stewart

Missy Elliott

JULY
Birthstone: Ruby

1 Missy Elliott, rapper, 1971
2 Lindsay Lohan, actress, 1986
3 Tom Cruise, actor, 1962
4 Neil Simon, playwright, 1927
5 P.T. Barnum, showman/circus founder, 1810
6 George W. Bush, 43rd president, 1946
7 Michelle Kwan, figure skater, 1980
8 John D. Rockefeller, industrialist, 1839
9 Tom Hanks, actor, 1956
10 Jessica Simpson, singer, 1980
11 E.B. White, author, 1899
12 Topher Grace, actor, 1978
13 Harrison Ford, actor, 1942
14 Matthew Fox, actor, 1966
15 Rembrandt van Rijn, artist, 1606
16 Will Farrell, actor, 1967
17 Donald Sutherland, actor, 1935
18 Kristin Bell, actress, 1980
19 Edgar Degas, artist, 1834
20 Sir Edmund Hillary, Everest climber, 1919
21 Josh Hartnett, actor, 1978
22 Selena Gomez, actress, 1992
23 Daniel Radcliffe, actor, 1989
24 Jennifer Lopez, actress/singer, 1969
25 Ray Billingsley, cartoonist, 1957
26 Kate Beckinsale, actress, 1973
27 Alex Rodriguez, baseball player, 1975
28 Beatrix Potter, author, 1866
29 Allison Mack, actress, 1982
30 Jaime Pressley, actress, 1977
31 J.K. Rowling, author, 1965

AUGUST
Birthstone: Peridot

1 Francis Scott Key, composer/lawyer, 1779
2 Isabel Allende, writer, 1942
3 Tom Brady, football player, 1977
4 Jeff Gordon, racecar driver, 1971
5 Neil Armstrong, astronaut, 1930
6 Andy Warhol, artist, 1928
7 Charlize Theron, actress, 1975
8 Roger Federer, tennis player, 1981
9 Eric Bana, actor, 1968
10 Antonio Banderas, actor, 1960
11 Stephen Wozniak, computer pioneer, 1950
12 Ann M. Martin, author, 1955
13 Alfred Hitchcock, filmmaker, 1899
14 Halle Berry, actress, 1966
15 Ben Affleck, actor, 1972
16 Steve Carell, actor, 1963
17 Robert De Niro, actor, 1943
18 Meriwether Lewis, explorer, 1774
19 Bill Clinton, 42nd president, 1946
20 Fred Durst, musician, 1970
21 Stephen Hillenburg, SpongeBob creator, 1961
22 Bill Parcells, football coach, 1941
23 Julian Casablancas, singer, 1978
24 Rupert Grint, actor, 1988
25 Marvin Harrison, football player, 1972
26 Branford Marsalis, musician, 1960
27 Alexa Vega, actress, 1988
28 Jack Black, actor, 1969
29 LeAnn Rimes, country singer, 1982
30 Andy Roddick, tennis player, 1982
31 Chris Tucker, actor, 1972

Francis Scott Key

SEPTEMBER
Birthstone: Sapphire

1 Conway Twitty, country singer, 1933
2 Keanu Reeves, actor, 1964
3 Shaun White, Olympic snowboarder, 1986
4 Beyoncé Knowles, singer/actress, 1981
5 Michael Keaton, actor, 1951
6 Mark Chesnutt, singer, 1963
7 Shannon Elizabeth, actress, 1973
8 Latrell Sprewell, basketball player, 1970
9 Charlie Stewart, actor, 1993
10 Bill O'Reilly, TV personality, 1949
11 Ludacris, rapper, 1977
12 Benjamin McKenzie, actor, 1978
13 Roald Dahl, author, 1916
14 Nas, rapper, 1973
15 Prince Harry of Great Britain, 1984
16 Alexis Bledel, actress, 1981
17 Rasheed Wallace, basketball player, 1974
18 Lance Armstrong, cyclist, 1971
19 Ryan Dusick, musician, 1977
20 Red Auerbach, basketball coach, 1917
21 Hiram Revels, first black U.S. senator, 1822
22 Tom Felton, actor, 1987
23 Ray Charles, musician, 1930
24 Paul Hamm, gymnast, 1982
25 Will Smith, actor/rapper, 1968
26 Serena Williams, tennis player, 1981
27 Avril Lavigne, singer, 1984
28 Hilary Duff, actress/singer, 1987
29 Kevin Durant, basketball player, 1988
30 Elie Wiesel, author, 1928

OCTOBER
Birthstone: Opal

1 William Boeing, founder of Boeing Company, 1881
2 Mohandas Gandhi, activist, 1869
3 Ashlee Simpson, singer, 1984
4 Rachael Leigh Cook, actress, 1979
5 Parminder Nagra, actress, 1975
6 Elisabeth Shue, actress, 1963
7 Simon Cowell, television personality, 1959
8 R. L. Stine, author, 1943
9 Brandon Routh, actor, 1979
10 Maya Lin, sculptor and architect, 1960
11 Michelle Trachtenberg, actress, 1985
12 Hugh Jackman, actor, 1968
13 Ashanti, singer, 1980
14 Usher, singer, 1978
15 Elena Dementieva, tennis player, 1981
16 John Mayer, musician, 1977
17 Mae Jemison, astronaut, 1956
18 Wynton Marsalis, musician, 1961
19 Ty Pennington, TV personality, 1965
20 Snoop Dogg, rapper/actor, 1971
21 Dizzy Gillespie, trumpet player, 1917
22 Ichiro Suzuki, baseball player, 1973
23 Tiffeny Milbrett, soccer player, 1972
24 Kevin Kline, actor, 1947
25 Ciara, singer, 1985
26 Jon Heder, actor, 1977
27 Teddy Roosevelt, 26th president, 1858
28 Bill Gates, computer pioneer, 1955
29 Winona Ryder, actress, 1971
30 John Adams, 2nd president of the United States, 1735
31 Juliette Gordon Low, Girl Scouts' founder, 1860

Maya Lin

Condoleezza Rice

NOVEMBER
Birthstone: Topaz

1 Bo Bice, singer, 1975
2 Nelly, rapper, 1974
3 Walker Evans, photographer, 1903
4 Sean Combs (Puff Daddy), rapper, 1969
5 Johnny Damon, baseball player, 1973
6 John Philip Sousa, composer, 1854
7 Marie Curie, scientist/Nobel laureate, 1867
8 Parker Posey, actress, 1968
9 Nick Lachey, singer, 1973
10 Brittany Murphy, actress, 1977
11 Leonardo DiCaprio, actor, 1974
12 Ryan Gosling, actor, 1980
13 Rachel Bilson, actress, 1981
14 Condoleezza Rice, American statesperson, 1954
15 Zena Grey, actress, 1988
16 Marg Helgenberger, actress, 1958
17 Reggie Wayne, football player, 1978
18 Owen Wilson, actor, 1968
19 Larry Johnson, football player, 1979
20 Dominque Dawes, Olympic gymnast, 1976
21 Jena Malone, actress, 1984
22 Jamie Lee Curtis, actress, 1958
23 Billy the Kid (William Bonney), outlaw, 1859
24 Katherine Heigl, actress, 1978
25 Christina Applegate, actress, 1971
26 Charles Schulz, cartoonist, 1912
27 Bill Nye, "The Science Guy," 1955
28 Jon Stewart, TV host, 1962
29 Louisa May Alcott, author, 1832
30 Mark Twain, author, 1835

DECEMBER
Birthstone: Turquoise

1 Richard Pryor, actor, 1940
2 Lucy Liu, actress, 1967
3 Brendan Fraser, actor, 1967
4 Tyra Banks, model/TV personality, 1973
5 Cliff Floyd, baseball player, 1972
6 Otto Graham, football player/coach, 1921
7 Aaron Carter, actor/singer, 1987
8 AnnaSophia Robb, actress, 1993
9 Felicity Huffman, actress, 1962
10 Raven, actress, 1985
11 Mos Def, actor/rapper, 1973
12 Edvard Munch, artist, 1863
13 Jamie Foxx, actor, 1967
14 Vanessa Hudgens, actress and singer, 1988
15 Adam Brody, actor, 1979
16 Ludwig van Beethoven, composer, 1770
17 Sean Patrick Thomas, actor, 1970
18 Brad Pitt, actor, 1963
19 Jake Gyllenhaal, actor, 1980
20 Rich Gannon, football player, 1965
21 Ray Romano, actor/comedian, 1957
22 Diane Sawyer, journalist, 1945
23 Alge Crumpler, football player, 1977
24 Ryan Seacrest, DJ/TV personality, 1974
25 Clara Barton, American Red Cross founder, 1821
26 Marcelo Rios, tennis player, 1975
27 Carson Palmer, football player, 1979
28 Denzel Washington, actor, 1954
29 Jude Law, actor, 1972
30 LeBron James, basketball player, 1984
31 Val Kilmer, actor, 1959

Clara Barton

Talkin' 'Bout Your **Generation**

Do you ever feel like your parents don't really get your slang or the clothes and music you like? Ever feel like you don't really get the stuff they like either? Maybe it's because you're from different generations.

A generation usually spans about 20 years. Not everyone agrees on which years each generation covers, but the labels can be helpful in describing the shared experiences and popular culture of a group of the population.

iGeneration (born about 2001 and up)

- Also known as "Generation Z" or "the Internet Generation"
- First generation to grow up with a lifelong use of communications technology such as the Internet, cell phones, and digital cameras
- First Americans to grow up with widespread equality between sexes at work and home

Generation Y (born about 1980-2000)

- Also known as "Millennials" or "Echo Boomers"
- About 27.8% of the U.S. population, or around 82 million people in 2005
- First generation to grow up fluent in—and some say too reliant on—digital technology
- Seen as confident and cooperative, eager to "fix" the world by solving its problems

Generation X (born about 1965-79)

- About 20.6% of the U.S. population, or around 61 million people in 2005
- Born during the so-called "Baby Bust," a drop in birthrates after the Baby Boom
- The best-educated generation in U.S. history, with women educated in equal numbers to men.
- Independent-minded and obsessed with pop culture

Baby Boomers (born about 1946-64)

- About 27.9% of the population, or around 83 million people in 2005
- The "Baby Boom" began right after World War II, as millions of soldiers returned home
- Witnessed the civil rights and women's rights movements, as well as the Vietnam War
- Seen as idealistic and free-spirited, used to getting what they want, and denying they are aging.

MOST POPULAR NAMES

Boys (born 1900)	Girls (born 1900)	Boys (born 2000)	Girls (born 2000)
1. John	1. Mary	1. Jacob	1. Emily
2. William	2. Helen	2. Michael	2. Hannah
3. James	3. Anna	3. Matthew	3. Madison
4. George	4. Margaret	4. Joshua	4. Ashley
5. Charles	5. Ruth	5. Christopher	5. Sarah

⌂ ●WAforKids.com ➔

Go to **www.WAforKids.com** and type **040** into the code box. Then you can:
- Enter your birth date, and find a whole list of famous people that share it.
- Follow links to great sites that will help you create your own family tree.

GENEALOGY TRACING YOUR FAMILY TREE

Genealogy is the study of one's family, tracing back through generations of relatives. The first place to start in your family genealogy is with yourself. Write down the answers to the following questions:

- What is your full name (include middle name)?
- When and where were you born (town, city, state, country)?

Next, write down the name, birth date, and place of birth for each of your parents (ask them or the adult who takes care of you). Then, interview your grandparents and other relatives. Get their birthdates and places of birth as well. If any of these people have died, record their date of death. You might also ask about interesting events in their lives.

Now, you have the beginnings of a family tree. Fill out as much of this chart as you can.

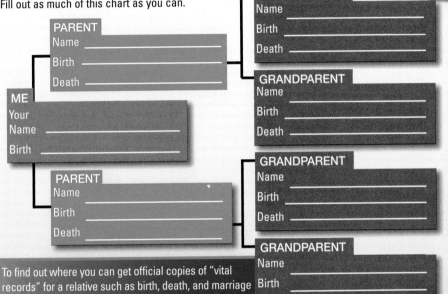

PARENT
Name
Birth
Death

ME
Your Name
Birth

PARENT
Name
Birth
Death

GRANDPARENT
Name
Birth
Death

GRANDPARENT
Name
Birth
Death

GRANDPARENT
Name
Birth
Death

GRANDPARENT
Name
Birth
Death

To find out where you can get official copies of "vital records" for a relative such as birth, death, and marriage certificates for a particular state, check the website of the U.S. National Center for Health Statistics (www.cdc. gov/nchs). Baptism, marriage, and burial records can often be found at family churches. Also, many libraries have U.S. Census records for 1790-1930. Make sure to keep copies of the documents you find.

Additional Sources

A good book for children to read is *Climbing Your Family Tree: Online and Off-Line Genealogy for Kids*, by Ira Wolfman. (***www.workman.com/familytree***)

The Church of Jesus Christ of Latter Day Saints (the Mormons) has Family History Centers throughout the world. There you can access their databases and programs, and possibly find members of your family.

More than 22 million immigrants passed through Ellis Island and the Port of New York as they entered the United States. The immigrants came by ship, which recorded each one's name on the ship's **manifest**, or passenger list. Now you can search the lists online at the Ellis Island website. *(http://www.ellisisland.org/)*

▲ Old family photos are a great way to explore your family history.

BOOKS

Who wrote the famous poem, "The Raven"? ➡ page 58

BOOK AWARDS, 2008

Newbery Medal
For the author of the best children's book
2008 winner: *Good Masters! Sweet Ladies! Voices from a Medieval Village* by Laura Amy Schlitz

Caldecott Medal
For the artist of the best children's picture book
2008 winner: *The Invention of Hugo Cabret* by Brian Selznick

Michael L. Printz Award
For excellence in literature written for young adults
2008 winner: *The White Darkness* by Geraldine McCaughrean

Coretta Scott King Award
For artists and authors whose works encourage expression of the African American experience

2008 winners:
Author Award: *Elijah of Buxton* by Christopher Paul Curtis
Illustrator Award: *Moses: Let It Shine* Illustrated by Ashley Bryan

Trenton Lee Stewart

NEW BOOK SPOTLIGHT

The Mysterious Benedict Society (2007) and *The Mysterious Benedict Society and the Perilous Journey* (2008) by Trenton Lee Stewart tell the story of four children who respond to an ad seeking "gifted children." In the first book, the children form the Mysterious Benedict Society and are trained by Mr. Benedict to foil the sinister Mr. Curtain's plans for taking over the world. In the second book, the fabulous foursome must rescue Mr. Benedict from his evil twin.

🏠 ●WAforKids.com ➡

Go to www.WAforKids.com and type 042 into the code box for more facts and fun:

• Are you a book-a-holic? Take the chapter quiz to find out.

• Learn all about comic books, and solve the Record-Breaking Books puzzle.

• Get more homework help on book awards and the history of books!

Famous Authors FOR KIDS

Author

Try the Book

E.L. Konigsburg (1930-), or Elaine Lobl Konigsburg, taught science before becoming an author. She has twice received the Newbery Medal, for *The View From Saturday* and *From the Mixed-Up Files of Mrs. Basil E. Frankweiler*, which she also illustrated. In fact, her drawings of that book's two main characters are based upon her daughter and younger son.

From the Mixed-Up Files of Mrs. Basil E. Frankweiler

C.S. Lewis (1898-1963), born Clive Staples Lewis, fought in World War I and later taught at Oxford University. The British author belonged to a literary group called The Inklings, whose members included J. R. R. Tolkien, author of *The Lord of the Rings*.

The Lion, the Witch, and the Wardrobe
(the first book in the Narnia series)

Christopher Paolini (1983-) began writing *Eragon* when he was 15. He read many fantasy and science fiction books and wanted to see if he could write one himself. By the time he was 20, *Eragon* was a bestseller. He and his younger sister Angela—who inspired the character of "Angela the herbalist" in his books—were home-schooled by their parents.

Eragon (the first book in the *Inheritance* series)

Gary Paulsen (1939-) worked a variety of jobs—including as an engineer, construction worker, and truck driver—before realizing he wanted to be a writer. His dedication to writing has led him to produce more than 175 books for children and adults. Three of his books have received the Newbery Honor award. In addition to writing, Paulsen trains dogs for the Iditarod sled race in Alaska, rides horses, and sails.

The Brian Saga: Hatchet, The River, Brian's Winter, and ***Brian's Return***

J.K. Rowling (1965-), whose initials stand for Joanne Kathleen, is the British author of the world-famous Harry Potter series. The idea for Harry Potter came to her suddenly during a train trip. She spent the next five years making an outline of the story and writing it out before *Harry Potter and the Sorcerer's Stone* was published.

Harry Potter and the Sorcerer's Stone
(first book in the Harry Potter series)

E.B. White (1899-1985) ("E. B." stands for Elwyn Brooks) worked as a reporter and then as an essay writer for a magazine. He created the character of Stuart Little after he had a dream about a mouse-like boy. He started telling stories about Stuart to his many nephews and nieces. Another book, *Charlotte's Web*, was inspired by the animals on his farm.

The Trumpet of the Swan

BOOKS TO READ

There are two major types of literature: fiction and nonfiction. A **fiction** book includes people, places, and events that might be inspired by reality but are mainly from an author's imagination. **Nonfiction** is about real things that actually happened. Nonfiction may be about a person's life, an event in history, or how something works.

Within these two groups there are smaller subgroups called genres (ZHAN-ruz).

Fiction

Mysteries, Thrillers, and Horror

These adventure stories will keep you up late, as you follow a main character who must uncover a secret.

Try These *Bunnicula,* by Deborah and James Howe; *The House With a Clock in Its Walls,* by John Bellairs

Fantasy and Science Fiction

This genre is one of the most popular for teen readers. You've heard of the Harry Potter books, but there are thousands of books for kids and teens in this genre.

Try These *The Hobbit,* by J.R.R. Tolkien; *The Little Prince,* by Antoine de Saint-Exupery

Realistic Fiction

Do you like stories that might have happened to you? Realistic fiction is about real-life situations that teens and kids deal with every day.

Try These *A Tree Grows in Brooklyn,* by Betty Smith; *Tales of a Fourth Grade Nothing,* by Judy Blume

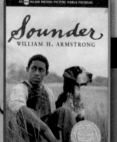

Historical Fiction

If you think history is just about facts, this is the genre for you. Authors take exciting historical events and put the most interesting fictional characters right in the middle of them.

Try These *My Brother Sam Is Dead,* by James Lincoln Collier and Christopher Collier; *Sounder,* by William H. Armstrong

Myths and Legends

These made-up stories go way back. Some are from nineteenth-century America, others are from ancient Greece and Africa.

Try These *The People Could Fly: American Black Folktales*, told by Virginia Hamilton

Graphic Novels, Comics, and Manga

Check out these adventure series that use drawings and text to tell complicated adventure stories.

Try These *Robot Dreams*, by Sara Varon; *Diary of a Wimpy Kid*, by Jeff Kinney

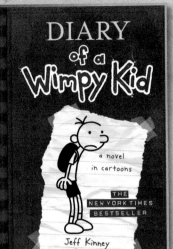

Nonfiction

Biographies, Autobiographies, and Memoirs

Do you like reading all about the details of a real person's life? This genre is for you.

Try These *The Many Rides of Paul Revere*, by James Cross Giblin; *Lincoln: A Photobiography*, by Russell Freedman

History

Books in this genre can be about an event, an era, a country, or even a war.

Try These *Team Moon: How 400,000 People Landed Apollo 11 on the Moon*, by Catherine Thimmesh

Reference

Books that supply facts and practical information on one topic or many, including almanacs, atlases, dictionaries, and encyclopedias

Try This *The World Almanac for Kids*

All About ... BOOKS

If a Roman emperor wanted to read a book, he had to unroll it. Books were written on long scrolls (kind of like a roll of paper towels) that you unrolled as you went along. This was clumsy, especially if you were looking for a certain passage. Around A.D. 100 the codex was invented. It was made up of a stack of pages stitched together at the side and protected by a cover. The codex was easier to carry around, to store, and to search through. Books we read today look something like a codex.

In the Middle Ages books were made by monks who copied them by hand onto prepared animal skins called parchment. The monks often decorated the pages with beautiful color illustrations called "illuminations." Books were scarce and very expensive, and few people who were not priests or monks could read.

A big change came with the use of paper and printing, which were first invented in China. Paper came into Europe through the Muslim world and was common by the 14th century. Johann Gutenberg of Germany perfected printing in the 1450s. Once books no longer had to be copied by hand and could be printed on paper, they became less expensive and reading became more common.

At first, books were still not easy to make and not cheap. Each letter was on a separate piece of type, and a typesetter had to put each letter into place individually. Once all the letters for the page were in place, they were covered with ink and printed, one page at a time, by hand on a press. By the 19th century, however, steam-powered presses could print out hundreds of pages at a time. Another invention was the linotype machine, which stamped out individual letters and set them up much faster than a typesetter could. Now books had become truly affordable, and the skill of reading was something that everyone was expected to learn. Today, with the use of computers, books can be easily transferred into electronic files, and read as e-books.

WHO AM I?

I was born in Boston in 1809. My parents died while I was still young, so I was raised by John Allan, a wealthy merchant. I attended college but left after less than a year due to lack of money. I served a few years in the Army before finding work as an editor and book reviewer for various magazines. I soon began publishing short stories and poems. In 1845, I became famous with the publication of my dramatic poem "The Raven." It begins with the lines:

Once upon a midnight dreary, while I pondered, weak and weary,
Over many a quaint and curious volume of forgotten lore,
While I nodded, nearly napping, suddenly there came a tapping,
As of someone gently rapping, rapping at my chamber door.
"'Tis some visitor," I muttered, "tapping at my chamber door;
Only this, and nothing more."

Answer: Edgar Allan Poe

ACTIVITY: MAKE YOUR OWN BOOK

▶ Materials

Paper:
- Construction paper for the cover
- Lighter paper stock for the inside pages

Stapler

Crayons/Markers

▶ Pick a topic: What are you interested in? Choose to write about something you enjoy. Remember, you're the author—you can write whatever you want, whether it's a short story, a book, or even a cookbook.

▶ Choose your audience: Before you begin to write, think about who will read the book. Are you writing an alphabet book for your 2-year-old cousin? Are you writing a biography of your grandmother? Are you writing a story for people your age?

▶ Write the text: Once you've decided on a topic, organize your thoughts. You can jot down your ideas on a piece of scrap paper. Another way of organizing is making an outline. An outline allows you to highlight your key thoughts and supporting ideas. If you're writing a short story, make a story map—write down your characters, the opening action of the story, the conflict, the climax, and the resolution. When you're done organizing, start writing.

▶ Revise the text: Once you feel done, read over what you wrote. Does it make sense? Is it interesting? Could your audience read it? Would they like it? Don't be afraid to make changes you think would be improvements. This might be a good time to show what you've written to a trusted reader, like a parent or friend. Consider any suggestions, but remember, you're the author. Then, read the text again. Look for grammar errors.

▶ Make the book: Now that you've written the text, you can decide how many words you'd like on each page, and how many pages your book will have. Remember to save the first page as a title page, where you can list your name as the author.

Once you've settled on a number of pages, assemble the book. Use the paper you want for the inside pages. Each sheet of paper will count as four book pages. For example, if you've decided to make a 12-page book, you'll need three pieces of paper.

1. Stack the paper.
2. Fold the stack of paper in half.
3. Take the heavy paper you want to use as a cover and place on the outside of the lighter paper.
4. Staple all the paper together along the crease, where the spine of the book would be.
5. You can also cut the paper to make your book smaller.

▶ Fill in the pages: Once you've bound the book, number the pages, and add your text and illustrations.

▶ Start reading: Share your book with others.

BUILDINGS

What structure is on the Cambodian flag? ➡ page 63

TALLEST BUILDINGS IN THE WORLD

Here are the world's tallest buildings, with the year each was completed. Heights listed here don't include antennas or other outside structures.

◀ **Dubai Tower**
Dubai, United Arab Emirates (2009, est.)
Projected height: 167 stories, 2,313 feet

Taipei 101
Taipei, Taiwan (2004)
Height: 101 stories, 1,667 feet

Petronas Towers 1 & 2
Kuala Lumpur, Malaysia (1998)
Height: each building is 88 stories, 1,483 feet

Sears Tower
Chicago, Illinois (1974)
Height: 110 stories, 1,451 feet

Jin Mao Tower
Shanghai, China (1999)
Height: 88 stories, 1,381 feet

Two International Finance Centre
Hong Kong, China (2003)
Height: 88 stories, 1,362 feet

WORLD'S TALLEST WHEN BUILT

Great Pyramid of Giza, Egypt
Built c. 2250 B.C. Height: 480 feet

Cologne Cathedral, Germany
Built 1248-1880. Height: 515 feet

Washington Monument, Washington D.C.
Built 1848-84. Height: 555 feet

Eiffel Tower, Paris, France
Built 1887-89. Height: 984 feet

Chrysler Building, New York, NY
Built 1930. Height: 1,046 feet

Empire State Building, New York, NY
Built 1931. Height: 1,250 feet ▶

Ostankino Tower, Moscow, Russia
Built 1963-67. Height: 1,771 feet

did you know?

The Dubai Tower in the United Arab Emirates keeps breaking records. In July, 2007 it became the world's tallest building when it passed a height of 1,667 feet. Then in 2008 it became the world's tallest structure, when it passed 2,063 feet. In 2009 the tower is expected to reach its final, record-breaking height of about half a mile (2,313 feet). The tower is Y-shaped to "confuse the wind" and keep it from bending. Extra concrete walls add support on the first 100 floors where people will live. Offices will be on the higher floors. Special balconies will let people go outside 152 floors up.

A Short History of Tall Buildings

For most of history, people built tall structures to honor gods, kings, and other powerful leaders, not as places to live. Building tall required lots of wealth and workers. But the biggest challenge was gravity. Each part of a wall had to support everything above it. Building higher required thicker walls at the base. Too many windows would weaken the building. The Great Pyramid required an area equal to 10 football fields and more than 2 million massive stone blocks. The Washington Monument, the last entirely stone structure to reach a record height, has walls 15 feet thick at its base.

By the 1880s, three **key factors in the evolution of tall buildings** were in place:

1. A NEED FOR SPACE Crowded cities had less space for building, and land got expensive. To create more space, buildings had to go up instead of out.

2. BETTER STEEL PRODUCTION Mass-producing steel meant more of it was available for construction. Long vertical **columns** and horizontal girders could be joined to form a strong cube-like grid that was lighter than a similar one made of stone or brick. Weight was also directed down the columns to a solid **foundation**, usually underground, instead of to walls.

3. THE ELEVATOR Tall buildings need elevators! The first elevator, powered by steam, was installed in a New York store in 1857. Electric elevators came along in 1880.

As buildings got taller, a new problem sprang up—**wind**. Too much movement could damage buildings or make the people inside uncomfortable. Some tall buildings, like New York's Citicorp Center, actually have a counter-weight near the top. A computer controls a 400-ton weight, moving it back and forth to lessen the building's sway.

In California and Japan, **earthquakes** are a big problem and special techniques are needed to make tall buildings safer from quakes.

IT'S NOT ALL ABOUT... TALL!

When it comes to buildings, the tall ones grab people's attention. But many other buildings are interesting and fun to look at. Here are a few really cool buildings.

EL TEMPLO DE LA SAGRADA FAMILIA, Barcelona, Spain

Architect Antonio Gaudí proved he had no shortage of imagination when he designed the "Temple of the Holy Family." Work began in 1883, and it is still in progress. This very detailed project has so many carvings and towers yet to be built that it may be many years before it's ever finished.

THE GLASS HOUSE, New Canaan, Connecticut

When architect Philip Johnson designed his own home in 1949, he created something beautiful and unique. What makes this house special is the structure: it is a steel frame with outside walls made of clear glass. This makes the house totally see-through. (Johnson did enclose the bathroom in brick!) In an interview, Johnson said, "It's the only house in the world where you can watch the sun set and the moon rise at the same time."

NATIONAL AQUATICS CENTER, Beijing, China

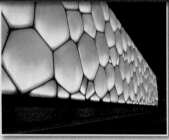

The "Water Cube" was built for the 2008 Olympic Games swimming and diving competitions. It's made to look natural and random, like soap bubbles or plant cells. The walls and roof are made of thousands of steel polygons fitted with inflated Teflon (plastic) bubbles. The bubbles make a greenhouse, capturing solar energy to heat the pools. Rain cleans the bubbles while the roof catches rainwater, which is reused inside. Each bubble has skin as thin as a pen tip but each could hold the weight of a car.

SYDNEY OPERA HOUSE, Sydney, Australia

Though it looks like a giant sea creature rising out of Sydney Harbor, architect Joern Utzon had the sections of an orange in mind when he designed this building. Finished in 1973, the shells are made of more than 2,000 concrete sections held together by 217 miles of steel cable. The roof cover—bolted on in 4,240 sections—is covered with 1.5 million ceramic tiles.

DOME OF THE ROCK
Jerusalem, Israel; 687 A.D.

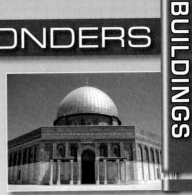

The Dome of the Rock is the oldest Islamic monument still standing. A shrine, it was built over a rock sacred to both Muslims and Jews. Its 25-meter dome is covered with gold. Because the structure is considered the center of the Earth for the Arabs who built it, there are exits leading north, east, south, and west.

ANGKOR WAT
Angkor, Cambodia; c. 1150 A.D.

This massive temple complex covers 400 acres and is surrounded by a big moat. The towers are shaped like lotus flowers. Every surface along its winding corridors is carved with Hindu tales. It's a source of pride for Cambodians, who have placed it on their flag.

CATHEDRAL NOTRE-DAME DE PARIS
Paris, France; 1163-1351

"Gothic" might stir up images of ghouls. However gothic architecture was meant to be uplifting, not scary. Instead of using thicker walls to build taller, the cathedral has pointed arches and rib-like supports called flying buttresses on the outside that lean into the walls to prop them up. Those buttresses also allow more space for bigger windows, usually stained glass, including large round "rose" windows. The scary monstrous statues along the rooftop are not Gothic. They're water spouts added in the 1800s.

FORBIDDEN CITY
Beijing, China; 1406-1420

This was the exclusive home for emperors of the Ming and Qing dynasties for 492 years. The palace grounds are the world's largest (178 acres). It was "forbidden" because people could not enter without the emperor's permission. The palace itself contains thousands of wooden chambers and great halls that cover 37 acres. Every roof is yellow, the color of Chinese royalty.

BRIDGES

There are four main bridge designs: beam, arch, truss, and suspension or cable-stayed.

BEAM

The beam bridge is the most basic kind. A log across a stream is a simple style of beam bridge. Highway bridges are often beam bridges. The span of a beam bridge, or the length of the bridge without any support under it, needs to be fairly short. Long beam bridges need many supporting poles, called piers.

ARCH

You can easily recognize an arch bridge, because it has arches holding it up from the bottom. The columns that support the arches are called abutments. Arch bridges were invented by the ancient Greeks.

TRUSS

The truss bridge uses mainly steel beams, connected in triangles to increase strength and span greater distances.

SUSPENSION

On suspension bridges, the roadway hangs from smaller cables attached to a pair of huge cables running over two massive towers. The ends of the giant cables are anchored firmly into solid rock or huge concrete blocks at each end of the bridge. The weight of the roadway is transferred through the cables to the anchors. On a cable-stayed bridge, the cables are attached directly from the towers (pylons) to the deck.

FAMOUS SHAPES PUZZLE

Can you match the names of the famous structures to their silhouettes?

1 Eiffel Tower
2 The Great Sphinx
3 Transamerica Pyramid Building
4 Stonehenge
5 Space Needle

ANSWERS ON PAGES 334-336. FOR MORE PUZZLES GO TO WWW.WAFORKIDS.COM

Anchorage Main cables are attached here, adding strength and stability

Deck Surface of the bridge

Main cable Primary load-bearing cables, secured by anchorages

Pier Supports for pylons

Pylon Tower supports that hold up cables and decks

Suspender cable Vertical cables that hold up the deck

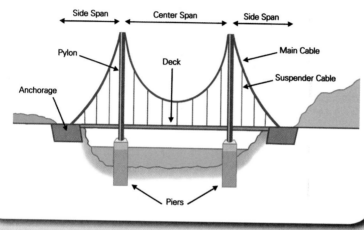

DAM FACTS

Dams are built to control the flow of rivers. They can provide water for drinking or farming, prevent flooding, and create electricity. The first dams were embankment dams built thousands of years ago out of walls of rocks and dirt to prevent flooding or to make lakes called reservoirs for irrigation. Embankment dams are still made but require a lot of land. To save space, most dams are now made of concrete. They sometimes use the same properties as bridges, like abutments, to help hold back water. "Hydroelectric" dams are used to generate electricity by channeling the force of rivers and waterfalls into tunnels in the dam to move enormous turbines (wheel-shaped engines).

CALENDAR

When is Independence Day? ➡ page 70

CALENDAR BASICS

Holidays and calendars go hand in hand. Using a calendar, you can see what day of the week it is and look for the next special day. Calendars divide time into days, weeks, months, and years. According to our calendar, also known as the Gregorian calendar, a year is the time it takes for one revolution of Earth around the Sun: 365¼ days. To make things easier, we just add an extra day, February 29, in "leap years," which happen every 4 years.

THE NAMES OF THE MONTHS

January	named for the Roman god Janus, guardian of gates (often shown with two faces, looking backward and forward)
February	named for Februalia, a Roman time of sacrifice
March	named for Mars, the Roman god of war (the end of winter meant fighting could begin again)
April	"aperire," Latin for "to open," as in flower buds
May	named for Maia, the goddess of plant growth
June	"Junius," the Latin word for the goddess Juno
July	named after the Roman ruler Julius Caesar
August	named for Augustus, the first Roman emperor
September	"septem," Latin for seven (the Roman year began in March)
October	"octo," the Latin word for eight
November	"novem," the Latin word for nine
December	"decem," the Latin word for ten

Other Calendars

The **Gregorian calendar** is used by the U.S. and much of the rest of the world. But some nations and religions use other calendars.

Islamic Calendar The Islamic calendar is used by Muslim people around the world. Twelve lunar months, each beginning with the new moon, make up the year. The year is 354 days long (355 days in leap years). Al-Hijra/Muharram (Islamic New Year) in Islamic year 1430 is estimated to fall on December 29, 2008.

Jewish Calendar The Jewish calendar has months of 29 and 30 days, and its years are either 12 or 13 months long. It is a lunar-solar calendar, which means its months are lunar, but its years adjust to the movement of the Earth around the Sun. It is the official calendar in Israel and is used as a religious calendar by Jewish people worldwide. Rosh Hashanah (New Year) in the year 5769 begins at sundown on September 30, 2008 on the Gregorian calendar.

Chinese Calendar The Chinese calendar is a lunar-solar calendar that runs on a 60-year cycle. Within the cycle, years are given one of twelve animal designations: Rat, Ox, Tiger, Rabbit, Dragon, Snake, Horse, Sheep, Monkey, Rooster, Dog, and Pig. On January 26, 2009, the Year of the Ox starts.

FORMAL HOLIDAYS

There are no official holidays for the entire U.S. But there are federal holidays, when the offices of the federal government are closed. Many other offices, most banks and schools, in the 50 states are closed on these days. There are also other holidays that may not be an occasion for a day off from school but are enthusiastically celebrated. Holidays marked with a * are federal holidays.

JANUARY 2009

January is National Oatmeal Month and National Skating Month. Learn how to ice skate—for free—at events at participating ice rinks nationwide. Grab a bowl of oatmeal beforehand for a nutritious way to stay warm from the inside out.

* January 1: New Year's Day
Until the year 1753, New Year's Day was celebrated on March 25 every year. When the Gregorian calendar was adopted in 1582, the date was switched to Jan. 1.

* January 19: Martin Luther King Day
Martin Luther King Jr., one of the civil rights movement's best-known leaders, was actually born on Jan. 15. Now, Martin Luther King Day is celebrated on the third Monday of January every year, in all 50 states.

January 26: Chinese New Year
The year 4707 begins on January 26 according to China's traditional lunar-solar calendar. The celebration lasts for 15 days, ending with the Lantern Festival.

FEBRUARY 2009

February is Black History Month and American Heart Month. Learn about the lives of some important African Americans that you may not have studied in school. See if your school is sponsoring a "Jump Rope for Heart" event, and be sure to wear red to raise heart disease awareness on National Wear Red Day, February 6.

February 2: Groundhog Day
Groundhog Day tradition holds that if a groundhog emerges from hibernation to see his shadow on February 2, six weeks of winter will follow. If there is no shadow, spring will come early.

February 14: Valentine's Day
Valentine's Day is mostly a way to celebrate those you care about—people have been exchanging Valentine cards with loved ones since the 1500s.

* February 16: Presidents' Day
Presidents' Day, on the 3rd Monday of every year, is really two holidays in one. The day does double-duty by honoring two former U.S. presidents, who were born just 10 days (and 77 years) apart: Presidents George Washington (born Feb. 22, 1732) and Abraham Lincoln (born Feb. 12, 1809).

MARCH 2009

In March, celebrate American Red Cross month by giving your time to a Red Cross project in your community (find a list of their local projects at *www.redcross.org*).

March is also National Frozen Food month: take the time to notice how many of the foods you eat are frozen—ice cream included!

March 17: St. Patrick's Day
This day celebrates the patron saint of Ireland. Many people, especially those with Irish heritage, consider St. Patrick's Day a time to remember their ancestors and eat traditional Irish foods.

March 20: First Day of Spring
Today marks the first day of Spring in the Northern Hemisphere. Also known as the Vernal Equinox, the first day of Spring is observed when the center of the sun appears directly above the Earth's equator.

APRIL 2009

April is National Humor Month and National Poetry Month. Be sure to laugh at any pranks on April Fools' Day, then try telling a new joke every day during the month. Visit the library for books of poetry (try *Where the Sidewalk Ends*, by Shel Silverstein), then try writing some of your own.

April 1: April Fools' Day
People have been celebrating April Fools' Day with pranks and gags for over 400 years. Have fun tricking your family or friends, but make sure that none of your pranks are cruel or harmful.

April 22: Earth Day
First celebrated on this date in 1970, Earth Day has been an occasion to bring attention to environmental issues ever since. Contact the Earth Day Network, *www.earthday.org*, for events near you if your school doesn't have anything planned. As little as making a commitment to recycle can make a difference.

MAY 2009

May is National Bike Month and National Hamburger Month. Enjoy a few hamburgers during May, and make sure you spend some time biking, too—whether you're trying to get somewhere or stay fit.

May 5: Cinco de Mayo
Mexicans remember May 5, 1862, when Mexico defeated the French army in the Battle of the Puebla.

May 10: Mother's Day
Mother's Day is celebrated every year on the second Sunday in May. By 2007, over 155 million Mother's Day cards were bought and given to moms across the U.S. every year. And that doesn't even include the homemade cards that many moms love most.

* May 25: Memorial Day
Also known as Decoration Day, this holiday falls on the last Monday in May. Originally celebrated in honor of members of the military that died during the Civil War, the day now honors all men and women who have died while serving in the U.S. military.

JUNE 2009

June is Great Outdoors Month. Be sure to get outside and get active at special events, from National Boating and Fishing Week to the Great American Backyard Campout, to celebrate the Great Outdoors.

June 14: Flag Day
Celebrated on June 14, this day remembers the adoption of the first version of the Stars and Stripes by the Continental Congress in 1777. Flag Day is not an official federal holiday, but many communities hold celebrations to honor the American flag.

June 19: Juneteenth
Juneteenth, also known as Emancipation Day, celebrates a military order on June 19, 1865, that formally completed the freeing of the slaves. People all over the country—especially in Texas, where it is a state holiday—spend Juneteenth celebrating freedom.

June 21: Father's Day
This day that celebrates fathers falls on the third Sunday in June.

June 21: First Day of Summer
The first day of summer in the Northern Hemisphere is observed on the Summer Solstice, when the sun rises and sets the farthest north on the horizon and daylight hours are longest.

JULY 2009

July is Cell Phone Courtesy Month and National Hot Dog Month. Cell Phone Courtesy Month reminds the 233 million cell phone users in the U.S. to be more aware of how cell phone use in public places affects other people. When your family barbecues, enjoy a hot dog—whether it's beef, pork, turkey, or tofu—it's a summertime tradition. Over 3 billion hot dogs are eaten in the U.S. every year.

July 1: Canada Day
Canada Day (called Dominion Day until 1982) celebrates the creation of the Dominion of Canada on July 1, 1867. Like the Fourth of July in the U.S., Canada Day is celebrated with parades and fireworks.

* July 4: Independence Day
Commonly known as the Fourth of July, this federal holiday marks the anniversary of the signing of the Declaration of Independence on July 4, 1776. Americans celebrate with picnics, parades, barbecues, and parties—and don't forget the fireworks!

July 14: Bastille Day
This holiday commemorates the beginning of the French Revolution by the storming of the Bastille, an event that eventually led to the formation of modern France.

AUGUST 2009

August is American Adventures Month and Happiness Happens Month. Celebrate vacations in North, South, and Central America, by going on one of your own or remembering a fun vacation you've taken in the past. Happiness Happens Month encourages people to appreciate happiness.

August 2: Friendship Day
This special day honors friendship.

August 26: Women's Equality Day
This holiday remembers the day that the 19th Amendment to the Constitution was ratified to grant women the right to vote.

SEPTEMBER 2OO9

September is Library Card Sign-Up Month and Hispanic Heritage Month (September 15-October 15). If you don't already have a library card, get one. And take advantage of the library to learn about the 500-year-old roots of Hispanic culture in the Americas.

* September 7: Labor Day
A federal holiday celebrated on the first Monday in September, Labor Day celebrates workers with a day off in their honor. Labor Day has its roots in the late 19th-century labor movement, when workers began to organize to demand shorter hours and fairer pay. It was made a federal holiday in 1894.

September 13: National Grandparents' Day
Grandparents' Day, celebrated on the Sunday after Labor Day, is a day to honor your grandparents and the knowledge they pass on.

September 17: Constitution or Citizenship Day
Citizenship Day occurs annually on the date of the signing of the U.S. Constitution in 1787, as a day to celebrate our rights and responsibilities as U.S. citizens.

September 22: First Day of Autumn
Today is the first day of autumn, or fall, in the Northern Hemisphere. Also known as the Autumnal Equinox, the first day of fall occurs when the center of the sun appears directly above the Earth's equator.

OCTOBER 2OO9

October is National Dental Hygiene Month and National Popcorn Poppin' Month. Snack on plenty of popcorn this month, and experiment by adding your own flavors or spices to the wholesome treat. If you get a kernel stuck in your teeth (or just eat too much Halloween candy!), brush and floss extra carefully.

* October 12: Columbus Day
Celebrated on the second Monday in October, Columbus Day marks Christopher Columbus's landing on an island in the Bahamas, then thought of as 'the New World,' in 1492.

October 31: Halloween
Halloween always falls on the last day of October. A holiday similar to Halloween has been celebrated since at least the seventh century. Today, global customs vary as much as costumes do, but trick-or-treating remains the most common way to celebrate in the U.S.

NOVEMBER 2009

November is National American Indian Heritage Month. Learn about Native Americans and their roles in American history.

* November 2: Election Day

The first Tuesday after the first Monday in November, Election Day is a mandatory holiday in some states.

* November 11: Veterans Day

Veterans Day honors veterans of wars for their service. It originally marked the "eleventh hour of the eleventh day of the eleventh month" in 1918. This is when World War I battles came to an end according to the conditions of an armistice (an agreement to stop fighting) signed earlier that morning.

* November 26: Thanksgiving

Every year on the fourth Thursday in November, Americans take the day to honor the people, events, and things in their lives for which they are thankful. Tradition calls for a big meal, shared with friends and family, before or after watching football and/or the televised Thanksgiving Day parade. But make sure you spend at least a few minutes honoring the real spirit of the day, and celebrate the things you are thankful for.

DECEMBER 2009

December is National Drunk and Drugged Driving Prevention Month. Impaired driving causes an injury every two minutes and a death every half hour. Contribute something to raise awareness of the danger of drunk and drugged driving this month.

December 21: First Day of Winter

The first day of winter, in the Northern Hemisphere, is observed on the Winter Solstice, when the sun rises and sets the farthest south on the horizon and daylight hours are shortest. Get outside for your favorite wintertime activity. Don't worry if the days seem too short—they'll be getting longer from this day on leading up to summer.

December 31: New Year's Eve

This day isn't technically a holiday, but you'll still find a lot of people celebrating the end of one year and the beginning of the next. Get a head start on making your New Year's resolutions before you go to bed.

OTHER HOLIDAYS

Here are a few other holidays that you can observe this year. Try celebrating the end of a successful school year on National Pizza Party Day with your class on May 15.

January 17: Kid Inventors' Day
Lots of young people came up with ideas that seemed crazy at first—but out of those "crazy" ideas came things like water skis, earmuffs, and popsicles.

February 1: Super Bowl XLIII
The year's biggest game—and most-watched TV program—takes place on February 1. Over 97.5 million people tuned in to Super Bowl XLII in 2008.

March 4: Do Something Day
The date says it all: March Forth! Do Something—ideally, something that will help you with a long term goal.

April 23: Take Our Daughters and Sons to Work Day
Kids (mostly between ages 8-12) have the opportunity today to go to work with an adult (not just moms and dads) and find out what their days are like.

May 5: Cartoonists Day
This day honors cartoonists everywhere, whether they animate your favorite TV shows and movies, or ink your favorite comic strips or books.

June 25: National Handshake Day
For adults in the business world, this is a day in honor of the idea that a firm handshake is an easy way to put your best foot forward.

July 19: National Ice Cream Day
Otherwise known as Sundae Sunday, National Ice Cream Day takes place on the third Sunday of every July.

August 19: National Aviation Day
Celebrated since 1939, this day honors aircraft and human flight on the anniversary of the birth date of Orville Wright, who piloted the first self-powered flight in history.

September 12: Video Games Day
Americans spent $18.8 billion on video games in 2007. Celebrate by playing, and thank your parents for the system, whether it's a Wii, PSP, Xbox, or other console.

October 2: National Diversity Day
National Diversity Day, which occurs on the first Friday in October, is a day to learn about, accept, and appreciate different cultures, religions, races, and genders.

November 10: National Young Reader's Day
Young Reader's Day encourages kids, teachers, and families to develop a love of books.

December 18: Underdog Day
Underdog Day celebrates past and present second bananas and unsung heroes—think Robin instead of Batman; Dr. Watson instead of Sherlock Holmes.

CRIME

INFAMOUS CRIMINALS

John Wilkes Booth

(1838-65) First presidential assassin. Booth was a famous actor but also a strong supporter of slavery and the South in the Civil War. On the night of April 14, 1865—five days after the South formally surrendered—President Abraham Lincoln attended a play at Ford's Theatre in Washington, DC. During the play *Our American Cousin*, Booth entered Lincoln's box seat and fired a single, fatal shot into the back of Lincoln's head. Booth shouted, "*Sic semper tyrannis*!" (Virginia's state motto, which means "Thus always to tyrants") and "The South is avenged!" He then jumped 12 feet from the box onto the stage, breaking one of his legs in the process, and escaped. He spent several days on the run before soldiers found him hiding in a barn in Virginia. When Booth refused to surrender, the soldiers set fire to the barn and shot him.

Jesse James (1847-1882)

The James family supported the Confederate Army during the Civil War. As a teenager, Jesse, joined a gang that attacked Union troops, robbed mail coaches, and terrorized and murdered those they considered to be anti-Confederate. The gang included his older brother Frank and his cousins, Cole and James Younger. After the war, Jesse and Frank became outlaws. Together with the Youngers, they formed a gang that robbed banks, trains, and stage-coaches, and sometimes killed. After the gang broke up, Jesse formed his own gang. Robert Ford, a member of the Jesse's gang, killed Jesse in his own home with a single shot to the back of the head.

Al Capone

(1899-1947) Notorious gangster. Born in Brooklyn, New York, Capone was known as "Scarface" because of a knife cut on his left cheek. He dropped out of school in the sixth grade and joined a gang. In 1925, Capone took over as leader of a Chicago criminal organization dealing in illegal liquor and gambling. This was during the era of Prohibition (1920-33), when most alcohol in the U.S. was illegal. Some of his men murdered seven members of a rival Chicago gang on February 14, 1929, in a crime dubbed the "St. Valentine's Day Massacre." Capone was never convicted of murder or other violent crimes, but in 1931 he was found guilty of not paying income taxes. He spent seven years in prison, some of that on Alcatraz Island, in San Francisco Bay.

LEGAL PROCESS

In the U.S., the federal and state governments have their own courts. The **federal courts**, or U.S. courts, hear cases such as those involving disputes between states. **State courts** hear other types of cases. Most of the legal work in this country occurs at the state level.

Different states organize their court systems differently. Below is a description of how a typical criminal case might proceed after a judge has determined there was sufficient reason to arrest a suspect (the person accused of a crime).

1 Grand jury. Citizens with no connection to the case review evidence and decide if there is enough to **indict**, or charge, the defendant with a crime.

2 Arraignment. A judge tells the defendant what crimes he or she has been charged with by the grand jury. The defendant can plead guilty, not guilty, or no contest. (No contest means the person will not fight the charges but does not admit to being guilty.)

3 Trial. A prosecutor presents evidence of the defendant's guilt. A defense attorney represents the defendant's best interests. Witnesses may testify about what they know. A jury listens to all the evidence and arguments. The judge makes sure everyone follows the rules.

Juvenile court cases follow different procedures than those used for adults. Juveniles are usually under 18. The top age for juveniles in the justice system varies from 15 to 17, depending upon the laws of the state. Juvenile cases are determined by a juvenile court judge. Sentencing options may include a fine, community service, restitution, placement in a group or foster home, probation, or referral for treatment.

4 Deliberations. Jury members discuss the evidence and try to agree on a **verdict**, or decision about the defendant's guilt. They must agree that the defendant is not guilty or is guilty "beyond a reasonable doubt." If they cannot agree, the defendant may receive a trial before a new jury.

5 Conviction and sentencing. If the defendant is found guilty, the judge sentences the person, or says how he or she will be punished.

6 Appeal. The defendant may appeal a guilty verdict to an **appellate court**, which may agree or disagree with the original verdict. It may send the case back to the lower court for a new trial.

DISASTERS

What is a tsunami? ➡ page 79

Hurricanes

Hurricanes—called typhoons or cyclones in the Pacific— are Earth's biggest storms. When conditions are right, they form over the ocean from collections of storms and clouds known as tropical disturbances. Strong winds create a wall of clouds and rain that swirl in a circle around a calm center called the **eye**.

Hurricane Categories

1: 74-95 mph

2: 96-110 mph

3: 111-130 mph

4: 131-155 mph

5: over 155 mph

The eye develops as **warm, moist air** is forced upward in the storm by **denser, cooler air**. From the outer edge of the storm to the inner eye, the pressure drops and wind speeds rise sharply, creating swirling **convection currents** around the eye. If wind speeds reach 39 mph, the storm is named. If wind speeds top 74 mph, the storm is called a **hurricane**.

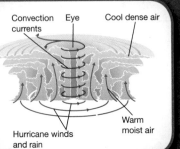

Convection currents   Eye   Cool dense air

Warm moist air

Hurricane winds and rain

Hurricanes can be up to 300 miles wide. On land, the storm can snap trees and tear buildings apart. Strong winds blowing toward shore can create a rise in the ocean water called a **storm surge**. It can combine with heavy rains to cause flooding and massive damage.

For the Atlantic Ocean, Caribbean Sea, and Gulf of Mexico, hurricane season runs from June 1 to November 30. Most hurricanes happen in August, September, and October, when the oceans are warmest.

Notable U.S. Hurricanes

Date	Location	What Happened?	Deaths
Sept. 8, 1900	Galveston, TX	Category 4 storm flooded the island with 15-foot waves.	8,000+
Sept. 19, 1938	NY, CT, RI, MA	"The Long Island Express," with storm surges rising 10-25 feet, caused $306 million in damages.	600+
Aug. 24-26, 1992	FL, LA	Hurricane Andrew swept across the Gulf of Mexico, leaving 250,000 homeless.	65
Aug. 25-29, 2005	LA, MS, AL, GA, FL	Hurricane Katrina, with 175 mph winds and a 25-foot high storm surge, caused about $125 billion in damage.	1,833

Hurricane Names

The U.S. began using women's names for hurricanes in 1953 and added men's names in 1979. When all letters (except Q, U, X, Y, and Z) are used in one season, any additional storms are named with Greek letters. Six Greek letters were needed to name 2005 storms.

2008 Names: Arthur, Bertha, Cristobal, Dolly, Edouard, Fay, Gustav, Hanna, Ike, Josephine, Kyle, Laura, Marco, Nana, Omar, Paloma, Rene, Sally, Teddy, Vicky, and Wilfred

Tornadoes

Tornadoes are rapidly spinning columns of air. They form when winds change direction, speed up, and spin around in or near a thunderstorm. They can also spin off from hurricanes.

Tornadoes can happen any time that the weather is right, but they are more common between March and July. They can happen in any state, but strong tornadoes touch down most often in the U.S. southeast or central plains.

According to the National Oceanic and Atmospheric Administration's (NOAA), an average of 1,200 tornadoes occur in the U.S. each year. They cause an average of 60 deaths and 1,500 injuries each year and over $400 million in damage.

Tornadoes are measured by how much damage they cause. In February 2007, the U.S. began using the Enhanced Fujita (EF) Scale (at left) to measure tornadoes. The EF-Scale provides an estimate of a tornado's wind speed based on the amount of damage. If a tornado doesn't hit anything, it may be hard to classify it.

Wind speeds are difficult to measure directly, because measuring instruments can be destroyed in more violent winds. The highest wind speed ever recorded— 302 mph—was taken in May 1999 in an Oklahoma tornado.

did you know? The U.S. city hit by the most tornadoes is Oklahoma City, with more than 100 recorded tornadoes.

Tornado Categories

WEAK

EF0: 65-85 mph

EF1: 86-110 mph

STRONG

EF2: 111-135 mph

EF3: 136-165 mph

VIOLENT

EF4: 166-200 mph

EF5: over 200 mph

U.S. Tornado Records (since record keeping began in 1950)

YEAR: The 1,819 tornadoes reported in 2004 topped the previous record of 1,424 in 1998.

MONTH: In May 2003, there were a total of 543 tornadoes, easily passing the old record of 399 set in June 1992.

TWO-DAY PERIOD: On April 3 and 4, 1974, 147 tornadoes touched down in 13 states.

WEB SITE For more information on storms and weather, go to the NOAA Education page: *www.education.noaa.gov/cweather.html*

EARTHQUAKES

There are thousands of earthquakes each year, but most are too small to be noticed. About 1 in 5 can be felt, and about 1 in 500 causes damage.

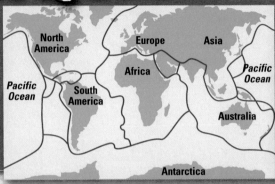

WHAT CAUSES EARTHQUAKES?

To understand earthquakes, imagine the Earth as an egg with a cracked shell. The cracked outer layer (the eggshell) is called the **lithosphere,** and it is divided into huge pieces called **plates** (see map above). Underneath the lithosphere is a softer layer called the **asthenosphere**. The plates are constantly gliding over this softer layer, moving away, toward, or past one another. Earthquakes result when plates collide.

The cracks in the lithosphere are called **faults**. Many quakes occur along these fault lines.

MAJOR EARTHQUAKES

The earthquakes listed here are among the largest and most destructive recorded in the past 50 years.

Year	Location	Magnitude	Deaths (estimated)
1960	near Chile	9.5	5,000
1970	Northern Peru	7.8	66,000
1976	Tangshan, China	8.0	255,000
1988	Soviet Armenia	7.0	55,000
1989	United States (San Francisco area)	7.1	62
1990	Western Iran	7.7	40,000
1994	United States (Los Angeles area)	6.8	61
1995	Kobe, Japan	6.9	5,502
1999	Western Turkey	7.4	17,200
2001	Western India	7.9	30,000
2004	Sumatra	9.1	227,898
2005	Pakistan and India	7.6	80,000
2008	Sichuan, China	7.9	87,652

VOLCANOES

ash and gas

crater

lava

magma

A volcano is a mountain or hill **(cone)** with an opening on top known as a **crater**. Hot melted rock **(magma)**, gases, and other material from inside the Earth mix together and rise up through cracks and weak spots. When enough pressure builds up, the magma can escape, erupting through the crater. Magma is called lava when it reaches the air. Lava may be hotter than 2,000°F. The cone of a volcano is often made of layers of lava and ash that have erupted, then cooled.

Some islands, like the Hawaiian Islands, are really the tops of undersea volcanoes.

Where is the Ring of Fire?

The hundreds of active volcanoes near the edges of the Pacific Ocean make up what is called the **Ring of Fire**. They mark the boundary between the plates under the Pacific Ocean and the plates under the surrounding continents. (Earth's plates are explained on page 78, with the help of a map.) The Ring of Fire runs from Alaska, along the west coast of South and North America, to the southern tip of Chile. The ring also runs down the east coast of Asia, starting in the far north. It continues down past Australia.

Some Famous Volcanic Eruptions

Year	Volcano (place)	Deaths (estimated)
79	Mount Vesuvius (Italy)	16,000
1586	Kelut (Indonesia)	10,000
1792	Mount Unzen (Japan)	14,500
1815	Tambora (Indonesia)	10,000
1883	Krakatau, or Krakatoa (Indonesia)	36,000
1902	Mount Pelée (Martinique)	28,000
1980	Mount St. Helens (U.S.)	57
1982	El Chichón (Mexico)	1,880
1985	Nevado del Ruiz (Colombia)	23,000
1986	Lake Nyos (Cameroon)	1,700
1991	Mount Pinatubo (Philippines)	800

TSUNAMIS

Tsunami (pronounced *tsoo-NAH-mee*) comes from two Japanese words: "tsu" (harbor) and "nami" (wave). These huge waves are sometimes called tidal waves, but they have nothing to do with the tides.

The strongest tsunamis happen when a big part of the sea floor lifts along a fault (see page 78), pushing up a huge volume of water. The resulting waves are long and low, and might not even be noticed in deep

water. They move at speeds of up to 500 miles per hour. As they near shore, they slow down and the great energy forces the water upward into big waves.

On December 26, 2004, a magnitude-9.3 earthquake off the Indonesian island of Sumatra triggered a tsunami in the Indian Ocean. The tsunami hit 12 countries. An estimated 226,000 people were killed, and 1.6 million were left homeless.

MAJOR DISASTERS

Here are some other disasters the world has faced.

Hindenburg *disaster*

Aircraft Disasters

Date	Location	What Happened?	Deaths
May 6, 1937	Lakehurst, NJ	German zeppelin (blimp) *Hindenburg* caught fire as it prepared to land.	36
Aug. 12, 1985	Japan	Boeing 747 jet collided with Mt. Osutaka. Japan's worst single-aircraft disaster in history.	520
March 27, 1977	Tenerife, Canary Islands	Two Boeing 747s collide on the runway of Los Rodeos airport.	582
Sept. 11, 2001	New York, NY; Arlington, VA; Shanksville, PA	Two hijacked planes crashed into the World Trade Center, one into the Pentagon, one went down in a PA field.	Nearly 3,000

Explosions and Fires

Date	Location	What Happened?	Deaths
June 15, 1904	New York City	*General Slocum,* wooden ship carrying church members up the East River, caught fire.	1,021
March 25, 1911	New York City	Triangle Shirtwaist Factory caught fire. Workers were trapped inside.	146
Nov. 28, 1942	Boston, MA	Fire swept through the Coconut Grove nightclub; patrons panicked. Deadliest nightclub fire in U.S. history.	146
Dec. 3, 1984	Bhopal, India	A pesticide factory explosion spread toxic gas; worst industrial accident in history.	15,000

Rail Disasters

Date	Location	What Happened?	Deaths
Jan. 16, 1944	León Prov., Spain	Train crashed in the Torro Tunnel.	500
March 2, 1944	Salerno, Italy	Passengers suffocated when train stalled in tunnel.	521
Feb. 6, 1951	Woodbridge, NJ	Commuter train fell through a temporary overpass.	84
June 6, 1981	Bihar, India	Train plunged off of a bridge into the river; India's deadliest rail disaster ever.	800

did you know?

One of the most unusual disasters ever occurred in Boston on January 15, 1919. A giant steel vat holding 2.3 million gallons of molasses ruptured. Thirty-foot waves of the gooey substance flooded the streets, killing 21 people and injuring 150.

Lusitania *disaster*

Ship Disasters

Date	Location	What Happened?	Deaths
April 14, 1912	near Newfoundland	Luxury liner *Titanic* collided with iceberg.	1,503
May 7, 1915	Atlantic Ocean, near Ireland	British steamer *Lusitania* torpedoed and sunk by German submarine.	1,198
Jan. 30, 1945	Baltic Sea	Liner *Wilhelm Gustloff* carrying German refugees and soldiers sunk by Soviet sub. Highest death toll for a single ship.	6,000 7,000
Aug. 12, 2000	Barents Sea	Explosions sank Russian submarine *Kursk*; multiple rescue attempts failed.	118
Sept. 26, 2002	Atlantic Ocean near The Gambia	Senegalese ferry capsized.	1,863
Feb. 3, 2006	Red Sea	Egyptian ferry returning from Saudi Arabia sank after fire broke out onboard.	1,000

Other Disasters

Date	Location	What Happened?	Deaths
Aug. 1931	China	Vast flooding on the Huang He River. Highest known death toll from a flood.	3,700,000
1984	Africa (chiefly Ethiopia)	Several years of severe drought caused one of the worst modern famines.	800,000
April 1986	Chernobyl, USSR (now Ukraine)	Explosions at a nuclear power plant leaked radioactive material. 135,000 people were exposed to harmful levels of radiation.	31
Summer 2003	Europe	A severe summer heat wave swept across Europe. More than 14,000 died in France alone.	35,000
Feb. 2006	The Philippines	Landslide on Leyte Island buries a village.	1,000

did you know?

One of the worst snowstorms in U.S. history happened March 11-14, 1888, just a week before the first day of spring. Much of the northeastern U.S. was buried in up to four feet of snow, with towering snowdrifts up to 30 feet high! At least 400 people died in the "Great White Hurricane," many of them in New York City. People were stranded by blocked streets, huge drifts, and powerless streetcars. There was no way to bring food or supplies into the city.

ENVIRONMENT

What is a renewable source of energy? ➡ page 91

HOME SWEET BIOME

A "biome" is a large natural area that is home to certain types of plants. The animals, climate, soil, and even the amount of water in the region also help distinguish a biome. There are more than 30 kinds of biomes in the world. But the following types cover most of Earth's surface.

Forests

Forests cover about one-third of Earth's land surface. Pines, hemlocks, firs, and spruces grow in the cool **evergreen forests** farthest from the equator. These trees are called **conifers** because they produce cones.

Temperate forests have warm, rainy summers and cold, snowy winters. Here **deciduous trees** (which lose their leaves in the fall and grow new ones in the spring) join the evergreens. Temperate forests are home to maple, oak, beech, and poplar trees, and to wildflowers and shrubs. These forests are found in the eastern United States, southeastern Canada, northern Europe and Asia, and southern Australia.

Still closer to the equator are the **tropical rain forests**, home to the greatest variety of plants on Earth. About 60 to 100 inches of rain fall each year. Tropical trees stay green all year. They grow close together, shading the ground. There are several layers of trees. The top, **emergent layer** has trees that can reach 200 feet in height. The **canopy**, which gets lots of sun, comes next, followed by the **understory**. The **forest floor**, covered with roots, gets little sun. Many plants cannot grow there.

Tropical rain forests are found mainly in Central America, South America, Asia, and Africa. They once covered as much as 12% of Earth's land surface or more than 8 million square miles. Today, because of destruction by humans, less than 5% or fewer than 2.5 million square miles of rain forest remain. More than half the plant and animal species in the world live there. Many kinds of plants from rain forests are used to make medicines. The Amazon rain forest is the world's largest tropical rain forest. It covers about 2 million square miles—roughly two-thirds the size of the United States.

When rain forests are burned, carbon dioxide is released into the air. This adds to the **greenhouse effect** (see page 70). As forests are destroyed, the precious soil is easily washed away by the heavy rains.

Emergent Layer

Canopy

Understory

Forest Floor

Tundra

Tundra, the coldest biome, is a treeless plain. The temperature rarely rises above 45°F. Water in the ground freezes the soil solid (permafrost) so plant and tree roots can't dig down. Most tundra plants are mosses and lichens without roots. In some areas, the soil thaws for about two months each year. This may allow wildflowers or small shrubs to grow. Artic tundra is located in the northernmost regions of North America, Europe, and Asia surrounding the Arctic Ocean. Alpine tundra is located on top of the world's highest mountains (such as the Himalayas, Alps, Andes, and Rockies).

What Is the Tree Line? On mountains there is an altitude above which trees will not grow. This is the **tree line** or **timberline**. Above the tree line, you can see low shrubs and small plants.

Deserts

The driest areas of the world are the **deserts**. Hot or cold (Antarctica has desert), they receive less than 10 inches of rain in a year. Many contain an amazing number of plants that store water in thick bodies or roots deep underground. Rain can spur fields of wildflowers to spontaneously bloom. Shrubby sagebrush and spiny cacti are native to dry regions of North and South America. Prickly pear, barrel, and saguaro cacti can be found in the southwestern United States. African and Asian deserts contain shrubs called euphorbias. Date palms grow in desert oases of the Middle East and North Africa.

Red Rock Canyon, Nevada

Prairie in Indiana

Grasslands

Areas that are too dry to have green forests, but not dry enough to be deserts, are **grasslands**. The most common plants are grasses. Cooler grasslands are found in the Great Plains of the United States and Canada, in the steppes of Europe and Asia, and in the pampas of Argentina. Drier grasslands called steppes have short grasses and are used for grazing cattle and sheep. In **prairies**, characterized by tall grasses, there is a little more rain. Wheat, rye, oats, and barley grow there. The warmer grasslands, called **savannas**, are found in central and southern Africa, Venezuela, southern Brazil, and Australia. Most savannas have moist summers and cool, dry winters.

Marine

Covering almost three-quarters of the earth, marine regions are the largest biome. The marine biome includes the **oceans, coastal areas, tidal zones,** and **coral reefs**. Reefs are found in relatively shallow warm waters. Like tropical rain forests, reefs are home to thousands of species of plant and animal life. Australia's Great Barrier Reef is the largest in the world.

The Great Barrier Reef, Australia

WATER, WATER EVERYWHERE

Earth is the water planet. More than two-thirds of its surface is covered with water, and every living thing on it needs water to live. Scientists looking for life on other planets start by looking for water. Water is not only part of our daily life (drinking, cooking, cleaning, bathing); it makes up 75% of our brains and 60% of our whole bodies! Humans can survive for about a month without food, but only for about a week without water. People also use water to produce power, to irrigate farmland, and for recreation.

HOW MUCH IS THERE TO DRINK?

Almost 97% of the world's water is salt water from the oceans and inland seas. Another 2% of the water is frozen in ice caps and glaciers. Half of the 1% left is too far underground to be reached. That leaves only 0.5% of freshwater for all the people, plants, and animals on Earth. This supply is renewable only by rainfall.

WHERE DOES DRINKING WATER COME FROM?

Most smaller cities and towns get their freshwater from **groundwater**—melted snow and rain that seeps deep into the ground and is drawn out from wells. Larger cities usually rely on lakes or rivers (and reservoirs) for their water. Areas of the world with little fresh water sometimes use a process called desalination (removing salt from seawater) for drinking water. But this process is slow and expensive.

THE HYDROLOGICAL CYCLE: Water's Endless Journey

Water is special. It's the only thing on Earth that exists naturally in **all three physical states**: solid (ice), liquid, and gas (water vapor). Although the water cycle has no starting or ending point, it is driven by the sun.

HOW DOES WATER GET INTO THE AIR?

Heat from the sun causes surface water in oceans, lakes, swamps, and rivers to turn into water vapor. This is called **evaporation**. Ice and snow can also **sublimate** (go from solid to gas with no liquid stage) into water vapor. Plants release water vapor into the air as part of the process called **transpiration**. Animals release a little bit when they breathe and when they perspire.

HOW DOES WATER COME OUT OF THE AIR?

Warm air holds more water vapor than cold air. As the air rises into the atmosphere, it cools and the water vapor **condenses**—changes back into tiny water droplets. These droplets form clouds. As the drops get bigger, gravity pulls them down as **precipitation** (rain, snow, sleet, fog, and dew are all types of precipitation). Precipitation, which falls mostly as rain, is the main route for water's return to Earth.

WHERE DOES THE WATER GO?

Depending on where the precipitation lands, it can: **1.** evaporate back into the atmosphere, **2.** run off into streams and rivers, **3.** be absorbed by plants, **4.** soak down into the soil as groundwater, or **5.** fall as snow on a glacier and be trapped as ice for thousands of years. Snowpack from winter snow in the mountains often melts in the spring and flows into streams as snowmelt.

WHY WE NEED WETLANDS

Wetlands are—you guessed it—wet lands. They are wet (covered with water, or with water at or near the surface) for at least part of every year. Bogs, swamps, and marshes are wet most of the year. Prairie potholes, are wet for only part of the year. Wetlands also include fens, wet meadows, vernal pools, playa lakes, and pocosins.

Wetlands have at least three important functions:

▶ **Storing water.** They absorb water like giant sponges and hold it in, releasing it slowly. During floods an acre of wetland can hold in 1.5 million gallons of water. As a result, wetlands help to control floods.

▶ **Cleaning up water.** They slow down water flow and let harmful sediments drop to the bottom. Plant roots and tiny organisms remove human and animal waste.

▶ **Providing habitats.** They are home to huge numbers of plants, fish, and wildlife. More than one-third of all threatened and endangered species in the U.S. live only in wetlands.

There are fewer than 100 million acres of wetlands left in the lower 48 states, less than half of what there were in 1600. Wetlands are lost when people drain and fill them in for farmland, dam them up to form ponds and lakes, or pave and build up surrounding areas.

Wetlands, Everglades National Park

WATER WOES

Pollution: Polluted water can't be used for drinking, swimming, or watering crops, nor can it provide a habitat for plants and animals. Even fish caught in polluted waters may be inedible if they contain high levels of toxins (poisons), such as mercury. Major sources of water pollutants are sewage, chemicals from factories, fertilizers and pesticides, and landfills that leak. In general, anything that anyone dumps on the ground finds its way into the water cycle. Each year, the United Nations promotes March 22 as "World Water Day" to remind people how important it is to protect precious freshwater.

Overuse: Using water faster than nature can pass it through the hydrological cycle can create other problems. When more water is taken out of lakes and reservoirs (for drinking, washing, watering lawns, and other uses) than is put back in, the water levels begin to drop. Combined with lower than normal precipitation, this can be devastating. In some cases, lakes become salty or dry up completely.

The Dreaded Dripping Faucet: Just one faucet, dripping very slowly (once a minute), can waste 38 gallons of water a year. Multiply that by several million houses and apartments, and you see a lot of water going down the drain!

WHERE GARBAGE GOES

The disposal of garbage is a serious issue. The problem is that we now produce more garbage than our natural environment can absorb. And many modern products, such as television sets and mobile phones, have parts that may never fully break down. The piles of garbage keep growing, and we add more to them every year.

What We Throw Out

Metal
7%

Plastic
16%

Food and Yard Waste
25%

Rubber and Leather
3%

Other Trash
25%

Paper
24%

*2006, after recycling

WHAT HAPPENS TO THINGS WE THROW AWAY?

Landfills

About half of our trash goes to places called landfills. A **landfill** (or dump) is a low area of land that is filled with garbage. Most modern landfills are lined with a layer of plastic or clay to try to keep dangerous liquids from seeping into the soil and groundwater supply. The number of landfills is one-fifth of what it was in 1988, but they're much larger.

The Problem with Landfills

Because of the unhealthy materials many contain, landfills do not make good neighbors. But where can we dispose of waste? How can hazardous waste — material that can poison air, land, and water — be disposed of in a safe way?

Incinerators

One way to get rid of trash is to burn it. Trash is burned in a furnace-like device called an **incinerator** to make energy. Incinerators burned a fifth of landfill-bound trash in 2005.

The Problem with Incinerators

Leftover ash and smoke from burning trash like rubber tires may contain harmful chemicals, called **pollutants**, including greenhouse gases. Pollutants can make it hard for some people to breathe. They can harm plants, animals, and people.

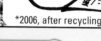
did you know?

In 2000, humans produced 13.9 billion tons of garbage, more than 2.2 tons per person. By 2050, we will probably produce 29.4 billion tons. That's a lot of garbage.

Reduce, Reuse, Recycle

Reducing garbage helps protect the environment. Avoid buying overly packaged goods. Reuse products. Buy durable and recyclable products or products made of recycled materials.

	TO REDUCE WASTE	TO RECYCLE
Paper	Use both sides of the paper. Use cloth towels instead of paper towels.	Recycle newspapers, magazines, comic books, and junk mail.
Plastic	Wash food containers and store leftovers in them. Reuse plastic bags.	Return soda bottles to the store. Recycle other plastics.
Glass	Keep bottles and jars to store other things.	Recycle glass bottles and jars.
Clothes	Give clothes to younger relatives or friends. Donate clothes to thrift shops.	Cut unwearable clothing into rags to use instead of paper towels.
Metal	Keep leftovers in storage containers instead of wrapping them in foil. Use glass or stainless steel pans instead of disposable pans.	Recycle aluminum foil, pans, and trays, and steel cans and containers. Return wire hangers to the dry cleaner.
Food/Yard Waste	Cut the amount of food you throw out. Try saving leftovers for snacks or meals later on.	Make a compost heap using food scraps, leaves, grass clippings, and the like.
Batteries	Use rechargeable batteries for toys and games, radios, music players, and flashlights.	Find out about your town's rules for recycling or disposing of batteries.

What Is Made From RECYCLED MATERIALS?

- *From* RECYCLED PAPER we get newspapers, cereal boxes, wrapping paper, cardboard containers, and insulation.
- *From* RECYCLED PLASTIC we get soda bottles, tables, benches, bicycle racks, cameras, backpacks, carpeting, shoes, and clothes.
- *From* RECYCLED STEEL we get steel cans, cars, bicycles, nails, and refrigerators.
- *From* RECYCLED GLASS we get glass jars and tiles.
- *From* RECYCLED RUBBER we get pencil cases, computer mousepads, shoe soles, bulletin boards, floor tiles, playground equipment, and speed bumps.

Producing an aluminum can from recycled material can save enough energy to run a television for three hours.

What is GLOBAL WARMING?

What Causes Global Warming?

Global warming is the gradual increase in Earth's temperature. The sun's rays heat the Earth. Some energy is absorbed by Earth's surface and converted into heat. More than one-third of this energy radiates back in to space. But some is prevented from escaping by **greenhouse gases** in the atmosphere. The most common greenhouse gases are carbon dioxide, methane, nitrous oxide, water vapor, and fluorinated gases. Most greenhouse gases occur naturally, and help to make life on Earth possible.

Without the natural greenhouse effect, the Earth would be about 60° colder than it is today.

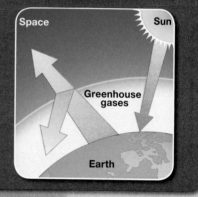

Since the mid-1800s, humans have been releasing more and more greenhouse gases into the atmosphere. Most of it comes from burning fossil fuels—like coal, natural gas, and oil—which produce carbon dioxide. Factories, farms, and landfills also add extra greenhouse gases. Deforestation adds to the problem, because trees absorb carbon dioxide.

There is more carbon dioxide and methane in the atmosphere today than has been normal for the last 650,000 years, trapping more of the sun's energy. The decade from 1998–2007 has been the warmest ever recorded. Scientists now find it very likely that humans are the primary cause of this global warming. They estimate that carbon dioxide has caused up to 70% of the enhanced greenhouse effect.

Where Greenhouse Gases Come From in the U.S. (2006)

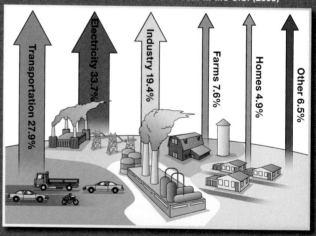

How Do We Know about Global Warming?

Worldwide records of climate have been kept since about 1850. Scientists have measured global increases in air and ocean temperatures, a rise in sea level, and melting glaciers. Today, weather balloons, ocean buoys, and satellites provide even more information.

Scientists drill thousands of feet into ice caps in Antarctica and Greenland to remove ice core samples. The layers of ice and air pockets trapped in them can be read like a timeline of climate change over the past 800,000 years.

What Will Happen?

Scientists have created computer climate models that identify patterns and make predictions. The best current estimates predict that by the year 2100, the Earth's average temperature will increase at least 3°F and oceans will rise 7 inches. The worst-case scenarios suggest that the Earth could warm by more than 11°F and sea levels could rise nearly 3 feet.

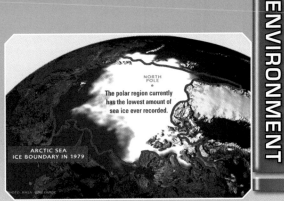

NORTH POLE

The polar region currently has the lowest amount of sea ice ever recorded.

ARCTIC SEA ICE BOUNDARY IN 1979

PHOTO: NASA, GODDARD

As the Earth warms, sea levels rise:

- Water expands slightly as it warms.

- The ice sheet covering Greenland and the Arctic Sea are melting. Also, chunks of ice (icebergs) are breaking away from ice sheets in Antarctica and Greenland.

- Glaciers and permafrost are melting in non-polar regions, producing more groundwater.

- As ice melts, it exposes darker land or sea, which is less reflective and absorbs more heat.

The Arctic region may be warming up more than other places because of the albedo effect, or a surface's power to reflect light. Ice reflects the sun's rays. With less ice on Earth, more of the sun's heat will be absorbed by the oceans. Warmer water raises sea levels and melts ice faster.

Warmer air affects the water cycle (see page 84). More water evaporates, and the atmosphere can hold more water vapor. Places with plenty of water will have more rain and floods. But in places where water is scarce, evaporation will dry out the land even more. Vapor will take more time to condense, meaning less rain and more droughts.

Rising sea levels already threaten coastal villages of Alaska and Russia and many small Pacific islands.

Many scientists believe that warmer oceans will lead to more tropical cyclones (also called hurricanes and typhoons).

As environments change, animals must find new homes or they may become extinct. Warmer global climates will allow more disease-carrying creatures like mosquitoes to spread to new places.

The World's ENERGY

Energy is all around us. You are using energy to turn the pages of this book. Energy cannot be created or destroyed, but it can change form. Heat, light, and electricity are forms of energy. The Sun's warmth is energy in the form of heat. Rubbing your hands together to keep warm is using energy to create heat. One important way we interact with our environment is by extracting energy from natural resources and putting it to use in everyday life, providing heat, electricity, and mechanical power. Some resources—like sunlight, water, and wind—will always be around. These are renewable resources. Nonrenewable resources come in limited supply, like fossil fuels and uranium. There will be no more once they're used up.

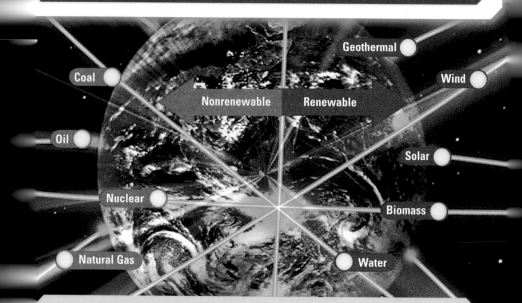

Nonrenewable / Renewable

Geothermal
Wind
Coal
Oil
Solar
Nuclear
Biomass
Natural Gas
Water

Who Produces and Uses the MOST ENERGY?

The United States produces about 15% of the world's energy—more than any other country—but it also uses 22% of the world's supply. The table on the left lists the world's top ten energy producers and the percent of the world's production that each nation was responsible for in 2005. The table on the right lists the world's top energy users and the percent of the world's energy that each nation consumed that same year.

TOP ENERGY PRODUCERS		TOP ENERGY USERS	
United States	15%	United States	22%
China	14%	China	14%
Russia	11%	Russia	7%
Saudi Arabia	6%	Japan	5%
Canada	4%	India	4%
Iran	3%	Germany	3%
India	3%	Canada	3%
Norway	2%	France	3%
Australia	2%	United Kingdom	2%
Mexico	2%	Brazil	2%

SOURCES OF ENERGY

Where Does Energy Come From?

Non-renewable resources come in limited supply. The "fossil fuels" **coal, oil, and natural gas are the most common**. Those are the decayed remains of ancient animals and plants that lived long before the dinosaurs (about 354 to 290 million years ago). They took millions of years to form and, if we run out, will take millions more for new supplies to be made. **Uranium**, the element that is split to power nuclear reactors, is more abundant than silver. However, U-235, the type of uranium used for fuel in nuclear plants, is relatively rare.

Uranium and coal are mined, either by digging huge pits or making tunnels that go deep underground. Oil and gas are pumped from wells drilled into the ground, sometimes at the bottom of the ocean. Oil fresh from the ground is called crude. It is sent to a refinery where it is separated into different types of fuel like gasoline, diesel, jet fuel, and other petroleum products. Natural gas, which consists mostly of methane, also includes propane and butane as by-products.

Renewable sources of energy will never run out. We can find many by just looking around. The force of moving water like a river or waterfall can create **hydropower**. It is one of the oldest sources of energy. **Ocean energy** uses the motion of the tides or the power of breaking waves to produce energy. The sun's light can be converted into **solar power**. Steady winds can be used to spin giant propellers, generating **wind power**. **Biomass**, or renewable material made from plants or animals like wood or garbage, can be burned to make energy. Heat from the Earth's mantle, called **geothermal energy**, can be collected at natural hot springs where magma boils surface water.

How Do We Power Homes?

The most common uses of energy in the home are to control heating and cooling and provide electricity for lighting and appliances.

Most electricity is generated at power stations by wheel-shaped engines called **turbines**. Water and wind both push turbines but usually a turbine is pushed with steam. Water is heated into steam by burning biomass or fossil fuels, or by splitting uranium atoms during nuclear fission. Half of America's electricity is generated from burning coal. But two-thirds of the energy stored in coal is lost when it is burned. Natural steam from hot springs can be used to spin turbines, but natural hot springs are rare.

Some homes have solar panels that use the sun's energy to heat water. Other types of panels use solar cells to convert sunlight into electricity. Many people have natural gas, the most widely used energy source in American homes, delivered to their home through pipes. The flames on stoves burn natural gas, which can also power home furnaces and hot water heaters.

Renewable Energy in Action:

Washington state is the nation's biggest producer of hydroelectricity and gets nearly three-quarters of its power from renewable resources. The Grand Coulee Dam that spans the Columbia River in northern Washington is the biggest hydroelectric dam in the U.S.

Iceland gets most of its heat from geothermal sources. Water is boiled in hot springs by underground volcanoes and piped into buildings like a giant radiator. Geothermal and hydropower sources provide 99% of the country's electricity.

Nuclear Fission is a complex and carefully controlled process where atoms are "split," or broken into two smaller atoms, to release huge bursts of energy that heat water into steam. One pencil-eraser-sized pellet of uranium can produce as much energy as 1,780 pounds of coal.

Producing Electricity: Pros & Cons

Nuclear Fission

👍 **Pros:** No greenhouse gases; big energy from a small amount of fuel; cannot explode like a nuclear bomb.

👎 **Cons:** Creates dangerous nuclear waste that takes thousands of years to become safe; meltdowns can contaminate large areas (like Chernobyl) with radiation; expensive.

Hydroelectric

👍 **Pros:** Does not pollute or heat the water or air; no waste products, runs non-stop; very inexpensive.

👎 **Cons:** Massive dams are expensive and difficult to build; alters the environment around the dam; can affect fish migratory patterns.

Biomass

👍 **Pros:** Reduces trash in landfills; cuts down on release of methane; plants, such as corn for ethanol, are a renewable resource.

👎 **Cons:** Burning some trash releases toxins and some greenhouse gases into the air; still leaves ash; plants require large farms and specific climate conditions; could raise food prices.

Wind

👍 **Pros:** Clean; land for wind farms can be used for other purposes like farming; can be built offshore.

👎 **Cons:** Wind farms take up a lot of space; can kill birds if placed in migratory paths; require winds of at least 12 to 14 mph; can be noisy.

Solar

👍 **Pros:** No pollution; little maintenance required.

👎 **Cons:** Solar panels are expensive and take up a lot of space; energy can't be gathered when the sun isn't shining; manufacturing the solar cells produces waste products.

A solar power home

Fossil Fuels
(primarily coal)

👍 **Pros:** Affordable because equipment is in wide use; needs smaller space to generate power compared to most other sources.

👎 **Cons:** Limited supply; major contributor to global warming; causes chemical reactions that create acid rain and smog; releases pollutants that cause breathing problems like asthma, can destroy land and pollute water.

WHERE DOES U.S. ENERGY COME FROM?

In 2007, about 86% of the energy used in the U.S. came from fossil fuels, mainly petroleum, natural gas, or coal. The rest came mostly from nuclear power, renewable resources such as hydroelectric power, geothermal, solar, and wind energy, and from alternative fuels such as biomass, and burning wood and animal waste.

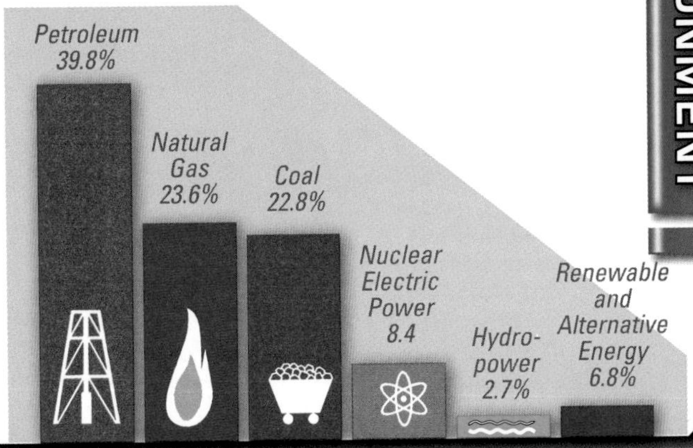

Petroleum
39.8%

Natural Gas
23.6%

Coal
22.8%

Nuclear Electric Power
8.4

Hydro-power
2.7%

Renewable and Alternative Energy
6.8%

ENVIRONMENT
SCRAMBLE

Unscramble these environment and energy terms and write them in the boxes at right. Then read down the light-blue boxes for the answer to the riddle!

What insulting name did the plumber call the leaky faucet?

T I C S A P L   O T L E T B

M U M L U A I N   A N C

S A S G L

R O A R D C D B A

A E P R P

E S T A I B T E R

T O M C O P S

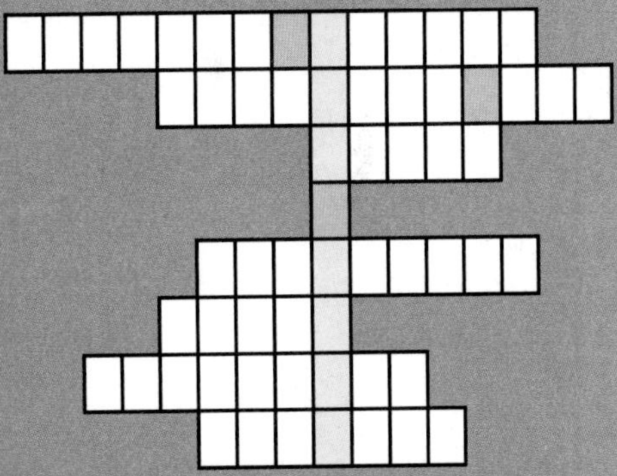

A nuclear power plant

ANSWERS ON PAGES 334-336.
FOR MORE PUZZLES GO TO
WWW.WAFORKIDS.COM

An offshore oil rig

FASHION

Where do you wear a hijab? ➤ **page 97**

Take a trip through fashion history over the last 100 years. What style do you like the best? It's a modern trend for the fashion-forward, especially kids, to borrow from the decades and make their own special styles.

1900s:
THE EDWARDIAN ERA

Women: "Formal" females favored custom-made dresses, tight corsets, lots of lace, and feathered hats.
Men: "High society" gents wore tailored wool suits, straw "boater" hats, and narrow shoes.

1920s:
THE ROARING TWENTIES

Women: "Flappers" had short, sleek hair and wore drop-waist sequined dresses and fancy costume jewelry.
Men: Distinguished men wore pastel-colored shirts, and silk ties that were secured with tie pins.

1940s:
MAKE DO AND MEND

Women: During World War II, "Rosie the Riveter" styles (blue jeans, baggy sweaters, and "drainpipe" trousers) were practical and patriotic. Stockings were a luxury.
Men: Materials were scarce during the war. Pillowcases and parachutes were used to make clothing. Instead of wool, suits were made of wood pulp and had fake pockets.

1960s:
FLOWER POWER

Women: A "groovy chick" would look mod in a bright colored miniskirt, blue eye shadow, white go-go boots, and super-long hair.
Men: A "hippie" guy might wear bell-bottom jeans, a paisley shirt, and a leather vest. Funky peace signs and flower patches were popular.

1970s:

DISCO DAYS

Women: Girls were "staying alive" in "hot pants," polyester pantsuits, bell-bottoms, and platform shoes.
Men: "Mr. Disco" wore polyester bell-bottoms, brightly colored shirts, and gold chains on the dance floor.

1990s:

ANYTHING GOES

Women: Dr. Martens big black boots, hooded sweatshirts, and layered T-shirts for the neo-hippie chick.
Men: "Grungy" guys kept themselves warm in lumberjack flannels and their money secure with trucker chain wallets. The "hip-hoppers," on the other hand, warmed up in puffy athletic jackets and sneakers.

2000s:

FROM HIP-HOP TO *GOSSIP GIRL*

Women: Girls start the decade in low-rise jeans, tight T-shirts with bare midriffs, and bell-bottoms. As the decade continues, girls turn to fashions from teen dramas such as television's *Gossip Girl*, adopting its glamorous yet funky styles.

Men: Hip-hop guys keep a beat in baggy pants, gold chains, and athletic gear. The *Gossip Girl* boys bring back prep-school fashions with their blazers, striped ties, and loafers.

did you know?

Starting in the 1500s, fashion designers crafted doll clothes to show their designs. The dolls used were one-half to one-third the size of humans. The designers clothed the "dress dolls" in miniature samples of their fashions. Clients could then view the dolls and pick the styles they liked. The clothes were then custom-made to fit the client exactly.

Fashion
AROUND THE WORLD

TOGAS

A toga is a robe that is draped and wrapped around one's body. The toga was worn by government officials in ancient Rome until about 100 A.D. Only men wore togas. Women wore a dress-like outfit called a stola. During winter, some Romans wore leggings to stay warm. There were many different styles of togas, but most were made from white wool. When Emperors passed laws requiring togas to be worn, they became a symbol of Roman citizenship. If a person was banished from the Roman Empire, he had to leave his toga behind.

BREECHCLOTHS AND BUCKSKIN DRESSES

Early Native Americans had their own distinctive style of dress, which varied from tribe to tribe. However, in most tribes, the men wore breechcloths, a long piece of hide or cloth held in place by a belt. In colder climates, they added leather leggings for warmth. Women often wore skirts and leggings. In some tribes, they wore dresses instead, such as the Cheyenne buckskin dress. Nearly all Native Americans wore the sturdy leather shoes called *moccasins* or a boot called a *mukluk*.

WIGS

People were wearing wigs as long ago as 3500 B.C. In ancient Egypt, people wore wigs made from vegetable matter and human hair to protect their heads from the sun. Wigs were common in Greek and Chinese theater, and were worn in ancient Roman, Assyrian, and Phoenician cultures. In Europe during the 16th and 17th centuries, wigs were associated with royalty or high fashion. Today, people wear wigs for fashion, convenience, or religious observance.

What Not to Wear *A sumptuary law is a law that applies to personal habits, including dress. Laws passed in Rome in 216 B.C. limited women to wearing no more than half an ounce of gold. Later, laws were passed that forbade men to wear silk. Around 1300 A.D. these kinds of laws were made in Europe. In Florence, people were not allowed to wear anything red or made from silk. In England, only knights were allowed to wear fur and only the royal family could wear purple. During the 16th century, French and English rulers often made these laws for religious or moral reasons. Sumptuary laws passed in colonial America in 1651 forbade colonists to wear gold, silk, lace, silver, or hats made from beaver fur.*

KIMONOS

Robes were first worn in Japan around 300 A.D. It was popular during the Heian period, around 800, for Japanese women to wear many layers of robes. Royalty wore up to 16 layers! The original Japanese word for clothing, *kimono*, stuck with the fashion. During the 15th century, warriors wore kimonos to represent their leader. Today they are worn for traditional festivals and special events, including weddings. A bridal kimono is called a *shiro-muku*.

VEILS

The tradition of covering one's face or head with a veil was practiced more than 5,000 years ago in the ancient kingdom of Sumeria, the modern-day Middle East. Veils were worn to protect the face from desert wind. But some veils revealed the origin, tribe, or even skills of a person. In this tradition, men of the northern African Tuareg tribe wear veils today as a status symbol, even as they eat and drink!

As early as the 1st century, some Hindu women wore veils to show modesty, as many Muslim women all over the world do today. A *hijab* is the most popular form of headscarf worn by Muslim women, and is not particular to a certain color or country. The *chador* is a long black shawl that covers the entire body and head. It is typically worn in Iran. The *burqa* is a robe that covers the entire body and face, and is worn mostly in Afghanistan.

The veil has made many appearances in Western history as well. In medieval Europe, women wore chest-length veils called wimples. Today veils are worn in Western cultures for weddings, mourning, and religious ceremonies.

MATCHING GAME

TRADITIONAL CLOTHING	COUNTRY OF ORIGIN
Lederhosen (short pants with suspenders)	Uganda
Pien-fu (2-piece robe)	Chile
Kikoi (sarong-type skirt)	China
Chamanto (knee-length poncho)	Germany
Kamiks (watertight boots)	Morocco
Kaftan (belted shirt-dress)	Arctic Inuit people

ANSWERS ON PAGES 334-336. FOR MORE PUZZLES GO TO WWW.WAFORKIDS.COM

GAMES

What was the name of the first fully interactive video game? ➡ page 99

ONLINE GAMES

Online games are more popular than ever. One-third of Internet users play a game at least once a week. Online gamers can build a virtual city with *Sim City*, play World Cup soccer, or explore a fantasy world in one of the exciting online role-playing games.

World of Warcraft is the most popular online role-playing game, with more than 10 million subscribers around the world. Thousands of people can play the game online at the same time.

The game takes place mainly on Azeroth, a planet peopled by an assortment of fantastic characters. To enter the game world, you create and name your own character. You can be a human, elf, orc, troll, or other imaginary creature.

Once you create your own character, you then work with other players on your side to explore the game world and complete quests. Meanwhile, you battle the players on the opposing side. Games can last for days or even weeks, with the player entering and leaving the game world as often as he or she wishes.

WEB CONNECT:
🔟 CAN'T MISS INTERNET GAMES

There are tons of great games that can be played on the internet. And most are free. Here are 10 that every kid should check out.

Battleships A computerized version of the board game Battleship. (www.miniclip.com/games/battleships/en/)

Bookworm Deluxe Find words in a jumble, but watch out for flaming blocks that can set fire to your library. (www.popcap.com/gamepopup.php?theGame=bookworm)

Hypervelocity Racer Drive a race car and avoid potholes and other race cars. (www.surfnetkids.com/games/hypervelocity_racing.htm)

Matchsticks You may have played this one in real life. Remove sticks to create shapes. (www.surfnetkids.com/games/matchsticks.htm)

Papa Louie Deliver pizzas while battling pizza monsters. (www.miniclip.com/games/papa-louie/en/)

Planetary Rescue Squad Use physics to deliver supplies to space explorers. (pbskids.org/dragonflytv/games/game_planetary.html)

Samorost All you have to do is click on the objects in the correct order to solve each puzzle. (www.samorost.net/samorost1)

3 Puck Chuck Sort of like a pool table with air hockey pucks instead of balls. (pbskids.org/zoom/games/3puckchuck/)

Viking Quest Construct a Viking boat, hire a crew, and raid England. (www.bbc.co.uk/history/ancient/vikings/launch_gms_viking_quest.shtml)

Whizzball A puzzle game where you have to get a marble to hit its target. You can also build puzzles for others to try. (kids.discovery.com/games/whizzball/whizzball.html)

VIDEO GAME TIME LINE

1962 Spacewar, played on an early microcomputer, is the first fully interactive video game.

1974 Atari's Pong, one of the first home video games, has "paddles" to hit a white dot back and forth on-screen.

1980 Pac-Man, Space Invaders, and Asteroids (first to let high scorers enter initials) invade arcades.

1985 Nintendo Entertainment System comes to the U.S. Super Mario Bros. is a huge hit!

1987 Legend of Zelda game released.

1989 Nintendo's handheld video game system, Game Boy, debuts.

1996 Nintendo 64 is released.

2000 Sony's PlayStation 2 arrives.

2001 Microsoft's Xbox and Nintendo's GameCube hit the shelves.

2005 Sony's PSP, a new handheld video game system, goes on sale.

2006 Nintendo Wii, which features a wand-like controller, is released.

2008 Nintendo Wii Fit, a balance board which allows you to exercise as you play games, goes on sale.

CONSOLE GAMES

Console games such as those popularized by Sony, Microsoft, and Nintendo are also widely popular. At home, these action-packed games may be played alone or with several of your friends. You can also connect to the Internet to engage with multiple players. If games like **Space Chimps** or **Blue Dragon** aren't your thing, you can practice anything from yoga to the hula hoop with Wii Fit.

It's fun to practice playing soccer with Wii Fit.

⌂ ●WAforKids.com ↱

Go to www.WAforKids.com for these activities:

• Puzzle out dozens of World Almanac for Kids games, both online and in easy-to-print pages.

• Take quizzes on fun topics like weird food around the world, sports, and more.

GEOGRAPHY

What chain of islands did James Cook explore? ➡ page 102

SIZING UP THE EARTH

The word "geography" comes from the Greek word *geographia*, meaning "writing about the Earth." It was first used by the Greek scholar Eratosthenes, who was head of the great library of Alexandria in Egypt. Around 230 B.C., when many people believed the world was flat, he did a remarkable thing. He calculated the circumference of the Earth. His figure of about 25,000 miles was close to the modern measurement of 24,901 miles!

Actually, the Earth is not perfectly round. It's flatter at the poles and bulges out a little at the middle. This bulge around the equator is due to Earth's rotation. Although Earth seems solid to us, it is really slightly plastic, or flexible. As the Earth spins, material flows toward its middle, piling up and creating a slight bulge. The Earth's diameter is 7,926 miles at the equator, but only 7,900 miles from North Pole to South Pole. The total surface area of the Earth is 196,940,000 square miles.

GEOGRAPHY 1 2 3

Longest Rivers	**1.** Nile (Egypt and Sudan)—4,160 miles
	2. Amazon (Brazil and Peru)—4,000 miles
	3. Chang (China)—3,964 miles (formerly called the Yangtze)
Tallest Mountains	**1.** Mount Everest (Tibet and Nepal)—29,035 feet
	2. K2 (Kashmir)—28,250 feet
	3. Kanchenjunga (India and Nepal)—28,208 feet
Biggest Islands	**1.** Greenland (Atlantic Ocean)—840,000 square miles
	2. New Guinea (Pacific Ocean)—306,000 square miles
	3. Borneo (Pacific Ocean)—280,100 square miles
Biggest Desert Regions	**1.** Sahara Desert (North Africa)—3.5 million square miles
	2. Australian Deserts—1.3 million square miles
	3. Arabian Peninsula—1 million square miles
Biggest Lakes	**1.** Caspian Sea (Europe and Asia)—143,244 square miles
	2. Superior (U.S. and Canada)—31,700 square miles
	3. Victoria (Kenya, Tanzania, Uganda)—26,828 square miles
Highest Waterfalls	**1.** Angel Falls (Venezuela)—3,212 feet
	2. Tugela Falls (South Africa)—2,800 feet
	3. Monge Falls (Norway)—2,540 feet

READING A MAP

▶ **DIRECTION** Maps usually have a **compass rose** that shows you which way is north. On most maps, like this one, it's straight up. The compass rose on this map is in the upper left corner.

▶ **DISTANCE** As you can see, the distances on a map are much shorter than the distances in the real world. The **scale** shows you how to estimate the real distance. This map's scale is in the lower left corner.

▶ **PICTURES** Maps usually have little pictures or symbols to represent real things like roads, towns, airports, or other points of interest. The map **legend** (or **key**) tells what they mean.

▶ **FINDING PLACES** Rather than use latitude and longitude to locate features, many maps, like this one, use a grid system with numbers on one side and letters on another. An index, listing place names in alphabetical order, gives a letter and a number for each. The letter and number tell you in which square to look for a place on the map's grid. For example, Landisville can be found at A-1 on this map.

▶ **Using the map** People use maps to help them travel from one place to another. What if you lived in East Petersburgh and wanted to go to the Hands-on-House Children's Museum? First, locate the two places on the map. East Petersburgh is C1, and the Hands-on House Children's Museum is E1. Next, look at the roads that connect them and decide on the best route. (There could be several different ways to go.) One way is to travel east on Route 722, then southeast on Valley Road until you see the Children's Museum.

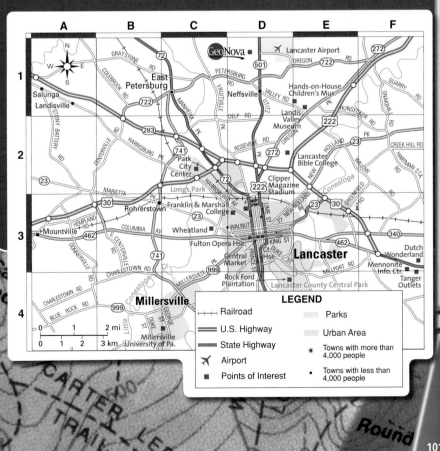

Note.

*he asterisk ❋ between th
of St Helena denotes the
hitherto ascertained . be

Early Exploration

AROUND 1000	**Leif Ericson**, from Iceland, explored "Vinland," which may have been the coasts of northeast Canada and New England.
1271-95	**Marco Polo** (Italian) traveled through Central Asia, India, China, and Indonesia.
1488	**Bartolomeu Dias** (Portuguese) explored the Cape of Good Hope in southern Africa.
1492-1504	**Christopher Columbus** (Italian) sailed four times from Spain to America and started colonies there.
1497-98	**Vasco da Gama** (Portuguese) sailed farther than Dias, around the Cape of Good Hope to East Africa and India.
1513	**Juan Ponce de León** (Spanish) explored and named Florida.
1513	**Vasco Núñez de Balboa** (Spanish) explored Panama and reached the Pacific Ocean.
1519-21	**Ferdinand Magellan** (Portuguese) sailed from Spain around the tip of South America and across the Pacific Ocean to the Philippines, where he died. His expedition continued around the world.
1519-36	**Hernando Cortés** (Spanish) conquered Mexico, traveling as far west as Baja California.
1527-42	**Alvar Núñez Cabeza de Vaca** (Spanish) explored the southwestern United States, Brazil, and Paraguay.
1532-35	**Francisco Pizarro** (Spanish) explored the west coast of South America and conquered Peru.
1534-36	**Jacques Cartier** (French) sailed up the St. Lawrence River to the site of present-day Montreal.
1539-42	**Hernando de Soto** (Spanish) explored the southeastern United States and the lower Mississippi Valley.
1603-13	**Samuel de Champlain** (French) traced the course of the St. Lawrence River and explored the northeastern United States.
1609-10	**Henry Hudson** (English), sailing from Holland, explored the Hudson River, Hudson Bay, and Hudson Strait.
1682	**Robert Cavelier, sieur de La Salle** (French), traced the Mississippi River to its mouth in the Gulf of Mexico.
1768-78	**James Cook** (English) charted the world's major bodies of water and explored Hawaii and Antarctica.
1804-06	**Meriwether Lewis and William Clark** (American) traveled from St. Louis along the Missouri and Columbia rivers to the Pacific Ocean and back.
1849-59	**David Livingstone** (Scottish) explored Southern Africa, including the Zambezi River and Victoria Falls.

arrows describe the velocity of the
Currents in Nautical Miles in 24 hrs?

Extent of Polar Ice
Floating Islands of Ice

SOME FAMOUS EXPLORERS

These explorers, and many others, risked their lives on trips to explore faraway and often unknown places. Some sought fame. Some sought fortune. Some just sought challenge. All of them increased people's knowledge of the world.

CHRISTOPHER COLUMBUS

(1451-1506), Italian navigator who sailed for Spain. He had hoped to find a fast route to Asia by going west from Europe. Instead he became the first European (other than the Vikings) to reach America, landing in the Bahamas in October 1492.

FERDINAND MAGELLAN (1480-1521),

Portuguese navigator and explorer who set sail from Spain in 1519, seeking a western route to the Spice Islands of Indonesia. He became the first European to cross the Pacific Ocean, but was killed by natives in the Philippines. However, because he passed the easternmost point he had reached on an earlier voyage, he is recognized as the first person to circumnavigate the Earth.

Hernando de Soto

(about 1500–1542), Spanish explorer. Searching for riches, he and his men explored present-day Florida, Georgia, North and South Carolina, and Tennessee. Unfortunately, his party carried fatal diseases from Europe which killed thousands of Indians. Ironically, de Soto himself died on the banks of the Mississippi River of an illness contracted in America. His exploration opened up America for other explorers.

MERIWETHER LEWIS (1774-1809) and WILLIAM CLARK

(1770-1838), American soldiers and explorers. In 1804-06 they led an expedition across the American West and back. Aided by a Shoshone woman, Sacagawea, they gained knowledge of the huge Louisiana Territory that the United States had bought from France.

Mary Henrietta Kingsley (1862–1900),

British explorer. At a time when women were discouraged from traveling into remote regions, she made two trips to West Africa, visiting areas never seen by Europeans. She studied and wrote about the customs and natural environment.

MATTHEW HENSON (1866-1955),

the first famous African American explorer. As an assistant to explorer Robert Peary (1856-1920), he traveled on seven expeditions to Greenland and the Arctic region. In April 1909, Peary and Henson became the first to reach, or nearly reach, the North Pole. (Recent research suggests they may have fallen short by about 30 to 60 miles.)

JACQUES COUSTEAU (1910-1997),

French undersea explorer and environmentalist. He helped invent the Aqualung, allowing divers to stay deep underwater for hours, and made award-winning films of what he found there.

ANN BANCROFT

(1955-), American educator and explorer. In 1986, she became the first woman to reach the North Pole by dogsled, and in 1992-93 was leader of the first all-woman expedition to reach the South Pole on skis.

BENEDICT ALLEN

(1960-), British explorer. He has published nine books about his journeys, through remote and extreme environments. While studying in New Guinea, he participated in a secret ceremony that left many scars on his body.

WEB SITE For a site about explorers with lots of useful links, try
www.kidinfo.com/American_History/Explorers.html

LOOKING AT OUR WORLD

THINKING GLOBAL

Shaped like a ball or sphere, a globe is a model of our planet. Like Earth, it's not perfectly round. It is an oblate spheroid (called a "geoid") that bulges a little in the middle.

In 1569, Gerardus Mercator found a way to project the Earth's curved surface onto a flat map. One problem with a Mercator map (like the one on page 105) is that land closer to the poles appears bigger than it is. Australia looks smaller than Greenland on this type of map, but in reality it's not.

North Pole

prime meridian
(0 degrees)

North America

40 degrees
north latitude

Africa

20 degrees
north latitude

South America

Equator

20 degrees
south latitude

40 degrees
south latitude

South Pole

LATITUDE AND LONGITUDE

Imaginary lines that run east and west around Earth, parallel to the equator, are called **parallels**. They tell you the **latitude** of a place, or how far it is from the equator. The equator is at 0 degrees latitude. As you go farther north or south, the latitude increases. The North Pole is at 90 degrees **north latitude**. The South Pole is at 90 degrees **south latitude**.

Imaginary lines that run north and south around the globe, from one pole to the other, are called **meridians**. They tell you the degree of **longitude**, or how far east or west a place is from the prime meridian (0 degrees).

Which Hemispheres Do You Live In?

Draw an imaginary line around the middle of Earth. This is the **equator**. It splits Earth into two halves called **hemispheres**. The part north of the equator, including North America, is the **northern hemisphere**. The part south of the equator is the **southern hemisphere**.

An imaginary line called the **Greenwich meridian** or **prime meridian** divides Earth into east and west. It runs north and south around the globe, passing through the city of Greenwich in England. North and South America are in the **western hemisphere**. Africa, Asia, and most of Europe are in the **eastern hemisphere**.

THE TROPICS OF CANCER AND CAPRICORN

If you find the equator on a globe or map, you'll often see two dotted lines running parallel to it, one above and one below (see pages 149 and 158–159). The top one marks the Tropic of Cancer, an imaginary line marking the latitude (about 23°27' North) where the sun is directly overhead on June 21 or 22, the beginning of summer in the northern hemisphere.

Below the equator is the Tropic of Capricorn (about 23°27' South). This line marks the sun's path directly overhead at noon on December 21 or 22, the beginning of summer in the southern hemisphere. The area between these dotted lines is the tropics, where it is consistently hot because the sun's rays shine more directly than they do farther north or south.

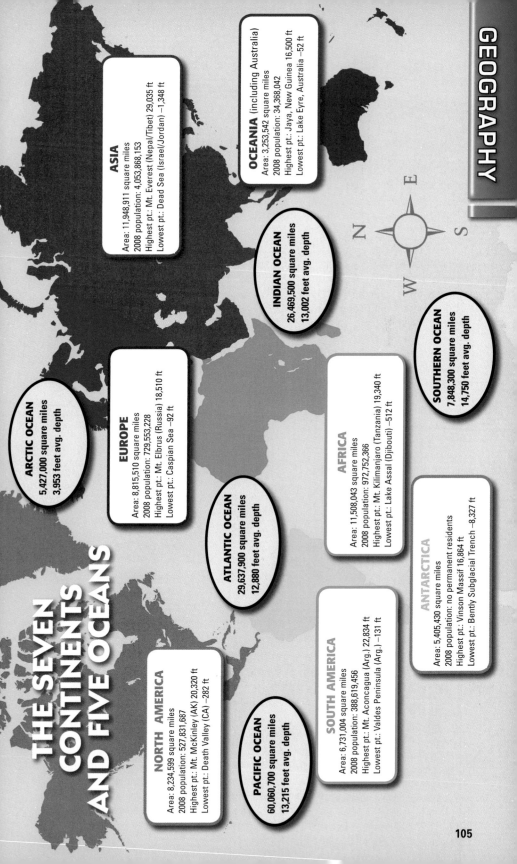

THE SEVEN CONTINENTS AND FIVE OCEANS

ASIA
Area: 11,948,911 square miles
2008 population: 4,053,868,153
Highest pt.: Mt. Everest (Nepal/Tibet) 29,035 ft
Lowest pt.: Dead Sea (Israel/Jordan) −1,348 ft

OCEANIA (including Australia)
Area: 3,253,542 square miles
2008 population: 34,368,042
Highest pt.: Jaya, New Guinea 16,500 ft
Lowest pt.: Lake Eyre, Australia −52 ft

INDIAN OCEAN
26,469,500 square miles
13,002 feet avg. depth

SOUTHERN OCEAN
7,848,300 square miles
14,750 feet avg. depth

ARCTIC OCEAN
5,427,000 square miles
3,953 feet avg. depth

EUROPE
Area: 8,815,510 square miles
2008 population: 729,553,228
Highest pt.: Mt. Elbrus (Russia) 18,510 ft
Lowest pt.: Caspian Sea −92 ft

AFRICA
Area: 11,508,043 square miles
2008 population: 972,752,366
Highest pt.: Mt. Kilimanjaro (Tanzania) 19,340 ft
Lowest pt.: Lake Assal (Djibouti) −512 ft

ATLANTIC OCEAN
29,637,900 square miles
12,880 feet avg. depth

ANTARCTICA
Area: 5,405,430 square miles
2008 population: no permanent residents
Highest pt.: Vinson Massif 16,864 ft
Lowest pt.: Bently Subglacial Trench −8,327 ft

NORTH AMERICA
Area: 8,234,599 square miles
2008 population: 527,831,687
Highest pt.: Mt. McKinley (AK) 20,320 ft
Lowest pt.: Death Valley (CA) −282 ft

PACIFIC OCEAN
60,060,700 square miles
13,215 feet avg. depth

SOUTH AMERICA
Area: 6,731,004 square miles
2008 population: 388,619,456
Highest pt.: Mt. Aconcagua (Arg.) 22,834 ft
Lowest pt.: Valdes Peninsula (Arg.) −131 ft

WHAT'S INSIDE THE EARTH?

Starting at the Earth's surface and going down you find the lithosphere, the mantle, and then the core.

The lithosphere, the rocky crust of the Earth, extends for about 60 miles.

The dense, heavy inner part of the Earth is divided into a thick shell, the mantle, surrounding an innermost sphere, the core. The mantle extends from the base of the crust to a depth of about 1,800 miles and is mostly solid.

Then there is the Earth's core. It has two parts: an inner sphere of scorchingly hot, solid iron almost as large as the moon and an outer region of molten iron. The inner core is much hotter than the outer core. The intense pressure near the center of Earth squeezes the iron in the inner core into a solid ball nearly as hot as the surface of the Sun. Scientists believe the core formed billions of years ago during the planet's fiery birth. Iron and other heavy elements sank into the planet's hot interior while the planet was still molten. As this metallic soup cooled over millions of years, crystals of iron hardened at the center.

lithosphere

mantle about 1,800 miles

outer core about 1,300 miles

core about 1,500 miles

In 1996, after nearly 30 years of research, it was found that, like the Earth itself, the inner core spins on an axis from west to east, but at its own rate, outpacing the Earth by about one degree per year.

Homework Tip

There are three types of rock:

1 IGNEOUS rocks form from underground magma (melted rock) that cools and becomes solid. Granite is an igneous rock made from quartz, feldspar, and mica.

2 SEDIMENTARY rocks form on low-lying land or the bottom of seas. Layers of small particles harden into rock such as limestone or shale over millions of years.

3 METAMORPHIC rocks are igneous or sedimentary rocks that have been changed by chemistry, heat, or pressure (or all three). Marble is a metamorphic rock formed from limestone.

CONTINENTAL DRIFT

The Earth didn't always look the way it does now. It was only in the early 20th century that a geologist named Alfred Lothar Wegener came up with the theory of continental drift. Wegener got the idea by looking at the matching rock formations on the west coast of Africa and the east coast of South America. He named the enormous first continent Pangaea. The continents are still moving, athough most move no faster than your fingernails grow—aout 2 inches a year.

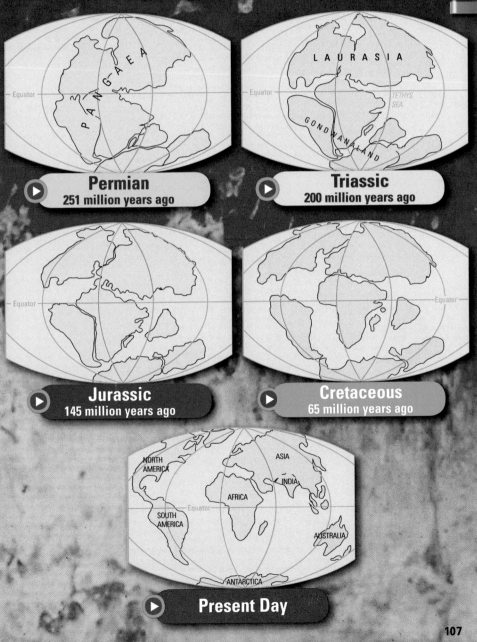

Permian
251 million years ago

Triassic
200 million years ago

Jurassic
145 million years ago

Cretaceous
65 million years ago

Present Day

107

KIDS' HEALTH ISSUES

ALLERGIES

Our immune systems protect us from harmful substances. Certain people's immune systems, however, try to fight off even harmless substances. Common **allergens**—the substances people are allergic to—include pollen and peanuts. If a person inhales, eats, or touches an allergen, he or she might have an allergic reaction. The person might look as if he or she has a cold or have trouble breathing. In severe cases, a person can die from an allergic reaction.

Some people are born more likely to have an allergy. They can control it by taking medication or staying away from whatever they're allergic to. Sometimes kids outgrow their allergies.

Carly Roman has severe allergies. She had to drink a medicated shake as her only food for 8 weeks.

ASTHMA

Asthma is a condition that makes breathing difficult. Allergens, polluted air, vigorous exercise, or stress can trigger an asthma attack. When someone has an attack, his or her airways narrow and can't carry as much air to the lungs.

An asthma attack might last up to a few hours. After one attack, another might not occur until hours, days, or years later. Asthma can't be cured, but people can take medication to prevent it and to treat it. They can also avoid things that trigger an attack. About 9% of American kids, or 7 million, had asthma in 2008.

OBESITY

When people eat more calories than they burn off through exercise, their bodies store that extra energy as fat. In 2003-04, 17% of all kids in the U.S., or more than 12 million, were overweight.

Someone is considered overweight if his or her **body mass index (BMI)** is above a certain number. If a person's BMI is even higher, he or she is considered obese. To calculate your BMI, visit **WEB SITE** *apps.nccd.cdc.gov/dnpabmi.*

EATING DISORDERS

About 8 million teenagers in the United States have an eating disorder. Some have **anorexia nervosa**, a condition in which the person has an overwhelming desire to be thin. **Anorexics** skip meals and drastically reduce the amount of food they eat. They lose so much weight that they endanger their health. About 5 percent of anorexics die from the disorder.

Other teenagers suffer from **bulimia nervosa**, also known as bulimia. **Bulimics** alternate between bingeing, when they eat huge amounts of food, and purging, when they empty their bodies of everything they've eaten. Unlike anorexics, who are significantly underweight, most bulimics are of normal or above-normal weight.

These disorders are most common among girls between the ages of 11 and 18. However, a growing number of teenage boys are developing eating disorders, too.

NEW FOOD PYRAMID

To stay healthy, it is important to eat the right foods and to exercise. In 2005, the U.S. government designed a new food pyramid to help people track what they should eat. The pyramid recommends different amounts of food depending on age, gender, and activity level. The colored parts of the pyramid stand for different foods. The width of each part shows you about how much of that food you should be eating. The figure on the steps reminds you to be physically active.

GRAINS
Make half of the grains you eat whole, such as whole-grain bread, cereal, brown rice, and pasta.

VEGETABLES
Try more dark green and orange vegetables. Eat more dry beans and peas.

FRUITS
Choose from fresh, frozen, canned, or dried fruit.

OILS
Not a food group but essential for good health. Get most of your fats from fish, nuts, and vegetable oils like corn and canola oil.

MILK
Get your calcium from low-fat or fat-free milk, yogurt, and cheese.

MEAT & BEANS
Eat lean meats. Don't forget to try fish, beans, peas, nuts, and seeds.

MyPyramid.gov STEPS TO A HEALTHIER YOU

To figure out what you should be eating, based on your age, gender, and activity level, use the calculator online: **WEB SITE** www.mypyramid.gov

For example, an active girl between the ages of 9 and 13 should eat between 1,800 and 2,200 calories daily, including:

Fruits	1.5-2 cups	Meat & Beans	5-6 ounces
Vegetables	2.5-3 cups	Milk	3 cups
Grains	6-7 ounces	Oils	5-6 teaspoons

YOUR BODY

Know What Goes Into It

NUTRITION FACTS: KNOWING HOW TO READ THE LABEL

Every food product approved by the Food and Drug Administration (FDA), whether it's a can of soup or a bag of potato chips, has a label that describes the nutrients derived from that product. For instance, the chips label on this page shows the total calories, fat, cholesterol, sodium, carbohydrate, protein, and vitamin content per serving.

A serving size is always defined (here, it is about 12 chips or 28 grams). This label shows that there are 9 servings per container. Don't be fooled by the calorie count of 140–these are calories per serving and not per container. If you ate the entire chips bag, you would have eaten 1,260 calories!

Nutrition Facts

Serving Size 1 oz. (28g/About 12 chips)
Servings Per Container About 9

Amount Per Serving	
Calories 140	Calories from Fat 60

	% Daily Value*
Total Fat 7g	**11%**
Saturated Fat 1g	**5%**
Trans Fat 0g	
Cholesterol 0mg	**0%**
Sodium 170mg	**7%**
Total Carbohydrate 18g	**6%**
Dietary Fiber 1g	**4%**
Sugars less than 1g	
Protein 2g	

Vitamin A 0%	•	Vitamin C 0%	
Calcium 2%	•	Iron 2%	
Vitamin E 4%	•	Thiamin 2%	
Riboflavin 2%	•	Vitamin B6 4%	
Phosphorus 6%	•	Magnesium 4%	

* Percent Daily Values are based on a 2,000 calorie diet. Your daily values may be higher or lower depending on your calorie needs:

		Calories:	2,000	2,500
Total Fat	Less than		65g	80g
Sat Fat	Less than		20g	25g
Cholesterol	Less than		300mg	300mg
Sodium	Less than		2,400mg	2,400mg
Total Carbohydrate			300g	375g
Dietary Fiber			25g	30g

Calories per gram:
Fat 9 • Carbohydrate 4 • Protein 4

Why You Need To Eat:

Fats are needed to help kids grow and to stay healthy. Fats contain nine calories per gram—the highest calorie count of any type of food. So you should limit (but not avoid) intake of fatty foods. Choose unsaturated fats, like the fat in nuts, over saturated fats and trans fats, like the fat in doughnuts.

Carbohydrates are a major source of energy for the body. Simple carbohydrates are found in white sugar, fruit, and milk. Complex carbohydrates, also called starches, are found in bread, pasta, and rice.

Cholesterol is a soft, fat-like substance produced by your body. It's also present in animal products such as meat, cheese, and eggs but not in plant products. Cholesterol helps with cell membrane and hormone production, but there are two main types. Bad cholesterol, or LDL, gets stuck easily in blood vessels, which can lead to a heart attack or stroke. Good cholesterol, or HDL, helps break down bad cholesterol.

Proteins help your body grow and make your immune system stronger. Lean meats and tofu are good options.

Vitamins and Minerals are good for all parts of your body. For example, vitamin A, found in carrots, promotes good vision; calcium, found in milk, helps build bones; and vitamin C, found in fruits, helps heal cuts.

SOME LOW-FAT FOODS

Bananas
Oatmeal
Plain popcorn
Apples
Sunflower seeds
Lentils

SOME FATTY FOODS

Ice cream
Cheeseburgers
Buttered popcorn
Chocolate candy
Potato chips

HAVE FUN GETTING FIT

Why Work Out?

Nearly one in five children in America today are overweight. Overweight kids run the risk of developing serious health problems including diabetes, asthma, and high blood pressure.

Exercise is a great way to prevent obesity and improve health. Children should get at least 60 minutes of exercise every day. But keep in mind that exercise should be fun. You can play soccer, ride a bike, dance, swim, or play catch with a friend. As long as you're moving, it's exercise!

HOW TO WORK OUT

▶ Begin with a five-minute warm-up! Warm-up exercises heat the body up, so that muscles become soft, limber, and ready for more intense activity. Warm-up exercises include jumping jacks, walking, and stretching.

▶ After warming up, do an activity that you like, such as running or playing basketball with your friends. This increases your heart rate.

▶ After working out, cool down for 5 to 10 minutes. Cooling down is like a reverse warm-up. It lets your heart rate slow gradually. Walking is an example of a cool-down activity. Afterward, do some stretching. This helps your muscles remove waste, such as lactic acid, that your muscles make while exercising. Also remember to drink plenty of water during and after your exercise.

▶ Building up strength through your workouts can be very beneficial. This doesn't mean you should lift the heaviest weights possible! It's better to do more lifts using light weights (1/2 lb or 1 lb) than fewer lifts with very heavy weights. Give your body time to recover between strength workouts.

It's becoming easier for people with all kinds of disabilities to take part in physical activities. Many groups across the U.S. help out by providing information and chances to compete. Special equipment uses the latest materials (such as light plastics) and improved design to let people with disabilities hold their own in almost any activity.

ACTIVITY

ACTIVITY	CALORIES PER MINUTE
Racquetball	10
Jogging (6 miles per hour)	8
Martial arts	8
Playing basketball	7
Playing soccer	6
Bicycling (10-12 miles per hour)	5
Raking the lawn	4
Skating or rollerblading (easy pace)	4
Swimming (25 yards per minute)	3
Walking (3 miles per hour)	3
Yoga	3
Playing catch	2

If you're interested in running, try (WEB SITE) www.kidsrunning.com
There you'll find advice, activities, stories, poems, and more—all about running.

BODY BASICS:

Your body is made up of many parts. Even though we are all individuals, our bodies share similar structures. These structures make up different systems in the body.

CIRCULATORY SYSTEM In the circulatory system, the **heart** pumps **blood**. Blood travels through tubes, called **arteries**, to all parts of the body. Blood carries oxygen and food that the body needs to stay alive. **Veins** carry blood back to the heart.

DIGESTIVE SYSTEM The digestive system moves food through the **esophagus**, **stomach**, and **intestines**. As food passes through, some of it is broken down into tiny particles called **nutrients**. Nutrients enter the bloodstream and are carried to all parts of the body. The digestive system changes whatever food isn't used into waste that is eliminated from the body.

ENDOCRINE SYSTEM The endocrine system includes **glands**. There are two kinds of glands. **Exocrine** glands produce liquids such as sweat and saliva. **Endocrine** glands produce chemicals called **hormones**. Hormones control body functions like growth.

NERVOUS SYSTEM
The nervous system enables us to think, feel, move, hear, and see. It includes the **brain**, the **spinal cord**, and **nerves** throughout the body. Nerves in the spinal cord carry signals between the brain and the rest of the body. The brain has three major parts. The **cerebrum** controls thinking, speech, and vision. The **cerebellum** is responsible for physical coordination. The **brain stem** controls the respiratory, circulatory, and digestive systems.

RESPIRATORY SYSTEM The respiratory system allows us to breathe. Air enters the body through the nose and mouth. It goes through the **windpipe**, or **trachea**, to two tubes called **bronchi**, which carry air to the **lungs**. Oxygen from the air is absorbed by tiny blood vessels in the lungs. The blood then carries oxygen to the heart, from where it is sent to the body's cells.

- Brain
- Trachea (windpipe)
- Esophagus
- Lungs
- Heart
- Liver
- Stomach
- Small intestine
- Large intestine

What the Body's Systems Do?

MUSCULAR SYSTEM
Muscles are made up of elastic fibers. There are three types of muscle: **skeletal**, **smooth**, and **cardiac**. Skeletal muscles help the body move—they are the large muscles we can see. Smooth muscles are found in our digestive system, blood vessels, and air passages. Cardiac muscle is found only in the heart. Smooth and cardiac muscles are **involuntary** muscles—they work without us having to think about them.

REPRODUCTIVE SYSTEM
Through the reproductive system, adult human beings are able to create new human beings. Reproduction begins when a man's **sperm** cell fertilizes a woman's **egg** cell.

URINARY SYSTEM
This system, which includes the **kidneys**, cleans waste from the blood and regulates the amount of water in the body.

IMMUNE SYSTEM
The immune system protects your body from diseases by fighting against certain outside substances, or **antigens**. This happens in different ways. For example, white blood cells called **B lymphocytes** learn to fight viruses and bacteria by producing **antibodies** to attack them. Sometimes, as with **allergies**, the immune system makes a mistake and creates antibodies to fight a substance that's really harmless.

BRAIN DIAGRAM

The typical human brain only weighs about three pounds. But it's like the control center of the body, responsible for making sure everything functions properly. Different parts of the brain do different things.

Right hemisphere of cerebrum
- Controls left side of body
- Location of things relative to other things
- Recognizes faces
- Music
- Emotions

Left hemisphere of cerebrum
- Controls right side of body
- Ability to understand language and speech
- Ability to reason
- Numbers

Cerebrum

Cerebellum
Controls coordination, balance

Brain stem
Regulates vital activities like breathing and heart rate

113

THE FIVE SENSES

Your senses gather information about the world around you. The five senses are **hearing**, **sight**, **smell**, **taste**, and **touch**. You need senses to find food, resist heat or cold, and avoid situations that might be harmful. Your ears, eyes, nose, tongue, and skin sense changes in the environment. Nerve receptors send signals about these changes to the brain, where the information is processed.

HEARING

1

eardrum

inner ear

middle ear

outer ear

auditory nerve

The human ear is divided into three parts—the outer, middle, and inner. The **outer ear** is mainly the flap we can see on the outside. Its shape funnels sound waves into the **middle ear**, where the eardrum is located. The **eardrum** vibrates when sound waves hit it, causing three tiny bones behind it to vibrate as well. These vibrations are picked up in the **inner ear** by tiny filaments of the **auditory nerve**. This nerve changes the vibrations into nerve impulses and carries them to the brain.

did you know?

You have several thousand taste buds on your tongue. Each taste bud is actually a tiny nerve ending that allows you to perceive different tastes. Although you probably know about the taste receptors for sweet, sour, salty, and bitter tastes, scientists recently located a fifth taste receptor as well, for **umami**. It's the savory flavor found in meats and cheeses, due to the glutamic acid in these foods. The word umami means "delicious" in Japanese.

SIGHT

2

The **lens** of the eye is the first stop for light waves, which tell you the shapes and colors of things around you. The lens focuses light waves onto the **retina**, located on the back wall of the eye. The retina has light-sensitive nerve cells. These cells translate the light waves into patterns of nerve impulses that travel along the **optic nerve** to your brain, where an image is produced. So in reality, all the eye does is collect light. It is the brain that actually forms the image.

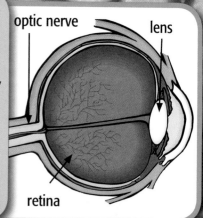

optic nerve

lens

retina

SMELL

3

In our noses are nerve cells called **olfactory receptors**. Tiny mucus-covered hairs from these receptors detect chemicals in the air. These chemicals make what we call odor, or scent. This information then travels along the **olfactory nerves** to the brain. Nerves from the olfactory receptors connect with the **limbic system**, the part of the brain that deals with emotions. That's why we tend to like or dislike a smell right away. The smell can leave a strong impression on our memory, and very often a smell triggers a particular memory.

TASTE

4

Taste buds are the primary receptors for taste. They are located on the surface and sides of the tongue, on the roof of the mouth, and at the back of the throat. These buds can detect five qualities— **sweet** (like sugar), **sour** (like lemons), **salty** (like chips), **bitter** (like coffee) **umami** or savory flavors (like meat). Taste signals come together with smell signals in the same part of your brain. That's why you need both senses to get a food's full flavor.

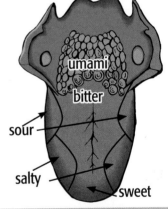

umami

bitter

sour

salty

sweet

TOUCH

5

Your sense of touch allows you to feel temperature, pain, and pressure. These environmental factors are all sensed by nerve fibers located in the **epidermis**, the outer layer of skin, and the **dermis**, the second layer of skin, throughout the body. As with all the other senses, nerves send information to the brain through the nervous system.

INVENTIONS

Invention TIME LINE

YEAR	INVENTION	INVENTOR (COUNTRY)
105	paper	Ts'ai Lun (China)
1440s	printing press/movable type	Johann Gutenberg (Germany)
1590	2-lens microscope	Zacharias Janssen (Netherlands)
1608	telescope	Hans Lippershey (Netherlands)
1616	reflecting telescope	Niccolo Zucchi
1714	mercury thermometer	Gabriel D. Fahrenheit (Germany)
1752	lightning rod	Benjamin Franklin (U.S.)
1783	parachute	Sebastien Lenormand (France)
1800	electric battery	Alessandro Volta (Italy)
1804	steam locomotive	Richard Trevithick (England)
1837	telegraph	Samuel F. B. Morse (U.S.)
1842	anesthesia (ether)	Crawford W. Long (U.S.)
1846	sewing machine	Elias Howe (U.S.) ▶
1870	telephone*	Antonio Meucci (Italy), Alexander G. Bell (U.S.)
1879	practical light bulb	Thomas A. Edison (U.S.)
1886	automobile (gasoline)	Karl Benz (Germany)
1891	escalator	Jesse W. Reno (U.S.)
1892	moving picture viewer	Thomas A. Edison & William K. Dickson (U.S.)
1895	X-ray	Wilhelm Roentgen (Germany)
1897	diesel engine	Rudolf Diesel (Germany)
1902	air conditioning	Willis Carrier (U.S.)
1922	insulin	Sir Frederick G. Banting & Charles Best (Canada)
1923	television**	Vladimir K. Zworykin (U.S.) ▶
1926	rocket engine	Robert H. Goddard (U.S.)
1928	tape recorder	Fritz Pfleumer (Germany)
1928	penicillin	Alexander Fleming (Scotland)
1933	FM radio	Edwin Armstrong (U.S.)
1939	jet airplane	Hans van Ohain (Germany)
1941	electronic computer	John V. Atanasoff & Clifford Berry (U.S.)
1955	Velcro®	George de Mestral (Switzerland)
1957	digital image	Russell Kirsch (U.S.)
1957	laser***	Gordon Gould (U.S.)
1971	CAT scanner	Godfrey N. Hounsfield (England)
1973	cellular telephone	Motorola/Martin Cooper (U.S.)
1975	digital camera	Steven Sasson (U.S.)
1975	personal computer IBM	E. Roberts, W. Yates, & J. Bybee (U.S.)
1990	handheld digital camera	Dycam (U.S.)
2001	Segway® Personal Transporter (PT)	Dean Kamen (U.S.)
2007	iPhone	Steve Jobs (U.S.) ▶

* Meucci developed a version of the telephone (early 1870s); Bell received a patent for another version.
** Others who helped invent the television include Philo T. Farnsworth (1927) and John Baird (1925).
*** First working laser built in 1960 by Theodore Maiman.

CURRENT Inventions

BIOMIMETICS: DESIGNED BY NATURE

Spider web silk is stronger than steel. A beetle in Africa's Namib Desert uses its bumpy wings to collect drinking water from fog. Sharks are covered in teeth-like scales that help them swim faster. Humans have made many great inventions but sometimes nature still does things better.

Researchers who study biomimetics look to natural abilities and designs for new advances in engineering, medicine, and other sciences. Their research mimics nature to create new inventions.

Swiss engineer George de Mestral could be called the father of biomimicry. Mestral liked to hike but he was always removing sticky seeds called burrs from his clothes and his dog's fur. Curious about their sticking power, he looked at one under a microscope and saw hundreds of tiny hooks. After several years of research, he made a tape with burr-like hooks that could stick to a tape of wool-like loops: Velcro.

Geckos feet aren't sticky but, thanks to millions of microscopic hairs, they can climb up most surfaces whether wet, dry, dirty, smooth, or bumpy. Ron Fearing and students at Berkley University have mimicked those tiny foot hairs with plastic microfibers (42 million per square centimeter) to create an adhesive, like tape. It attaches by sliding instead of pushing. A simple pull in another direction (releasing the stress) can remove it. It leaves no sticky gunk and does not stick to itself.

Watch a fly lift off. It certainly doesn't fly like an airplane. Flies flap their wings much like the way people tread water, in twisting movements and with varying force. Robert Wood at Harvard University has created a flying microrobot that copies the basic makeup of a fly. It's the size of a penny and weighs 60 milligrams. Its wings, which flap 120 times a second, are made of carbon fiber and polymer. In the future, the robot could be used in rescues and exploration.

did you know?

George Washington Carver (1864–1943) was an inventor who created hundreds of new products (such as cheese, milk, flour, and soap) from peanuts and other legumes. This made the peanut one of the country's leading cash crops, and helped to revitalize farming in the American south. Carver, whose parents were slaves, went on to advise many world leaders, including Presidents Calvin Coolidge and Franklin D. Roosevelt.

LANGUAGE

Do you see with your *ojos* or your *orejas*? ➡ page 121

TOP LANGUAGES

Mandarin, the principal language of China, has the most native speakers of any language. Spanish ranks second as the most common native, or first, language in the world.*

LANGUAGE	KEY PLACES WHERE SPOKEN	NATIVE SPEAKERS
Mandarin	China, Taiwan	873,014,298
Spanish	South America, Spain	322,299,171
English	U.S., Canada, Britain, Australia	309,352,280
Hindi	India	180,764,791
Portuguese	Portugal, Brazil	177,457,180
Bengali	Bangladesh, India	171,070,202
Russian	Russia	145,031,551
Japanese	Japan	122,433,899

Which LANGUAGES Are SPOKEN in the UNITED STATES?

Most Americans speak English at home. But since the beginning of American history, immigrants have come to the U.S. from all over the world. Many have brought other languages with them.

"¡Hola!" That's how more than 28 million Spanish-speaking Americans say "hi" at home.

The table at the right lists the most frequently spoken languages in the U.S., as of the 2000 census.

	LANGUAGE USED AT HOME	SPEAKERS OVER 5 YEARS OLD
1	Speak only English	215,423,557
2	Spanish, Spanish Creole	28,101,052
3	Chinese	2,022,143
4	French	1,643,838
5	German	1,382,613
6	Tagalog (Philippines)	1,224,241
7	Vietnamese	1,009,627
8	Italian	1,008,370
9	Korean	894,063
10	Russian	706,242
11	Polish	667,414
12	Arabic	614,582
13	Portuguese	564,630
14	Japanese	477,997
15	French Creole	453,368
16	Greek	365,436
17	Hindi	317,057
18	Persian	312,085
19	Urdu	262,900
20	Gujarathi (from India & parts of Africa)	235,988

LANGUAGE EXPRESS

Ciao! (Italian)
Hello! (English)
Konnichi wa! (Japanese)

Surprise your friends and family with words from other languages.

English	Italian	French	German	Chinese
January	gennaio	janvier	Januar	yi-yue
February	febbraio	février	Februar	er-yue
March	marzo	mars	Marz	san-yue
April	aprile	avril	April	si-yue
May	maggio	mai	Mai	wu-yue
June	giugno	juin	Juni	liu-yue
July	luglio	juillet	Juli	qi-yue
August	agosto	août	August	ba-yue
September	settembre	septembre	September	jiu-yue
October	ottobre	octobre	Oktober	shi-yue
November	novembre	novembre	November	shi-yi-yue
December	dicembre	decembre	Dezember	shi-er-yue
blue	azzurro	bleu	blau	lan
red	rosso	rouge	rot	hong
green	verde	vert	grün	lu
yellow	giallo	jaune	gelb	huang
black	nero	noir	schwarz	hei
white	bianco	blanc	weiss	bai
happy birthday!	buon compleanno!	joyeux anniversaire!	Glückwunsch zum Geburtstag!	sheng-ri kuai le!
hello!	ciao!	bonjour!	hallo!	ni hao!
good-bye!	arrivederci!	au revoir!	auf Wiedersehen!	zai-jian!
fish	pesci	poisson	Fisch	yu
bird	uccello	oiseau	Vogel	niao
horse	cavallo	cheval	Pferd	ma
one	uno	un	eins	yi
two	due	deux	zwei	er
three	tre	trois	drei	san
four	quattro	quatre	vier	si
five	cinque	cinq	fünf	wu

⌂ ●WAforKids.com ➤

Go to www.WAforKids.com and type 120 into the code box for these activities:
- Take a fun quiz about "Weird Words and Phrases" and show what you know about quotes with a "Who Said It?" quiz.
- Are you a wonderful wordsmith? Find out with a chapter quiz.
- Get even more facts about figures of speech, what it's like to be a writer, and what your name means.

¡SAY IT EN ESPAÑOL!

Spanish is the most commonly spoken language in the U.S. after English. More than 28 million people speak Spanish at home. That's almost 10 percent of all people in the U.S.

Pronouncing **Spanish** Words

In Spanish, the vowels only make one type of sound. The sound each vowel makes in Spanish is the same sound it makes in the English words at right.

Also, if you see the letters J, G, or X followed by a vowel, pronounce them like the English "H." So, "Frijoles" sounds like "Free-hole-ace." "Ejecutivo" sounds like "Eh-he-coo-tee-vo." "Región" sounds like "Ray-hee-own."

Try your pronunciation on the words and phrases on this page.

A	water
E	bet
I	feet (like you are saying the letter *e*)
O	slow
U	tube

Sister
Languages

There are some words that sound alike in both Spanish and English. These are called cognates. See if you can guess how each kid listed at right answered the question: **What do you want to be when you grow up?**

Julio	Yo quiero ser *músico*.
Maria	Un dia, yo quisiera ser *autora*.
Juan	Yo quiero ser *banquero*.
Olivia	Un dia, yo quisiera ser *doctora*.
Jose	Yo quiero ser *presidente*.

Answers: Julio—musician; Maria—author; Juan—banker; Olivia—doctor; Jose—president.

Food

Next time you're having dinner, ask your brother to pass the *arroz*.

Basic Spanish Phrases

Hello	Hola
Goodbye	Adiós
How are you?	¿Cómo estás?
Please	Por favor
Thank you	Gracias
It's nice to meet you.	Mucho gusto en conocerte.

Salad **Ensalada**

Juice **Jugo**

Beans **Frijoles**

Rice **Arroz**

Chicken **Pollo**

Your Body
Es Su Cuerpo

Use your *boca* to say these parts of the body (*cuerpo*). Use your *cabeza* to remember how to say them!

Head	Cabeza
Face	Cara
Eyes	Ojos
Mouth	Boca
Ears	Orejas
Neck	Cuello
Hair	Cabello
Arm	Brazo
Belly	Barriga
Hand	Mano
Leg	Pierna
Knee	Rodilla
Foot	Pie

Numbers

1	uno	6	seis
2	dos	7	siete
3	tres	8	ocho
4	cuatro	9	nueve
5	cinco	10	diez

Joke en Español

Teacher ¿Como se escribe "nariz" en inglés? (How do you write "nose" in English?)

Student No sé. (I don't know.)

Teacher ¡Correcto! (Correct!)

THE ENGLISH LANGUAGE

Facts About English

- According to the *Oxford English Dictionary*, the English language contains between 250,000 and 750,000 words. (The number depends on whether you count different meanings of the same word as separate words and on how many obscure technical terms you count.)

- The most frequently used letters of the alphabet are E, T, A, and O, in that order.

- Here are the 30 most common English words: the, of, and, a, to, in, is, that, it, was, he, for, as, on, with, his, be, at, you, I, are, this, by, from, had, have, they, not, or, one. Try to make a sentence with just these words. Here's an example: "I had to be with it for that is not the one they have."

New Words

English is always changing as new words are born and old ones die out. Many new words come from the fields of electronics and computers, from the media, or from slang.

hoodie: a hooded sweatshirt, usually with a zipper down the front

manga: a Japanese comic book or graphic novel

ollie: a skateboarding or snowboarding maneuver in which the board rises off the ground

qigong: pronounced chee-gong, this is a Chinese philosophy of exercise. *Qi*, or *chi*, is the Chinese term for "vital life energy."

ringtone: a sound or song programmed in or downloaded to ring from a cell phone.

supersize: to increase the amount of, as in food

In Other Words: SIMILES

Similes are comparisons of two dissimilar things that use "as" or "like." Here are some to wrap your brain around:

graceful as a swan—"smooth and elegant." Swans are admired for their long necks and the way they quietly glide through the water. Ballerinas are often compared to swans, with their extended, smooth movements on the stage.

quiet as a mouse—"almost too quiet to hear." Mice are quiet and shy, and good at hiding. Even their squeaks are practically too soft to hear.

strong as an ox—"stronger than most people." Oxen are cattle that are trained to pull very heavy loads.

GETTING TO THE ROOT

Many English words and parts of words can be traced back to Latin or Greek. If you know the meaning of a word's parts, you can probably guess what it means. A root (also called a stem) is the part of the word that gives its basic meaning but can't be used by itself. Roots need other word parts to complete them: either a prefix at the beginning, or a suffix at the end, or sometimes both. The following tables give some examples of Greek and Latin roots, prefixes, and suffixes.

LATIN

root	basic meaning	example
-alt-	high	altitude
-dict-	to say	dictate
-port-	to carry	transport
-scrib-/ -script-	to write	prescription
-vert-	turn	invert

prefix	basic meaning	example
de-	away, off	defrost
in-/im-	not	invisible
non-	not	nontoxic
pre-	before	prevent
re-	again, back	rewrite
trans-	across, through	trans-Atlantic

suffix	basic meaning	example
-ation	(makes verbs into nouns)	invitation
-fy/-ify	make or cause to become	horrify
-ly	like, to the extent of	highly
-ment	(makes verbs into nouns)	government
-ty/-ity	state of	purity

GREEK

root	basic meaning	example
-anthrop-	human	anthropology
-biblio-	book	bible
-bio-	life	biology
-dem-	people	democracy
-phon-	sound	telephone
-psych-	soul	psychology

prefix	basic meaning	example
anti-/ant-	against	antisocial
auto-	self	autopilot
biblio-/ bibl-	book	bibliography
micro-	small	microscope
tele-	far off	television

suffix	basic meaning	example
-graph	write, draw, describe, record	photograph
-ism	act, state, theory of	realism
-ist	one who believes in, practices	capitalist
-logue/ -log	speech, to speak	dialogue
-scope	see	telescope

JOKES AND RIDDLES

1. Who is President if the Vice President dies?

2. A farmer combined four bales of hay with two bales of hay. How many bales does he have?

3. What keeps the beat for your head?

4. How do you make the number one disappear?

5. What do you lose when you stand up?

6. What's the last thing you take off before you go to bed?

7. Why was the chef arrested?

8. Why is the letter E like London?

9. What happens to a white hat when you throw it in the Red Sea?

10. Why do birds fly south for the winter?

11. Think of words ending in "gry." Two are "angry" and "hungry." There are three words in "the English language." What is the third word? *HINT:* Everyone uses it every day and if you've listened closely, I've already said the answer.

12. What did one traffic light say to the other?

13. Two mothers and their two daughters went shopping. They each bought something, but came home with only three new things. Why?

14. What does everyone do at the same time, all day long, every day?

15. What can you put in a wooden box so that it's lighter?

16. How does the solar system hold up its pants?

17. You can keep it only after giving it to someone else. What is it?

18. What's black and white and read all over?

19. What has wheels and flies but never leaves the ground?

20. What type of dog can jump higher than a skyscraper?

21. What comes once in a minute, twice in a moment, but never in a billion years?

22. Why did the boy put a ruler under his pillow before he went to bed?

23. What can you hold without using your limbs?

24. What did one microchip say to the other when he wouldn't give him back his toy?

25. Why do seagulls fly over the sea?

26. How many birthdays does the average person have?

27. Some months have 31 days, some months only have 30. How many have 28 days?

28. What is light as a feather but not even the strongest man can hold it for long?

29. A herder had 11 sheep. All but 9 died. How many were left?

30 Why can't a man living in Cincinnati be buried south of the Ohio River?

31 What has four eyes but cannot see?

32 What goes up when the rain comes down?

33 What do you get when you cross a rooster and a duck?

34 What kind of horses go out after dark?

35 What time is it when an elephant sits on a fence?

36 When is a car not a car?

37 What has arms but can't hug?

38 You're the driver of a bus. You stop on a corner and pick up 6 people. At the second stop, 4 people get on and 3 people get off. When you stop again, 5 people get on and 2 people get off. At the last stop, 5 people get on and 1 person gets off. How old is the bus driver?

39 You live in a one-story purple house. Everything in the house is purple. The walls are purple, the refrigerator is purple, the plates are purple, etc. What color are the stairs?

40 What do you get when you cross the world's best fairy tale with the world's biggest mammal?

WORD-CONNECT

Synonyms are words that have the same meaning. For example, "funny" and "comic" are synonyms. The answers to this crossword puzzle are all synonyms of the clues given below. See if you can fill in all the blanks.

ACROSS
1 Unbelievable
5 Point
7 Accept
8 Paddle
9 Tale
11 Bill
13 Mad
15 Even [straight]

DOWN
2 Performer
3 Fly
4 Container
6 Toss
8 Choice
10 Journey
12 Child
14 Shout

ANSWERS ON PAGES 334-336. FOR MORE PUZZLES GO TO WWW.WAFORKIDS.COM

MILITARY

What medal is the highest honor for U.S. soldiers? ➡ page 129

American Revolution

Why? The British king sought to control American trade and tax the 13 colonies without their consent. The colonies wanted independence.

Who? British and American loyalists vs. American revolutionaries with French support

When? 1775-1783

Result? The colonies gained independence.

War of 1812

Why? Britain interfered with American commerce and forced American sailors to join the British navy.

Who? Britain vs. United States

When? 1812-1814

U.S.S. Constitution

Result? There was no clear winner. The U.S. unsuccessfully invaded Canada, a British colony. The British burned Washington, D.C., and the White House but were defeated in other battles.

did you know? The lyrics to the "The Star Spangled Banner," were written by Francis Scott Key in 1814 after seeing the British attack on Fort McHenry and the resulting American victory during the War of 1812.

Mexican War

Why? The U.S. annexed Texas. It also sought control of California, a Mexican province.

Who? Mexico vs. United States

When? 1846-1848

Result? Mexico ceded land in Texas, California, and New Mexico. The U.S. paid Mexico millions of dollars in return.

Civil War

Why? The Southern states seceded from the U.S. The U.S. fought to keep them.

Who? Confederacy vs. Union

When? 1861-1865

Result? The United States remained a unified country. Slavery was abolished.

Spanish-American War

Why? The Americans supported Cuban independence from Spain.

Who? United States vs. Spain

When? 1898

Result? Spain handed the Philippines, Guam, and Puerto Rico over to the U.S. Cuba became independent.

The Charge of San Juan Hill

did you know? Future President Theodore Roosevelt led the charge of San Juan Hill.

126

World War I

Why? Colonial and military competition between European powers.

Who? Allies (including the U.S., Britain, France, Russia, Italy, and Japan) vs. Central Powers (including Germany, Austria-Hungary, and Turkey)

When? 1914-1918 (The U.S. entered in 1917)

Result? The Allies defeated the Central Powers. An estimated 8 million soldiers and close to 10 million civilians were killed.

World War II

Why? The Axis sought world domination.

Who? Axis (including Germany, Italy, and Japan) vs. Allies (including the U.S., Britain, France, and the Soviet Union). The U.S. did not enter the war until Japan attacked Pearl Harbor in 1941.

When? 1939-1945 (U.S. dropped atomic bombs on Hiroshima and Nagasaki.)

Result? The Allies defeated the Axis. The Holocaust (the Nazi effort to wipe out the Jews and other minorities) was stopped. The U.S. helped rebuild Western Europe and Japan. The Soviet Union set up Communist governments in Eastern Europe.

Yalta summit in 1945 with Winston Churchill, Franklin Roosevelt and Josef Stalin

 The Allied invasion of Nazi-occupied France on June 6, 1944, known as D-Day, was the biggest invasion in world history. More than 150,000 American, British, and Canadian soldiers stormed the beaches of Normandy.

Korean War

Why? North Korea invaded South Korea. In many ways, the conflict was part of the Cold War between the Communist and non-Communist nations.

Who? North Korea with support from China and the Soviet Union vs. South Korea backed by the United States and its allies.

When? 1950-1953

Result? The war ended with a cease-fire agreement. North Korean forces retreated north of the 38th parallel. Korea remains divided.

Nonmetallic body armor was used for the first time during the Korean War.

Vietnam War

Why? Communists (Viet Cong) backed by North Vietnam attempted to overthrow South Vietnam's government.

Who? North Vietnam with support from the Soviet Union and China vs. South Vietnam with support from the U.S. and its allies

When? 1959-1975

Result? The U.S. withdrew its troops in 1973. In 1975, South Vietnam surrendered. Vietnam became a unified Communist country

Two thirds of the men who served in Vietnam were volunteers.

Persian Gulf War

Why? Iraq invaded and annexed Kuwait. It refused to withdraw despite United Nations demands.

Who? Iraq vs. U.S.-led coalition

When? 1991

Result? The coalition drove out Iraqi forces from Kuwait.

A-10A Thunderbolt II ground attack plane flying during Desert Storm, 1991

Where Are We Now?

Afghanistan War

Why? The U.S. demanded that Afghanistan's Taliban regime turn over Osama bin Laden, the man who planned the 9/11 terrorist attacks. The Taliban claimed not to know bin Laden's whereabouts.

Who? Taliban regime vs. Afghani Northern Alliance fighters, supported by the U.S. and its allies

When? 2001-

Result? The Taliban regime was defeated, but U.S. troops are still fighting Taliban resisters and hunting for bin Laden.

did you know? Small handheld or gun-mounted cameras, powered by two AA batteries and weighing less than a pound, allow U.S. soldiers to see in total darkness or through smoke or fog.

Iraq War

Why? The U.S. accused Iraq of hiding weapons of mass destruction (WMDs) and supporting terrorists.

Who? Iraq vs. United States, Great Britain, and their allies

When? 2003-

Result? Saddam Hussein's government was toppled. Hussein was captured, put on trial, and hanged. No WMDs were found. Attacks from different groups on U.S. troops and Iraqi civilians have been ongoing.

TOP ⑩ NATIONS WITH LARGEST ARMED FORCES

1.	China	2,255,000	6.	South Korea	687,000
2.	United States	1,438,000	7.	Pakistan	619,000
3.	India	1,325,000	8.	Turkey	515,000
4.	North Korea	1,106,000	9.	Vietnam	484,000
5.	Russia	1,237,000	10.	Egypt	469,000

Source: International Institute for Strategic Studies, 2005-06. Figures are for active troops.

MEDALS

The **MEDAL OF HONOR** is the nation's highest medal for any branch of the military. It's awarded by the President and Congress to a person who risks his or her life by going "above and beyond the call of duty" in battle. The five-pointed star is worn around the neck. It's been awarded about 3,467 times since 1863.

The **PURPLE HEART** is given to any soldier who is wounded or killed in battle. It is the oldest American decoration for military merit, first awarded by General George Washington in 1782. Washington's face has been on the medal since 1932.

MODERN-DAY HEROES

The heroes below were each awarded the country's highest decoration for valor in combat, the Medal of Honor, posthumously (after death). Each one died in selfless, courageous acts of bravery that saved other lives.

WAR IN AFGHANISTAN

MICHAEL P. MURPHY (1976-2005) Lieutenant, United States Navy

OPERATION IRAQI FREEDOM

JASON L. DUNHAM (1981-2004) Corporal, United States Marine Corps

ROSS A. McGINNIS (1987-2006) ▶ Private First Class, United States Army

MICHAEL A. MONSOOR (1981-2006) Master-At-Arms Second Class (Sea, Air, and Land), United States Navy

PAUL R. SMITH (1969-2003) Sergeant First Class, United States Army

money

What does the pyramid on the dollar bill mean? ➡ **page 132**

World's Ten Richest People*

Name	Age	Country	Industry	Worth (in billions)
Warren Buffett	77	United States	Investments	62.0
Carlos Slim Helu	68	Mexico	Communications	60.0
Bill Gates	52	United States	Software (Microsoft)	58.0
Lakshmi Mittal	57	United Kingdom	Manufacturing - Steel	45.0
Mukesh Ambani	50	India	Manufacturing - Oil	43.0
Anil Ambani	48	India	Investments	42.0
Ingvar Kamprad	81	Switzerland	Retail - IKEA	31.0
KP Singh	76	India	Real Estate	30.0
Oleg Deripaska	40	Russia	Diversified Investments	28.0
Karl Albrecht	88	Germany	Retail – Aldi	27.0

*As of March 2008 (Source www.forbes.com)

Youngest Billionaires (2008)

Name	Age	Country	Industry	Worth (in billions)
Sergey Brin	34	United States	Technology – Google	18.7
Yang Huiyan	26	China	Real Estate	7.4
Kostyantin Zhevago	34	Ukraine	Banking/Mining	3.4
Xiaofeng Peng	33	China	Solar Energy	2.5
Albert von Thurn und Taxis	24	Germany	Diversified Investments	2.3
Fahd Hariri	27	France	Diversified Investments	2.3
Aymin Hariri	29	Saudi Arabia	Technology	2.3
Mark Zuckerberg	23	United States	Technology-Facebook	1.5
Hind Hariri	24	Lebanon	Diversified Investments	1.1
Begumhan Dogan Faralyali	31	Turkey	Media/Entertainment	1

PRESIDENT DOLLARS

ew gold colored dollar coins honoring the nation's presidents are now being circulated. The U.S. Mint has started making one-dollar coins that show the faces of our presidents in the order they served in office. The Mint will issue four presidential $1 coins per year through 2016.

The George Washington dollar coin was the first. It was released on February 15, 2007. Coins with Presidents John Adams, Thomas Jefferson, and James Madison were also released in 2007. In 2008, the coins honor Presidents James Monroe, John Quincy Adams, Andrew Jackson, and Martin Van Buren. So far, the coins have been released mid-month in February, May, August, and November.

Tails

Look for Presidents William Henry Harrison, John Tyler, James K. Polk, and Zachary Taylor in 2009. The coin honoring President Lincoln will be available in late 2010.

The size, weight, and metal composition of the new coins are identical to the Sacagawea Golden dollar first minted in 2000. The heads side design of each coin shows a picture and the name of the President, his term in office, and the numerical order in which he served. The tails side design has a picture of the Statue of Liberty to represent Liberty, a term that appears on all other coins in circulation. The tail side design is the same for all these Presidential coins. Inscriptions that traditionally appear on the face of other U.S. coins are located on the edge of the Presidential $1 coins.

As they are introduced into circulation, the Presidential $1 coins will be available from banks, credit unions, and thrift institutions. The program is modeled after the 50 States Quarter Program, in which state quarters were introduced into circulation over a 10-year period from 1999 through 2008. For more information and a Presidential Dollar coin release schedule, visit the U.S. Mint's website at www.usmint.gov.

The U.S. $1 Bill: AN OWNER'S MANUAL

Everybody knows that George Washington is on the U.S. one-dollar bill, but did you ever wonder what all that other stuff is?

Plate position
Shows where on the 32-note plate this bill was printed.

The Treasury Department seal: The balancing scales represent justice. The pointed stripe across the middle has 13 stars for the original 13 colonies. The key represents authority.

Plate serial number
Shows which printing plate was used for the face of the bill.

Serial number
Each bill has its own.

Federal Reserve District Number
Shows which district issued the bill.

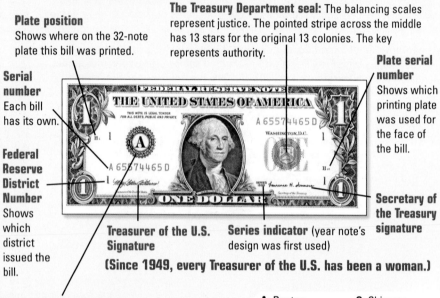

Treasurer of the U.S. Signature

Series indicator (year note's design was first used)

Secretary of the Treasury signature

(Since 1949, every Treasurer of the U.S. has been a woman.)

Federal Reserve District Seal
The name of the Federal Reserve Bank that issued the bill is printed in the seal. The letter tells you quickly where the bill is from. Here are the letter codes for the 12 Federal Reserve Districts:

A: Boston	**G**: Chicago
B: New York	**H**: St. Louis
C: Philadelphia	**I**: Minneapolis
D: Cleveland	**J**: Kansas City
E: Richmond	**K**: Dallas
F: Atlanta	**L**: San Francisco

Front of the Great Seal of the United States: The bald eagle is the national bird. The shield has 13 stripes for the 13 original colonies. The eagle holds 13 arrows (symbol of war) and an olive branch (symbol of peace). Above the eagle is the motto "E Pluribus Unum," Latin for "out of many, one," and a constellation of 13 stars.

Plate serial number
Shows which plate was used for the back.

Back of the Great Seal of the United States:
The pyramid symbolizes something that lasts for ages. It is unfinished because the U.S. is always growing. The eye, known as the "Eye of Providence," probably comes from an ancient Egyptian symbol. The pyramid has 13 levels; at its base are the Roman numerals for 1776, the year of American independence. "Annuit Coeptis" is Latin for "God has favored our undertaking." "Novus Ordo Seclorum" is Latin for "a new order of the ages." Both phrases are from the works of the Roman poet Virgil.

WORLD CURRENCY

An exchange rate is the price of a country's currency in terms of another. For example, one U.S. dollar cost, or could buy, 6.86 yuan in China in August 2008. These rates are based on a country's economy, the value of products it makes and buys, and inflation, the increase in how much money is needed to buy goods.

When people in one country want to buy goods or services from someone in another country, they need to exchange, or buy, their currency. Many people who study economies (economists) believe that an item should cost the same in every country once the currency is exchanged, a theory called Purchasing Power Parity (PPP).

The most famous example of Purchasing Power Parity was given by the *Economist* Magazine as the Big Mac index. Using the Big Mac index, we determine the cost of a Big Mac in a number of countries and can then conclude an exchange rate based on this index. For example, if a Big Mac costs $3 in the US, and 9,000 riel in Cambodia, we can determine that the exchange rate is $1 for 3,000 riel. We would then use this indexed exchange rate to determine relative value of other items.

THE McCURRENCY MENU

Country	Big Mac prices	
	In local currency	in dollars (exchange rate for July 2008)
United States	$3.57	3.57
Australia	A $3.45	3.36
Brazil	Real 7.50	4.73
Britain	Pound 2.29	4.57
Canada	C $4.09	4.08
China	Yuan 12.5	1.83
Japan	Yen 280	2.62
Mexico	Peso 32.0	3.15
Russia	Ruble 59.0	2.54

McDonald's restaurants are in about 120 countries. The price of a Big Mac should cost the same wherever you go ($3.57). This is rarely the case. In China, a Big Mac costs 12.5 Yuan. According to PPP, 12.5 Yuan should equal $3.57, the cost of a Big Mac in America, but the exchange rate is $1 to 6.86 Yuan. An American buying the burger in China would only pay $1.83.
Source: www.economist.com

Most countries make their own currency. Some may have the same name but each one is different and may have a different value. Most are decorated with cultural symbols and important historic figures. Colorful and educational, the detailed images also aim to prevent counterfeiting.

MOVIES & TV

What book is *The Wizard of Oz* movie based on? ➤ page 136

MOVIE & TV FACTS

What a Night! *The Dark Knight* holds the record for highest one-day box office sales in the U.S. It also set a record for highest opening-day sales. The movie made $66.4 million when it opened in theaters on July 18, 2008.

Giving Credit *The Lord of the Rings: The Return of the King* (2003) has one of the longest closing credits of any movie. Hundreds of people, including a horse makeup artist, are listed in the credits, which last for nearly 10 minutes.

A Good Run Before *The Simpsons, The Flintstones* held the record for TV's longest running prime-time animated series. The cartoon, about two Stone Age families, lasted six seasons, from 1960 to 1966. *The Simpsons*, which has been on air since 1989, is currently in its 19th season.

The Simpsons ▶

ALL-TIME TOP ANIMATED MOVIES*			ALL-TIME TOP MOVIES*		
1	*Shrek 2* (2004)	$436.7	1	*Shrek 2* (2004)	$436.7
2	*Finding Nemo* (2003)	339.7	2	*E.T. the Extra-Terrestrial* (1982)	435.0
3	*The Lion King* (1994)	328.5	3	*Star Wars: Episode I— The Phantom Menace* (1999)	435.0
4	*Shrek the Third* (2007)	322.7	4	*Finding Nemo* (2003)	339.7
5	*Shrek* (2001)	267.7	5	*The Lion King*	328.4
6	*The Incredibles* (2004)	261.4	6	*Shrek the Third* (2007)	322.7
7	*Monsters, Inc.* (2001)	255.9	7	*Harry Potter Sorcerer's Stone* (2001)	317.6
8	*Toy Story 2* (1999)	245.9	8	*Star Wars: Episode II— Attack of the Clones* (2002)	310.7
9	*Cars* (2006)	244.1	9	*Star Wars: Episode VI— Return of the Jedi* (1993)	309.2
10	*WALL-E* (2008)	220.1	10	*The Chronicles of Narnia: The Lion, the Witch, and the Wardrobe* (2005)	291.7

Source: *The Nielsen Group 2008*
*Through September 2008. Gross in millions of dollars based on box office sales in the U.S. and Canada.

TOP TV SHOWS IN 2007-08

AGES 6-11

NETWORK
1. *American Idol*
2. *Wipeout*
3. *Survivor: China*
4. *I Survived a Japanese Game Show*
5. *Friday Night Smackdown*

CABLE
1. *Camp Rock*
2. *FOP Movie: Fairly Odd Baby*
3. *High School Musical 2*
4. *Cheetah Girls: One World*

▲ *Survivor*

AGES 12-17

NETWORK
1. *American Idol*
2. *House*
3. *Family Guy*
4. *Moment of Truth*
5. *Heroes*

CABLE
1. *Camp Rock*
2. *The Secret Life of the American Teen*
3. *Goodbye Zoey*
4. *High School Musical 2*

Source: *The Nielsen Group 2008*

did you know? The strike by the the Writers Guild of America against the Alliance of Motions Picture and Television Producers lasted from November 5, 2007 to February 12, 2008. Due to the strike, new programs for weekly shows came to a halt. The Writers Strike caused ratings to fall, especially for the big networks. In response to the strike, many television viewers chose alternative forms of entertainment.

HITTING THEATERS IN 2008...

- In *The Spiderwick Chronicles*, three siblings discover a magical world of faeries after moving into the rundown Spiderwick estate. (February).

- Based on the Dr. Seuss book, *Horton Hears a Who* is about an elephant who hears voices coming from a speck of dust—except no one believes him. (March).

- *Nim's Island*, a story of courage and love, follows 11-year old Nim as she searches for her missing father. Based on the book by Wendy Orr. (April)

- The Pixar computer animated science fiction film, *WALL-E*, is about the adventures of a lonely, curious robot seeking love. (June)

- Don't miss *High School Musical 3: Senior Year* with Troy, Gabriella, and their friends. (October)

- In this sequel, *Madagascar 2*, the escaped zoo animals land in Africa. (November)

...AND IN 2009

- *Coraline*, voiced by Dakota Fanning, is an animated fantasy film that comes out in February.

- *The Princess and the Frog*, a traditional animated film based on the classic fairy tale will hit screens in December.

- The next movie due in the series, *Harry Potter and the Half-Blood Prince* will be released in July.

- A remake of the *Swiss Family Robinson*, based on the novel by John Wyss, is scheduled for 2009.

BOOKS TO FILM

Movie: *The Wizard of Oz* (1939)
Book: *The Wonderful Wizard of Oz* by L. Frank Baum (1900)

The making of the classic film *The Wizard of Oz* was delayed by script problems. No one knew exactly how to make L. Frank Baum's magical story come to life on screen. Another problem was that 16-year-old Judy Garland was much older than the Dorothy Gale character that Baum had written about. When filming first began, Garland was dressed in a blond wig and childish make-up to make her look younger, but that idea was quickly scrapped.

Readers of *The Wonderful Wizard of Oz* could easily spot where changes were made to adapt the movie for the big screen. In Baum's story, Dorothy's slippers were silver, but ruby slippers looked more dramatic in technicolor! Baum's book was also pretty violent for a children's book—the Wizard sends Dorothy to kill the Wicked Witch, not just to get her broomstick. The Tin Man (Tin Woodsman, in the book) uses his ax on forest creatures. In the end, the filmmakers didn't think that moviegoers would buy all of Baum's fantasy, and they changed the story so Dorothy would wake up at the end as if it were all a dream.

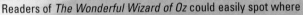

Movies: *Willy Wonka and the Chocolate Factory* (1971); *Charlie and the Chocolate Factory* (2005)
Book: *Charlie and the Chocolate Factory* by Roald Dahl (1964)

Charlie and the Chocolate Factory was first adapted to the big screen in 1971. Dahl himself wrote the original screenplay, but it was heavily changed. By the time the movie came out, much of Dahl's original story had been altered, and he was rumored to have hated the film. During Veruca Salt's downfall in the book, she is judged a "bad nut" by nut-selecting squirrels; in the first film version, she is judged a bad egg by the golden egg machine.

Fortunately, in the Hollywood movie business, there's usually a second chance! The screenwriter for the 2005 remake *Charlie and the Chocolate Factory* had never seen the original film before he began writing. He wrote a script working solely from Dahl's novel. The squirrel scene was reinstated. But other changes were made. For instance, in the book, Willy Wonka never mentions his father, but in the movie, his candy-hating dentist father becomes a big part of the story. There's much debate among Charlie fans over which movie follows the book more closely—and whether that's important.

Movie: *Harry Potter and the Order of the Phoenix (2007)*
Book: *Harry Potter and the Order of the Phoenix (2003)*

Each of the books in the tremendously popular Harry Potter series, by J.K. Rowling has been or will be made into a movie. The movie stories follow the basic plots of the books closely. The movies have also been very popular.

Harry Potter Retrospective

1 *Harry Potter and the Sorcerer's Stone* (book: 1997; movie: 2001)

2 *Harry Potter and the Chamber of Secrets* (book: 1998; movie: 2002)

3 *Harry Potter and the Prisoner of Azkaban* (book: 1999; movie: 2004)

4 *Harry Potter and the Goblet of Fire* (book: 2000; movie: 2005)

5 *Harry Potter and the Order of the Phoenix* (book: 2003; movie: 2007)

6 *Harry Potter and the Half-Blood Prince* (book: 2005; movie: 2009)

7 *Harry Potter and the Deathly Hollows* (book: 2007; movie: 2010 and 2011)

Image from Harry Potter and the Order of the Phoenix

Movie: *The Chronicles of Narnia: Prince Caspian (2008)*
Book: *The Chronicles of Narnia: Prince Caspian (1951)*

The Chronicles of Narnia is a series of seven books written by C.S. Lewis. *The Lion, the Witch, and the Wardrobe* is the first book in the series and *Prince Caspian* is the second book. (A movie version of *The Voyage of the Dawn Treader*, the next book in the series, is expected to come out in May 2010.)

Both the book and movie follow four siblings who return to the land of Narnia. It has been one year in their world but 1,300 years have passed in Narnia. The Pevensie children help the rightful heir, Prince Caspian, reclaim his throne. There are some differences between the movie and the book. Peter and Caspian have a bit of a rivalry. Susan also plays a more active role as an archer in battle in the movie version.

Image from The Chronicles of Narnia: Prince Caspian

movies & tv match-ups

Match these duos with the movie or TV show in which they belong.

DUOS	MOVIE OR TV SHOW
Mac & Blooregard	*Wizards of Waverly Place*
Katara & Sokka	*Pirates of the Caribbean*
Will & Elizabeth	*Howl's Moving Castle*
Alex & Justin	*Ironman*
Susan & Reed	*Foster's Home for Imaginary Friends*
Sophie & Calcifer	*Zoey 101*
Tony & Pepper	*Fantastic Four*
Quinn & Lola	*Avatar: The Last Airbender*

ANSWERS ON PAGES 334-336. FOR MORE PUZZLES GO TO WWW.WAFORKIDS.COM

MUSEUMS

Which is one of the most popular exhibits at the Metropolitan Museum of Art ? ➡ page 139

Museums collect things of great interest, such as works of art or everyday objects from different times in the past, and show them off to visitors. Some museums teach you all about science and technology.

The American Museum of Natural History, in New York City, dates back to 1869, and is the biggest natural science museum in the world. It has huge dinosaur skeletons, lifelike scenes of animals in different environments, and exhibits that show humans as they lived tens of thousands of years ago. The museum's **Rose Center for Earth and Space** (pictured at right) contains interactive exhibits about astronomy and astrophysics, as well as the world's most advanced star projector. Inside the Hayden Planetarium, the projector takes you on a journey through a virtual re-creation of the Milky Way Galaxy.
WEB SITE *www.amnh.org*

Exploratorium, in San Francisco, California, is a place to learn about everything from frogs to earthquakes to space weather. Grope through darkness in the Tactile Dome, where the sense of touch is your only guide. There are "hands-on" exhibits in all areas of science, with plenty of things to look at, pick up, and tinker with. **WEB SITE** *www.exploratorium.com*

The Smithsonian Institution, in Washington, DC, is not just one museum, but 18 museums, most of them located along the Mall in Washington. It's the biggest museum complex in the world, holding about 142 million objects, from First Ladies' dresses to the first airplane flown by the Wright Brothers. The Smithsonian includes the National Air and Space Museum, the National Portrait Gallery, and the National Zoo.
WEB SITE *www.si.edu*

SANDRA PRIE

MUSEUMS OF ALL KINDS

The **Newseum** in **Washington, DC**, opened in 2008. This interactive museum allows visitors to explore how and why news is made. The exhibits blend five centuries of news history with modern technology to illustrate the importance of the news. The museum has 14 major galleries, 8 sections of the Berlin Wall, 7 levels, and 2 television studios. **WEB SITE** *www.newseum.org*

Jamestown Settlement in **Williamsburg, Virginia**. This "living museum" includes re-creations of an Indian village, a fort, and the first permanent English settlement in America. Museum staff wear costumes and show what life was like for colonists 400 years ago.
WEB SITE *www.historyisfun.org*

The International UFO Museum and Research Center in **Roswell, New Mexico**, is dedicated to research into UFOs, or "unidentified flying objects" from outer space. Some say that a UFO crashed in the nearby desert back in 1947.
WEB SITE *www.iufomrc.com*

The **Buffalo Bill Historical Center** in **Cody, Wyoming**, includes five museums and a research library devoted to the American west. The museums include artworks of the American West, Plains Indian art and artifacts, and a natural history museum that provides a multidisciplinary perspective on the Greater Yellowstone Ecosystem, its surrounding area, and human interactions. **WEB SITE** *www.bbhc.org*

National Museum of Health and Medicine in **Washington, DC**. Founded during the Civil War as the Army Medical Museum, it holds specimens for research in military medicine and surgery. One of the most popular exhibits has artifacts from President Lincoln's assassination, including the bullet. **WEB SITE** *nmhm.washingtondc.museum*

did you **know**?

The Temple of Dendur is one of the most popular exhibits at the Metropolitan Museum of Art in NYC. It was built in 15 BC to honor the goddess Isis. The temple was a gift to the United States from Egypt in gratitude for American help in saving monuments from ancient Egypt. It had to be moved because a dam was built near its original location. The building was taken apart and shipped to the US. Engineers used detailed drawings to reconstruct the original temple inside the museum.

AMERICAN MUSEUM OF NATURAL HISTORY

MUSEUMS

139

MUSIC & DANCE

Who was named Top New Male Vocalist by the Academy of Country Music in 1997? ➡ page 141

TOP ALBUMS OF 2007

① *Daughtry*........................... Chris Daughtry ▶
② *Konvicted*.......................... Akon
③ *The Dutchess* .... Fergie
④ *Hannah Montana Soundtrack* .... Hannah Montana
   (Miley Cyrus)
⑤ *Some Hearts* .... Carrie Underwood
⑥ *All the Right Reasons* .... Nickelback
⑦ *Future Sex/Lovesounds* .... Justin Timberlake
⑧ *High School Musical 2 Soundtrack*.... High School Musical 2
⑨ *Now 23* .... Various Artists
⑩ *Minutes to Midnight* .... Linkin Park

Source: Billboard 200, Billboard Magazine

All About ≫ *American Idol*

American Idol is a popular television reality-competition show. The program's goal is to discover the best singer in the country. Auditions are held in various cities across the nation. The show's judges, Paula Abdul, Simon Crowell, and Randy Jackson select a group of semifinalists who sing each week on the program. The judges offer comments after each performance. Then the viewing public votes by phone or text message to decide who advances or who goes home. The results are announced the following night. Eventually, only two finalists are left to compete for the title of American Idol. In 2008, the winner was **David Cook**. Winners from previous seasons are Kelly Clarkson, Ruben Studdard, Fantasia Barrino, Carrie Underwood, Taylor Hicks, and Jordin Sparks. Many of the runners-up and other contestants have gone on to successful musical and recording careers, including Chris Daughtry, who topped the Billboard

WHO'S HOT NOW

ALICIA KEYS

Born: January 25, 1981, in New York City, New York

Albums: *Songs in A Minor* (2001),
The Diary of Alicia Keys (2003), *Unplugged* (2005),
As I Am (2007)

This R&B star grew up with her mother on the west
side of Manhattan in Hell's Kitchen, a rough area
between Times Square and the Hudson River.
Although she is of mixed race, Alicia grew up
feeling she could be part of any group.

Alicia started piano lessons at the age of seven. As a teenager, she began writing her
own songs and attended Professional Performing Arts High School.

Alicia's first album, *Songs in A Minor*, came out in 2001, when she was only 20 years
old. The album topped the charts and the song "Fallin" was a number-one single. In
2002, she won five Grammy Awards, including Best New Artist. As Alicia hit the road
on tour, she wrote many of the songs that appeared on her second album, *The Diary
of Alicia Keys*. This became her second number-one pop album. Alicia took home four
more Grammy awards in 2005. Grammy voters chose *Diary* as best R&B album.

Although success is great, music still comes first for Alicia. "I definitely see myself
growing in a lot of ways musically," she says. "This music thing, me and you, we're
gonna do this for a long time."

KENNY CHESNEY

Born: March 26, 1968, in Knoxville, Tennessee

Albums: *In My Wildest Dreams* (1993), *All I Need to Know* (1995), *Me & You* (1996),
Everywhere We Go (1999), *No Shoes No Shirt No Problems* (2002), *When the Sun Goes
Down* (2004), *The Road and the Radio* (2005), *Live Those Songs Again* (2006), *Just Who I
Am: Poets & Pirates* (2007)

This country music singer got a special Christmas present when he came home
from college in 1987: a guitar. It changed his life. He decided he wanted to make
his living playing music. He went to college full time but he also practiced music.
After he graduated from college, Kenny kept working on his music.

In 1993, he got a recording contract for his first album. That
album and his second album were popular. His third album, *Me
And You*, went "gold" (sold more than 500,000 copies).

In 1997, Kenny was named the Top New Male Vocalist by
the Academy of Country Music. In 2003, he was named the
Top Male Vocalist by the Academy of Country Music. In
2005 and 2006, the Academy named him the Entertainer of
the Year. In 2007, Kenny won the People's Choice Award as
Favorite Male Singer.

Connecting with people is what it's all about for Kenny.
When people are waiting in line to get into his concerts,
he often goes out, talks, shakes hands, and signs
autographs.

141

MUSICAL INSTRUMENTS

There are many kinds of musical instruments. Instruments in an orchestra are divided into four groups, or sections: string, woodwind, brass, and percussion.

PERCUSSION INSTRUMENTS Percussion instruments make sounds when they are struck. They include drums, cymbals, triangles, gongs, bells, and xylophones. Keyboard instruments, like the piano, are sometimes included in percussion instruments.

BRASSES Brass instruments are hollow inside. They make sounds when air is blown into a mouthpiece. The trumpet, French horn, trombone, and tuba are brasses.

WOODWINDS Woodwinds are cylindrical and hollow inside. They make sounds when air is blown into them. The clarinet, flute, oboe, bassoon, and piccolo are woodwinds.

STRINGS Stringed instruments make sounds when the strings are either stroked with a bow or plucked with the fingers. The violin, viola, cello, bass, and harp are used in an orchestra. The guitar, banjo, and mandolin are other stringed instruments.

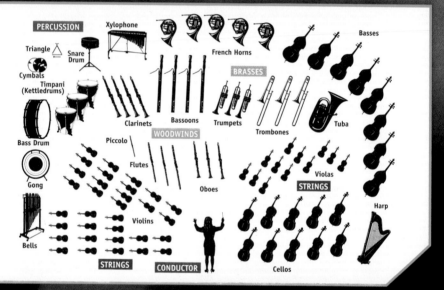

UNUSUAL MUSICAL INSTRUMENTS

The Aeolian Wind Harp, also called a harmonic harp, is an ancient musical instrument that is played by the wind. It dates back to ancient Greece and is named for the Greek god of the wind, Aeolus. It is designed to play only pure harmonic tones. Changes in wind velocity create higher or lower harmonics at louder or softer volumes. Aeolian wind harps are still hand-crafted today.

The Sea Organ is a musical instrument that is played by the sea. It was created by Nikoa Basic in 2005. The Sea Organ is a pipe organ with 35 organ pipes built under concrete along the shores of Zadar, Croatia. Sea water and wind movements push air through the pipes to create a variety of random, beautiful musical sounds.

DANCING WITH THE STARS

Dancing with the Stars is a television reality-competition show that pairs a celebrity with a professional ballroom dancer. The professional dancer teaches the celebrity how to perform various ballroom dances. Among these dances are the foxtrot, cha-cha-cha, quickstep, jive, tango, paso doble, rumba, samba, and waltz.

Each pair dances live on the show every week. The dancers receive scores from three professional dance judges. Program viewers may also cast their votes by calling a toll-free number, online at the ABC website, or by text messaging. The judges' scores and the viewer votes are combined to create a score. The pair with the lowest score is eliminated from the competition each week.

The winners of the 2008 season were **Kristi Yamaguchi** (1992 Olympic Gold Medalist in figure skating) and professional dancer **Mark Ballas**. Yamaguchi earned the highest scores of any competitor thus far on the show.

SALSA DANCING

Salsa dancing is a mix of different Latin American dance forms. Here are the basic steps in salsa dancing:

You will be the leader. Face your partner, and take their right hand with your left hand. Put your right hand around your partner and rest it in the middle of his/her back. Your partner should put his/her left hand on your right shoulder.

1. Stand with your feet together. This is the starting position. Slide your left foot forward. At the same time, your partner steps back with the right foot.

2. Shift your weight to your right foot, and slide your left foot back to starting position. At the same time, your partner shifts his/her weight to the left foot and slides the right foot forward to starting position.

3. Slide your right foot back, while your partner steps forward with the left foot.

4. Shift your weight onto your left foot, and bring your right foot back to starting position. Your partner shifts his/her weight to the right foot and slides the left foot back to starting position.

MYTHOLOGY

Who was the first woman created by the Greek gods? ➡ page 145

MYTHS OF THE GREEKS

As the ancient Greeks went about their daily lives, they believed that a big family of gods and goddesses were watching over them from Mount Olympus. Farmers planting crops, sailors crossing the sea, and poets writing verses thought that these powerful beings could help or harm them. Stories of the gods and goddesses are called **myths**. Some of the oldest myths come from the *Iliad* and *Odyssey*, long poems in Greek composed around 700 B.C.

After the Romans conquered Greece in 146 B.C., they adopted Greek myths but gave Roman names to the main gods and goddesses. The planets in our solar system are named after Roman gods.

The family of Greek and Roman gods and goddesses was large. Their family tree would have more than 50 figures on it. The deities listed are the Olympian gods, the most important of the gods, who lived on Mount Olympus. Those with * are children of Zeus (Jupiter).

Greek Name	Roman Name	Description
Aphrodite	Venus	Goddess of beauty and of love
*Apollo	Phoebus	God of prophecy, music, and medicine
*Ares	Mars	God of war; protector of the city
*Artemis	Diana	Goddess of the Moon; and of the Hunt
*Athena	Minerva	Goddess of wisdom and of war
Cronus	Saturn	Father of Zeus (Jupiter), Poseidon (Neptune), Hades (Pluto), Hera (Juno), and Demeter (Ceres)
Demeter	Ceres	Goddess of crops and harvest, sister of Zeus (Jupiter)
*Dionysus	Bacchus	God of wine, dancing, and theater
Hades	Pluto	Ruler of the Underworld, brother of Zeus (Jupiter)
Hephaestus	Vulcan	God of fire
Hera	Juno	Queen of the gods, wife of Zeus (Jupiter), goddess of marriage
*Hermes	Mercury	Messenger god, had winged helmet and sandals
Poseidon	Neptune	God of the sea and of earthquakes, brother of Zeus (Jupiter)
Zeus	Jupiter	Sky god, ruler of gods and mortals

Greek & Roman Gods

MAKING SENSE of the WORLD

Unlike folklore or fables, myths were once thought to be true. Most ancient peoples explained many things in nature by referring to gods and heroes with superhuman qualities. To the Greeks a rough sea meant that POSEIDON was angry. Lightning was THOR'S hammer in Norse mythology. Ancient Egyptians believed that the sun, as it rose and set everyday, was a lifetime for RE, the creator and ruler of the universe. In Japan, AMATERASU was the Shinto sun goddess who gave light to the land. Her brother SUSANOO was the storm god who ruled the sea.

There are even stories of gods or heroes who chose brain over brawn to get what they wanted. COYOTE was wild and cunning, a true trickster for many Native American tribes throughout the West. He was usually a loner and was never simply good or bad. ANANSI was a spider in the stories of the Akan tribes of West Africa. The tiny spider used his wits to capture the hornet, python, and leopard. In return the sky god NYAME let him own every story ever told.

Myths have remained popular long after people knew they weren't real because the stories hold important life lessons and morals for cultures around the world. Myths have also inspired countless stories and works of art.

Re

Greek & Roman Heroes

Besides stories about the gods, Greek and Roman mythology has many stories about other heroes with amazing qualities.

- **ODYSSEUS**, the king of Ithaca, was a hero of the Trojan War in the *Iliad*. It was his idea to build a huge wooden horse, hide Greek soldiers inside, and smuggle them into the city of Troy to capture it. The *Odyssey* is the story of his long and magical trip home after the war.

- **PANDORA** was the first woman created by the Greek gods. Zeus ordered Hephaestus to create a beautiful woman out of earth. All the Olympian gods gave her gifts (her name means "gifts of all"). Hera's gift was curiosity. When Pandora was finished, she received a box which she was never to open. Her curiosity could not resist and Pandora opened the box to release all the evil spirits upon the world.

- **JASON** and the Argonauts set out on a quest to find the golden fleece, so Jason can reclaim his rightful throne. Among the Argonauts were Herakles and Orpheus. After many adventures and with the help of Medea, Jason slays the Minotaur and claims the fleece. He later betrays Medea

and eventually dies when a beam from his ship, the Argo, falls off and hits him on the head.

Hercules

The most popular hero was Herakles, or **Hercules**. The most famous of his deeds were his 12 labors. They included killing the **Hydra**, a many-headed monster, and capturing the three-headed dog **Cerberus**, who guarded the gates of the Underworld. Hercules was so great a hero that the gods granted him immortality. When his body lay on his funeral pyre, Athena came and carried him off to Mount Olympus in her chariot.

NATIONS

What country has more than a thousand underground caves?

➡ page 180

GOVERNMENTS

Among the world's 195 independent nations there are various kinds of governments.

Totalitarianism In **totalitarian** countries the rulers have strong power, and the people have little freedom. North Korea currently has a totalitarian government.

Monarchy A country with a king or queen can be called a **monarchy**. Monarchies are almost always hereditary, meaning the throne is passed down in one family.

Democracy The word **democracy** comes from the Greek words *demos* ("people") and *kratos* ("rule"). In a democracy, the people rule. In most modern democracies, there are too many people to agree on everyday decisions. So people make decisions through the leaders they choose. These democracies are called **representative** democracies. If people are unhappy with their leaders, they can vote them out of office. Winston Churchill, a former British prime minister, probably had that in mind when he said, "Democracy is the worst form of government except all those other forms that have been tried from time to time."

UN SECRETARY-GENERAL BAN KI-MOON of South Korea became the eighth secretary-general of the United Nations January 1, 2007, succeeding Kofi Annan. So what does the secretary-general do?

The secretary-general heads the Secretariat, which has a staff of thousands from all different countries. The Secretariat oversees the UN's day-to-day operation. The secretary-general makes sure that programs and policies the UN has agreed on, such as peacekeeping operations, are running smoothly. He also functions as a diplomat. He tries to resolve disputes between countries. In addition, the secretary-general is an advocate for those who are less fortunate. He learns what social and economic problems exist around the world and prepares reports on them. As a leader, the secretary-general upholds the UN's commitment to world peace.

The secretary-general is appointed by the General Assembly on the Security Council's recommendation. The term of office is five years, which can be renewed.

Before becoming secretary-general, Ban served in the South Korean government. (Ban is his family name, Ki-moon is his personal name.) He can speak Korean, English, and French.

A COMMUNITY OF NATIONS

The **United Nations (UN)** was started in 1945 after World War II. The first members were 51 nations, 50 of which met in San Francisco, California. They signed an agreement known as the UN Charter. The UN now has 192 members, including Montenegro, which joined in 2006. Only two independent nations—Taiwan and Vatican City—are not members.

The UN emblem shows the world surrounded by olive branches of peace.

HOW THE UN IS ORGANIZED

➤ **GENERAL ASSEMBLY** **What It Does:** Discusses world problems, admits new members, appoints the secretary-general, decides the UN budget. **Members:** All UN members; each country has one vote.

➤ **SECURITY COUNCIL** **What It Does:** Handles questions of peace and security. **Members:** Five permanent members (China, France, UK, Russia, U.S.) who must all vote the same way before certain proposals can pass; ten elected by the General Assembly to two-year terms. In 2008, the ten were Belgium, Indonesia, Italy, Panama, and South Africa (terms ending Dec. 31, 2008) and Burkina Faso, Costa Rica, Croatia, Libya, and Viet Nam (terms ending Dec. 31, 2009).

➤ **ECONOMIC AND SOCIAL COUNCIL** **What It Does:** Deals with issues related to economic development, population, education, health, and human rights. **Members:** 54 member countries elected to three-year terms.

➤ **INTERNATIONAL COURT OF JUSTICE (WORLD COURT)** located in The Hague, Netherlands. **What It Does:** UN court for disputes between countries. **Members:** 15 judges, each from a different country, elected to nine-year terms.

➤ **SECRETARIAT** **What It Does:** Carries out the UN's day-to-day operations. **Members:** UN staff, headed by the secretary-general.

For more information, e-mail inquiries@un.org *or write to:* Public Inquiries Unit, Dept. of Public Information, United Nations, Room GA-57, New York, NY 10017

WEB SITE www.un.org

did you know? The United Nations Headquarters is in New York City but the land and buildings are considered international territory. The United Nations flies its own flag and has its own post office—which sells UN postage stamps. Six official languages are spoken at the UN—Arabic, Chinese, English, French, Russian and Spanish.

WAforKids.com

Go to **www.WAforKids.com** and type **143** into the code box for more facts and fun:

• Quiz yourself (or your parents!) on flags from around the globe

• Download crossword puzzles filled with fun facts about other countries

• Get homework tips on every nation of the world

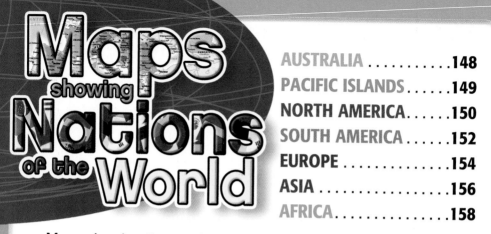

Maps showing Nations of the World

Maps showing the continents and nations of the world appear on pages 148-159. Flags of the nations appear on pages 160-185. A map of the United States appears on pages 290-291.

AUSTRALIA

⊛ National Capital

★ State Capital

• Other City

1:40,886,000

0   250   500 mi

0   250   500 km

Two-Point Equidistant Projection

© GeoNova

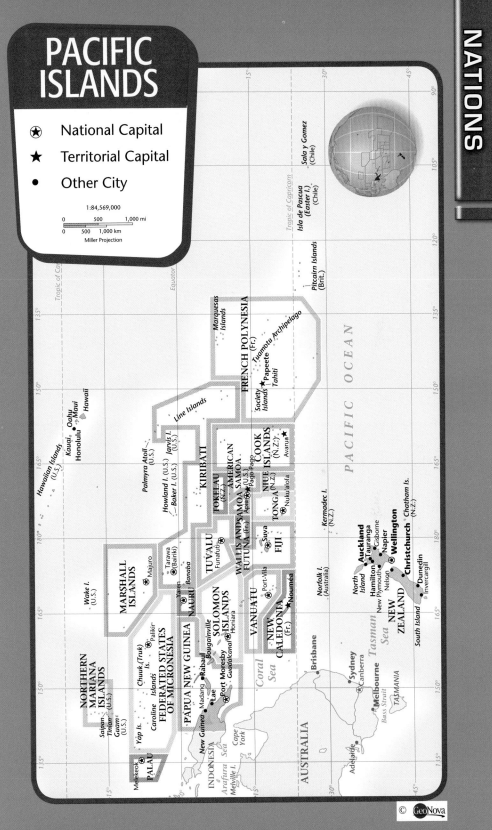

PACIFIC ISLANDS

National Capital ⊛

Territorial Capital ★

Other City ●

1:84,569,000

0   500   1,000 mi

0   500   1,000 km

Miller Projection

Tropic of Cancer

Equator

Tropic of Capricorn

Sala y Gomez
(Chile)

Isla de Pascua
(Easter I.)
(Chile)

Pitcairn Islands
(Brit.)

FRENCH POLYNESIA
(Fr.)

Marquesas
Islands

Tuamotu Archipelago

Society ★ Papeete
Islands   Tahiti

Line Islands

PACIFIC OCEAN

Hawaiian Islands
(U.S.)

Kauai   Oahu   Maui
  Honolulu ●   ● Hawaii

Palmyra Atoll
(U.S.)

Howland I. (U.S.)
Baker I. (U.S.)

Jarvis I.
(U.S.)

KIRIBATI

**COOK
ISLANDS**
(N.Z.)
Avarua ★

TOKELAU
(N.Z.)

**AMERICAN
SAMOA**
(U.S.)
Pago Pago ●

NIUE
(N.Z.)

Wake I.
(U.S.)

**MARSHALL
ISLANDS**

● Majuro

Tarawa
(Bairiki) ⊛

Banaba

TUVALU
Funafuti ⊛

SAMOA ⊛
Apia

WALLIS AND
FUTUNA (Fr.)

TONGA
Nuku'alofa ⊛

Suva ●
FIJI

Kermadec I.
(N.Z.)

**NORTHERN
MARIANA
ISLANDS**
(U.S.)

Saipan
Tinian
Guam
(U.S.)

Yap Is.
Chuuk (Truk)
Is. ● Palikir
Caroline Islands

**FEDERATED STATES
OF MICRONESIA**

Yaren ⊛

NAURU

**SOLOMON
ISLANDS**
Honiara ⊛
Guadalcanal

Bougainville

VANUATU ⊛
Port-Vila

**NEW
CALEDONIA**
(Fr.)
Nouméa ★

Norfolk I.
(Australia)

North
Island
New Plymouth
Nelson

Auckland ●
Tauranga ●
Hamilton ● ● Gisborne
● Napier
Wellington ⊛

Chatham Is.
(N.Z.)

PAPUA NEW GUINEA

New Guinea
Madang ●
Lae ●
Port Moresby ⊛

Rabaul ●

Brisbane ●

Sydney ●
Canberra ⊛

Melbourne ●

*Coral
Sea*

*Tasman
Sea*

**NEW
ZEALAND**

South Island

Christchurch ●
● Dunedin
● Invercargill

PALAU
Melekeok ⊛

INDONESIA
Melville I.

*Arafura
Sea*

Cape
York

AUSTRALIA

Bass Strait

TASMANIA

Adelaide ●

© GeoNova

SWEDEN

NORWAY

UNITED KINGDOM

ICELAND

Greenland Sea

Denmark Strait

Spitsbergen

Nord

Cape Morris Jessup

North Pole

+

Arctic Ocean

Tasiilaq

Cape Farewell

GREENLAND (KALAALLIT NUNAAT) (Den.)

Labrador Sea

NEWFOUNDLAND AND LABRADOR

St. Anthony

Island of Newfoundland

St. John's

Corner Brook

St. Pierre & Miquelon (Fr.)

Anticosti I.

N.B.

N.E.W.F.L.D.

Sydney

N.F.L.D.

N.E.W. P.E.I.

Happy Valley-Goose Bay

Hebron

QUEBEC

Schefferville

Labrador City

Sept-Îles

Chibougamau

Nuuk

Davis Strait

Knud Rasmussen Land

Qaanaaq (Thule)

Ellesmere I.

Grise Fiord

Arctic Bay

Pond Inlet

Baffin Bay

Baffin Island

Pangnirtung

Iqaluit

Hudson Strait

Ungava Peninsula

Povungnituk

Belcher Is.

James Bay

ONTARIO

CANADIAN SHIELD

Cape Morris Jessup

Alert

Queen Elizabeth Islands

Resolute

Holman

Victoria I.

Cambridge Bay

Kugluktuk

Repulse Bay

Southampton I.

Hudson Bay

Churchill

York Factory

MANITOBA

Thompson

Flin Flon

L. Winnipeg

Banks I.

Sachs Harbour

Beaufort Sea

Inuvik

Fort McPherson

Great Bear L.

Déline

Mackenzie R.

Great Slave L.

Fort Simpson

Yellowknife

Hay River

Fort Smith

Uranium City

L. Athabasca

Fort McMurray

La Loche

La Ronge

SASK.

Prince Albert

Saskatoon

Saskatchewan R.

Regina

RUSSIA

Point Barrow

Point Hope

Kotzebue

Barrow

BROOKS RANGE

Yukon

Fort Yukon

Fairbanks

Dawson

Mayo

Carmacks

Whitehorse

YUKON

Watson Lake

NORTHWEST TERRITORIES

BRITISH COLUMBIA

Peace River

ALBERTA

Peace R.

Edmonton

N. Saskatchewan R.

Calgary

Jasper

G R E A T

R O C K Y

Prince George

Williams Lake

Columbia R.

Fraser R.

RANGE

Nome

Bethel

ALASKA

Mt. McKinley 6,194 m. (20,320 ft.)

ALASKA RANGE

Anchorage

Kenai

Seward

Valdez

Kodiak

Gulf of Alaska

Mt. Logan 5,959 m. (19,551 ft.)

Yakutat

Skagway

Juneau

Sitka

COAST MOUNTAINS

Prince Rupert

Queen Charlotte Is.

Ketchikan

Kitimat

Vancouver I.

Victoria

Vancouver

Bering Strait

Arctic Circle

Bering Sea

NUNAVUT

CANADA

ATLANTIC OCEAN

Bermuda (Brit.)

BARBADOS
GUADELOUPE (Fr.)
ANTIGUA & (Fr.)
BARBUDA
DOMINICA
MARTINIQUE (Fr.)
ST. LUCIA
ST. VINCENT &
GRENADA
THE GRENADINES
TRINIDAD & TOBAGO
Port-of-Spain

ST. KITTS & NEVIS
VIRGIN IS.(U.S.,Brit.)
PUERTO RICO (U.S.)
San Juan
TURKS &
CAICOS IS. (Brit.)
Santo Domingo
HAITI
Port-au-Prince

VENEZUELA

COLOMBIA

BRAZIL

Bonaire (Neth.)
Curaçao (Neth.)
Aruba (Neth.)

Boston
MASS.
R.I.
CONN.
New York City
NEW JERSEY
Philadelphia
Baltimore PENN.
DELAWARE
MARYLAND
Washington, D.C.
Richmond

Rochester
Buffalo
Toronto
Cleveland
Pittsburgh
OHIO
Cincinnati
W. VA. VA.
Raleigh
N.C.
Charlotte

THE BAHAMAS
Nassau

Santiago de Cuba
CUBA
Havana
Kingston
JAMAICA

Caribbean Sea

Panama City
PANAMA
COSTA RICA
San José
NICARAGUA
Managua
HONDURAS
Tegucigalpa

MICH.
Detroit
MINN.
Minneapolis
S. DAK.
Rapid City
Milwaukee
Chicago
IOWA
ILL.
IND.
Indianapolis
OHIO
St. Louis
MO.
KY.
Louisville
Nashville
TENN.
Memphis
Birmingham
ALA.
Mobile
GA.
Atlanta
S.C.
Savannah
Jacksonville
FLA.
Tampa
St. Petersburg
Miami
Straits of Florida

APPALACHIAN MTS.

CAYMAN IS. (Brit.)

Omaha
NEB.
KANSAS
Wichita
Kansas City
OKLA.
Oklahoma City
ARK.
Little Rock
MISS.
Jackson
LA.
Baton Rouge
New Orleans
Shreveport

UNITED STATES

Gulf of Mexico

BELIZE
Belmopan
Campeche
Bay of Campeche
GUATEMALA
Guatemala City
EL SALVADOR
San Salvador

WIS.
Michigan
Ontario

PACIFIC OCEAN

Tropic of Cancer

Eureka
CALIF.
Sacramento
San Francisco
Reno
NEVADA
Las Vegas
Fresno
Mt. Whitney 4,418 m. (14,494 ft.)
SIERRA NEVADA
Santa Barbara
Los Angeles
San Diego
Tijuana
Mexicali

COAST RANGES

Boise
Pocatello
bia
Plateau
OREG.
Snake
Great Salt L.
Salt Lake City
UTAH
Colorado Plateau
ARIZONA
Phoenix
Nogales
Hermosillo
Ciudad Obregón
BAJA CALIFORNIA
Gulf of California
La Paz
Mazatlán

WYO.
Casper
Cheyenne
Denver
COLORADO
NEW MEXICO
Albuquerque
El Paso
Ciudad Juárez
Chihuahua
Durango
SIERRA MADRE OCCIDENTAL

MOUNTAINS

Platte
Arkansas
Rio Grande

TEXAS
Dallas
Austin
San Antonio
Houston
Monterrey
Torreón
SIERRA MADRE ORIENTAL
San Luis Potosí
León
Guadalajara
MEXICO
Mexico City
Puebla
Orizaba Pk. (18,405 ft) 5,610 m
Veracruz
Villahermosa
Tuxtla Gutiérrez
Acapulco
Oaxaca
Mérida
YUCATÁN PENINSULA

© GeoNova

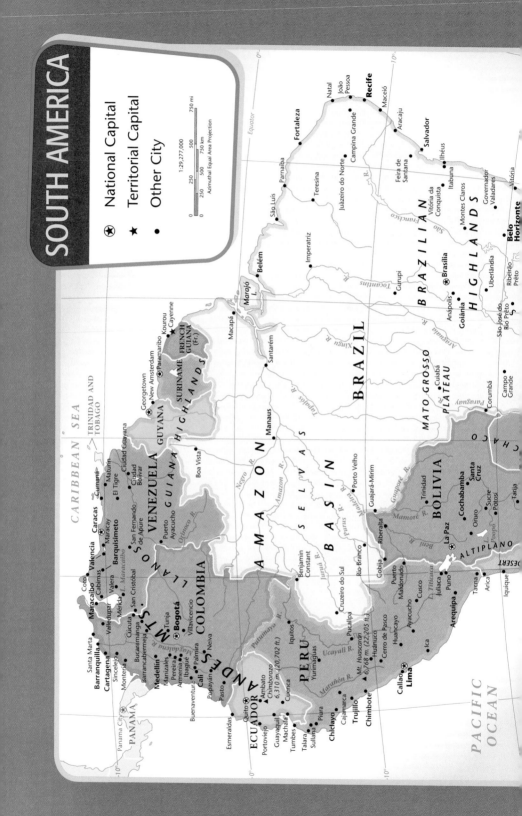

SOUTH AMERICA

Legend:
- ⊛ National Capital
- ★ Territorial Capital
- • Other City

1:29,277,000

0 — 250 — 500 — 750 km
0 — 250 — 500 — 750 mi

Azimuthal Equal Area Projection

Labels on map

CARIBBEAN SEA

TRINIDAD AND TOBAGO

PACIFIC OCEAN

PANAMA
Panama City

COLOMBIA
Santa Marta
Barranquilla
Cartagena
Sincelejo
Montería
Coro
Maracaibo
Cabimas
Valledupar
Valera
Mérida
L. Maracaibo
San Cristóbal
Cúcuta
Bucaramanga
Barrancabermeja
Medellín
Manizales
Pereira
Armenia
Ibagué
Cali
Palmira
Buenaventura
Popayán
Tunja
⊛ Bogotá
Villavicencio
Neiva
Pasto

VENEZUELA
Caracas
Cumaná
Maturín
El Tigre
Ciudad Bolívar
Ciudad Guayana
Maracay
Valencia
Barquisimeto
San Fernando de Apure
Puerto Ayacucho
Orinoco R.

GUYANA
Georgetown
New Amsterdam

SURINAME
Paramaribo

FRENCH GUIANA (Fr.)
Cayenne
Kourou

GUIANA HIGHLANDS

LLANOS

ANDES MTS.

Boa Vista

ECUADOR
Quito
Esmeraldas
Portoviejo
Guayaquil
Machala
Tumbes
Ambato
Chimborazo 6,310 m. (20,702 ft.)
Cuenca

PERU
Talara
Sullana
Piura
Chiclayo
Cajamarca
Trujillo
Chimbote
Mt. Huascarán ▲ 6,768 m. (22,205 ft.)
Yurimaguas
Iquitos
Pucallpa
Cruzeiro do Sul
Cerro de Pasco
Huánuco
Callao ⊛ Lima
Huancayo
Ica
Ayacucho
Cusco
Puno
Arequipa

Yurúa R.
Ucayali R.
Marañón R.
Putumayo R.
Napo R.
Magdalena R.
Cauca R.

BRAZIL
Macapá
Marajó I.
Belém
Santarém
Imperatriz
Gurupi
São Luís
Parnaíba
Teresina
Juàzeiro do Norte
Campina Grande
Fortaleza
Parnaíba
Natal
João Pessoa
Recife
Maceió
Aracaju
Salvador
Ilhéus
Itabuna
Feira de Santana
Vitória da Conquista
Montes Claros
Governador Valadares
Vitória
Belo Horizonte
Brasília ⊛
Anápolis
Goiânia
Uberlândia
São José do Rio Prêto
Ribeirão Prêto
Manaus
Porto Velho
Cuiabá

BRAZILIAN HIGHLANDS

AMAZON BASIN

SELVAS

MATO GROSSO PLATEAU

Equator

São Francisco R.
Tocantins R.
Xingu R.
Tapajós R.
Madeira R.
Negro R.
Amazon R.
Juruá R.
Araguaia R.

BOLIVIA
Guajará-Mirim
Riberalta
Cobija
Puerto Maldonado
Trinidad
Cochabamba
Santa Cruz
Sucre
Potosí
Oruro
La Paz
L. Titicaca
Juliaca
Tacna
Arica
Iquique
Benjamin Constant
Rio Branco

Mamoré R.
Beni R.
Guaporé R.
Paraguay R.

ALTIPLANO
DESERT
CHACO
Campo Grande
Corumbá
Lago Poopó
L. Titicaca
Tarija

South Polar Region

ATLANTIC OCEAN

PACIFIC OCEAN

ATLANTIC OCEAN

Cape Horn
Drake Passage
South Shetland Is.
South Orkney Is.

Bellingshausen Sea
Antarctic Peninsula
Weddell Sea
Riiser Larsen Ice Shelf
Fimbul Ice Shelf

Alexander I.
Thurston I.
Ellsworth Land
Vinson Massif 4,897 m (16,067 ft.)
Ronne Ice Shelf
Filchner Ice Shelf
Berkner I.

Amundsen Sea
Marie Byrd Land
ELLSWORTH MTS.
PENSACOLA MTS.
South Pole
ANTARCTICA
Queen Maud Land

Siple I.
ROCKEFELLER PLATEAU
QUEEN MAUD MTS.
PRINCE ALBERT MTS.
PRINCE CHARLES MTS.
Edgeworth Land

Ross Ice Shelf
Roosevelt I.
Ross I.
McMurdo
American Highland
Amery Ice Shelf
West Ice Shelf

Scott Island
Cape Adare
Ballery Is.
TRANSANTARCTIC MOUNTAINS
Wilkes Land
Shackleton Ice Shelf
Davis Sea

INDIAN OCEAN
Cape Poinsett

Curitiba
Ponta Grossa
Joinville
Florianópolis
Caxias do Sul
Passo Fundo
Santa Maria
Porto Alegre
Pelotas

Ciudad del Este
Posadas
Encarnación
Santo Tomé
Rivera
Minas
Melo
Montevideo
Paraná R.
Asunción
Formosa
Resistencia
Corrientes
Curuzú Cuatiá
Santa Fé
Paraná
Rosario
Salto
Paysandú
URUGUAY
Concordia
La Plata
Rio de la Plata
Mar del Plata

San Miguel de Tucumán
Santiago del Estero
Catamarca
La Rioja
Córdoba
San Juan
Río Cuarto
San Rafael
Mendoza
Junín
Buenos Aires
Avellaneda
Santa Rosa
Punta Alta
Bahía Blanca
Viedma

ARGENTINA

Falkland Is. (Islas Malvinas) (Brit.) (claimed by Arg.)
★ Stanley

Valdés Peninsula
Rawson
Trelew
Comodoro Rivadavia

Mt. Ojos del Salado 6,880 m. (22,572 ft.)
Copiapó
La Serena

Mt. Aconcagua 6,960 m. (22,834 ft.)
Viña del Mar
Valparaíso
Santiago
San Bernardo
Rancagua
Talca
Chillán
Talcahuano
Concepción

CHILE

ANDES MTS.
PATAGONIA

San Carlos de Bariloche
Esquel
Neuquén
San Rafael

Temuco
Valdivia
Osorno
Puerto Montt
Chiloé I.
Los Chonos Archipelago
Taitao Peninsula

Río Gallegos
Punta Arenas
Strait of Magellan
Tierra del Fuego
Ushuaia
Cape Horn

San Félix I. (Chile)
San Ambrosio I. (Chile)
Juan Fernández Is. (Chile)

EUROPE

- ⊛ National Capital
- • Other City

1:22,107,000

0   250   500 mi
0   250   500 km
Azimuthal Equal Area Projection

ICELAND
Reykjavik ⊛   Akureyri

Norwegian   *Sea*

Faroe Is.
(Den.)

Shetland Is.
(Brit.)

Trom

Bodø

Trondheim

Sundsvall

NORWAY
Bergen

SWEDEN

Stavanger   Oslo ⊛   Uppsala
Skagerrak   **Stockholm**
Linköping
Göteborg   Gotland

Jutland   Århus   Ölar
Copenhagen ⊛ Helsingborg
DENMARK   Odense   Malmö
Bal

Orkney
Is.

Aberdeen

Hebrides

Glasgow   Edinburgh

Belfast
Dublin ⊛   Newcastle
IRELAND   Liverpool
Cork   Manchester   Leeds
Birmingham   Sheffield

UNITED KINGDOM
(GREAT BRITAIN)

Irish
Sea

North
Sea

Gdańsk
Hamburg   Szczecin

ATLANTIC
OCEAN

Land's End

Cardiff   Bristol
Portsmouth   ⊛ **London**
English Channel
Channel Is.
(Brit.)   Le Havre
Brest   Rouen

NETHERLANDS
Amsterdam
Rotterdam   Hannover
Antwerp
Brussels   Essen   **GERMANY**   ⊛ **Berlin**
Lille   Cologne   Poznań
BELGIUM   Bonn   Leipzig   Dresden   Wro
LUXEMBOURG   Frankfurt
Paris ⊛   Luxembourg   Mannheim   **Prague** ⊛   Katowice
  CZECH REP.   Brno   Ostra

Bremen

Hamburg
Liège

Elbe
Oder

Nantes

Loire

Strasbourg   Stuttgart
FRANCE   Dijon   Munich   Linz   **Vienna**   Bratislav
Bern ⊛   Zürich   **LIECHTENSTEIN**   **SLOVA**
Geneva   **SWITZERLAND**   **AUSTRIA**   Graz
  Lyon   *Mt. Blanc*   **A L P S**   Ljubljana   **SLOVENIA**   **HUNGA**
  4807 m   **Milan**   Verona   Pécs
  (15,771 ft)   **Turin**   Venice   Zagreb

Rhine
Danube

SLOVENIA
Budap

Cape Finisterre

Gijón

Vigo

Porto

Bay
of
Biscay

Bordeaux

Toulouse

PYRENEES

Bilbao   Zaragoza
Valladolid   *Pico de Aneto*
  3404 m
  (11,168 ft)   **ANDORRA**

Genoa
Verona   Bologna   **CROATIA**   **BOSNIA &**
Nice   Florence   San   **HERZEGOVI**
Marseille   **MONACO**   **MARINO**   Sarajevo
Toulon   *Ligurian Sea*   Split
  Rome ⊛   **MONTENEG**
Corsica   *Elba*   **VATICAN**   Dubrovnik
(Fr.)   **CITY**   Podgoric

APENNINES
Po
Adriatic

DINARIC
ALPS

PORTUGAL   **IBERIAN**
Lisbon ⊛
Badajoz   **PENINSULA**
  Tagus   ⊛ **Madrid**
  SPAIN   Valencia   **Barcelona**
Córdoba   *Balearic Sea*
Sevilla   *Majorca*
Alicante   Palma   *Minorca*
Granada   *Balearic Is.*
Málaga   *(Sp.)*

Sardinia
(It.)

ITALY
Naples   Bari
Salerno

Tyrrhenian
Sea

Co
Ioni
Se

Cape
St. Vincent   Cádiz
Strait of   **GIBRALTAR**
Gibraltar   *(Brit.)*

Cagliari

Palermo   Catania   ▲ *Mt. Etna*
  3323 m
  Sicily   *(10,902 ft)*

⊛ Rabat
Casablanca

MOROCCO

⊛ Algiers

A T L A S   **M O U N T A I N S**
ALGERIA

M e d i t e r r a n e a n

Tunis ⊛

TUNISIA

Valletta
⊛ **MALTA**

S e a

154

North Cape
mmerfest
Barents Sea
Nar'yan-Mar
Pechora
Ob
LAND
Murmansk
KOLA PENINSULA
Apatity
Pechora
Irtysh
Arctic Circle
Ukhta
URAL
R U S S I A
Arkhangel'sk
Serov
Oulu
Belomorsk
Syktyvkar
Berezniki
Petropavl
Divina
Kotlas
Yekaterinburg
FINLAND
Lake Onega
Kirov
Perm'
Chelyabinsk
Tampere
Petrozavodsk
Izhevsk
Ufa
Qostanay
Lahti
Lake Ladoga
Vologda
Naberezhnyye Chelny
Magnitogorsk
Helsinki
St. Petersburg
Cherepovets
Kazan
Tallinn
Velikiy Novgorod
Yaroslavl'
Nizhniy Novgorod
ESTONIA
Ivanovo
Tartu
Pskov
EUROPEAN
Tver
Ul'yanovsk
Tol'yatti
Orenburg
Orsk
Moscow
Ryazan'
Saransk
Samara
LATVIA
PLAIN
Penza
Daugavpils
Volga
Aktobe
HUANIA
Vitsyebsk
Smolensk
Tula
Tambov
Ural
Oral
KAZAKHSTAN
nas
Vilnius
Mahilyow
Lipetsk
Saratov
Aral Sea
ad
Minsk
Bryansk
Voronezh
HERN
Hrodna
BELARUS
Kursk
Atyraū
Brest
Homyel'
saw
Volgograd
UZBEKISTAN
ND
Kyiv
Kharkiv
Luhans'k
Astrakhan
Aktaū
L'viv
Dnieper
Donets'k
UKRAINE
Dniester
Dnipropetrovs'k
Don
Caspian Sea
ice
Chernivtsi
Zaporizhzhia
ATHIAN
Kryvyy Rih
Mariupol'
MOLDOVA
Sea of Azov
Stavropol'
Groznyy
Makhachkala
TURKMENISTAN
ebrecen
Iaşi
Mykolaiv
Krasnodar
Mt. Elbrus
Türkmenbashy
ROMANIA
Chişinău
Odesa
CRIMEA
5642 m
(18,510 ft)
C A U C A S U S
mişoara
Simferopol'
GEORGIA
Ploieşti
Sevastopol'
Baku
Bucharest
Constanţa
Tbilisi
AZERBAIJAN
ade
Black Sea
ARMENIA
Danube
Varna
Trabzon
Yerevan
ristina
BULGARIA
Burgas
Tabriz
Skopje
Sofia
Plovdiv
Tehran
ONIA
İstanbul
IRAN
Thessaloniki
Ankara
TURKEY
N
ULA
Larisa
İzmir
EECE
Adana
PONNESE
Athens
Cyclades
SYRIA
Baghdad
Sea of Crete
Rhodes
Nicosia
Euphrates
Crete
Iraklion
CYPRUS
LEBANON
IRAQ
Beirut
Damascus
Tigris
Persian Gu

155

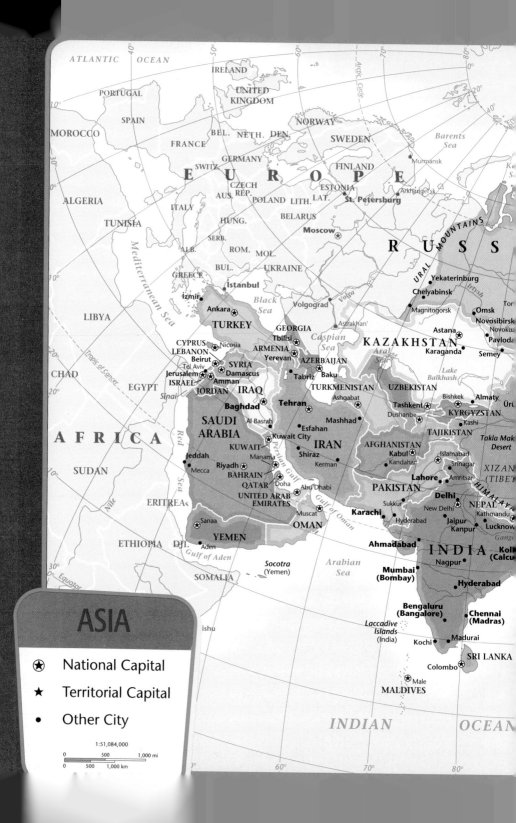

ATLANTIC OCEAN

IRELAND

PORTUGAL

UNITED KINGDOM

SPAIN

NORWAY

MOROCCO

FRANCE

BEL. NETH. DEN.

SWEDEN

Barents Sea

ALGERIA

SWITZ.

GERMANY

FINLAND

Murmansk

ITALY

CZECH

AUS.

POLAND LITH. LAT.

ESTONIA

Arkhangel'sk

EUROPE

St. Petersburg

TUNISIA

HUNG.

BELARUS

Moscow ⊛

RUSS

SERB.

LIBYA

ALB.

ROM.

MOL.

UKRAINE

URAL MOUNTAINS

Yekaterinburg

BUL.

Chelyabinsk

GREECE

İstanbul

Volgograd

Volga

Irtysh

Magnitogorsk

Omsk

İzmir

Ankara ⊛

Black Sea

Caspian

Astrakhan'

Astana ⊛

Novosibirsk

CHAD

TURKEY

GEORGIA

Tbilisi ⊛

Sea

KAZAKHSTAN

Karaganda

Novoku

Paylod

EGYPT

CYPRUS

Nicosia

ARMENIA

Yerevan ⊛

AZERBAIJAN

Aral Sea

Semey

LEBANON

Beirut ⊛

SYRIA

Baku ⊛

Lake Balkhash

Üri

Sinai

Tel Aviv

Damascus ⊛

Tabriz

TURKMENISTAN

UZBEKISTAN

Bishkek ⊛

Almaty

Jerusalem ⊛

Amman ⊛

IRAQ

Tehran ⊛

Ashgabat ⊛

Tashkent ⊛

KYRGYZSTAN

Kashi

ISRAEL

JORDAN

Baghdad ⊛

Mashhad

Dushanbe ⊛

Takla Mak

Esfahan

TAJIKISTAN

Desert

AFRICA

SAUDI

Al-Basrah

Kuwait City

IRAN

AFGHANISTAN

Islamabad ⊛

XIZAN

ARABIA

KUWAIT ⊛

Shiraz

Kabul ⊛

Srinagar

(TIBET

Manama ⊛

Kandahar

Lahore

Amritsar

HIMALAYA

SUDAN

Jeddah

Riyadh ⊛

Kerman

PAKISTAN

Delhi ⊛

NEPAL ⊛

Mecca

BAHRAIN

Sukkur

New Delhi

Kathmandu ⊛

QATAR

Doha ⊛

Abu Dhabi ⊛

Karachi

Jaipur

Lucknow

ERITREA

UNITED ARAB

Hyderabad

Kanpur

Gange

Sanaa ⊛

EMIRATES

Muscat ⊛

Ahmadabad

INDIA

Kolk

ETHIOPIA

DJI.

YEMEN

OMAN

Gulf of Oman

Nagpur

(Calcu

Aden

Gulf of Aden

Arabian

Mumbai

Hyderabad

Socotra

(Yemen)

Sea

(Bombay)

SOMALIA

Bengaluru

(Bangalore)

Chennai

(Madras)

ishu

Laccadive Islands

(India)

Kochi

Madurai

SRI LANKA

Colombo ⊛

MALDIVES

Male ⊛

INDIAN

OCEAN

North Pole

ARCTIC OCEAN

180°

160°

140°

120°

Chukchi Sea

East Siberian Sea

Laptev Sea

Anadyr

Bering Sea

ALASKA

170°

180°

KAMCHATKA PENINSULA

Magadan

Petropavlovsk-Kamchatskiy

Sea of Okhotsk

170°

SIBERIA

Lena

Sakhalin

Kuril Islands (Russia)

160°

Krasnoyarsk

Bratsk

Lake Baikal

Chita

Komsomolsk na Amure

Khabarovsk

Sapporo

Irkutsk

Ulan-Ude

Harbin

Vladivostok

Sea of Japan (East Sea)

JAPAN

Sendai

Ulaanbaatar

Changchun

Shenyang

N. KOREA

Tokyo

Yokohama

Kyoto

150°

MONGOLIA

GOBI DESERT

Hohhot

Beijing

Pyongyang

Dalian

Seoul

Kobe

Osaka

ALTAY MTS.

Yellow (Huang)

Tianjin

S. KOREA

Hiroshima

XINJIANG

Jinan

Qingdao

Nagasaki

Taiyuan

Yellow Sea

PACIFIC OCEAN

Lanzhou

Zhengzhou

CHINA

Xi'an

Nanjing

Shanghai

East China Sea

Everest 29,035 ft.

Chengdu

Wuhan

Changsha

Wenzhou

Ryukyu Islands

Okinawa (Japan)

Lhasa

Chongqing

Yangtze (Chang)

Fuzhou

BHUTAN

Xiamen

Taipei

BANGLADESH

Kunming

Guangzhou

Hong Kong

TAIWAN

Dhaka

Nanning

Macao

Philippine Sea

Mandalay

Hanoi

Gulf of Tonkin

LUZON

MYANMAR (BURMA)

Nay Pyi Taw

LAOS

Vientiane

Da Nang

Manila

PHILIPPINES

Yangon (Rangoon)

THAILAND

VIETNAM

South China Sea

Cebu

MINDANAO

Bangkok

CAMBODIA

Davao

Andaman Sea

Phnom Penh

Ho Chi Minh City

Sulu Sea

Kota Kinabalu

Celebes Sea

Manado

NEW GUINEA

Nicobar Islands (India)

Bandar Seri Begawan

BRUNEI

Irian Jaya

Medan

MALAYSIA

Kuching

BORNEO

INDONESIA

Banda Sea

Arafura Sea

Kuala Lumpur

SINGAPORE

Singapore

SUMATRA

Banjarmasin

Makassar

Timor Sea

Padang

Java Sea

Dili

TIMOR-LESTE

Palembang

Jakarta

Surabaya

Kupang

AUSTRALIA

Bandung

JAVA

100°

110°

120°

130°

140°

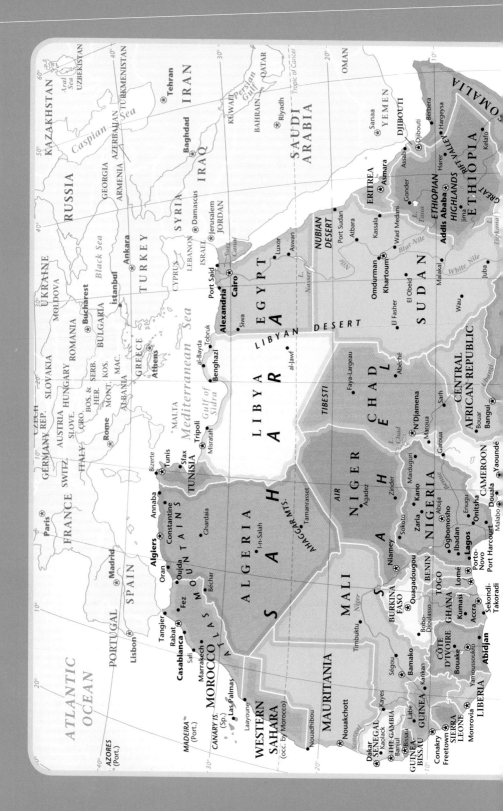

INDIAN OCEAN

Kosi Bay°

Antsiranana

Toamasina

MADAGASCAR

COMOROS
Moroni

Antananarivo
Fianarantsoa

Toliara

Mombasa

Nairobi
Kilimanjaro
5895 m (19,340 ft)
SERENGETI
PLAIN
Mwanza
Arusha

Tanga
Zanzibar
Dar es Salaam

Mtwara
Nacala-
Porto
Nampula

Mozambique Channel

Tropic of Capricorn

Nairobi

TANZANIA
Dodoma
Tabora
Mbeya

RWANDA
Kigali
BURUNDI
Bujumbura
Bukavu

L. Victoria

L. Tanganyika

Mweru

GREAT RIFT VALLEY

DEMOCRATIC
REPUBLIC OF
THE CONGO

MALAWI
Lilongwe
Chipata
Blantyre

Lake
Nyasa

Quelimane

MOZAMBIQUE

Beira

Inhambane

Maputo
Mbabane
SWAZILAND
Newcastle
Pietermaritzburg
Durban

Lubumbashi
Likasi
Kolwezi
Kabwe
KATANGA
PLATEAU

Kananga
Mbuji-Mayi

ZAMBIA
Ndola
Lusaka

L. Kariba

Kitwe

Livingstone

ZIMBABWE
Harare
Mutare
Bulawayo

Francistown

BOTSWANA
KALAHARI
DESERT
Gaborone

Limpopo

Pretoria
Johannesburg
Klerksdorp
Kimberley
Bloemfontein
LESOTHO
Maseru

East London
Port Elizabeth

SOUTH
AFRICA

Cape
Agulhas

Kinshasa
Kikwit
Tshikapa

THE CONGO
CONGO
Brazzaville
GABON
Franceville

Pointe-Noire

Cabinda
(Ang.)

Port-
Gentil

Kasai

Matadi

Luanda

Lobito
Benguela

Namibe

ANGOLA
Malanje
Huambo

Menongue

Cunene

Grootfontein

NAMIBIA
Windhoek

NAMIB DESERT

Walvis Bay

Lüderitz

Cape Town
Cape of Good Hope

Orange

ATLANTIC
OCEAN

ASCENSION
(Brit.)

ST. HELENA
(Brit.)

AFRICA

⊛ National Capital

• Other City

1:39,550,000

0   250   500   750 mi

0   250   500   750 km

Azimuthal Equal Area Projection

© GeoNova

FACTS About NATIONS

Here are basic facts about each of the 195 independent nations in the world. The color of the heading for each country tells you what continent it belongs in. The population is an estimate for mid-2008. The language entry gives official languages and other common languages.

COLOR KEY
- Africa
- Asia
- Australia
- Europe
- North America
- Pacific Islands
- South America

Afghanistan

- **Capital:** Kabul
- **Population:** 32,738,376
- **Area:** 250,001 sq mi (647,500 sq km)
- **Language:** Afghan Persian (Dari), Pashtu
- **Did You Know?** The national sport *buzkashi* is played on horseback and literally means "goat grabbing."

Albania
- **Capital:** Tirana
- **Population:** 3,619,778
- **Area:** 11,100 sq mi (28,748 sq km)
- **Language:** Albanian, Greek
- **Did You Know?** The double-headed eagle on Albania's flag was a symbol of the Byzantine Empire, to which Albania once belonged.

Algeria

- **Capital:** Algiers (El Djazair)
- **Population:** 33,769,669
- **Area:** 919,595 sq mi (2,381,740 sq km)
- **Language:** Arabic, French, Berber dialects
- **Did You Know?** Algeria's desert region contains large "sand seas" called *ergs*, which feature constantly shifting dunes up to 2,000 feet high.

Andorra
- **Capital:** Andorra la Vella
- **Population:** 82,627
- **Area:** 181 sq mi (468 sq km)
- **Language:** Catalan, French, Castilian
- **Did You Know?** The average lifespan of people in Andorra is 83.5 years, the highest of any country in the world.

Angola

- **Capital:** Luanda
- **Population:** 12,531,357
- **Area:** 481,354 sq mi (1,246,700 sq km)
- **Language:** Portuguese, African languages
- **Did You Know?** Angola is the second largest oil-producer in sub-Saharan Africa after Nigeria.

Antigua & Barbuda

- **Capital:** St. John's
- **Population:** 84,522
- **Area:** 171 sq mi (443 sq km)
- **Language:** English
- **Did You Know?** On Aug. 1, 1834, Antigua became the first of the British Caribbean colonies to free its slaves.

BEACH IN AUSTRALIA

Argentina

▶ **Capital:** Buenos Aires
▶ **Population:** 40,481,998
▶ **Area:** 1,068,302 sq mi (2,766,890 sq km)
▶ **Language:** Spanish, English, Italian, German, French
▶ **Did You Know?** About 90% of Argentina's population is urban; one-third of the total population lives in the capital alone.

Armenia

▶ **Capital:** Yerevan
▶ **Population:** 2,968,586
▶ **Area:** 11,506 sq mi (29,800 sq km)
▶ **Language:** Armenian, Russian
▶ **Did You Know?** Armenia considers itself the first country to have formally adopted Christianity as a state religion, in the year 301.

Australia

▶ **Capital:** Canberra
▶ **Population:** 21,007,310
▶ **Area:** 2,967,909 sq mi (7,686,850 sq km)
▶ **Language:** English, Aboriginal languages
▶ **Did You Know?** The world's biggest rock—Uluru (also called Ayers Rock)—is located here, a monolith that stands more than 1,000 feet tall.

Austria

▶ **Capital:** Vienna
▶ **Population:** 8,205,533
▶ **Area:** 32,382 sq mi (83,870 sq km)
▶ **Language:** German, Slovene, Croatian, Hungarian
▶ **Did You Know?** Austria's Hohe Tauern National Park is one of Europe's largest protected natural areas.

Azerbaijan

▶ **Capital:** Baku
▶ **Population:** 8,177,717
▶ **Area:** 33,436 sq mi (86,600 sq km)
▶ **Language:** Azeri, Russian, Armenian
▶ **Did You Know?** Although Nagorno-Karabakh, a region in Azerbaijan whose population is mostly Armenian, declared its independence in 1991, Azerbaijan does not recognize its claim.

The Bahamas

▶ **Capital:** Nassau
▶ **Population:** 307,451
▶ **Area:** 5,382 sq mi (13,940 sq km)
▶ **Language:** English, Creole
▶ **Did You Know?** About two-thirds of the population lives on New Providence, one of The Bahamas' nearly 700 islands.

Bahrain

▶ **Capital:** Manama
▶ **Population:** 718,306
▶ **Area:** 257 sq mi (665 sq km)
▶ **Language:** Arabic, English, Farsi, Urdu
▶ **Did You Know?** Groundwater and treated seawater are the only sources of freshwater in Bahrain.

WAforKids.com Go to *www.WAforKids.com* for more facts about nations.

Bangladesh

▶ **Capital:** Dhaka
▶ **Population:** 153,546,901
▶ **Area:** 55,599 sq mi (144,000 sq km)
▶ **Language:** Bangla, English
▶ **Did You Know?** About one-third of Bangladesh floods each year during monsoon season, between June and early October.

Barbados

▶ **Capital:** Bridgetown
▶ **Population:** 281,968
▶ **Area:** 166 sq mi (431 sq km)
▶ **Language:** English
▶ **Did You Know?** Considered one of the Seven Wonders of Barbados, the grapefruit is believed to have been developed in Barbados from other fruits.

Belarus

▶ **Capital:** Minsk
▶ **Population:** 9,685,768
▶ **Area:** 80,155 sq mi (207,600 sq km)
▶ **Language:** Belarusian, Russian
▶ **Did You Know?** Contamination from the 1986 Chernobyl nuclear power plant explosion, in neighboring Ukraine, continues to affect Belarus. High numbers of children have been diagnosed with cancer. Many people are unemployed because land that was contaminated could no longer be farmed.

Belgium

▶ **Capital:** Brussels
▶ **Population:** 10,403,951
▶ **Area:** 11,787 sq mi (30,528 sq km)
▶ **Language:** Dutch, French, German
▶ **Did You Know?** Belgium produces about 172,000 tons of chocolate every year, supporting 290 chocolate makers and over 2,000 shops.

Belize

▶ **Capital:** Belmopan
▶ **Population:** 301,270
▶ **Area:** 8,867 sq mi (22,966 sq km)
▶ **Language:** English, Spanish, Mayan, Garifuna, Creole
▶ **Did You Know?** Belize Barrier Reef is the second largest coral reef system (a diverse underwater habitat) in the world.

Benin

▶ **Capital:** Porto-Novo (constit.); Cotonou (admin.)
▶ **Population:** 8,532,547
▶ **Area:** 43,483 sq mi (112,620 sq km)
▶ **Language:** French, Fon, Yoruba
▶ **Did You Know?** About 4 million people in Benin practice Vodun (also known as Voodoo), one of the country's official religions.

Bhutan

▶ **Capital:** Thimphu
▶ **Population:** 682,321
▶ **Area:** 18,147 sq mi (47,000 sq km)
▶ **Language:** Dzongkha, Tibetan dialects
▶ **Did You Know?** Bhutan had been under the rule of an absolute monarchy since 1907 but became a democracy in 2008.

Bolivia

▶ **Capital:** La Paz (admin.); Sucre (legislative/judiciary)
▶ **Population:** 9,247,816
▶ **Area:** 424,164 sq mi (1,098,580 sq km)
▶ **Language:** Spanish, Quechua, Aymara
▶ **Did You Know?** Bolivia's administrative capital, La Paz, is the highest capital city in the world, at about 13,000 feet above sea level.

COLOR KEY

● Africa
● Asia
● Australia
● Europe
● North America
● Pacific Islands
● South America

Bosnia and Herzegovina

- **Capital:** Sarajevo
- **Population:** 4,590,310
- **Area:** 19,741 sq mi (51,129 sq km)
- **Language:** Bosnian, Croatian, Serbian
- **Did You Know?** This country has three presidents, who serve consecutive eight-month terms.

Botswana

- **Capital:** Gaborone
- **Population:** 1,842,323
- **Area:** 231,804 sq mi (600,370 sq km)
- **Language:** Setswana, English
- **Did You Know?** Chobe National Park is home to about 100,000 elephants, possibly the largest elephant population in the world.

Brazil

- **Capital:** Brasília
- **Population:** 196,342,587
- **Area:** 3,286,488 sq mi (8,511,965 sq km)
- **Language:** Portuguese, Spanish, English, French
- **Did You Know?** Brazil has won 5 men's World Cup soccer tournaments, the most of any country.

Brunei

- **Capital:** Bandar Seri Begawan
- **Population:** 381,371
- **Area:** 2,228 sq mi (5,770 sq km)
- **Language:** Malay, English, Chinese
- **Did You Know?** The same royal family has ruled Brunei since the 1400s.

Bulgaria

- **Capital:** Sofia
- **Population:** 7,262,675
- **Area:** 42,823 sq mi (110,910 sq km)
- **Language:** Bulgarian, Turkish
- **Did You Know?** The image of a man on horseback that appears on some Bulgarian coins is based on an 8th-century rock carving called the Madara Rider.

Burkina Faso

- **Capital:** Ouagadougou
- **Population:** 15,264,735
- **Area:** 105,869 sq mi (274,200 sq km)
- **Language:** French, indigenous languages
- **Did You Know?** "Burkina Faso" means "land of honest people."

Burundi

- **Capital:** Bujumbura
- **Population:** 8,691,005
- **Area:** 10,745 sq mi (27,830 sq km)
- **Language:** Kirundi, French, Swahili
- **Did You Know?** The Twa, a Pygmy group (adult males average about 5 feet tall), are thought to be Burundi's original inhabitants.

Cambodia

- **Capital:** Phnom Penh
- **Population:** 14,241,640
- **Area:** 69,900 sq mi (181,040 sq km)
- **Language:** Khmer, French, English
- **Did You Know?** About 75% of Cambodian families are subsistence farmers, growing just enough food for themselves.

BRUSSELS, BELGIUM

Chad

- **Capital:** N'Djamena
- **Population:** 10,111,337
- **Area:** 495,755 sq mi (1,284,000 sq km)
- **Language:** French, Arabic, Sara
- **Did You Know?** The surface area of Lake Chad was nearly 10,000 sq mi in 1963. Forty years later, the lake had shrunk to one-twentieth of that size (about 500 sq mi) due to climate change and human use.

Cameroon

- **Capital:** Yaoundé
- **Population:** 18,467,692
- **Area:** 183,568 sq mi (475,440 sq km)
- **Language:** English, French, African languages
- **Did You Know?** "Cameroon" comes from the Portuguese word camarões, meaning "shrimps," which early Portuguese explorers found in abundance in Cameroon's Wouri River.

Chile

- **Capital:** Santiago
- **Population:** 16,454,143
- **Area:** 292,260 sq mi (756,950 sq km)
- **Language:** Spanish
- **Did You Know?** Chile is about 2,500 miles long but only 93 miles wide.

Canada

- **Capital:** Ottawa
- **Population:** 33,212,696
- **Area:** 3,855,103 sq mi (9,984,670 sq km)
- **Language:** English, French
- **Did You Know?** The 2010 Olympic Winter Games will be held in Vancouver, British Columbia.

China

- **Capital:** Beijing
- **Population:** 1,330,044,605
- **Area:** 3,705,407 sq mi (9,596,960 sq km)
- **Language:** Mandarin, and many dialects
- **Did You Know?** China's economy is the second largest in the world, behind the top-ranked United States. China made about $7 trillion in 2007.

Cape Verde

- **Capital:** Praia
- **Population:** 426,998
- **Area:** 1,557 sq mi (4,033 sq km)
- **Language:** Portuguese, Crioulo
- **Did You Know?** More Cape Verdeans live abroad than live on the nation's islands. Severe droughts in the late 20th century forced many to leave.

Colombia

- **Capital:** Bogotá
- **Population:** 45,013,674
- **Area:** 439,736 sq mi (1,138,910 sq km)
- **Language:** Spanish
- **Did You Know?** Colombia is the only South American country that touches both the Caribbean Sea and the Pacific Ocean.

Central African Republic

- **Capital:** Bangui
- **Population:** 4,444,330
- **Area:** 240,535 sq mi (622,984 sq km)
- **Language:** French, Sangho
- **Did You Know?** With only about 18 people per square mile, this is one of Africa's least densely populated nations.

GREAT WALL OF CHINA

Comoros

- **Capital:** Moroni
- **Population:** 731,775
- **Area:** 838 sq mi (2,170 sq km)
- **Language:** Arabic, French, Shikomoro
- **Did You Know?** The endangered Livingstone's flying fox, a fruit bat native to the islands of Comoros, has a wing span of more than 4 feet.

Congo, Democratic Republic of the

- **Capital:** Kinshasa
- **Population:** 66,514,506
- **Area:** 905,568 sq mi (2,345,410 sq km)
- **Language:** French, Lingala, Kingwana, Kikongo, Tshiluba
- **Did You Know?** In 2006, the Democratic Republic of the Congo held its first free, democratic multi-party elections since 1960.

Congo, Republic of the

- **Capital:** Brazzaville
- **Population:** 3,903,318
- **Area:** 132,047 sq mi (342,000 sq km)
- **Language:** French, Lingala, Monokutuba, Kikongo
- **Did You Know?** The production and export of crude oil makes up a major part of the Congolese economy.

Costa Rica

- **Capital:** San José
- **Population:** 4,195,914
- **Area:** 19,730 sq mi (51,100 sq km)
- **Language:** Spanish, English
- **Did You Know?** At its narrowest point, between the Pacific Ocean and Caribbean Sea, Costa Rica is only about 75 miles wide. The country's name means "rich coast" in Spanish.

Côte d'Ivoire (Ivory Coast)

- **Capital:** Yamoussoukro
- **Population:** 20,179,602
- **Area:** 124,503 sq mi (322,460 sq km)
- **Language:** French, Dioula
- **Did You Know?** There are about 60 native ethnic groups in Côte d'Ivoire. The largest group is the Akan.

Croatia

- **Capital:** Zagreb
- **Population:** 4,491,543
- **Area:** 21,831 sq mi (56,542 sq km)
- **Language:** Croatian, Serbian
- **Did You Know?** Croatia has more than 1,000 islands off its coast in the Adriatic Sea. Only about 50 are inhabited.

Cuba

- **Capital:** Havana
- **Population:** 11,423,952
- **Area:** 42,803 sq mi (110,860 sq km)
- **Language:** Spanish
- **Did You Know?** Havana hosts one of the largest annual film festivals in Latin America.

Cyprus

- **Capital:** Nicosia
- **Population:** 792,604
- **Area:** 3,571 sq mi (9,250 sq km)
- **Language:** Greek, Turkish, English
- **Did You Know?** Halloumi, a salty cheese made from a mixture of goat and sheep milk, is a traditional food in Cyprus.

COLOR KEY
- Africa
- Asia
- Australia
- Europe
- North America
- Pacific Islands
- South America

Czech Republic

- Capital: Prague
- Population: 10,220,911
- Area: 30,450 sq mi (78,866 sq km)
- Language: Czech, Slovak
- Did You Know? The so-called "Velvet Revolution" brought about the end of communism in Czechoslovakia in 1989. The term "Velvet Divorce" was used to describe the 1993 division of the Czech Republic and Slovakia.

Denmark

- Capital: Copenhagen
- Population: 5,484,723
- Area: 16,639 sq mi (43,094 sq km)
- Language: Danish, Faroese
- Did You Know? Each year in Copenhagen, around 1 million people visit a statue depicting the Little Mermaid from Hans Christian Andersen's famous fairy tale.

Djibouti

- Capital: Djibouti
- Population: 506,221
- Area: 8,880 sq mi (23,000 sq km)
- Language: French, Arabic, Somali, Afar
- Did You Know? Most of the country is barren. It receives little rainfall, and few plants survive in Djibouti's rocky deserts.

Dominica

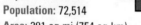

- Capital: Roseau
- Population: 72,514
- Area: 291 sq mi (754 sq km)
- Language: English, French patois
- Did You Know? Mary Eugenia Charles, who governed from 1980 to 1995, was the first female prime minister in the Caribbean.

Dominican Republic

- Capital: Santo Domingo
- Population: 9,507,133
- Area: 18,815 sq mi (48,730 sq km)
- Language: Spanish
- Did You Know? Merengue, a lively music and dance, originated here. A combination of African and European styles of dancing, the merengue is now a popular ballroom dance.

Ecuador

- Capital: Quito
- Population: 13,927,650
- Area: 109,483 sq mi (283,560 sq km)
- Language: Spanish, Quechua
- Did You Know? Observations of the wildlife on Ecuador's Galapagos Islands helped scientist Charles Darwin come up with his theory of evolution.

Egypt

- Capital: Cairo
- Population: 81,713,517
- Area: 386,662 sq mi (1,001,450 sq km)
- Language: Arabic, English, French
- Did You Know? In the Western Desert, the sand dunes often shift due to the wind, moving up to 300 feet and covering homes in mounds of sand.

El Salvador

- Capital: San Salvador
- Population: 7,066,403
- Area: 8,124 sq mi (21,040 sq km)
- Language: Spanish, Nahua
- Did You Know? El Salvador is the most densely-populated country in the mainland of the Americas, with about 883 people per square mile.

COLOR KEY

- Africa
- Asia
- Australia
- Europe
- North America
- Pacific Islands
- South America

Equatorial Guinea

- **Capital:** Malabo
- **Population:** 616,459
- **Area:** 10,831 sq mi (28,051 sq km)
- **Language:** Spanish, French, Fang, Bubi
- **Did You Know?** Equatorial Guinea is the only African country in which Spanish is an official language.

Eritrea

- **Capital:** Asmara
- **Population:** 5,502,026
- **Area:** 46,842 sq mi (121,320 sq km)
- **Language:** Afar, Arabic, Tigre, Kunama, Tigrinya
- **Did You Know?** Eritrea was once a colony of Italy, then occupied by British forces, and finally annexed by Ethiopia before it achieved independence in 1993.

Estonia

- **Capital:** Tallinn
- **Population:** 1,307,605
- **Area:** 17,462 sq mi (45,226 sq km)
- **Language:** Estonian, Russian
- **Did You Know?** Despite its small geographic size, Estonia has more than 1,400 lakes and 1,500 islands.

Ethiopia

- **Capital:** Addis Ababa
- **Population:** 82,544,838
- **Area:** 435,186 sq mi (1,127,127 sq km)
- **Language:** Amharic, Tigrinya, Oromigna, Guaragigna, Somali, Arabic
- **Did You Know?** Ethiopian children traditionally take their father's first name as their last name.

Fiji

- **Capital:** Suva
- **Population:** 931,741
- **Area:** 7,054 sq mi (18,270 sq km)
- **Language:** English, Fijian, Hindustani
- **Did You Know?** Wearing a hat is a sign of disrespect in Fijian culture.

Finland

- **Capital:** Helsinki
- **Population:** 5,244,749
- **Area:** 130,559 sq mi (338,145 sq km)
- **Language:** Finnish, Swedish
- **Did You Know?** Finland is home to several odd competitions, including the Wife-Carrying World Championships and the Mobile-Phone-Throwing World Championships.

France

- **Capital:** Paris
- **Population:** 64,057,790
- **Area:** 211,209 sq mi (547,030 sq km)
- **Language:** French
- **Did You Know?** France produces more films each year than any other European country.

Gabon

- **Capital:** Libreville
- **Population:** 1,485,832
- **Area:** 103,347 sq mi (267,667 sq km)
- **Language:** French, Fang, Myene, Nzebi
- **Did You Know?** Omar Bongo, Gabon's president since 1967, is currently Africa's longest-serving head of state.

The Gambia

- **Capital:** Banjul
- **Population:** 1,735,464
- **Area:** 4,363 sq mi (11,300 sq km)
- **Language:** English, Mandinka, Wolof
- **Did You Know?** The Gambia is the smallest country by area on the continent of Africa.

Georgia

- **Capital:** T'bilisi
- **Population:** 4,630,841
- **Area:** 26,911 sq mi (69,700 sq km)
- **Language:** Georgian, Russian, Armenian, Azeri, Abkhaz
- **Did You Know?** The Georgian alphabet is one of only a few alphabets still in use today. It is believed to have been created in the 5th century.

Germany

- **Capital:** Berlin
- **Population:** 82,369,548
- **Area:** 137,847 sq mi (357,021 sq km)
- **Language:** German
- **Did You Know?** Germany is the second most populous country in Europe, after Russia.

Ghana

- **Capital:** Accra
- **Population:** 23,382,848
- **Area:** 92,456 sq mi (239,460 sq km)
- **Language:** English, Akan, Moshi-Dagomba, Ewe, Ga
- **Did You Know?** In 1957, the British colony known as the Gold Coast was merged with another territory to form Ghana.

Greece

- **Capital:** Athens
- **Population:** 10,722,816
- **Area:** 50,942 sq mi (131,940 sq km)
- **Language:** Greek, English, French
- **Did You Know?** Democracy was invented in Greece in the 5th century B.C.

Grenada

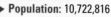

- **Capital:** Saint George's
- **Population:** 90,343
- **Area:** 133 sq mi (344 sq km)
- **Language:** English, French patois
- **Did You Know?** Grenada is sometimes referred to as the "Spice of the Caribbean" because its top export is nutmeg.

Guatemala

- **Capital:** Guatemala City
- **Population:** 13,002,206
- **Area:** 42,043 sq mi (108,890 sq km)
- **Language:** Spanish, Amerindian languages
- **Did You Know?** Before the arrival of the Spanish, the Mayan Indian empire flourished for more than 1,000 years in what is today Guatemala.

Guinea

- **Capital:** Conakry
- **Population:** 9,806,509
- **Area:** 94,926 sq mi (245,857 sq km)
- **Language:** French, Susu, Pulaar, Malinke
- **Did You Know?** Guinea has had only two presidents since attaining independence in 1958.

TAJ MAHAL AT AGRA, INDIA

Guinea-Bissau

- **Capital:** Bissau
- **Population:** 1,503,182
- **Area:** 13,946 sq mi (36,120 sq km)
- **Language:** Portuguese, Crioulo, African languages
- **Did You Know?** Most of the nation's farmers grow cashew nuts, providing a vital cash crop and accounting for 90% of Guinea-Bissau's exports.

Guyana

- **Capital:** Georgetown
- **Population:** 770,794
- **Area:** 83,000 sq mi (214,970 sq km)
- **Language:** English, Amerindian dialects, Creole, Hindi
- **Did You Know?** Guyana is the only Latin American country whose official language is English.

Haiti

- **Capital:** Port-au-Prince
- **Population:** 8,924,553
- **Area:** 10,714 sq mi (27,750 sq km)
- **Language:** French, Creole
- **Did You Know?** Haiti gained independence from France in 1804 and, after the U.S., is the second oldest country in the Americas.

Honduras

- **Capital:** Tegucigalpa
- **Population:** 7,639,327
- **Area:** 43,278 sq mi (112,090 sq km)
- **Language:** Spanish, Amerindian dialects
- **Did You Know?** Christopher Columbus was the first recorded European to reach Honduras, where he landed in 1502.

Hungary

- **Capital:** Budapest
- **Population:** 9,930,915
- **Area:** 35,919 sq mi (93,030 sq km)
- **Language:** Hungarian (Magyar)
- **Did You Know?** Budapest was originally two separate cities, Buda and Pest. The two areas are separated by the Danube River.

Iceland

- **Capital:** Reykjavik
- **Population:** 304,367
- **Area:** 39,769 sq mi (103,000 sq km)
- **Language:** Icelandic, English
- **Did You Know?** The Althingi, Iceland's general assembly, was established in the year 930 and is the world's oldest surviving parliament.

India

- **Capital:** New Delhi
- **Population:** 1,147,995,898
- **Area:** 1,269,346 sq mi (3,287,590 sq km)
- **Language:** Hindi, English, Bengali, Urdu
- **Did You Know?** Jammu and Kashmir—part of a region in dispute between India, Pakistan, and China—is India's only Muslim-majority state.

Indonesia

- **Capital:** Jakarta
- **Population:** 237,512,355
- **Area:** 741,100 sq mi (1,919,440 sq km)
- **Language:** Bahasa Indonesian, English, Dutch, Javanese
- **Did You Know?** About one-seventh of the world's active volcanoes are found on this nation of islands.

Iran

- **Capital:** Tehran
- **Population:** 65,875,223
- **Area:** 636,296 sq mi (1,648,000 sq km)
- **Language:** Farsi (Persian), Turkic, Kurdish
- **Did You Know?** Although Arabs are the majority ethnic group in some Middle East countries, they are a minority in Iran. About half of all Iranians are Persian.

Iraq

- **Capital:** Baghdad
- **Population:** 28,221,181
- **Area:** 168,754 sq mi (437,072 sq km)
- **Language:** Arabic, Kurdish
- **Did You Know?** The Sumer, one of the world's oldest known civilizations, lived in the Tigris-Euphrates Valley in the 4th millennium B.C.

Ireland

- **Capital:** Dublin
- **Population:** 4,156,119
- **Area:** 27,135 sq mi (70,280 sq km)
- **Language:** English, Irish
- **Did You Know?** The country of Ireland occupies only 83% of the "Emerald Isle." The rest of the island is part of the United Kingdom and is called Northern Ireland.

Israel

- **Capital:** Jerusalem
- **Population:** 7,112,359
- **Area:** 8,019 sq mi (20,770 sq km)
- **Language:** Hebrew, Arabic, English
- **Did You Know?** Hebrew, Israel's official language, was revived as a spoken language in the 19th and 20th centuries; it was last spoken widely in 3rd century B.C.

Italy

- **Capital:** Rome
- **Population:** 58,145,321
- **Area:** 116,306 sq mi (301,230 sq km)
- **Language:** Italian, German, French, Slovenian
- **Did You Know?** Italy has one of the highest cell-phone-use rates in the world, with about 123 cell-phone subscriptions for every 100 Italians.

Jamaica

- **Capital:** Kingston
- **Population:** 2,804,332
- **Area:** 4,244 sq mi (10,991 sq km)
- **Language:** English, Jamaican Creole
- **Did You Know?** Jamaica's name comes from the Arawak Indian word *Xaymaca*, which means "land of wood and water."

Japan

- **Capital:** Tokyo
- **Population:** 127,288,419
- **Area:** 145,883 sq mi (377,835 sq km)
- **Language:** Japanese
- **Did You Know?** With the world's third-largest economy (after the U.S. and China), Japan is also one of the largest and most technologically advanced producers of cars and electronic equipment.

Jordan

- **Capital:** Amman
- **Population:** 6,198,677
- **Area:** 35,637 sq mi (92,300 sq km)
- **Language:** Arabic, English
- **Did You Know?** The Dead Sea, on the Israel-Jordan border, is 6 to 10 times saltier than the ocean.

COLOR KEY

- Africa
- Asia
- Australia
- Europe
- North America
- Pacific Islands
- South America

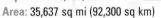

Kazakhstan

- **Capital:** Astana
- **Population:** 15,340,533
- **Area:** 1,049,155 sq mi (2,717,300 sq km)
- **Language:** Kazakh, Russian
- **Did You Know?** Baikonur Cosmodrome, one of the Russian Space Agency's launch facilities, is located in Kazakhstan.

Kenya

- **Capital:** Nairobi
- **Population:** 37,953,838
- **Area:** 224,962 sq mi (582,650 sq km)
- **Language:** Kiswahili, English
- **Did You Know?** Fossils of our human ancestors dating from more than 1 million years ago have been found in Kenya. Its National Museum is home to one of the world's best collections of human ancestral bones.

Kiribati

- **Capital:** Tarawa
- **Population:** 110,356
- **Area:** 313 sq mi (811 sq km)
- **Language:** English, I-Kiribati
- **Did You Know?** Kiribati's islands are spread across an area of the Pacific Ocean about the same size as the continental U.S.

Korea, North

- **Capital:** Pyongyang
- **Population:** 23,479,089
- **Area:** 46,541 sq mi (120,540 sq km)
- **Language:** Korean
- **Did You Know?** North and South Korea have officially been at war for more than 50 years. A ceasefire has maintained the peace since 1953.

Korea, South

- **Capital:** Seoul
- **Population:** 48,379,392
- **Area:** 38,023 sq mi (98,480 sq km)
- **Language:** Korean
- **Did You Know?** The martial art of tae kwon do is the national sport. It means "way of the foot and fist."

Kosovo

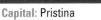

- **Capital:** Pristina
- **Population:** 2,126,708 (2007 est.)
- **Area:** 4,212 sq mi (10,887 sq km)
- **Language:** Albanian, Serbian, Bosnian, Turkish, Roma
- **Did You Know?** In 2008, the Kosovo Assembly declared its independence from Serbia, making it the world's newest country.

Kuwait

- **Capital:** Kuwait City
- **Population:** 2,596,799
- **Area:** 6,880 sq mi (17,820 sq km)
- **Language:** Arabic, English
- **Did You Know?** In 2005, women were granted full political rights, including the right to vote and run in parliamentary elections.

Kyrgyzstan

- **Capital:** Bishkek
- **Population:** 5,356,869
- **Area:** 76,641 sq mi (198,500 sq km)
- **Language:** Kyrgyz, Russian
- **Did You Know?** The 40 "rays of light" on Kyrgyzstan's flag represent the country's various Kyrgyz tribes.

SAVANNA IN KENYA

BOH TEA PLANTATION IN MALAYSIA

Laos

- **Capital:** Vientiane
- **Population:** 6,677,534
- **Area:** 91,429 sq mi (236,800 sq km)
- **Language:** Lao, French, English
- **Did You Know?** The first kingdom in what is now Laos was called *Lan Xang*, or "Kingdom of the Million Elephants."

Latvia

- **Capital:** Riga
- **Population:** 2,245,423
- **Area:** 24,938 sq mi (64,589 sq km)
- **Language:** Latvian, Russian, Lithuanian
- **Did You Know?** Latvia calls itself the "Land that Sings." Choirs and dance groups compete each year for a place in the Nationwide Latvian Song and Dance Celebration which attracts more than 30,000 dancers, singers, and musicians.

Lebanon

- **Capital:** Beirut
- **Population:** 3,971,941
- **Area:** 4,015 sq mi (10,400 sq km)
- **Language:** Arabic, French, English, Armenian
- **Did You Know?** The cedar of Lebanon is one of four cedar species in the world. The tree is mentioned in myths and even appears on the country's flag.

Lesotho

- **Capital:** Maseru
- **Population:** 2,128,180
- **Area:** 11,720 sq mi (30,355 sq km)
- **Language:** English, Sesotho, Zulu, Xhosa
- **Did You Know?** The Kingdom of Lesotho is completely surrounded by South Africa.

Liberia

- **Capital:** Monrovia
- **Population:** 3,334,587
- **Area:** 43,000 sq mi (111,370 sq km)
- **Language:** English, ethnic languages
- **Did You Know?** Liberia was founded in 1822 by freed African slaves from the U.S. It became an independent republic in 1847.

Libya

- **Capital:** Tripoli
- **Population:** 6,173,579
- **Area:** 679,362 sq mi (1,759,540 sq km)
- **Language:** Arabic, Italian, English
- **Did You Know?** In 1922, Libya reached 136°F, the highest temperature ever recorded.

Liechtenstein

- **Capital:** Vaduz
- **Population:** 34,498
- **Area:** 62 sq mi (160 sq km)
- **Language:** German, Alemannic dialect
- **Did You Know?** Liechtenstein is one of only two countries in the world (Uzbekistan is the other) that is "doubly landlocked." It has no coastline and is surrounded by countries without coastlines.

Lithuania

- **Capital:** Vilnius
- **Population:** 3,565,205
- **Area:** 25,174 sq mi (65,200 sq km)
- **Language:** Lithuanian, Russian, Polish
- **Did You Know?** Basketball is one of the country's most popular sports. Lithuania's men's Olympic basketball team won the bronze medal at three Summer Olympic games.

Luxembourg

- **Capital:** Luxembourg
- **Population:** 486,006
- **Area:** 998 sq mi (2,586 sq km)
- **Language:** French, German, Luxembourgish
- **Did You Know?** Luxembourg's per capita gross national product (GDP) is more than $80,000, the highest in the world.

Macedonia

- **Capital:** Skopje
- **Population:** 2,061,315
- **Area:** 9,781 sq mi (25,333 sq km)
- **Language:** Macedonian, Albanian, Turkish
- **Did You Know?** Macedonia's Albanian and Turkish minorities are legacies of the Ottoman Empire, which ended its rule of Macedonia in 1913 after 500 years in power.

Madagascar

- **Capital:** Antananarivo
- **Population:** 20,042,551
- **Area:** 226,657 sq mi (587,040 sq km)
- **Language:** Malagasy, French
- **Did You Know?** Madagascar is the world's fourth largest island after Greenland, New Guinea, and Borneo. Because of its isolation from mainland Africa, most of its wildlife and plants exist nowhere else on Earth.

Malawi

- **Capital:** Lilongwe
- **Population:** 13,931,831
- **Area:** 45,745 sq mi (118,480 sq km)
- **Language:** English, Chichewa
- **Did You Know?** Malawi means "flaming waters" and is named for the sun setting on Lake Malawi, Africa's third largest lake.

Malaysia

- **Capital:** Kuala Lumpur
- **Population:** 25,274,133
- **Area:** 127,317 sq mi (329,750 sq km)
- **Language:** Malay, English, Chinese, Tamil
- **Did You Know?** About half of Malaysia's exports are electronics.

Maldives

- **Capital:** Male
- **Population:** 385,925
- **Area:** 116 sq mi (300 sq km)
- **Language:** Maldivian Divehi, English
- **Did You Know?** The capital island of this 1,190-island nation is so overcrowded that Hulhumale, an artificial island, was created nearby.

Mali

- **Capital:** Bamako
- **Population:** 12,324,029
- **Area:** 478,767 sq mi (1,240,000 sq km)
- **Language:** French, Bambara
- **Did You Know?** The Grand Mosque in Djenné is the largest mud-brick building in the world.

Malta

- **Capital:** Valletta
- **Population:** 403,532
- **Area:** 122 sq mi (316 sq km)
- **Language:** Maltese, English
- **Did You Know?** This island nation is located midway between Europe and Africa, but it considers itself part of Europe and joined the European Union in 2004.

COLOR KEY

- ● Africa
- ● Asia
- ● Australia
- ● Europe
- ● North America
- ● Pacific Islands
- ● South America

173

Marshall Islands

- **Capital:** Majuro
- **Population:** 63,174
- **Area:** 4,577 sq mi (11,854 sq km)
- **Language:** English, Marshallese
- **Did You Know?** The United States occupied this island nation for several decades after World War II and the country still uses the U.S. dollar as its currency.

Mauritania

- **Capital:** Nouakchott
- **Population:** 3,364,940
- **Area:** 397,955 sq mi (1,030,700 sq km)
- **Language:** Arabic, Wolof, Pulaar
- **Did You Know?** Since 80% of the country is covered by desert, most farming takes place on the banks of the Senegal River.

Mauritius

- **Capital:** Port Louis
- **Population:** 1,274,189
- **Area:** 788 sq mi (2,040 sq km)
- **Language:** Creole, Bhojpuri, French, English
- **Did You Know?** About 70% of the people are descended from immigrants who came from India to work on Mauritius's sugar plantations.

Mexico

- **Capital:** Mexico City
- **Population:** 109,955,400
- **Area:** 761,606 sq mi (1,972,550 sq km)
- **Language:** Spanish, Mayan languages
- **Did You Know?** Before 1848, Mexico included the area now covered by Arizona, California, Nevada, New Mexico, western Colorado, Texas, and Utah.

Micronesia

- **Capital:** Palikir
- **Population:** 107,665
- **Area:** 271 sq mi (702 sq km)
- **Language:** English, Trukese, Pohnpeian, Yapese
- **Did You Know?** There are no formal political parties in Micronesia.

Moldova

- **Capital:** Chisinau
- **Population:** 4,324,450
- **Area:** 13,067 sq mi (33,843 sq km)
- **Language:** Moldovan, Russian
- **Did You Know?** On March 1, Moldovans celebrate the beginning of spring by wearing a pin with braided threads of red (symbolizing blood) and white (symbolizing life).

Monaco

- **Capital:** Monaco
- **Population:** 32,796
- **Area:** 1 sq mi (1.95 sq km)
- **Language:** French, English, Italian, Monegasque
- **Did You Know?** Except for a period of time when France annexed Monaco, the House of Grimaldi has been in power since 1297.

Mongolia

- **Capital:** Ulaanbaatar
- **Population:** 2,996,081
- **Area:** 603,909 sq mi (1,564,116 sq km)
- **Language:** Khalkha Mongolian
- **Did You Know?** Mongolia was founded more than 360 years ago, but its capital has changed locations more than 20 times.

Montenegro

- **Capital:** Cetinje; Podgorica (admin.)
- **Population:** 678,177
- **Area:** 5,415 sq mi (14,026 sq km)
- **Language:** Serbian, Bosnian, Albanian, Croatian
- **Did You Know?** Montenegro adopted its first constitution in 2007, a little more than a year after it declared its independence from Serbia. Both countries had been a part of Yugoslavia.

Morocco

- **Capital:** Rabat
- **Population:** 34,343,219
- **Area:** 172,414 sq mi (446,550 sq km)
- **Language:** Arabic, Berber dialects, French
- **Did You Know?** One of the world's most grueling foot races is the Marathon des Sables ("Marathon of Sands"), a 7-day, 143-mile trek across the Sahara Desert in Morocco.

Mozambique

- **Capital:** Maputo
- **Population:** 21,284,701
- **Area:** 309,496 sq mi (801,590 sq km)
- **Language:** Portuguese, Bantu languages
- **Did You Know?** Mozambique has been hurt by colonial rule, civil war and famine. But after a peace deal in 1992 ended 16 years of civil conflict, the country has enjoyed a period of rapid economic growth.

Myanmar (Burma)

- **Capital:** Yangon (Rangoon); Nay Pyi Taw (admin.)
- **Population:** 47,758,181
- **Area:** 261,970 sq mi (678,500 sq km)
- **Language:** Burmese
- **Did You Know?** The Mogok Stone Tract is known for producing some of the world's most brilliant rubies.

Namibia

- **Capital:** Windhoek
- **Population:** 2,088,669
- **Area:** 318,696 sq mi (825,418 sq km)
- **Language:** Afrikaans, English, German
- **Did You Know?** Until it gained independence from South Africa in 1990, Namibia was known as South-West Africa.

Nauru

- **Capital:** Yaren district
- **Population:** 13,770
- **Area:** 8 sq mi (21 sq km)
- **Language:** Nauruan, English
- **Did You Know?** Named "Pleasant Island" by its first European visitors, this island nation is the world's smallest republic.

Nepal

- **Capital:** Kathmandu
- **Population:** 29,519,114
- **Area:** 56,827 sq mi (147,181 sq km)
- **Language:** Nepali, Maithali, Bhojpuri, English
- **Did You Know?** In Nepali, Mt. Everest is called Sagarmatha, which translates as "Goddess of the Sky."

Netherlands

- **Capital:** Amsterdam; The Hague (admin.)
- **Population:** 16,645,313
- **Area:** 16,033 sq mi (41,526 sq km)
- **Language:** Dutch, Frisian
- **Did You Know?** There are twice as many bikes as cars in this country.

COLOR KEY
- Africa
- Asia
- Australia
- Europe
- North America
- Pacific Islands
- South America

CUPOLAS OF THE CHAPEL OF CHRIST IN THE KREMLIN, MOSCOW, RUSSIA

New Zealand

- **Capital:** Wellington
- **Population:** 4,173,460
- **Area:** 103,738 sq mi (268,680 sq km)
- **Language:** English, Maori
- **Did You Know?**

This wealthy Pacific nation has two main cultural groups: people of European descent who arrived in the last 200 years, and the Maori, whose ancestors arrived from Polynesia around 1,000 years ago.

Nicaragua

- **Capital:** Managua
- **Population:** 5,785,846
- **Area:** 49,998 sq mi (129,494 sq km)
- **Language:** Spanish, Miskito, indigenous languages
- **Did You Know?** The islands of the Miskito Cays, once an area for pirate hideouts, is now a protected area for coral reefs and wildlife.

Niger

- **Capital:** Niamey
- **Population:** 13,272,679
- **Area:** 489,192 sq mi (1,267,000 sq km)
- **Language:** French, Hausa, Djerma
- **Did You Know?** Niger was a crossroads of ancient trade in Africa. Caravans would stop here on their way to Timbuktu, Mali.

Nigeria

- **Capital:** Abuja
- **Population:** 146,255,306
- **Area:** 356,669 sq mi (923,768 sq km)
- **Language:** English, Hausa, Yoruba, Ibo
- **Did You Know?** In the tradition of Nigeria's Yoruba people, the birth of twins brings good luck to their parents.

Norway

- **Capital:** Oslo
- **Population:** 4,644,457
- **Area:** 125,021 sq mi (323,802 sq km)
- **Language:** Norwegian, Sami
- **Did You Know?** Norway's coast is known for its many fjords—narrow sea inlets surrounded by steep slopes.

Oman

- **Capital:** Muscat
- **Population:** 3,311,640
- **Area:** 82,031 sq mi (212,460 sq km)
- **Language:** Arabic, English, Indian dialects
- **Did You Know?** As part of their traditional clothing, Omani men carry an ornate dagger called a khanjar tucked in the front of a special belt.

Pakistan

- **Capital:** Islamabad
- **Population:** 172,800,051
- **Area:** 310,403 sq mi (803,940 sq km)
- **Language:** Urdu, English, Punjabi, Sindhi
- **Did You Know?** After gaining its independence from Britain in 1947, Pakistan was divided into two sections, nearly 1,000 miles apart on opposite sides of India. In 1971, East Pakistan declared its independence as the country of Bangladesh.

BERGEN, NORWAY

Palau

- **Capital:** Melekeok
- **Population:** 21,093
- **Area:** 177 sq mi (458 sq km)
- **Language:** English, Palauan, Sonsoral, Tobi, Angaur
- **Did You Know?** Palau's marine life is among the world's most diverse—more than 1,400 species of fish and 500 species of coral can be found here.

Panama

- **Capital:** Panama City
- **Population:** 3,309,679
- **Area:** 30,193 sq mi (78,200 sq km)
- **Language:** Spanish, English
- **Did You Know?** Panama is the shortest link between the Atlantic and Pacific Oceans in the Americas, making its 50-mile-long (80-km) canal of great strategic importance.

Papua New Guinea

- **Capital:** Port Moresby
- **Population:** 5,931,769
- **Area:** 178,704 sq mi (462,840 sq km)
- **Language:** English, Motu, Melanesian pidgin
- **Did You Know?** More than 700 ethnic groups, each with its own language and customs, live in this country.

Paraguay

- **Capital:** Asunción
- **Population:** 6,831,306
- **Area:** 157,047 sq mi (406,750 sq km)
- **Language:** Spanish, Guarani
- **Did You Know?** One of the world's largest hydroelectric power plants by capacity is Itaipu, located in Paraguay and Brazil.

Peru

- **Capital:** Lima
- **Population:** 29,180,899
- **Area:** 496,226 sq mi (1,285,220 sq km)
- **Language:** Spanish, Quechua, Aymara
- **Did You Know?** Peru's rich heritage includes Machu Picchu, the beautiful and mysterious ruins of an Incan city high in the Andes Mountains.

Philippines

- **Capital:** Manila
- **Population:** 96,061,683
- **Area:** 115,831 sq mi (300,000 sq km)
- **Language:** Filipino, English
- **Did You Know?** The Philippines are vulnerable to many natural hazards, including tropical cyclones (known as typhoons), landslides, earthquakes, tsunamis, and volcanic eruptions.

Poland

- **Capital:** Warsaw
- **Population:** 38,500,696
- **Area:** 120,728 sq mi (312,685 sq km)
- **Language:** Polish, Ukrainian, German
- **Did You Know?** In 1989, the Polish people voted in eastern Europe's first post-communist government.

Portugal

- **Capital:** Lisbon
- **Population:** 10,676,910
- **Area:** 35,672 sq mi (92,391 sq km)
- **Language:** Portuguese
- **Did You Know?** The national style of music, called *fado*, originated in Lisbon. It has a sad and longing sound.

COLOR KEY

- Africa
- Asia
- Australia
- Europe
- North America
- Pacific Islands
- South America

Qatar

- **Capital:** Doha
- **Population:** 824,789
- **Area:** 4,416 sq mi (11,437 sq km)
- **Language:** Arabic, English
- **Did You Know?** North Field, one of the largest natural gas reservoirs in the world, is just off the coast of Qatar.

Romania

- **Capital:** Bucharest
- **Population:** 22,246,862
- **Area:** 91,699 sq mi (237,500 sq km)
- **Language:** Romanian, Hungarian, German
- **Did You Know?** Prince Vlad Tepes ("the Impaler"), who once ruled part of Romania, was the inspiration for the fictional Dracula.

Russia

- **Capital:** Moscow
- **Population:** 140,702,094
- **Area:** 6,592,772 sq mi (17,075,200 sq km)
- **Language:** Russian, many minority languages
- **Did You Know?** The Trans-Siberian Railroad is the world's longest railway line, stretching 5,778 miles from Moscow east to Vladivostok.

Rwanda

- **Capital:** Kigali
- **Population:** 10,186,063
- **Area:** 10,169 sq mi (26,338 sq km)
- **Language:** French, English, Kinyarwanda, Kiswahili
- **Did You Know?** Volcanoes National Park is home to one of only two remaining mountain gorilla populations in the world.

Saint Kitts and Nevis

- **Capital:** Basseterre
- **Population:** 39,817
- **Area:** 101 sq mi (261 sq km)
- **Language:** English
- **Did You Know?** The islands of St. Kitts and Nevis declared independence from Britain in 1983. They are inhabited mainly by descendants of enslaved West Africans.

Saint Lucia

- **Capital:** Castries
- **Population:** 159,585
- **Area:** 238 sq mi (616 sq km)
- **Language:** English, French patois
- **Did You Know?** The Caribbean island is a popular spot to visit because of its beautiful beaches, unusual plants and the Qualibou volcano with its boiling sulphur springs.

Saint Vincent and the Grenadines

- **Capital:** Kingstown
- **Population:** 118,432
- **Area:** 150 sq mi (389 sq km)
- **Language:** English, French patois
- **Did You Know?** The deadly Soufrière volcano on St. Vincent island last erupted in 1979.

Samoa (formerly Western Samoa)
- **Capital:** Apia
- **Population:** 217,083
- **Area:** 1,137 sq mi (2,944 sq km)
- **Language:** English, Samoan
- **Did You Know?** In 1962, Samoa (then known as Western Samoa) became the first South Pacific island nation to achieve independence.

San Marino
- **Capital:** San Marino
- **Population:** 29,973
- **Area:** 24 sq mi (61 sq km)
- **Language:** Italian
- **Did You Know?** According to legend, San Marino was founded in 301 A.D. by a Christian stonemason, Marinus, for whom the country was named.

São Tomé and Príncipe

- **Capital:** São Tomé
- **Population:** 206,178
- **Area:** 386 sq mi (1,001 sq km)
- **Language:** Portuguese, Creole
- **Did You Know?** Cocoa makes up 80% of all the country's exports.

Saudi Arabia

- **Capital:** Riyadh
- **Population:** 28,146,657
- **Area:** 756,985 sq mi (1,960,582 sq km)
- **Language:** Arabic
- **Did You Know?** Saudi Arabia is the world's leading exporter of oil.

Senegal

- **Capital:** Dakar
- **Population:** 12,853,269
- **Area:** 75,749 sq mi (196,190 sq km)
- **Language:** French, Wolof, Pulaar
- **Did You Know?** Dakar is the westernmost point on the continent of Africa.

Serbia
- **Capital:** Belgrade
- **Population:** 10,159,046
- **Area:** 34,116 sq mi (88,361 sq km)
- **Language:** Serbian, Albanian, Romanian
- **Did You Know?** The Roma (Gypsies), one of Serbia's largest minority groups, have helped to maintain the country's folk music tradition.

COLOR KEY
- Africa
- Asia
- Australia
- Europe
- North America
- Pacific Islands
- South America

TOWER BRIDGE IN LONDON, ENGLAND

179

Seychelles

> **Capital:** Victoria
> **Population:** 82,247
> **Area:** 176 sq mi (455 sq km)
> **Language:** Creole, English, French

> **Did You Know?** The colors of Seychelles' flag represent the sky and sea (blue), the sun (yellow), the people and their work (red), social justice and harmony (white), and the environment (green).

Sierra Leone

> **Capital:** Freetown
> **Population:** 6,294,774
> **Area:** 27,699 sq mi (71,740 sq km)
> **Language:** English, Mende, Temne, Krio
> **Did You Know?** Diamonds are one of this country's major exports.

Singapore

> **Capital:** Singapore
> **Population:** 4,608,167
> **Area:** 267 sq mi (693 sq km)
> **Language:** Chinese, Malay, Tamil, English
> **Did You Know?** The Port of Singapore is the world's busiest by tons of cargo shipped. Its merchant fleet is the largest in Asia and fifth largest in the world.

Slovakia

> **Capital:** Bratislava
> **Population:** 5,455,407
> **Area:** 18,859 sq mi (48,845 sq km)
> **Language:** Slovak, Hungarian
> **Did You Know?** Bryndzové halušky, or potato dumplings with sheep's milk cheese, is considered Slovakia's national dish.

Slovenia

> **Capital:** Ljubljana
> **Population:** 2,007,711
> **Area:** 7,827 sq mi (20,273 sq km)
> **Language:** Slovenian, Serbo-Croatian
> **Did You Know?** Slovenia has more than a thousand underground caves. The famous Postojna Cave system has about 13 miles of known passageways.

Solomon Islands

> **Capital:** Honiara
> **Population:** 581,318
> **Area:** 10,985 sq mi (28,450 sq km)
> **Language:** English, Melanesian pidgin
> **Did You Know?** Because so many different languages are spoken in the Solomon Islands, many people communicate using a simplified English called Melanesian pidgin.

Somalia

> **Capital:** Mogadishu
> **Population:** 9,558,666
> **Area:** 246,201 sq mi (637,657 sq km)
> **Language:** Somali, Arabic, Italian, English
> **Did You Know?** Iman, a supermodel from Somalia, speaks five languages and studied political science in college.

South Africa

- **Capital:** Pretoria (admin.); Cape Town (legis.); Bloemfontein (judicial)
- **Population:** 48,782,755
- **Area:** 471,011 sq mi (1,219,912 sq km)
- **Language:** Afrikaans, English, Ndebele, Sotho, Zulu, Xhosa
- **Did You Know?** Racial segregation was law between 1948 and 1994. In the era of apartheid (Afrikaans for "apartness"), only whites could vote or run for public office. The rest of the population held limited political rights.

Spain

- **Capital:** Madrid
- **Population:** 40,491,051
- **Area:** 194,897 sq mi (504,782 sq km)
- **Language:** Castilian Spanish, Catalan, Galician
- **Did You Know?** Spain produces and exports the most olives and olive oil in the world.

Sri Lanka

- **Capital:** Colombo
- **Population:** 21,128,773
- **Area:** 25,332 sq mi (65,610 sq km)
- **Language:** Sinhala, Tamil, English
- **Did You Know?** Ceylon tea takes its name from this country, which used to be called Ceylon while under European rule.

Sudan

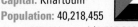

- **Capital:** Khartoum
- **Population:** 40,218,455
- **Area:** 967,499 sq mi (2,505,810 sq km)
- **Language:** Arabic, Nubian, Ta Bedawie
- **Did You Know?** The ancient kingdom of Kush, whose civilization reflected Egyptian and African influences, once thrived in Sudan.

Suriname

- **Capital:** Paramaribo
- **Population:** 475,996
- **Area:** 63,039 sq mi (163,270 sq km)
- **Language:** Dutch, English, Sranang Tongo
- **Did You Know?** Many Surinamers are descended from escaped West African slaves, who were brought to Suriname when it was still a Dutch colony.

Swaziland

- **Capital:** Mbabane
- **Population:** 1,128,814
- **Area:** 6,704 sq mi (17,363 sq km)
- **Language:** English, siSwati
- **Did You Know?** Swaziland's king is one of the few remaining absolute monarchs in the world. Although a new constitution was adopted in 2006, political parties are still officially banned.

Sweden

- **Capital:** Stockholm
- **Population:** 9,045,389
- **Area:** 173,732 sq mi (449,964 sq km)
- **Language:** Swedish, Sami, Finnish
- **Did You Know?** Sweden has not participated in any wars since 1814, when it ceased fighting in the Napoleonic Wars.

SKYLINE OF SINGAPORE

Tajikistan

- **Capital:** Dushanbe
- **Population:** 7,211,884
- **Area:** 55,251 sq mi (143,100 sq km)
- **Language:** Tajik, Russian
- **Did You Know?** Tajikistan's main source of energy is hydroelectricity. Its Nurek Dam is the highest dam in the world.

Tanzania

- **Capital:** Dar es Salaam Dodoma (legislative)
- **Population:** 40,213,162
- **Area:** 364,900 sq mi (945,087 sq km)
- **Language:** Kiswahili (Swahili), English, Arabic
- **Did You Know?** Tanzania's Mt. Kilimanjaro, which peaks at 19,340 feet, is the highest point in Africa.

Thailand

- **Capital:** Bangkok
- **Population:** 65,493,298
- **Area:** 198,457 sq mi (514,000 sq km)
- **Language:** Thai, English
- **Did You Know?** Formerly known as Siam, after a 19th-century king, Thailand is the only country in Southeast Asia to have never been colonized. Thailand means "land of the free."

Switzerland

- **Capital:** Bern (admin.); Lausanne (judicial)
- **Population:** 7,581,520
- **Area:** 15,942 sq mi (41,290 sq km)
- **Language:** German, French, Italian, Romansch
- **Did You Know?** Switzerland has long remained neutral during wars, giving it a political stability that has helped it become one of the world's wealthiest countries. Banking is one of its most important industries.

Syria

- **Capital:** Damascus
- **Population:** 19,747,586
- **Area:** 71,498 sq mi (185,180 sq km)
- **Language:** Arabic, Kurdish, Armenian
- **Did You Know?** Tablets found in the ancient city of Ugarit contain one of the world's oldest alphabets, dating back to around 1400 B.C.

Taiwan

- **Capital:** Taipei
- **Population:** 22,920,946
- **Area:** 13,892 sq mi (35,980 sq km)
- **Language:** Mandarin Chinese, Taiwanese
- **Did You Know?** Although Taiwan set up its own government in 1949, China considers Taiwan to be one of its provinces and still under its control.

COLOR KEY
- Africa
- Asia
- Australia
- Europe
- North America
- Pacific Islands
- South America

Timor-Leste (East Timor)

- **Capital:** Dili
- **Population:** 1,108,777
- **Area:** 5,794 sq mi (15,007 sq km)
- **Language:** Tetum, Portuguese, Indonesian, English
- **Did You Know?** This country occupies the eastern half of Timor island; the island's western half (except for an area on the coast) belongs to Indonesia.

Togo

- **Capital:** Lomé
- **Population:** 5,858,673
- **Area:** 21,925 sq mi (56,785 sq km)
- **Language:** French, Ewe, Mina, Kabye, Dagomba
- **Did You Know?** In October 2007, a record 85% of registered voters turned out for Togo's first free and fair parliamentary elections since 2002.

Tonga

- **Capital:** Nuku'alofa
- **Population:** 119,009
- **Area:** 289 sq mi (748 sq km)
- **Language:** Tongan, English
- **Did You Know?** Tonga is ruled by the only surviving monarchy in Polynesia, though it does have a parliament in which most of the members are elected.

Trinidad and Tobago

- **Capital:** Port-of-Spain
- **Population:** 1,047,366
- **Area:** 1,980 sq mi (5,128 sq km)
- **Language:** English, Hindi, French, Spanish
- **Did You Know?** Steel drums were invented on the island of Trinidad around the time of World War II, using recycled metal containers such as oil drums.

Tunisia

- **Capital:** Tunis
- **Population:** 10,383,577
- **Area:** 63,170 sq mi (163,610 sq km)
- **Language:** Arabic, French
- **Did You Know?** Lamb is the basis of most meat dishes in Tunisia. Long, social meals frequently begin with lamb soup.

Turkey

- **Capital:** Ankara
- **Population:** 7,892,807
- **Area:** 301,384 sq mi (780,580 sq km)
- **Language:** Turkish, Kurdish, Arabic
- **Did You Know?** Hisarlik, an archaeological site in northwest Turkey, contains the ancient city of Troy, site of the legendary Trojan War.

VIEW OF THE SWISS ALPS FROM JUNGFRAU, SWITZERLAND

Turkmenistan

- **Capital:** Ashgabat
- **Population:** 5,179,571
- **Area:** 188,456 sq mi (488,100 sq km)
- **Language:** Turkmen, Russian, Uzbek
- **Did You Know?** This desert nation has the smallest population of the five former Soviet republics in Central Asia, but possesses the world's fifth largest reserves of natural gas as well as large deposits of oil.

Tuvalu

- **Capital:** Funafuti
- **Population:** 12,177
- **Area:** 10 sq mi (26 sq km)
- **Language:** Tuvaluan, English
- **Did You Know?** One of Tuvalu's main exports is copra, the dried coconut meat from which coconut oil is made.

Uganda

- **Capital:** Kampala
- **Population:** 31,367,972
- **Area:** 91,136 sq mi (236,040 sq km)
- **Language:** English, Ganda, Swahili
- **Did You Know?** The crested crane is a national symbol and appears on Uganda's flag.

Ukraine

- **Capital:** Kiev
- **Population:** 45,994,287
- **Area:** 233,090 sq mi (603,700 sq km)
- **Language:** Ukrainian, Russian
- **Did You Know?** Ukraine was once known as the "bread basket of the Soviet Union" for its exports of wheat. It is still one of the world's top wheat producers.

United Arab Emirates

- **Capital:** Abu Dhabi
- **Population:** 4,621,399
- **Area:** 32,000 sq mi (82,880 sq km)
- **Language:** Arabic, Persian, English, Hindi, Urdu
- **Did You Know?** The approximately 2,313-feet tall Burj Dubai (*Burj* is Arabic for "tower") in Dubai will be the tallest building in the world upon its completion in 2009.

United Kingdom (Great Britain)

- **Capital:** London
- **Population:** 60,943,912
- **Area:** 94,526 sq mi (244,820 sq km)
- **Language:** English, Welsh, Scottish Gaelic
- **Did You Know?** At the height of its power during the 19th century, the British Empire controlled one-fourth of all the land in the world and more than one-fourth of the world's population.

United States

- **Capital:** Washington, DC
- **Population:** 303,824,646
- **Area:** 3,718,712 sq mi (9,631,420 sq km)
- **Language:** English, Spanish
- **Did You Know?** The U.S. is the world's leading economic and military power. It is also a major source of entertainment: American TV, films, and music are all popular around the globe.

Uruguay

- **Capital:** Montevideo
- **Population:** 3,477,778
- **Area:** 68,039 sq mi (176,220 sq km)
- **Language:** Spanish, Portunol
- **Did You Know?** The leaves of the *yerba maté* shrub are used to brew a popular drink in Uruguay. The tea is often drunk from a gourd using a metal straw.

COLOR KEY
- Africa
- Asia
- Australia
- Europe
- North America
- Pacific Islands
- South America

Uzbekistan

- **Capital:** Tashkent
- **Population:** 27,345,026
- **Area:** 172,742 sq mi (447,400 sq km)
- **Language:** Uzbek, Russian, Tajik
- **Did You Know?** Samarkand, in east-central Uzbekistan, is one of Central Asia's oldest cities. It was once an important trading center on the Silk Road between Asia and the West.

Vanuatu

- **Capital:** Port-Vila
- **Population:** 215,446
- **Area:** 4,710 sq mi (12,200 sq km)
- **Language:** French, English, Bislama, local languages
- **Did You Know?** More than 100 local languages and dialects are spoken on the 80-plus islands that make up this Pacific nation.

Vatican City

- **Population:** 824
- **Area:** .17 sq mi (.44 sq km)
- **Language:** Italian, Latin, French
- **Did You Know?** Not only is Vatican City the world's smallest country, it also has the smallest population of any country—824 people.

BURJ AL ARAB IN DUBAI

Venezuela

- **Capital:** Caracas
- **Population:** 26,414,815
- **Area:** 352,144 sq mi (912,050 sq km)
- **Language:** Spanish, indigenous dialects
- **Did You Know?** The highest waterfall on Earth, Angel Falls, is in Venezuela, dropping 3,212 feet over the side of a mountain.

Vietnam

- **Capital:** Hanoi
- **Population:** 86,116,559
- **Area:** 127,244 sq mi (329,560 sq km)
- **Language:** Vietnamese, English, French, Chinese
- **Did You Know?** Vietnam endured a long civil war that drew in first France, then the U.S. before ending in 1976. But the nation now has one of Asia's fastest-growing economies.

Yemen

- **Capital:** Sana'a
- **Population:** 23,013,376
- **Area:** 203,850 sq mi (527,970 sq km)
- **Language:** Arabic
- **Did You Know?** One of Yemen's chief crops is coffee. "Mocha" coffee beans take their name from the Yemeni port city of Mocha.

Zambia

- **Capital:** Lusaka
- **Population:** 11,669,534
- **Area:** 290,586 sq mi (752,614 sq km)
- **Language:** English, indigenous languages
- **Did You Know?** Victoria Falls, one of the world's largest waterfalls, provides Zambia with a source of hydroelectric power.

Zimbabwe

- **Capital:** Harare
- **Population:** 11,350,111
- **Area:** 150,804 sq mi (390,580 sq km)
- **Language:** English, Shona, Sindebele
- **Did You Know?** The nation takes its name from the famous stone ruins of Great Zimbabwe, a city built by wealthy Shona-speaking cattlemen between the 13th and 14th centuries.

NATIVE AMERICANS

Who spoke the unbreakable code during World War II? ➡ page 189

native Americans are thought to have arrived in the Americas 18,000 years ago, most likely from northeast Asia. Although their population decreased significantly through the 17th, 18th, and 19th centuries from disease and war, there are still hundreds of tribes or nations, each with its own unique language and traditions. From the names of states and towns to foods like corn and squash, the influence of Native American cultures can be found everywhere in America.

TIME LINE NORTH AMERICAN INDIANS

1492	Christopher Columbus made contact with Taino tribes on the island he named Hispaniola.
c.1600	Five tribes—Mohawk, Oneida, Onondaga, Cayuga, and Seneca—formed the Iroquois Confederacy in the Northeast.
1754-63	Many Native Americans fought with both French and British troops in the French and Indian War.
1804-06	Sacagawea served as an interpreter and guide for Lewis and Clark. It's doubtful that the expedition could have succeeded without her.
1821	Sequoyah completed an alphabet for the Cherokee language.
1827	Cherokee tribes in what is now Georgia formed the Cherokee Nation with a constitution and elected governing officials.
1830	Congress passed the Indian Removal Act, the first law that forced tribes to move so that U.S. citizens could settle certain areas of land.
1834	Congress created the Indian Territory for tribes removed from their lands. It covered the present-day states of Oklahoma, Kansas, and Nebraska.
1912	Jim Thorpe, a Native American, wins the decathalon and the pentathalon in the 1912 Olympic Games.
1924	Congress granted all Native Americans U.S. citizenship.
1929	Charles Curtis, a member of the Kaw nation, became the first American of Indian ancestry elected vice president.
1985	Wilma Mankiller became the first female chief of the Cherokee Nation.

MAJOR CULTURAL AREAS OF NATIVE NORTH AMERICANS

Climate and geography influenced the culture of the people who lived in these regions. On the plains, for example, people depended on the great herds of buffalo for food. For Aleuts and Eskimos in the far north, seals and whales were an important food source. There are more than 560 tribes officially recognized by the U.S. government today and more than 56 million acres of tribal lands. Below are just a few well-known tribal groups that have lived in these areas.

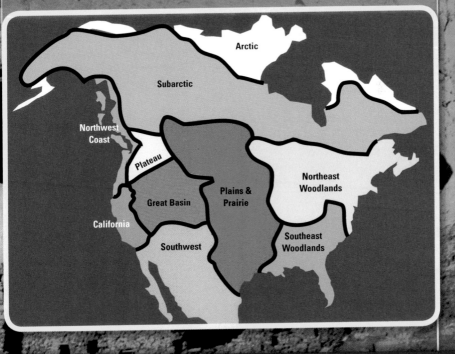

NORTHEAST WOODLANDS
The Illinois, Iroquois (Mohawk, Onondaga, Cayuga, Oneida, Seneca, and Tuscarora), Lenape, Menominee, Micmac, Narragansett, Potawatomi, Shawnee

SOUTHEAST WOODLANDS
The Cherokee, Chickasaw, Choctaw, Creek, Seminole

PLAINS & PRAIRIE
The Arapaho, Blackfoot, Cheyenne, Comanche, Hidatsa, Kaw, Mandan, Sioux

SOUTHWEST
The Apache, Navajo, Havasupai, Mojave, Pima, Pueblo (Hopi, Isleta, Laguna, Zuñi)

GREAT BASIN
The Paiute, Shoshoni, Ute

CALIFORNIA
The Klamath, Maidu, Miwok, Modoc, Patwin, Pomo, Wintun, Yurok

PLATEAU
The Cayuse, Nez Percé, Okanagon, Salish, Spokan, Umatilla, Walla Walla, Yakima

NORTHWEST COAST
The Chinook, Haida, Kwakiutl, Makah, Nootka, Salish, Tillamook, Tlingit, Tsimshian

SUBARCTIC
The Beaver, Chipewyan, Chippewa, Cree, Ingalik, Kaska, Kutchin, Montagnais, Naskapi, Tanana

ARCTIC
The Aleut, Eskimo (Inuit and Yipuk)

1. Cherokee, 301,750
2. Navajo, 296,076
3. Sioux, 116,737
4. Chippewa, 109,149
5. Choctaw, 79,236
6. Pueblo, 75,679
7. Apache, 71,737
8. Lumbee, 61,394
9. Eskimo, 47,985
10. Iroquois, 47,004

*2006 U.S. Census estimates. Figures are for people reporting only one tribal grouping.

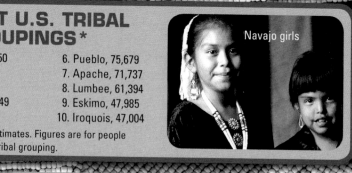

Navajo girls

Native American Populations by State*

State	Population	State	Population
Alabama	23,799	Nebraska	17,103
Alaska	103,497	Nevada	34,813
Arizona	294,118	New Hampshire	3,458
Arkansas	21,635	New Jersey	27,970
California	421,346	New Mexico	190,826
Colorado	54,626	New York	104,936
Connecticut	12,497	North Carolina	111,148
Delaware	3,454	North Dakota	34,190
Florida	80,369	Ohio	27,546
Georgia	30,893	Oklahoma	287,728
Hawaii	6,378	Oregon	51,209
Idaho	20,897	Pennsylvania	24,077
Illinois	41,231	Rhode Island	6,574
Indiana	18,603	South Carolina	16,849
Iowa	11,145	South Dakota	66,665
Kansas	27,374	Tennessee	18,733
Kentucky	9,988	Texas	163,455
Louisiana	27,042	Utah	33,663
Maine	7,582	Vermont	2,386
Maryland	18,584	Virginia	26,020
Massachusetts	19,044	Washington	104,405
Michigan	60,820	West Virginia	4,045
Minnesota	60,491	Wisconsin	51,937
Mississippi	13,816	Wyoming	12,668
Missouri	28,332	Wash., DC	2,161
Montana	60,725	U.S. total	2,902,851

*2006 U.S. Census estimates. Figures do not include people who reported belonging to other ethnic groups in addition to Native American.

TOTEM POLES

Northwest Coast Indians carve totem poles with painted images of animals and human faces. The carvings represent animals and spirits and may also tell stories about specific people or events. The poles are carved from tree trunks or smaller pieces of wood and may be used as memorials, gravemarkers, and as welcome signs in front of homes. The tallest totem pole, erected in 1994 and dismantled in 1997, was located in Victoria, British Columbia, Canada. It was 180 feet, 3 inches tall.

NATIVE AMERICAN GROUPS

THE SIOUX NATION

The Sioux Nation is comprised of the Lakota or Titonwan, the Dakota or Santee, and the Nakota or Yankton. The Sioux were nomadic (moved often), lived in teepees, and many of the tribes roamed the Great Plains. Their lands included the Black Hills (in western South Dakota). When gold was discovered in the Black Hills, the U.S. government wanted to buy or rent the land from the Lakota Sioux. These lands were sacred to the Sioux and they refused to sell. General George Custer was supposed to remove the Sioux to reservations. On June 15, 1876, the Battle of the Little Big Horn between Custer's cavalry and the Lakota and their allies was fought. The Sioux Nation won a victory in this battle. The last conflict between the Lakota Sioux and the U.S. government was the Massacre at Wounded Knee on December 29, 1890.

Great Sioux leaders include Chief Red Cloud, Sitting Bull, Crazy Horse, and Black Elk.

Chief Sitting Bull

NAVAJO NATION (DINE)

The Navajo Nation spans 27,000 square miles across Arizona, New Mexico, and Utah and is America's most populated reservation with about 175,000 residents. Many Dine (dee-NAY), as they call themselves, still speak a highly descriptive and unique language called Athapaskan. It was used as a code in World War II and never cracked. Local radio still broadcasts sports in Athapaskan, including New Mexico State University's football games. High school sports, especially basketball and cross country, are important to the Navajo. The Dine belong to clans within their nation, which are passed down from a mother to her children.

SENECA

The Seneca are one of the nations that formed the Iroquois Confederacy. There are about 7,200 people who make up the Seneca Nation today. Most live on one of two reservations in western New York. People inherit their Seneca clan status through their mothers. Women have always been important in their society. When clan families used to share wooden longhouses, which could extend more than 100 feet, the oldest woman was always the leader. Corn, beans, and squash are traditional foods. Lacrosse is a traditional sport popular today. A lesser known sport is snowsnake, a game where a polished staff is thrown down an iced snow track.

NUMBERS

What pattern is used to create Pascal's Triangle? ➡ page 192

From 0 to Infinity

The set of numbers includes whole numbers like 8, negative numbers like –23, fractions like 2/27, decimals like 46.9 and even "irrational" numbers that cannot be expressed as a fraction. Zero and infinity are two particularly interesting numbers.

Zero

In Roman Numerals, I stands for 1 and X stands for 10. Do you know the Roman numeral for "0"? Probably not, because there isn't one. The Babylonians in Asia, Hindus in India, and Mayans in the Americas were among the first to use the idea of zero as a "placeholder." In our number system "10" means 1 "ten" and 0 "ones." The 0 in 10 is a "placeholder" in the ones column.

A "numeral" is a symbol that represents a number. The Babylonians used place value and the idea of zero. But at first they didn't have a numeral for zero, so they just left a blank space where a zero should be, like writing 10,301 as 1 3 1. That was confusing because there was no numeral "to hold the place." Later they used two wedges to stand for zero. The Mayans used a symbol that looks like an eye.

Zero has some cool properties. Any number multiplied by 0 equals zero. Any number added to 0 equals the original number.

Babylonian Zero

Mayan Zero

Infinity

∞ This symbol, which looks like an 8 lying on its side, represents infinity. Infinity can be very hard to picture, because it never ends. For example, infinity is just as far from the number 1 as it is from 1 million, or even from a 1 with 100 zeroes after it (known as a googol).

In math, numbers are thought of as infinite because you can always imagine a larger number. For example, what's the biggest number you know? Add 1 to that number; you have a bigger number. Negative numbers are infinite too.

Here's a puzzler: which is larger, the set of all counting numbers (1, 2, 3, 4…) or the set of all even numbers (2, 4, 6, 8…)? According to mathematicians' concept of infinity, they are the same size, infinite. For every counting number (for example, 1), there is a corresponding even number (for example, 2).

NUMERALS
in Ancient Civilizations

People have been counting since the earliest of times.
This is what some numerals look like in different cultures.

Modern	1	2	3	4	5	6	7	8	9	10	20	50	100
Egyptian	I	II	III	IIII	III-II	III-III	IIII-III	IIII-IIII	IIII-IIII-I	∩	∩∩	∩∩∩∩∩	9
Babylonian	Y	YY	YYY	ᵞᵞ	ᵞᵞᵞ	ᵞᵞᵞ	ᵞᵞᵞᵞ	ᵞᵞᵞ	ᵞᵞᵞ	<	≪	≪≪	Y≪
Greek	A	B	Γ	Δ	E	F	Z	H	θ	I	K	N	P
Mayan	•	••	•••	••••	—	⋅—	⋅⋅—	⋅⋅⋅—	⋅⋅⋅⋅—	═	👁	≝	👁
Chinese	一	二	三	四	五	六	七	八	九	十	二十	五十	百
Hindu	1	2	3	8	y	ς	)	<	ξ	10	20	yo	100
Arabic	1	2	3	۳	۶	۶	٧	٨	9	1o	2o	٤o	100

ROMAN NUMERALS

Roman numerals are still used today.
They are built up from different letters.

I stands for 1　　　　V stands for 5
X stands for 10　　　L stands for 50
C stands for 100　　 D stands for 500
M stands for 1,000

If one Roman numeral is followed
by one with a greater value, the first
is subtracted from the second. For
example, IX means 10 – 1 = 9. Think of
it as "one less than ten." On the other
hand, if a Roman numeral is followed by
one or more others that are equal or of
lesser value, add them together. Thus,
LXI means 50 + 10 + 1 = 61.

What year is it now? Write the number
in Roman numerals?

The Colosseum in Rome probably fit
about 50,000 people. Write that number
in roman numerals? This will probably
give you a clue as to why Roman
numerals lost popularity.

1	I	14	XIV	90	XC
2	II	15	XV	100	C
3	III	16	XVI	200	CC
4	IV	17	XVII	300	CCC
5	V	18	XVIII	400	CD
6	VI	19	XIX	500	D
7	VII	20	XX	600	DC
8	VIII	30	XXX	700	DCC
9	IX	40	XL	800	DCCC
10	X	50	L	900	CM
11	XI	60	LX	1,000	M
12	XII	70	LXX	2,000	MM
13	XIII	80	LXXX	3,000	MMM

ANSWERS ON PAGES 334-336.
FOR MORE PUZZLES GO TO
WWW.WAFORKIDS.COM

Pascal's Triangle

Row 0
Row 1
Row 2
Row 3
Row 4
Row 5
Row 6
Row 7
Row 8

mathematicians spend a lot of time looking for patterns. Sometimes, they find a pattern of numbers that can be useful for all sorts of things. Pascal's Triangle is just that kind of pattern.

How Is The Triangle Constructed?

Notice that all of the numbers on the sides of the triangle are the number 1. The top row is called row 0, the second, row 1, the third, row 2. Look at row 2. The number 2 in the middle of the row comes from adding the two numbers directly above it (1 + 1). This is the way the triangle works—as you go down the rows, each number is the sum of the two numbers directly above it. Look for yourself and check to see if it's true. Can you figure out what the numbers in row 8 will be?

What Can This Triangle Do?

This triangle can help you with probability and combinations. All of the numbers in the triangle have a place. To name the place, count in from the left, starting at 0. So, the first "2", closest to the top would be in row 2 (remember, rows start at 0, too), place 1.

Who Was Pascal?

Blaise Pascal was a mathematician from the seventeenth century. He wrote his first book on mathematics when he was only 16 years old, in 1639. He spent his life trying to solve problems in math and science.

Here's a Question This Triangle Can Help You Solve

You are taking a special trip for your birthday and you can only invite two friends. But you have five friends you would enjoy taking along with you. How many choices do you have for the combination of friends on your birthday trip? Or, simply—how many different ways can you pick two things from a set of five things?

The answer is the number in row 5, place 2. There are ten different combinations of friends you could bring.

That's just the start. You can use this triangle for many other mathematical problems. Look up Pascal's Triangle at **WEB SITE** mathforum.org

PRIME TIME

A prime number is a number that can only be divided by itself and the number 1. So, prime numbers include: 2, 3, 5, 7, 11, 13, 17, and so on. All other positive numbers (other than 1) are called composite numbers, because they have at least two factors (numbers they can be divided by) other than 1. For example, 6 is a composite number: its factors are 1, 2, 3, and 6.

Mathematicians around the world participate in the Great Internet Mersenne Prime Search (GIMPS) project. These mathematicians use powerful computers to search for the biggest prime number.

In September 2008, mathematicians at UCLA found the largest prime number yet discovered. It's expressed as a power. Powers work by multiplying the base number by as many times as the raised exponent number shows.

So, $2^3 = 2 \times 2 \times 2 = 8$.

The prime number they found is $2^{43,112,609}$ minus 1. The number has 12,978,189 digits, enough to fill more than 10 *World Almanacs for Kids*.

SUDOKU

A Sudoku puzzle is usually made up of nine rows and nine columns of numbers. The rows and columns make up mini-grids within the boundary of the puzzle. Each row, column, and region (mini-grid) can only have the numbers 1 through 9. Duplicate numbers are not permitted in any row, column, or region. Solving Sudoku is a great way to practice logical and deductive reasoning skills.

The basic rule for Sudoku is: complete the puzzle so that each row, column, and region contains the numbers 1 through 9 only once.

		7		5			3	
6	8	1	4	7	3	5	9	2
		3	2		6			
7		5		3		4		8
		8		4		2		
2		4		1		6		7
		2	3		7			
	5	9	1		4	8	7	
		6		8		1		

ANSWERS ON PAGES 334-336.
FOR MORE PUZZLES GO TO
WWW.WAFORKIDS.COM

The OLYMPIC Games

Which country won the silver medal in women's soccer? ➡ page 197

The first Olympics were held in Greece more than 2,500 years ago. In 776 B.C. they featured one event — a footrace. The Olympic Games were held every four years for more than 1,000 years, until 393 A.D., when the Roman emperor Theodosius stopped them. The first modern games were held in Athens in 1896. Since then the Summer Olympic Games take place every four years at a different location. Winter Olympics were added in 1924.

2008 SUMMER OLYMPICS: BEIJING, CHINA

The 2008 Summer Olympic Games or the Games of the Olympiad, were an international multi-sport event. Beijing, China, played host to about 10,500 athletes from around the world for the Games of the XXIX Olympiad (August 8–24, 2008).

Bird's Nest

2008 SUMMER OLYMPIC SPORTS

Archery	Equestrian	Rowing	Tennis
Badminton	(dressage, jumping,	Sailing	Track and Field
Baseball	3-day event)	Shooting	Trampoline
Basketball	Fencing	Soccer	Triathlon
Beach volleyball	Field Hockey	Softball	Volleyball
Boxing	Gymnastics	Swimming	(beach, indoor)
Canoe/Kayak	(artistic, rhythmic,	Synchronized	Water Polo
Cycling	trampoline)	Swimming	Weightlifting
(road, mountain,	Handball	Table Tennis	Wrestling
bike, track)	Judo	(ping-pong)	
Diving	Modern Pentathlon	Tae Kwon Do	

RECORD-BREAKING FEAT

...ricans—and much of the world—the big story at the 29th
... was the astounding feat by swimmer Michael Phelps.
...ear-old from Maryland won eight gold medals,
... the record for a single Olympics held by fellow
... Mark Spitz for 36 years.

...as won a total of 12 gold medals in his career
... the most of any Olympian in any sport. His
...competitors, Carl Lewis and Paavo Nurmi,
...ch won 9 gold medals in track and field.

Gold Medals, Single Games

Country	Medals Won	Year	Sport
...Phelps, U.S.	8	2008	Swimming
...tz, U.S.	7	1972	Swimming
...to, East Germany	6	1988	Swimming
...erbo, Unified Team	6	1992	Gymnastics

The United States also did well overall, winning the
greatest number of medals for a total of 110, followed
closely by the Chinese, who netted 100 medals,
including 51 gold medals, the most of any nation.

Top 10 Medal Winners by Country

COUNTRY	Gold	Silver	Bronze	TOTAL
UNITED STATES	36	38	36	110
CHINA	51	21	28	100
RUSSIA	23	21	28	72
BRITAIN	19	13	15	47
AUSTRALIA	14	15	17	46
GERMANY	16	10	15	41
FRANCE	7	16	17	40
SOUTH KOREA	13	10	8	31
ITALY	8	10	10	28
UKRAINE	7	5	15	27

*Michael Phelps eats 10,000 to 12,000 calories a day when he's
training. That's at least five times the calories a typical man
needs per day. He also trains for five hours a day, burning off
all that energy in the swimming pool and weight room.*

Results of
Selected Events

Event	Gold	Silver	Bronze
Archery (Men's Team)	Korea	Italy	China
Archery (Women's Team)	Korea	China	France
Baseball	Korea	Cuba	USA
Basketball (Men's)	USA	Spain	Argentina
Basketball (Women's)	USA	Australia	Russia
Beach volleyball (Men's)	USA (Dalhausser/Rogers)	Brazil (Araujo/Magalhaes)	Brazil (Santos/Rego)
Beach volleyball (Women's)	USA (Walsh/May)	China (Wang/Tian)	China (Xue/Zhang)
Boxing (Welterweight)	Kazakhstan (B. Sarsekbayev)	Cuba (C. Banteaux Suarez)	Korea (J. Kim)/China (S. Hanati)
Cycling (Men's Road Race)	Spain (S. Sanchez)	Italy (D. Rebellin)	Switzerland (F. Cancellara)
Cycling (Women's Road Race)	Britain (N. Cooke)	Sweden (E. Johansson)	Italy (T. Guderzo)
Diving—10 Meter Platform (Men's)	Australia (M. Mitcham)	China (L. Zhou)	Russia (G. Galperin)
Diving—10 Meter Platform (Women's)	China (R. Chen)	Canada (E. Heymans)	China (X. Wang)
Equestrian (Dressage Team)	Germany	Netherlands	Denmark
Field Hockey (Men's)	Germany	Spain	Australia
Field Hockey (Women's)	Netherlands	China	Argentina
Gymnastics (Men's Team All-around)	China	Japan	USA
Gymnastics (Women's Team All-around)	China	USA	Romania
Gymnastics (Men's Individual All-around)	China (Y. Wei)	Japan (K. Uchimura)	France (B. Caranobe)
Gymnastics (Women's Individual All-around)	USA (N. Liukin)	USA (S. Johnson)	China (Y. Yilin)
Rhythmic Gymnastics (Women's Team)	Russia	China	Belarus
Handball (Men's)	France	Iceland	Spain
Handball (Women's)	Norway	Russia	Korea

Event	Gold	Silver	Bronze
Pentathlon (Men's Modern)	Russia (A. Moiseev)	Lithuania (E. Krungolcas)	Lithuania (A. Zadneprovskis)
Pentathlon (Women's Modern)	German (L. Schoneborn)	Britain (H. Fell)	Ukraine (V. Tereshuk)
Rowing (Men's Eight with Coxswain)	Canada	Britain	USA
Rowing (Women's Eight with Coxswain)	USA	Netherlands	Romania
Soccer (Men's)	Argentina	Nigeria	Brazil
Soccer (Women's)	USA	Brazil	Germany
Softball	Japan	USA	Australia
Swimming (Men's 100 m Butterfly)	USA (M. Phelps)	Servia (M. Cavic)	Australia (A. Lauterstein)
Swimming (Women's's 100 m Butterfly)	Australia (L. Trickett)	USA (C. Magnuson)	Australia (J. Schipper)
Swimming (Men's 200 m Individual Medley)	USA (M. Phelps)	Hungary (L. Cseh)	USA (R. Lochte)
Swimming (Women's 200 m Medley)	Australia (S. Rice)	Zimbabwe (K. Coventry)	USA (N. Coughlin)
Tennis (Women's Singles)	Russia (E. Dementieva)	Russia (D. Safina)	Russia (V. Zvonareva)
Track and Field (Men's 100 m)	Jamaica (U. Bolt)	Trinidad & Tobago (R. Thompson)	USA (W. Dix)
Track and Field (Women's 100 m)	Jamaica (S. Fraser)	Jamaica (S. Simpson)	Jamaica (K. Stewart)
Track and Field (Men's 400 m)	USA (L. Merritt)	USA (J. Wariner)	USA (D. Neville)
Track and Field (Women's 400 m)	Britain (C. Ohuruogu)	Jamaica (S. Williams)	USA (S. Richards)
Triathlon (Men's)	Germany (J. Frodeno)	Canada (S. Whitfield)	New Zealand (B. Docherty)
Triathlon (Women's)	Australia (E. Snowsill)	Portugal (V. Fernandes)	Australia (E. Moffatt)
Volleyball (Men's)	USA	Brazil	Russia
Volleyball (Women's)	Brazil	USA	China
Water Polo (Men's)	Hungary	USA	Serbia
Water Polo (Women's)	Netherlands	USA	Australia
Weightlifting (Men's over 105 kg)	Germany (M. Steiner)	Russia (E. Chigishev)	Latvia (V. Scerbatihs)
Weightlifting (Women's over 75 kg)	Korea (M. Jang)	Ukraine (O. Korobka)	Kazakhstan (M. Grabovetskaya)
Wrestling (Men's Freestyle, 55 kg)	USA (H. Cejudo)	Japan (T. Matsunaga)	Bulgaria (R. Velikov)/Russia (B. Kudukhov)

Odd Olympic Events

Whether it's platform diving, the 4 x 100 relay (on land or in the pool), or the gymnastic floor exercises, many people look forward to watching their favorite summer Olympic event every four years. Even though some events are seemingly timeless, others are cancelled from the program during planning, and new events take their place. For example, in 2006 the International Olympic Committee voted to discontinue baseball and softball (Olympic events since 1992 and 1996, respectively) as of the 2012 Games.

Baseball and softball could possibly be reinstated as Olympic events, as early as the 2016 Games. However, dozens of other events haven't been so lucky—many of them stranger than baseball and softball—have been discontinued and never seen at the Olympics again.

Tug of War (1900–1920)

Teams of eight went head-to-head in this battle of brute strength in the first few modern Olympic Games. Countries often fielded more than one team, since the teams came from champion athletic clubs. The United States won the tug-of-war in 1904, represented by a team from the Milwaukee Athletic Club. But in 1908, a British team made up of London policemen defeated the U.S. in just a few seconds. The U.S. team challenged the win, noting that all of the officers were wearing spiked boots. A stocking-feet rematch was held, but the U.S. was ultimately defeated again, while Great Britain went on to take the gold medal.

Motor Boating (1908)

The Games were supposed to have been held in Rome, Italy, in 1908; however, a 1906 eruption at Mount Vesuvius forced the move to Britain, where foggy weather cancelled six out of nine scheduled races. Operating at speeds of around 19 mph, the motor boating events at the 1908 Olympic Games in London weren't exactly high-speed thrill fests.

 There may be only 192 countries in the world, but there are 205 states/territories eligible to participate in the Olympic Games. This includes all 192 United Nations member states and 13 territories (or other entities not recognized as sovereign states). The 13 are: Taiwan, Palestine, American Samoa, Guam, Puerto Rico, U.S. Virgin Islands, Bermuda, British Virgin Islands, Cayman Islands, Aruba, Netherlands Antilles, Hong Kong, Cook Islands. At the 2008 Beijing Olympic Games 204 states/territories participated. The only one missing was Bunei, which intended to have two athletes take part, but failed to register them in time.

Michael Phelps might have been getting most of the attention as he raced for his eight gold medals, but another Olympic swimmer deserves notice too. Maarten Van der Weijden, swimming for Netherlands, won the first men's 10-kilometer open water marathon. His victory was even more remarkable in that he battled leukemia for much of 2001. He came back in 2003 and began swimming faster than ever before. The 6 ft 9 in. swimmer also works to increase awareness about leukemia, and raised $73,670 with a charity swim in 2004.

American gymnast Anastasia "Nastia" Liukin ▶ had her own Olympic triumph. First, she helped the Americans win a silver medal in the team competition. Then she won the gold medal in the individual all-around competition, edging out teammate Shawn Johnson by just six-tenths of a point. For Nastia, gymnastics is the family business. Her parents, Valeri and Anna, were also champion gymnasts and she grew up in the gym where they worked training other gymnasts. Her father Valeri—who is also her coach—won 2 gold medals and 2 silver medals for the Soviet Union in 1988.

Maarten Van der Weijden ▶

SOME MODERN OLYMPIC FIRSTS

1896 The first modern Olympic Games were held in Athens, Greece. A total of 312 athletes from 13 nations participated in nine sports.

1900 Women competed in the Olympic Games for the first time.

1908 For the first time, medals were awarded to the first three people to finish each event—a gold for first, a silver for second, and a bronze for third.

1920 The Olympic flag was raised for the first time, and the Olympic oath was introduced. The five interlaced rings of the flag represent: Africa, America, Europe, Asia, and Australia.

1924 The first Winter Olympic events, featuring skiing and skating, were held.

The Olympic flame was introduced at the Olympic Games. A relay of runners carries a torch with the flame from Olympia, Greece, to the site of each Olympics.

1994 Starting with the 1994 Winter Olympics, the winter and summer Games have alternated every two years, instead of being held in the same year, every fourth year.

POPULATION

In what year did the U.S. population reach 300 million? ➡ page 203

WHERE DO PEOPLE LIVE?

In 1959, there were three billion people in the world. In 1999, there were six billion. According to United Nations (UN) estimates, the world population reached 6.6 billion by mid-2007 and will grow to 9.4 billion by 2050.

It's a big world out there! Our planet has about 196.9 million square miles of surface area, but about 70% of that is water. The total land area, 57.5 million square miles, is about 16 times the land area of the U.S.

Russia is the largest nation with over 6.5 million square miles of land. China is a distant second with 3.6 million square miles. The smallest countries are Vatican City and Monaco.

Populations

Largest (2008)

1. **China***
   1,330,044,605
2. **India**
   1,147,995,898
3. **United States**
   303,824,646
4. **Indonesia**
   237,512,355
5. **Brazil**
   191,908,598

* Excluding Taiwan, pop. 22,920,946; Hong Kong, pop. 7,018,636; and Macau, pop. 460,823.

Smallest (2008)

	COUNTRY	POPULATION
1.	Vatican City	824
2.	Tuvalu	12,177
3.	Nauru	13,770
4.	Palau	21,093
5.	San Marino	29,973

Source: U.S. Census Bureau, CIA *The World Factbook 2008*

MOST SPARSELY POPULATED

	COUNTRY	PERSONS PER SQ MI
1.	Mongolia	4.9
2.	Namibia	6.4
3.	Australia	6.9
4.	Suriname	7.6
5.	Iceland	7.8

To get the population density, divide the population by the area. Density is calculated here according to land area, based on 2008 population.

MOST DENSELY POPULATED

	COUNTRY	PERSONS PER SQ MI*
1.	Monaco	32,671
2.	Singapore	17,265
3.	Vatican City	4,833
4.	Malta	3,294
5.	Maldives	3,181

* For comparison, New Jersey is the most densely populated state, with about 1,184 people per square mile in 2008.

FIVE LARGEST CITIES IN THE WORLD

Here are the five cities that had the most people, according to revised UN estimates for 2007. Numbers include people from the built-up area around each city (metropolitan area), not just the city. (See page 202 for the 10 biggest U.S. cities.)

CITY, COUNTRY	POPULATION	CITY, COUNTRY	POPULATION
1. Tokyo, Japan	35,676,000	4. Mumbai, India	18,978,000
2. New York, NY, U.S.	19,040,000	5. Sao Paulo, Brazil	18,845,000
3. Mexico City, Mexico	19,028,000		

All About >>
POPULATION GROWTH

There are more people in the world now than ever before. About four in every 10 people on Earth live in China or India. Historically, population growth rates were low but started to increase in the 17th and 18th centuries. Now, the UN estimates that approximately 76 million people are added to the planet each year. The world population is expected to reach 9.4 billion in 2050.

Most of the growth will be from population increases in poorer countries. In some developed countries like Japan and Russia, population is declining because families are having fewer children. Japan's population is projected to decline 22%, from 127.5 million in 2007 to 99.9 million in 2050. People aged 65 or older will make up 34% of the population.

India is expected to overtake China to become the world's most populous country by 2030. Its population is projected to climb an estimated 60% between 2007 and 2050, to 1.8 billion. Only about 17% of its population will be 65 or older. About 57% will be between 20 and 64.

What does all that mean? For Japan, there might be fewer workers and fewer people to take care of the elderly. Having more workers might help India develop its economy. But some people think high population growth puts a strain on the planet. More land has to be developed to provide people with housing and more food has to be grown.

POPULATION OF THE UNITED STATES, 2007

as of July 1, 2007

RANK & STATE NAME	POPULATION	RANK & STATE NAME	POPULATION
1. California (CA)	36,553,215	27. Oregon (OR)	3,747,455
2. Texas (TX)	23,904,380	28. Oklahoma (OK)	3,617,316
3. New York (NY)	19,297,729	29. Connecticut (CT)	3,502,309
4. Florida (FL)	18,251,243	30. Iowa (IA)	2,988,046
5. Illinois (IL)	12,852,548	31. Mississippi (MS)	2,918,785
6. Pennsylvania (PA)	12,432,792	32. Arkansas (AR)	2,834,797
7. Ohio (OH)	11,466,917	33. Kansas (KS)	2,775,997
8. Michigan (MI)	10,071,822	34. Utah (UT)	2,645,330
9. Georgia (GA)	9,544,750	35. Nevada (NV)	2,565,382
10. North Carolina (NC)	9,061,032	36. New Mexico (NM)	1,969,915
11. New Jersey (NJ)	8,685,920	37. West Virginia (WV)	1,812,035
12. Virginia (VA)	7,712,091	38. Nebraska (NE)	1,774,571
13. Massachusetts (MA)	6,449,755	39. Idaho (ID)	1,499,402
14. Washington (WA)	6,468,424	40. Maine (ME)	1,317,207
15. Indiana (IN)	6,313,520	41. New Hampshire (NH)	1,315,828
16. Arizona (AZ)	6,338,755	42. Hawaii (HI)	1,283,388
17. Tennessee (TN)	6,156,719	43. Rhode Island (RI)	1,057,832
18. Missouri (MO)	5,878,415	44. Montana (MT)	957,861
19. Maryland (MD)	5,618,344	45. Delaware (DE)	864,764
20. Wisconsin (WI)	5,601,640	46. South Dakota (SD)	796,214
21. Minnesota (MN)	5,197,621	47. Alaska (AK)	663,661
22. Colorado (CO)	4,861,515	48. North Dakota (ND)	639,715
23. Alabama (AL)	4,627,851	49. Vermont (VT)	621,254
24. South Carolina (SC)	4,407,709	50. District of Columbia (DC)	588,292
25. Louisiana (LA)	4,293,204	51. Wyoming (WY)	522,830
26. Kentucky (KY)	4,241,474	**TOTAL U.S. POPULATION**	**301,621,157**

Largest Cities in the United States

Cities grow and shrink in population. Below is a list of the largest cities in the United States in 2007 compared with their populations in 1950. Populations are for people living within the city limits only.

RANK & CITY	2007	1950
1. New York, NY	8,274,527	7,891,957
2. Los Angeles, CA	3,834,340	1,970,358
3. Chicago, IL	2,836,658	3,620,962
4. Houston, TX	2,208,180	596,163
5. Phoenix, AZ	1,552,259	106,818
6. Philadelphia, PA	1,449,634	2,071,605
7. San Antonio, TX	1,328,984	408,442
8. San Diego, CA	1,266,731	334,387
9. Dallas, TX	1,240,499	434,462
10. San Jose, CA	939,899	95,280

2007 Population Estimates US Census Bureau

The Growing U.S. Population

1790: 3,929,214	1970: 203,211,926
1850: 23,191,876	1990: 248,709,873
1900: 76,212,168	2000: 281,421,906
1930: 123,202,660	2007: 300,912,947
1950: 151,325,798	2008: 303,824,646

300,000,000
250,000,000
200,000,000
150,000,000
100,000,000
50,000,000

1790 1820 1850 1880 1910 1940 1970 2007

POPULATION TIME LINE

1790 Most populous state: Virginia, 692,000

1850 Most populous state: New York, 3.1 million

1900 Life expectancy at birth: 47.3 years
Population of Florida, 33rd most populous state: 529,000
Top country of birth of foreign-born population: Germany, 2.7 million
Percent of women participating in labor force: 20.6%
Number of cars registered in the U.S.: 8,000

1910 14.7% of U.S. population is foreign-born, highest percentage on record.
Population of Phoenix, Arizona: 11,134

1915 U.S. population reaches 100 million.

1930 Life expectancy at birth: 59.7 years
Top country of birth of foreign-born population: Italy, 1.8 million
Number of cars and trucks registered in the U.S.: 26.7 million

1950 Life expectancy at birth: 68.2 years
Population of Florida, 20th most populous state: 2.8 million
Percent of women participating in labor force: 29%
Number of cars and trucks registered in the U.S.: 48.9 million

1960 Population of Phoenix, Arizona, 29th most populous city: 439,170

1967 U.S. population reaches 200 million.

1970 4.7% of U.S. population is foreign-born, lowest percentage on record.

2000 Life expectancy at birth: 77 years
Population of Florida, 4th most populous state: 16 million
Top country of birth of foreign-born population: Mexico, 9.2 million
Percent of women participating in labor force: 59.9%
Number of cars and trucks registered in the U.S.: 220.7 million

2006 U.S. population reaches an estimated 300 million on October 17.
Population of Phoenix, Arizona, 6th most populous U.S. city: 1.5 million

2039 U.S. population projected to reach 400 million

The Many Faces of America:
IMMIGRATION

The number of people in the U.S. who were born in another country (foreign-born) reached 35.2 million in 2005, or about 11.7% of the population. This percentage has been rising since 1970, when it was at a low of 4.7%, and is at its highest since 1930. In the early 1900s, most immigrants came from Europe; in 2007, 36% of the foreign-born population was born in Asia, and 32% was born in North America.

Immigrants come for various reasons, such as to escape poverty or oppression and to make better lives for themselves and their children. The figures below, from the Department of Homeland Security, cover legal immigrants only. The U.S. government estimates that in the 1990s about 350,000 people each year came across the border illegally or overstayed a temporary visa. (Visas are official government documents that grant permission for a person to visit, work, or attend school in another country.) The Pew Hispanic Center estimated there were 11.5 to 12 million unauthorized immigrants in the U.S. in 2007, with the majority coming from Mexico.

What Countries Do Immigrants Come From?

Below are some of the birth countries of immigrants to the U.S. in 2007. Legal immigration from all countries to the U.S. totaled 1,052,415 in 2007.

COUNTRY	Number	Percent of total
Mexico	148,640	14.1
China, People's Republic	76,655	7.3
India	65,353	6.2
Colombia	33,187	3.2
Haiti	30,405	2.9
Cuba	29,104	2.8
Vietnam	28,691	2.7
Dominican Republic	28,024	2.7
Korea	22,405	2.1
El Salvador	21,127	2.0
Jamaica	19,375	1.8
Guatemala	17,908	1.7
Peru	17,699	1.4
Canada	15,495	1.5

Where Do Immigrants Settle?

In 2007, about 63% of all immigrants to the U.S. moved to the states below. California received roughly one-third of all immigrants born in Vietnam, Mexico, and the Philippines and one-fourth of immigrants born in China and Korea. Florida received 85% of immigrants born in Cuba, over half of those born in Haiti, and about one-third of those born in Colombia. Nearly half of those born in the Dominican Republic chose to settle in New York.

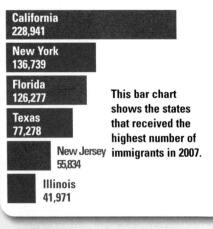

California 228,941

New York 136,739

Florida 126,277

Texas 77,278

New Jersey 55,834

Illinois 41,971

This bar chart shows the states that received the highest number of immigrants in 2007.

◀ Immigrants entering the U.S. at Ellis Island in New York, early 1900s

All About >> Hispanic AMERICANS

Hispanics are people who trace their heritage to Mexico, Puerto Rico, Cuba, or other Central or South American or Spanish cultures. They may be of any race. In 2007, there were approximately 45.5 million Hispanics in the U.S., making up about 15.1% of the population. Almost 60% were born in the U.S. The rest were born in another country.

Hispanic immigrants made up about 31% of the 1.3 million immigrants to the U.S. in 2006. Approximately 148,640 (14.1% of immigrants that year), were from Mexico. Large numbers of immigrants also came from Colombia, Cuba, El Salvador, and Guatemala.

As of July 2006, California had the largest Hispanic population of any state: 13.1 million. Texas ranked second with a Hispanic population of 8.4 million. Florida followed with 3.6 million of all Hispanics.

New Mexico had the highest percentage of Hispanics in its population. In 2006, close to 44% of New Mexico's population was Hispanic. California and Texas had the second- and third-highest percentage of Hispanics in their populations, with about 36% each.

U.S. Hispanic Population by Country of Origin, 2006

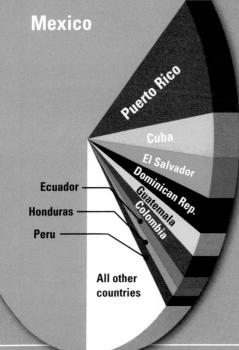

Country	Number	Percent of All Hispanics
Mexico	28,339,354	64.0
Puerto Rico	3,987,947	9.0
Cuba	1,520,276	3.4
El Salvador	1,371,666	3.1
Dominican Rep.	1,217,225	2.8
Guatemala	874,799	2.0
Colombia	801,363	1.8
Ecuador	490,317	1.1
Honduras	498,705	1.1
Peru	435,368	1.0
All other countries	4,715,258	10.7
Total U.S. Hispanic Population	**44,252,278**	100.0

Source: American Community Survey, U.S. Census Bureau

PRIZES & CONTESTS

What's the prize for winning the Duct Tape Prom Contest? ➡ page 209

NOBEL PRIZES

The Nobel Prizes are named after Alfred B. Nobel (1833–1896), a Swedish scientist who invented dynamite, and left money for these prizes. They are given every year for promoting peace, as well as for physics, chemistry, medicine, physiology, literature, and economics.

In 2007, former US Vice-President **Albert Arnold (Al) Gore Jr.** and the Intergovernmental Panel on Climate Change (IPCC) were awarded the Nobel Peace Prize "for their efforts to build up and disseminate greater knowledge about man-made climate change, and to lay the foundations for the measures that are needed to counteract such change."

Past winners of the Nobel Peace Prize include:

2006 Grameen Bank and its founder Muhammad Yunis, for making "micro-credit" available to the poor (mostly women) in Bangladesh to help them start a small business

2004 Wangari Maathai, activist, her Green Belt Movement in Kenya planted more than 30 million trees and promoted education, nutrition, and family planning.

2002 Jimmy Carter, former U.S. president and peace negotiator

1997 Jody Williams and the International Campaign to Ban Landmines

1993 Nelson Mandela, leader of South African blacks; **F.W. de Klerk** president of South Africa

1989 Dalai Lama, Tibetan Buddhist leader, forced into exile in 1959

1986 Elie Wiesel, holocaust survivor and author

1979 Mother Teresa, leader of the order of the Missionaries of Charity, who care for the sick and dying in India

1964 Martin Luther King Jr., civil rights leader

1954 Albert Schweitzer, missionary, surgeon

1919 Woodrow Wilson, U.S. president who played a key role in founding the League of Nations

1905 Baroness Bertha von Suttner, early advocate of peace through international cooperation; first woman to win the prize. ▼

ENTERTAINMENT *Awards*

2008 KIDS' CHOICE AWARDS

The 2008 Kids' Choice Awards were held Saturday, March 29, 2008, and hosted by ◀Jack Black. For more information, go to:

WEB SITE www.nick.com

KIDS' CHOICE AWARDS

More than 88 million votes were cast by kids in the 2008 Nickelodeon's Kids' Choice Awards. Winners included:

- Music Group . . . . The Jonas Brothers
- Movie . . . . *Alvin and the Chipmunks*
- Book . . . . The Harry Potter Series
- Video Game . . . . *Madden NFL '08*
- Favorite Reality
  TV Show . . . . *American Idol*
- Favorite TV Show . . . . . *Drake & Josh*
- Cartoon . . . . *Avatar: The Last Airbender*
- TV Actor . . . . Drake Bell
- TV Actress . . . . Miley Cyrus ▶
- Movie Actor . . . . Johnny Depp
- Movie Actress . . . . Jessica Alba
- Animated Movie . . . . . . *Ratatouille*
- Favorite Voice from
  an Animated Movie . . . Eddie Murphy (*Shrek the Third*)
- Male Singer . . . . Chris Brown
- Female Singer . . . . Miley Cyrus
- Song . . . . Girlfriend (Avril Lavigne)
- Male Athlete . . . . Tony Hawk
- Female Athlete . . . . Danica Patrick
- Wannabe Award . . . . . Cameron Diaz

20

BEE INVOLVED

If you have a knack for spelling or an interest in world geography, then these two national contests may be for you.

National Spelling Bee

The **National Spelling Bee** was started in Louisville, Kentucky, by the *Courier-Journal* in 1925. Today, newspapers across the U.S. run spelling bees for kids 15 and under. Winners may qualify for the Scripps National Spelling Bee held in Washington, D.C., in late May or early June. If interested, ask your school principal to contact your local newspaper. (For a behind-the-scenes look at the National Spelling Bee, try the 2002 film *Spellbound*.)

Sameer Mishra, 13, from Lafayette, Indiana won the 80th annual Scripps National Spelling Bee contest on May 30, 2008. After 20 rounds, he won the bee by correctly spelling the word "guerdon," which rather appropriately means "reward." This is the fourth time Sameer has competed in the National Spelling Bee. He finished by tying for 16th place in 2007.

WEB SITE www.spellingbee.com

Here are the words Sameer spelled on his way to the top. Some of them are just a little bit difficult!

sudation
demitasse
quadrat
diener
hyssop
macedoine
basenji

sinicize
hyphaeresis
taleggio
esclandre
nacarat
chorion
numnah

National Geographic Bee

After 9 rounds, the winner is . . .

Akshay Rajagopal, an 11-year-old from Lincoln, Nebraska. After 9 rounds of regular questions and a lightning elimination set, Akshay advanced to the championship round. He won by answering the question: The urban area of Cochabamba has been in the news in recent years due to protests over the privatization of the municipal water supply and regional autonomy issues. Cochabamba is the third largest conurbation in what country? (The answer: Bolivia. The dictionary definition of a *conurbation* is "a continuous network of urban communities.")

Akshay won a $25,000 scholarship for college and a lifetime membership in the National Geographic Society. "I think I just got lucky," Akshay said after his win. He knew all the answers except one which he guessed: What country lies east of Iran and holds the city of Balkh--the supposed birthplace of the ancient 13th-century Persian poet Rumi? Akshay's guess Afghanistan was right. For the second year in a row, the National Geographic Bee champion did not miss one question.

This contest draws five million contestants from nearly 15,000 schools from the U.S., Puerto Rico, U.S. Virgin Islands, and the Pacific Territories. To enter, you must be in grade 4-8. School-level bees are followed by state-level bees and then the nationals. For more information: **WEB SITE** www.nationalgeographic.com/geobee

Odd Contests

It just seems to be part of human nature to find out who is the best at something, no matter what it is! There are state, national, and international competitions in a wide variety of events. Most of them are normal ones such as foot races, trivia contests, and such. But then there are others that are just plain weird. Here are a few contests that are not very ordinary.

ROTTEN SNEAKER CONTEST

Held annually in Montpelier, Vermont, the Odor-Eaters Rotten Sneaker Contest was won in March 2008 by fifteen-year-old Benjamin Russell from Eagle River, Alaska. He made his shoes smelly because he plays hard: fishing, hunting, and camping in his sneakers over two summers. The sneakers almost made the panel of expert sniffers pass out. Ben won $2,500, the Golden Sneaker Award trophy, a lifetime supply of Odor-Eaters®, and a trip to New York City. His sneakers joined other winners' in the Odor-Eaters "Hall of Fumes." For more information, visit **WEB SITE** www.odoreaters.com

DUCT TAPE PROM OUTFITS

Couples entering the Duck® Brand Duct Tape Stuck on Prom Contest must attend a high school prom wearing complete outfits and accessories made from duct tape. The winning couple is chosen based on originality, workmanship, quantity of Duck Tape used, use of colors, and creative use of accessories. The first place couple each receives a $3,000 scholarship and a $3,000 cash prize is awarded to the school that hosted the prom. **WEB SITE** www.stuckatprom.com

NATHAN'S FAMOUS FOURTH OF JULY HOT DOG EATING CONTEST

Joey Chestnut of San Jose, California, won the famous hot dog eating contest in 2008. He beat Takeru Kobayashi of Nagano, Japan in overtime after both ate 59 Nathan's Famous hot dogs and buns in the initial 10-minute match. In the overtime round, each finalist was given a plate of five hot dogs and buns. Chestnut was the first to finish.

RELIGION

Which religion has Nirvana Day? ➡ page 213

How did the universe begin? Why are we here on Earth? What happens to us after we die? For most people, religion provides answers to questions like these. Believing in a God or gods, or in a higher power, is one way people make sense of the world around them. Religion can also help guide people's lives.

Different religions have different beliefs. For example, Christians, Jews, and Muslims are monotheists, meaning they believe in only one God. Hindus are polytheists, meaning they believe in many gods. On this page and the next are some facts about the world's major religions.

Christianity

WHO STARTED CHRISTIANITY? Christianity is based on the teachings of Jesus Christ. He was born in Bethlehem between 8 B.C. and 4 B.C. and died about A.D. 29.

WHAT WRITINGS ARE THERE? The **Bible**, consisting of the Old Testament and New Testament, is the main spiritual text in Christianity.

WHAT DO CHRISTIANS BELIEVE? There is only one God. God sent his Son, Jesus Christ, to Earth. Jesus died to save humankind but later rose from the dead.

HOW MANY ARE THERE? Christianity is the world's biggest religion. In 2005, there were more than 2.1 billion Christians worldwide.

WHAT KINDS ARE THERE? More than one billion Christians are **Roman Catholics**, who follow the Pope's leadership. **Orthodox Christians** accept similar teachings but follow different leadership. **Protestants** disagree with many Catholic teachings. They believe in the Bible's authority.

Buddhism

WHO STARTED BUDDHISM? Siddhartha Gautama (the Buddha), around 525 B.C.

WHAT WRITINGS ARE THERE? The **Tripitaka**, or "Three Baskets," contains three collections of teachings, rules, and commentaries. There are also other texts, many of which are called **sutras**.

WHAT DO BUDDHISTS BELIEVE? Buddha taught that life is filled with suffering. Through meditation and deeds, one can end the cycle of endless birth and rebirth and achieve a state of perfect peace known as **nirvana**.

HOW MANY ARE THERE? In 2005, there were about 376 million Buddhists in the world, 98% of them in Asia.

WHAT KINDS ARE THERE? There are two main kinds: **Theravada** ("Way of the Elders") Buddhism, the older kind, is more common in countries such as Sri Lanka, Myanmar, and Thailand. **Mahayana** ("Great Vehicle") Buddhism is more common in China, Korea, Japan, and Tibet.

Hinduism

WHO STARTED HINDUISM? The beliefs of Aryans, who migrated to India around 1500 B.C., intermixed with the beliefs of the people who already lived there.

WHAT WRITINGS ARE THERE? The **Vedas** ("Knowledge") collect the most important writings in Hinduism, including the ancient hymns in the **Samhita** and the teachings in the **Upanishads**. Also important are the stories the **Bhagavad-Gita** and the **Ramayana**.

WHAT DO HINDUS BELIEVE? There is one divine principle, known as **brahman**; the various gods are only aspects of it. Life is an aspect of, yet separate from the divine. To escape a meaningless cycle of birth and rebirth (**samsara**), one must improve one's **karma** (the purity or impurity of one's past deeds).

HOW MANY ARE THERE? In 2005, there were about 900 million Hindus, mainly in India and places where people from India have immigrated to.

WHAT KINDS ARE THERE? Most Hindus are primarily devoted to a single deity, the most common being the gods **Vishnu** and **Shiva** and the goddess **Shakti**.

Islam

WHO STARTED ISLAM? Muhammad, the Prophet, about A.D. 622.

WHAT WRITINGS ARE THERE? The **Koran** (*al-Qur'an* in Arabic), regarded as the word of God. The **Sunna**, or example of the Prophet, is recorded in the **Hadith**.

WHAT DO MUSLIMS BELIEVE? People who practice Islam are known as Muslims. There is only one God. God revealed the Koran to Muhammad so he could teach humankind truth and justice. Those who "submit" (literal meaning of "Islam") to God will attain salvation.

HOW MANY ARE THERE? In 2005, there were approximately 1.5 billion Muslims, mostly in parts of Africa and Asia.

Judaism

WHO STARTED JUDAISM? Abraham is thought to be the founder of Judaism, one of the first monotheistic religions. He probably lived between 2000 B.C. and 1500 B.C.

WHAT WRITINGS ARE THERE? The most important is the **Torah** ("Law"), comprising the five books of Moses. The **Nevi'im** ("Prophets") and **Ketuvim** ("Writings") are also part of the Hebrew Bible.

WHAT DO JEWS BELIEVE? There is one God who created and rules the universe. One should be faithful to God and observe God's laws.

HOW MANY ARE THERE? In 2005, there were close to 14 million Jews around the world. Many live in Israel and the United States.

WHAT KINDS ARE THERE? In the U.S. there are three main forms: **Orthodox**, **Conservative**, and **Reform**. Orthodox Jews are the most traditional, following strict laws about dress and diet. Reform Jews are the least traditional. Conservative Jews are somewhere in-between.

Major Holy Days

FOR CHRISTIANS, JEWS, MUSLIMS, BUDDHISTS, AND HINDUS

CHRISTIAN HOLY DAYS

	2009	2010	2011
Ash Wednesday	February 25	February 17	March 9
Good Friday	April 10	April 2	April 22
Easter Sunday	April 12	April 4	April 24
Easter for Orthodox Churches	April 19	April 4	April 24
Christmas	December 25	December 25	December 25

*Russian and some other Orthodox churches celebrate Christmas in January.

JEWISH HOLY DAYS

The Jewish holy days begin at sundown the night before the first full day of the observance. The dates of first full days are listed below.

	2009-10 (5770)	2010-11 (5771)	2011-12 (5772)
Rosh Hashanah (New Year)	September 19, 2009	September 9, 2009	September 29, 2011
Yom Kippur (Day of Atonement)	September 28, 2009	September 18, 2010	October 8, 2011
Hanukkah (Festival of Lights)	December 12, 2009	December 2, 2010	December 21, 2011
Passover	March 30, 2010	April 19, 2011	April 7, 2012

ISLAMIC (MUSLIM) HOLY DAYS

The Islamic holy days begin at sundown the night before the first full day of the observance. The dates of first full days are listed below.

	2008-09 (1430)	2009-2010 (1431)	2010-11 (1432)
Muharram 1 (New Year)	December 28, 2008	December 18, 2009	December 7, 2010
Mawlid (Birthday of Muhammad)	March 9, 2009	February 26, 2010	February 15, 2011
Ramadan (Month of Fasting)	August 21, 2009	August 11, 2010	August 1, 2011
Eid al-Fitr (End of Ramadan)	September 20, 2009	September 10, 2010	August 30, 2011
Eid al-Adha	November 27, 2009	November 16, 2010	November 6, 2011

NIRVANA DAY, February: Marks the death of Siddhartha Gautama (the Buddha).

VESAK OR VISAKAH PUJA (BUDDHA DAY), April/May: Celebrates the birth, enlightenment, and death of the Buddha.

ASALHA PUJA (DHARMA DAY), July: Commemorates the Buddha's first teaching

MAGHA PUJA OR SANGHA DAY, February: Commemorates the day when 1,250 of Buddha's followers (**sangha**) visited him without his calling them.

VASSA (RAINS RETREAT), July-October: A three-month period during Asia's rainy season when monks travel little and spend more time on meditation and study. Sometimes called Buddhist Lent

HINDU HOLY DAYS

Different Hindu groups use different calendars. A few of the many Hindu festivals and the months in which they may fall are listed below.

MAHA SHIVARATRI, February/March: Festival dedicated to Shiva, creator and destroyer.

HOLI, February/March: Festival of spring

RAMANAVAMI, March/April: Celebrates the birth of Rama, the seventh incarnation of Vishnu.

DIWALI, October/November: Festival of Lights

All About ›› *Islam: Sunni and Shiite*

There are two major groups of Muslims, the Sunnis and the Shiites. About 83% of the world's 1.3 billion Muslims are Sunni. They live all over the world but mostly in the Middle East, Africa, and Asia. Shiites make up the majority of Muslims in several countries, including Iran, Iraq, and Lebanon. The differences between these groups go back to the early years of Islam. The Sunnis accept an early follower of Muhammad, Abu Bakr, as Muhammad's successor. The Shiites believe that Ali ibn Abi Talib, the son-in-law and cousin of Muhammad, was Muhammad's rightful successor. Today, Sunnis and Shiites still follow different religious leaders and celebrate some different holidays. Historically, the Sunnis and Shiites have been opposed to each other, and even today, there is conflict in some areas between the two groups. The country of Iraq is an example of this. Minority Sunnis ruled and persecuted Shiites under the government of Saddam Hussein. Now Shiites represent the majority in government, and conflicts between the two groups have become violent.

Grand Ayatollah Ali al-Sistani, Iraqi Shiite religious leader ▶

213

SCIENCE

What common substance contains calcium carbonite? ➡ page 217

THE WORLD OF Science

The Latin root of the word "science" is *scire,* meaning "to know." There are many kinds of knowledge, but when people use the word *science* they usually mean a kind of knowledge that can be discovered and backed up by observation or experiments.

The branches of scientific study can be loosely grouped into four main branches: Physical Science, Life Science (Biology), Earth Science, and Social Science. Each branch has more specific areas of study. For example, zoology includes entomology (study of insects), which in turn includes lepidopterology (the study of butterflies and moths)!

In answering questions about our lives, our world, and our universe, scientists must often draw from more than one discipline. Biochemists, for example, deal with the chemistry that happens inside living things. Paleontologists study fossil remains of ancient plants and animals. Astrophysicists study matter and energy in outer space. And mathematics, considered by many to be both an art and a science, is used by all scientists.

Physical Science

ASTRONOMY—stars, planets, outer space

CHEMISTRY—properties and behavior of substances

PHYSICS—matter and energy

Life Science (Biology)

ANATOMY—structure of the human body

BOTANY—plants

ECOLOGY—living things in relation to their environment

GENETICS—heredity

PATHOLOGY—diseases and their effects on the human body

PHYSIOLOGY—the body's biological processes

ZOOLOGY—animals

Earth Science

GEOGRAPHY—Earth's surface and its relationship to humans

GEOLOGY—Earth's structure

HYDROLOGY—water

METEOROLOGY—Earth's atmosphere and weather

MINERALOGY—minerals

OCEANOGRAPHY—the sea, including currents and tides

PETROLOGY—rocks

SEISMOLOGY—earthquakes

VOLCANOLOGY—volcanoes

Social Science

ANTHROPOLOGY—human cultures and physical characteristics

ECONOMICS—production and distribution of goods and services

POLITICAL SCIENCE—governments

PSYCHOLOGY—mental processes and behavior

SOCIOLOGY—human society and community life

HOW DO SCIENTISTS MAKE DISCOVERIES? *THE SCIENTIFIC METHOD*

The scientific method was developed over many centuries. You can think of it as having five steps:

1. Ask a question.
2. Gather information through observation.
3. Based on that information, make an educated guess (hypothesis) about the answer to your question.
4. Design an experiment to test that hypothesis.
5. Evaluate the results.

If the experiment shows that your hypothesis is wrong, make up a new hypothesis. If the experiment supports your hypothesis, then your hypothesis may be correct! However, it is usually necessary to test a hypothesis with many different experiments before it can be accepted as a scientific law—something that is generally accepted as true.

You can **apply the scientific method** to problems in everyday life. For example, suppose you plant some seeds and they fail to sprout. You would probably **ask** yourself, "Why didn't they sprout?"—and that would be step one of the scientific method. The next step would be to make **observations**; for example, you might take note of how deep the seeds were

planted, how often they were watered, and what kind of soil was used. Then, you would make an **educated guess** about what went wrong—for example, you might hypothesize that the seeds didn't sprout because you didn't water them enough. After that, you would **test** your hypothesis—perhaps by trying to grow the seeds again, under the exact same conditions as before, except that this time you would water them more frequently.

Finally, you would wait and **evaluate** the results of your experiment. If the seeds sprouted, then you could conclude that your hypothesis may be correct. If they didn't sprout, you'd continue to use the method to find a scientific answer to your original question.

did you know?

More than 6,000 people die everyday because they don't have safe drinking water. A lot of those people are kids. In some countries, even water that looks clean can be full of bacteria. These bacteria cause serious illnesses like typhoid, dysentery, and cholera. That's why LifeStraw, a drinking straw that filters out harmful bacteria, was invented in 2005. The LifeStraw, which is about the size of a fat pencil, uses a combination of mesh filters, iodine beads, and active carbon to make water drinkable and taste better. It is designed for both adults and children older than 3 years. They dip the Lifestraw into a water source and suck on it to drink the purified water. The best part? When the company starts mass-producing the LifeStraw, it should only cost about $2 per person every year.

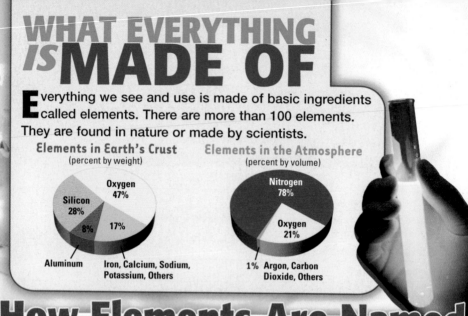

WHAT EVERYTHING *IS* MADE OF

Everything we see and use is made of basic ingredients called elements. There are more than 100 elements. They are found in nature or made by scientists.

Elements in Earth's Crust
(percent by weight)

Oxygen 47%
Silicon 28%
8%
17%
Aluminum
Iron, Calcium, Sodium, Potassium, Others

Elements in the Atmosphere
(percent by volume)

Nitrogen 78%
Oxygen 21%
1% Argon, Carbon Dioxide, Others

How Elements Are Named

Elements are named after places, scientists, figures in mythology, or properties of the element. But no element gets a name until the International Union of Pure and Applied Chemistry (IUPAC) accepts it. In November 2004, the 111th element was approved and named. Roentgenium, with symbol Rg, was discovered by German scientists in 1995.

NAME	SYMBOL	WHAT IT IS	WHEN FOUND	NAMED FOR
Argon	Ar	gas	1894	the Greek word *argos* which means inactive or lazy; it is one of the least reactive of all elements
Californium	Cf	radioactive metal	1950	state of California, and the University of California
Hydrogen	H	non-metal	1766	the Greek words *hydro* and *genes* which mean water and forming
Iodine	I	nonmetallic solid	1811	the Greek word *iodes*, meaning violet
Iridium	Ir	transitional metal	1804	the Latin word *iridis*, meaning rainbow
Lutetium	Lu	metal	1907	an ancient name for the city of Paris, *Lutetia*
Nickel	Ni	transitional metal	1774	the German word *kupfernickel*, meaning devil's copper
Selenium	Se	non-metal	1817	the Greek word for the moon, *selene*
Tungsten	W	transitional metal	1783	the Swedish words *tung sten*, meaning heavy stone.
Vanadium	V	metal	1801	Vandis, the Scandinavian Goddess of Beauty; its salts have beautiful colors

ALL ABOUT...
Compounds

Carbon, hydrogen, nitrogen, and oxygen are the most common chemical elements in the human body. Many other elements may be found in small amounts. These include calcium, iron, phosphorus, potassium, and sodium.

When elements join together, they form compounds. Water is a compound made up of hydrogen and oxygen. Salt is a compound made up of sodium and chlorine.

Common Name	Contains the Compound	Contains the Elements
Chalk	calcium carbonate	calcium, carbon, oxygen
Fool's Gold	iron disulfide	iron, sulfur
Marble	calcium carbonate	calcium, carbon, oxygen
Rust	iron oxide	iron, oxygen
Sugar	sucrose	carbon, hydrogen, oxygen
Toothpaste	sodium fluoride	sodium, fluorine
Vinegar	acetic acid	carbon, hydrogen, oxygen

CHEMICAL SYMBOLS ARE SCIENTIFIC SHORTHAND

When scientists write the names of elements, they often use a symbol instead of spelling out the full name. The symbol for each element is one or two letters. Scientists write O for oxygen and He for helium. The symbols usually come from the English name for the element (C for carbon). The symbols for some of the elements come from the element's Latin name. For example, the symbol for gold is Au, which is short for *aurum*, the Latin word for gold.

CRIME SCENE INVESTIGATOR:

YOU DO IT

Crime scene investigation can be dirty work. How do investigators know how to clean things? They use trial and error. Collect four pennies that are too tarnished to read (ask your parents to help you find some). Then, experiment with the solutions below.

Which one is best for disolving tarnish off a copper penny?
(Hint: Let the pennies soak for awhile. And make sure you have a clear space and clean towels for this experiment.)

> Ranch salad dressing
> Maple syrup
> Vinegar and baking soda
> Warm salt water

Physical Science

SOUND *and* LIGHT

What is Sound?

Sound is a form of energy that is made up of waves traveling through mass. When you "hear" a sound, it is actually your ear detecting the vibrations of molecules as the sound wave passes through. To understand sound, you first have to understand waves. Take a bowl full of water and drop a penny into the middle of it. You'll see little circular waves move away from the area where the penny hit, spread out toward the bowl's edges, and bounce back. Sound moves in the same way. The waves must travel through a gas, liquid, or a solid. In the vacuum of space, there is no sound because there are no molecules to vibrate. When you talk, your vocal chords vibrate to produce sound waves.

What is Light?

Light is a little tricky. It is a form of energy known as electromagnetic radiation that is emitted from a source. It travels as waves in straight lines and spreads out over a larger area the farther it goes. Scientists also think it goes along as particles known as photons. Light is produced in many ways, but mostly it comes from electrons that vibrate at high frequencies when heated to a high enough temperature.

Regular white light is made up of all the colors of the spectrum from red to violet. Each color has its own frequency. When you see a color on something, such as a red apple, that means that the apple absorbed all other colors of the spectrum and only reflected the red light. Things that are white reflect almost all the light that hits them. Things that are black, on the other hand, absorb all the light that hits them.

Light vs. Sound

Sound travels fast but light travels a whole lot faster. You've probably noticed that when you see lightning, you don't hear thunder until several seconds later. That's because the light reaches you before the sound. The speed of sound varies depending on temperature and air pressure (it also travels faster through liquids and solids). A jet traveling at about 761 miles per hour is considered to be flying at the "speed of sound." But this is nothing compared to light. It goes 186,000 miles per *second*! It goes the same speed no matter what. Scientists don't think anything in the universe can travel faster.

How Simple Machines Work

Simple machines are devices that make our lives easier. Cars could not run, skyscrapers couldn't be built, and elevators couldn't carry people up—if it weren't for simple machines.

Inclined Plane When trying to get a refrigerator onto the back of a truck, a worker will use a ramp, or inclined plane. Instead of lifting something heavy a short distance, we can more easily push it over a longer distance, but to the same height.
Examples: escalators, staircases, slides

Lever Any kind of arm, bar, or plank that can pivot on something (known as a fulcrum), is a lever. Depending on where the fulcrum is located on the lever, it can be used for different things.
Examples: shovel, bottle opener, "claw" part of a hammer used for prying out nails, seesaw

Wedge These machines are two inclined planes fastened onto each other to make a point. Wedges are used to pull things apart and even cut.
Examples: axes, knives

Wheel and Axle This is another kind of lever, but instead of going up and down, it goes around. The wheel is the lever and the axle on which it turns is the fulcrum.
Examples: cars, bicycles, wagons

Pulley A pulley is similar to a wheel and axle, except that there's no axle. It can be used to change both the direction and level force needed to move an object. The best example is a crane. An object is tied to a cable, which goes up and around the pulley, and down to the crane engine which is pulling it.
Examples: a block and tackle, a flag pole, tow trucks

Screw A screw is an inclined plane wrapped around a cylinder. In the case of a wood screw, as it is turned it travels deeper into the piece of wood. Another use of a screw is to hold things in place such as the lid on a jar.
Examples: drills, corkscrews

Biological Science

WHAT ARE LIVING THINGS MADE OF?

Plant cell

Cells are sometimes called the "building blocks" of all living things. Complex life forms have many cells. There are trillions of them in the human body.

There are two main kinds of cells: **eukaryotic** and **prokaryotic**. All the cells in your body— along with the cells of other animals, plants, and fungi—are eukaryotic. These contain several different structures, called **organelles**. Like tools in a toolbox, each kind of organelle has its own function. The **nucleus**, for example, contains most of the cell's DNA, while the **mitochondria** provide energy for the cell. The **ribosomes** are involved in making proteins.

Though both plant and animal cells are eukaryotic, they are different in a few ways. Animal cells rely only on mitochondria for energy, but plant cells also make use of another kind of organelle called a **chloroplast**. Chloroplasts contain chlorophyll, a green chemical plants use to make oxygen and energy from sunlight and water. This process is called **photosynthesis**. Unlike animal cells, plant cells are surrounded by a nonliving, rigid cell wall made of **cellulose**.

Prokaryotes (organisms with prokaryotic instead of eukaryotic cells) are all around you—and even inside of you. Most prokaryotes, such as bacteria, are single-celled. They don't have the variety of organelles that eukaryotic cells do.

WHAT IS DNA?

Every cell in every living thing (or organism) has **DNA**, a molecule that holds all the information about that organism. The structure of DNA was discovered in 1953 by the British scientist Francis Crick and the American scientist James Watson. James Watson was a *World Almanac* reader as a kid.

Lengths of connected DNA molecules, called **genes**, are tiny pieces of code. They determine what each organism is like. Almost all the DNA and genes come packaged in thread-like structures called **chromosomes**.

Humans have 46. There are 22 almost identical pairs, plus the X and Y chromosomes, which determine whether a human is male (one X chromosome and one Y chromosome) or female (two X chromosomes).

Genes are passed on from parents to children, and no two organisms (except clones or identical twins) have the same DNA.

Many things—the color of our eyes or hair, whether we're tall or short, our chances of getting certain diseases—depend on our genes.

What is the Human Genome?

The human genome contains 20,000 to 25,000 genes. A genome is all the DNA in an organism, including its genes. That's fewer than the 50,000-plus genes of a rice plant! Human genes can produce more than one kind of protein. Proteins perform most life functions and make up a large part of cellular structures.

By studying human genes, scientists can learn more about hereditary diseases and get a better idea of how humans evolved.

Tiny Creatures

Microbes Anton van Leeuwenhoek (pronounced Lay-wen-ook) made the first practical microscope in 1674. When he looked through it, he saw tiny bacteria, plant cells, and fungi, among other things. When he wrote about his findings, Leeuwenhoek called the creatures "wee beasties." We call them **microorganisms** ("micro" means *little*), or microbes. Before the microscope, people had no idea that there were millions of tiny living things crawling all over them.

Amoebas Amoebas (uh-ME-buhz) are eukaryotic jelly-like blobs of protoplasm that ooze through their microscopic world. They eat by engulfing their food and slowly digesting it. To move around, the cell extends a part of its goo to create something called a **pseudopod** (SOO-doh-pod), which means "false foot." The amoeba uses this to pull the rest of its "body" along. Amoebas normally live in water or on moist surfaces. In humans, most kinds of amoebas are harmless, but some cause diseases.

Diatoms Diatoms are one-celled algae that make glass shells to protect themselves. When they die, their shells collect at the bottom of the ocean in great numbers and form something called **diatomaceous earth**. It's gritty like sandpaper. Diatomaceous earth was once used in toothpaste to help scrape plaque off teeth. Nowadays, among other things, it is used as a pesticide—when sprayed in the air, it gets caught in the lungs of insects and slowly suffocates them.

CRIME SCENE INVESTIGATOR:

YOU DO IT

Crime scene investigation can involve dealing with blood. How do you know what you're looking at is blood, though, and not some other substance? Ask a parent to help you find Hemastix at a drug store. Then, ask a parent to prepare the solutions below for you. They should put a few drops on a plate for you.

> ketchup and water, mixed

> red watercolor paint

> blood (you can get this from a meat container)

Test each solution with a Hemastix. You can tell which one is blood because the Hemastix changes color.

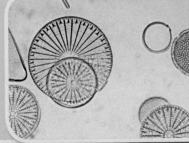

HOW STRONG IS GRAVITY? Compared to other forces, gravity is weak. It may feel powerful on Earth, where it takes lots of energy for airplanes and rockets to leave the ground. But this is only because the planet is so massive that it pulls everything toward its center. Magnets use a force stronger than gravity when they stick on metal. Static electricity defies gravity when it makes your hair stand on end.

WHY CAN'T SCUBA DIVERS GO TO THE BOTTOM OF THE OCEAN? Pressure, that's why. On dry land at sea level, there is about 14.7 pounds per square inch (psi) of atmospheric pressure pressing down on you. That's like having a 14.7 pound weight placed on top of you. We don't feel it because we've adapted to it. In water, the pressure increases the deeper you go. For every 33 feet a person dives, it goes up by 14.7 psi. The pressure can get to be so great that it literally crushes people. Scuba divers don't normally go deeper than 100 feet without specialized equipment. Even then, it's hard to go lower than 300 feet because of the effects of pressure on the human body. Instead, people use specially-built submarines to reach the deepest parts of the oceans.

WHY DON'T OIL AND WATER MIX? Water and oil don't mix because they are made up of different kinds of molecules. Water molecules are polar, meaning that their negatively charged particles (electrons) are bunched up on one side, and their positively charged particles (protons in the atoms' nuclei) are bunched on the other. In oil molecules, on the other hand, positive and negative particles are spread out evenly, with no bunching. These molecules are nonpolar. Opposite charges attract each other, so water molecules cling to each other and not to oil molecules. Scientists actually call nonpolar molecules "hydrophobic," which means "fearful of water."

IS QUICKSAND FOR REAL? Yes, but it's not as deadly as it is in the movies. Quicksand forms when sand gets mixed with too much water and becomes loosened and soupy. It may look like normal sand, but if you were to step on it, the pressure from your foot would cause the sand to act more like a liquid, and you'd sink right in. In quicksand, the more you struggle, the more you'll sink. But if you remain still, you'll start to float. So if you ever do fall into quicksand, remember to stay calm, and don't move until you've stopped sinking. Then very slowly try to get flat on your stomach and crawl out. Quicksand isn't very common, but if you were to step in some, you're not likely to sink deeper than up to your waist.

SOME FAMOUS SCIENTISTS

NICOLAUS COPERNICUS (1473-1543), Polish scientist who is known as the founder of modern astronomy. He came up with the theory that Earth and other planets revolve around the Sun. But most thinkers continued to believe that Earth was the center of the universe.

JOHANNES KEPLER (1571-1630), German astronomer who developed three laws of planetary motion. He was the first to propose a force (later named gravity) that governs planets' orbits around the Sun.

KEPPLER

BENJAMIN BANNEKER (1731-1806), African-American astronomer, mathematician, and writer. Banneker taught himself astronomy at the age of 58 and began publishing daily star and planet positions in his own almanac in 1792. He correctly predicted a 1789 solar eclipse that more famous astronomers missed. Banneker used his renown to argue against slavery, and exchanged letters with Thomas Jefferson on the topic.

CHARLES DARWIN (1809-1882), British scientist who is best known for his theory of **evolution by natural selection**. According to this theory, living creatures, by gradually changing so as to have the best chances of survival, slowly developed over millions of years into the forms they have today.

SVANTE ARRHENIUS (1859-1927), Swedish scientist who was the first person to investigate the effect that heat-absorbing gases, such as carbon dioxide, would have on global climate. In 1903, he was awarded the Nobel Prize for Chemistry.

ALBERT EINSTEIN (1879-1955), German-American physicist who developed revolutionary theories about the relationships between time, space, matter, and energy. Probably the most famous and influential scientist of the 20th century, he won a Nobel Prize in 1921.

NIELS BOHR (1885-1962), Danish physicist who studied the structure of properties of atoms. His work led to the development of quantum mechanics. In 1922, he won the Nobel Prize for Physics for his work on atomic structure.

RACHEL CARSON (1907-1964), U.S. biologist and leading environmentalist whose 1962 book *Silent Spring* warned that chemicals used to kill pests were killing harmless wildlife. Eventually, DDT and certain other pesticides were banned in the U.S.

JANE GOODALL (1934-), British scientist who is a leading authority on chimpanzee behavior. Goodall discovered that chimpanzees use tools, such as twigs to "fish" for ants. She also found that chimpanzees have complex family structures and personalities. She has written widely and is an advocate for the preservation of wild habitats.

STEPHEN HAWKING (1942-), British physicist and leading authority on **black holes**—dense objects in space whose gravity is so strong that not even light can escape them. Hawking has also written best-selling books, including *A Brief History of Time* (1988) and *The Universe in a Nutshell* (2001).

SPACE

Which planet is shrinking? ➡ p. 226

The Solar System

Mercury Venus Earth Mars Jupiter Saturn Uranus Neptune

—— Planets

Ceres

Pluto Eris

—— Dwarf Planet

The SUN Is a STAR

Did you know that the Sun is a star, like the other stars you see at night? It is a typical, medium-size star. But because the Sun is much closer to our planet than any other star, we can study it in great detail. The diameter of the Sun is 865,000 miles—more than 100 times Earth's diameter. The gravity of the Sun is nearly 28 times the gravity of Earth.

How hot is the Sun? The surface temperature of the sun is close to 10,000° F, and it is believed that the Sun's inner core may reach temperatures around 28 million degrees! The Sun provides enough light and heat energy to support all forms of life on our planet.

Homework Tip

Here's a useful way to remember the names of planets in order of their distance from the Sun. Think of this sentence: My Very Excellent Mother Just Sent Us Nachos.

M = Mercury, **V** = Venus, **E** = Earth, **M** = Mars, **J** = Jupiter, **S** = Saturn, **U** = Uranus, **N** = Neptune

The Planets Are in Motion

The planets move around the Sun along elliptical paths called **orbits**. One complete path around the Sun is called a **revolution**. Earth takes one year, or 365¼ days, to make one revolution around the Sun. Planets that are farther away from the Sun take longer. Most planets have one or more moons. A moon orbits a planet in much the same way that the planets orbit the Sun. Each planet also spins or rotates on its axis. An axis is an imaginary line running through the center of a planet. The time it takes Earth to rotate on its axis equals one day.

Saturn

Largest planet:
 Jupiter (88,732 miles diameter)

Smallest planet:
 Mercury (3,032 miles diameter)

Shortest orbit:
 Mercury (88 days)

Longest orbit:
 Neptune (164.8 years)

Tallest mountain:
 Mars (Olympus Mons, 15 miles high)

Hottest planet:
 Venus (867° F)

Coldest planet:
 Neptune (–330° F)

Shortest day:
 Jupiter (9 hours, 55 minutes, 30 seconds)

Longest day:
 Mercury (175.94 days)

No moons:
 Mercury, Venus

Most moons:
 Jupiter (63 known satellites)

WHAT IS AN ECLIPSE?

During a solar eclipse, the Moon casts a shadow on Earth. A total solar eclipse is when the Sun is completely blocked out. When this happens, the halo of gas around the Sun, called the **corona**, can be seen.

The next total solar eclipse will occur on July 22, 2009, but will only be seen in India, China, Japan, and other Asian countries.

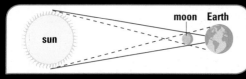

Sometimes Earth casts a shadow on the Moon. During a total lunar eclipse, the Moon remains visible, but it looks dark, often with a reddish tinge (from sunlight bent through Earth's atmosphere).

In 2009, there will be four lunar eclipses. However, all of them are minor eclipses, so will be visible as only slight shading on the moon. The next total lunar eclipse will not happen until December 21, 2010. It will be seen throughout North America.

THE PLANETS

① MERCURY

Average distance from the Sun: 36 million miles
Diameter: 3,032 miles
Average temp.: 333° F
Surface: silicate rock
Time to revolve around the Sun: 88 days
Day (synodic—midday to midday): 175.94 d
Number of moons: 0

 Until recently, we had photos of less than half of Mercury's surface, taken in 1975. But in 2008 the Messenger probe took photos of another 30 percent of the planet. The photos showed signs that Mercury is shrinking.

② VENUS

Average distance from the Sun: 67 million miles
Diameter: 7,521 miles
Average temp.: 867° F
Surface: silicate rock
Time to revolve around the Sun: 224.7 days
Day (synodic): 116.75 d
Number of moons: 0

 From Earth, Venus usually appears brighter than any other planet or star. At certain times, Venus can even be seen in daylight.

③ EARTH

Average distance from the Sun: 93 million miles
Diameter: 7,926 miles
Average temp.: 59° F
Surface: water, basalt, and granite rock
Time to revolve around the Sun: 365 ¼ days
Day (synodic): 24 h
Number of moons: 1

 Earth is a "water planet" with about 71 percent of its surface covered by water. However, most of that are oceans—too salty for drinking. Only about 3 percent of Earth's water is fresh and suitable for us to drink.

④ MARS

Average distance from the Sun: 142 million miles
Diameter: 4,213 miles
Average temp.: −81° F
Surface: iron-rich basaltic rock
Time to revolve around the Sun: 687 days
Day (synodic): 24 h 39 min 35 s
Number of moons: 2

 Phobos ('fear') and Deimos ('panic') are the names of the two moons orbiting Mars. They were named for the horses that pulled a chariot for the Greek god Ares, the counterpart of the Roman god of war, Mars.

⑤ JUPITER

Average distance from the Sun: 484 million miles
Diameter: 88,732 miles
Average temp.: −162° F
Surface: liquid hydrogen
Time to revolve around the Sun: 11.9 years
Day (synodic): 9 h 55 min 30 s
Number of moons: 63

Giant fragments of a comet struck Jupiter in 1994, leaving impact 'bruises' the size of Earth. One of the largest fragments collided with a force that was estimated as 100,000 times greater than the force released by the largest nuclear device ever exploded.

⑥ SATURN

Average distance from the Sun: 887 million miles
Diameter: 74,975 miles
Average temp.: −218° F
Surface: liquid hydrogen
Time to revolve around the Sun: 29.5 years
Day (synodic): 10 h 20 min 28 s
Number of moons: 56

 Saturn may be famous for its rings, but it is not the only planet with that feature. Jupiter, Uranus, and Neptune are all circled by less dramatic rings.

❼ URANUS

Average distance from the Sun: 1.8 billion miles
Diameter: 31,763 miles
Average temp.: −323° F
Surface: liquid hydrogen and helium
Time to revolve around the Sun: 84 years
Day (synodic): 17 h 14 min 23 s
Number of moons: 27

William Herschel, who discovered Uranus in 1781, worked as a music teacher and organist until a stipend from King George III allowed him to study astronomy full-time in 1782. He went on to make several other important discoveries.

❽ NEPTUNE

Average distance from the Sun: 2.8 billion miles
Diameter: 30,603 miles
Average temp.: −330° F
Surface: liquid hydrogen and helium
Time to revolve around the Sun: 164.8 years
Day (synodic): 16 d 6 h 37 min
Number of moons: 13

Triton, the largest of Neptune's moons, is considered the coldest object yet measured in the solar system, with an average temperature of −391° F.

Dwarf Planets and Plutoids

As of August 24, 2006, Pluto was no longer a planet. Pluto was reclassified a "dwarf planet" by the International Astronomical Union (IAU) when the organization changed the definition of 'planet.' The definition now says that a planet must "clear the neighborhood" around its orbit, which Pluto does not do. But Pluto is in good company. Two other bodies meet the new dwarf planet standards.

PLUTO

Average distance from the Sun: 3.6 billion miles
Diameter: 1,485 miles
Average temp.: −369° F
Surface: rock and frozen gases
Time to revolve around the Sun: 247.7 years
Day (synodic): 6 d 9 h 17 min
Number of moons: 3

Pluto is a special kind of dwarf planet called a plutoid. The IAU recently announced the creation of the term "plutoid" for a dwarf planet beyond the orbit of Neptune. There is only one plutoid other than Pluto: Eris.

CERES, which orbits the sun in the asteroid belt between Mars and Jupiter, was also considered a planet for a short time after its discovery in the 1800s. It was then called an asteroid until it was named a dwarf planet in August 2006.

ERIS is the third (and largest) dwarf (plutoid) planet. Eris was only discovered in 2003, so scientists are still learning a lot about its features. It is believed to have a rocky, speckled landscape similar to Pluto's and is the most distant object ever found to orbit the sun.

PLANET EARTH
SEASONS

The Earth spins on its axis of rotation. That's how we get day and night. But the Earth's axis isn't straight up and down. It is tilted about 23½ degrees. Because of this tilt, different parts of the globe get different amounts of sunlight during the year as the Earth orbits the Sun. This is why we have seasons.

23.5° **Ax**

WINTER Winter begins at the winter solstice (around December 21) in the Northern Hemisphere (north of the equator, where we live). Our hemisphere is tilted away from the Sun, so the Sun's rays reach us less directly. While days get longer during winter, they are still shorter than in spring and summer, so it's cold. Everything is reversed in the Southern Hemisphere, where it's summer!

SPRING At the vernal equinox (around March 21), daylight is 12 hours long throughout the world because Earth is not tilted toward or away from the sun. Days continue to get longer and the sunlight gets more direct in the Northern Hemisphere during spring.

Vernal Equinox

Summer
Solstice

Winter
Solstice

Autumnal Equinox

SUMMER The summer solstice (around June 21) marks the longest day of year in the Northern Hemisphere and the beginning of summer. The build-up of heat caused by more-direct sunlight during the long late spring and early

FALL After the autumnal equinox (around September 21) the Northern Hemisphere tilts away from the sun; sunlight is less direct and lasts less than 12 hours. The hemisphere cools off approaching winter.

THE MOON

The Moon is about 238,900 miles from Earth. It is 2,160 miles in diameter and has no atmosphere. The dusty surface is covered with deep craters. It takes the same time for the Moon to rotate on its axis as it does to orbit Earth (27 days, 7 hours, 43 minutes). This is why one side of the Moon is always facing Earth. The Moon has no light of its own but reflects light from the Sun. The lighted part of the Moon that we see changes in a regular cycle, waxing (growing) and waning (shrinking). It takes the Moon about 29½ days to go through all the "phases" in this cycle. This is called a lunar month.

PHASES OF THE MOON

| New Moon | Waxing Crescent | First Quarter | Waxing Gibbous | Full Moon | Waning Gibbous | Last Quarter | Waning Crescent | New Moon |

MOON Q&A

Why are there dark spots on the face of the Moon?

The dark spots you see on the face of the Moon are called *maria*. Maria are low plains made out of basalt, a fine, dark volcanic rock. The paler areas are mountains on the Moon's surface.

Does the Moon really cause the ocean tides?

Yes. Because the Moon is so big, its gravity causes the water in our seas and oceans to rise and fall as the Moon revolves around Earth. The Sun's gravitational pull also has an effect on ocean tides, but it is much weaker than the Moon's. That's because the Moon is so much closer to Earth than the Sun.

Are there any plans to go back to the Moon?

Right now, NASA is planning for another manned mission on the Moon no later than 2020. Other future Moon plans include a permanent lunar space station on the surface, probably on one of the Moon's poles. To prepare for this, an unmanned spacecraft was to be launched in early 2009 to search for water (in the form of ice) in the area near the Moon's south pole.

SOME UNMANNED MISSIONS
in the Solar System

LAUNCH DATE	Mission
1962	**Mariner 2** First successful flyby of Venus
1964	**Mariner 4** First probe to reach Mars, 1965
1972	**Pioneer 10** First probe to reach Jupiter, 1973
1973	**Mariner 10** Only U.S. probe to reach Mercury, 1974
1975	**Viking 1 and 2** Landed on Mars in 1976
1977	**Voyager 1** Reached Jupiter in 1979 and Saturn in 1980
1977	**Voyager 2** Reached Jupiter in 1979, Saturn in 1981, Uranus in 1986, Neptune in 1989
1989	**Magellan** Orbited Venus and mapped its surface
1989	**Galileo** Reached Jupiter, 1995
1996	**Mars Global Surveyor** Began mapping surface in 1999
1996	**Mars Pathfinder** Landed on Mars. Carried a roving vehicle (Sojourner)
1997	**Cassini** Reached Saturn in June 2004
2001	**Mars Odyssey** Began mapping and studying Mars in early 2002
2003	**Mars rovers Spirit and Opportunity** Landed on Mars in early 2004
2004	**Messenger** Flew past Mercury in 2008. Sent back first up-close data since 1975
2005	**Deep Impact** Reached comet Tempel 1 July 4, 2005
2006	**New Horizons** Launched January 19. Due to reach Pluto in 2015
2007	**Phoenix** Landed in 2008 to search for signs that Mars once held life

Phoenix Mars Lander

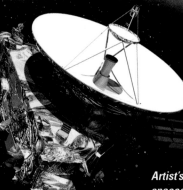

Artist's concept of the New Horizons spacecraft as it approaches Pluto and its three moons

Milestones
in Human Spaceflight

The U.S. formed NASA in 1958. It was in response to the Soviet Union's launching of the first artificial satellite *Sputnik I* on October 4, 1957. Since then, more than 400 astronauts have made trips into space to conduct research, visit orbiting space stations, and explore the Moon. Below are some of the biggest moments in human space flight.

1961	On April 12, Soviet cosmonaut Yuri Gagarin, in *Vostok 1*, became the first person to orbit Earth. On May 5, U.S. astronaut Alan B. Shepard Jr. during the *Mercury 3* mission became the first American in space.
1962	On February 20, U.S. astronaut John H. Glenn Jr. during the *Mercury 6* mission became the first American to orbit Earth.
1963	From June 16 to 19, the Soviet spacecraft *Vostok 6* carried the first woman into space, Valentina V. Tereshkova.
1965	On March 18, Soviet cosmonaut Aleksei A. Leonov became the first person to "walk" in space.
1966	On March 16, U.S. *Gemini 8* became the first craft to dock with (become attached to) another vehicle (an unmanned Agena rocket).
1969	On July 20, U.S. *Apollo 11's* lunar module *Eagle* landed on the Moon's surface in the area known as the Sea of Tranquility. Neil Armstrong was the first person ever to walk on the Moon.
1970	In April, *Apollo 13* astronauts returned safely to Earth after an explosion damaged their spacecraft and prevented them from landing on the moon.
1973	On May 14, the U.S. put its first space station, *Skylab*, into orbit. The last *Skylab* crew left in January 1974.
1975	On July 15, the U.S. launched an *Apollo* spacecraft and the Soviet Union launched a *Soyuz* spacecraft. Two days later, the American and Soviet crafts docked, and for several days their crews worked and spent time together in space.
1981	*Columbia* was launched and became the first space shuttle to reach space.
1986	On January 28, space shuttle *Challenger* exploded 73 seconds after takeoff. All seven astronauts, including teacher Christa McAuliffe, died. In February, the Soviet space station *Mir* was launched into orbit.
1998	In December, *Endeavour* was launched with *Unity*, a U.S.-built part of the International Space Station (ISS). The crew attached it to the Russian-built *Zarya* control module. The first ISS crew arrived in November 2000.
2001	The 15-year Russian *Mir* program ended.
2003	On February 1, space shuttle *Columbia* disintegrated during its reentry into the Earth's atmosphere, killing the seven-member crew. China launched its first manned spacecraft on October 15.
2004	On June 21, Mike Melvill piloted *SpaceShipOne,* the first privately funded spacecraft, into space.
2005	Space shuttle *Discovery* was launched July 26. Its 13-day mission was to test new safety upgrades to the shuttle.
2007	Construction begins on projects which will send people to the Moon, where they will build a permanent outpost.

SPACE NEWS 2009
The Age of Space Tourism Blasts Off

NASA selected its first astronauts in 1959, but none of them made it into space until 1961. Now, less than 50 years later, space tourism is taking off. Five "space tourists" have already made the voyage to space.

The VSS *Enterprise:* SpaceShipTwo

Virgin Galactic now expects to begin offering its first space tourism service sometime in 2009. The flights, which will launch from desert spaceports in the American Southwest, will last about 2.5 hours and will cost each passenger $200,000!

The spaceliner, based on the prize-winning SpaceShipOne (2004) design, is actually several different crafts. The WhiteKnightTwo "mothership" will carry two SpaceShipTwo rockets (each with room for six passengers and two pilots) to launch position at about 50,000 feet (around 9.5 miles) above Earth's surface. Then, the SpaceShipTwo crafts will detach from the mothership and fire up hybrid rocket engines to actually reach outer space. Passengers will travel about 68 miles above Earth's surface, experiencing weightlessness in a zero-gravity environment.

Going to outer space isn't just a matter of buying a ticket and heading to the airport. Passengers will have to pass rigorous health exams and training—similar to what astronauts are put through. There will also be three days of pre-flight training.

Mars Rover Redux

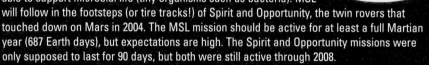

In late 2009, NASA plans to launch the Mars Science Laboratory (MSL) rover, which is expected to touch down on Mars in 2010. The mission aims to investigate if Mars ever was—or is today— able to support microbial life (tiny organisms such as bacteria). MSL will follow in the footsteps (or tire tracks!) of Spirit and Opportunity, the twin rovers that touched down on Mars in 2004. The MSL mission should be active for at least a full Martian year (687 Earth days), but expectations are high. The Spirit and Opportunity missions were only supposed to last for 90 days, but both were still active through 2008.

At about 9 feet long and 6 feet tall, the Mars Science Laboratory rover is roughly three times larger than Spirit and Opportunity. But the improvements between the generations of rovers aren't just on the surface. Spirit and Opportunity were cushioned for landing with airbags. But MSL will be lowered via "sky crane" from its traveling vessel after entering Mars's atmosphere. MSL can perform on-board chemical analysis on the rock and soil samples it collects. Another new feature is a laser that can vaporize a thin surface layer from a rock in order to analyze what makes up the material underneath.

WHAT'S OUT THERE?

M100, a spiral galaxy similar in shape to our home galaxy, the Milky Way

What else is in space besides planets?

A GALAXY is a group of billions of stars held close together by gravity. The universe may have as many as 100 billion galaxies! The one we live in is called the Milky Way. Our Sun and planets are only a small part of it. Scientists think there are as many as 200 billion stars in the Milky Way!

NEBULA is the name astronomers give to any fuzzy patch in the sky, even galaxies and star clusters. Planetary nebulas come from the late stages of some stars, while star clusters and galaxies are groups of stars. Emission nebulas, reflection nebulas, and dark dust clouds are regions of gas and dust that may be hundreds of light-years wide and are often birthplaces of stars. Emission nebulas often give off a reddish glow, caused when their hydrogen gas is heated by hot, newly formed stars nearby. Dust particles in some areas reflect hot blue starlight and appear as reflection nebulas. Dark dust clouds, though still mainly gas, contain enough dust to absorb starlight and appear as dark nebulas.

BLACK HOLE is the name given to a region in space with gravity so strong that nothing can get out—not even light. Many black holes are probably formed when giant stars at least 20 times as massive as our Sun burn up their fuel and collapse, creating very dense cores. Scientists think bigger, "supermassive" black holes may form from the collapse of many stars in the centers of galaxies. Astronomers can't see black holes, because they do not give off light. They watch for signs, such as effects on the orbits of nearby stars, or X-ray bursts from matter being sucked into the black hole.

SATELLITES are objects that move in an orbit around a planet. Moons are natural satellites. Artificial satellites, launched into orbit by humans, are used as space stations and observatories. They are also used to take pictures of Earth's surface and to transmit communications signals.

ASTEROIDS are solid chunks of rock or metal that range in size from small boulders to hundreds of miles across. Some asteroids orbit other asteroids. Hundreds of thousands of asteroids orbit the Sun in the main asteroid belt between Mars and Jupiter.

COMETS are moving chunks of ice, dust, and rock that form huge gaseous heads and tails as they move nearer to the Sun. One of the most well-known is Halley's Comet. It can be seen about every 76 years and will appear again in the year 2061.

Comet Hale-Bopp, discovered in 1995

METEOROIDS are small pieces of stone or metal traveling in space. Most meteoroids are fragments from comets or asteroids that broke off from crashes in space with other objects. A few are actually chunks that blew off the Moon or Mars after an asteroid hit.

When a meteoroid enters the Earth's atmosphere, it usually burns up completely. This streak of light is called a **meteor**, or **shooting star**. If a piece of a meteoroid survives its trip through our atmosphere and lands on Earth, it is called a **meteorite**.

SPORTS

When was the first indoor pro football game? ➡ page 242

Can you bend it like Beckham? Drive through the paint all the way to the hoop? Nail a 360°? Whether you play in a league or with friends in the neighborhood, prefer a solo bike trip or a hike through a nearby park, there are lots of awesome ways to stay fit, have fun, and get your game on.

FAVORITE SPORTS

Here are some favorite sports or activities, and the number of U.S. kids who enjoy each .

Boys (ages 6–17)		Girls (ages 6–17)	
1. Bicycling	12.3 million	1. Bicycling	5.1 million
2. Bowling	11.9 million	2. Bowling	5.0 million
3. Basketball	10.7 million	3. Walking/Hiking	4.2 million
4. Freshwater Fishing	10.5 million	4. Freshwater Fishing	3.9 million
5. Baseball	9.2 million	5. Running/Jogging	3.8 million
6. Running/Jogging	8.8 million	6. Soccer	2.9 million
7. Walking/Hiking	7.5 million	7. Basketball	2.9 million
8. Skateboarding	7.3 million	8. Inline Skating	2.8 million
9. Billiards/Pool	7.3 million	9. Ice Skating	2.6 million
10. Soccer	7.0 million	10. Gymnastics	2.6 million

Source: Sporting Goods Manufacturers Association, 2006

LITTLE LEAGUE

Little League Baseball is the largest youth sports program in the world. It began in 1939 in Williamsport, Pennsylvania, with 45 boys playing on three teams. Now about 2.6 million boys and girls ages 5 to 18 play on nearly 200,000 Little League teams in more than 80 countries.

WEB SITE *www.littleleague.org*

STRANGE SPORTS

Most American kids are familiar with sports like soccer, basketball, baseball, and football, because they see them (and play them) all the time. But some sports are seldom played on American fields, courts, or gridirons. Imagine yourself playing one of these somewhat unfamiliar sports.

FOOTVOLLEY

Footvolley is a game that combines soccer and beach volleyball. People started playing it on Brazilian beaches in the 1960s, but it has become popular in other countries, too. The net is the same as the one used in beach volleyball, but players use a soccer ball instead of a volleyball. Unlike volleyball, players cannot use their hands. They may use only their feet, heads, and chests to get the ball over the net. Otherwise, the rules are the same as those in beach volleyball. Tournaments are held all over the world.

BICYCLE POLO

Bicycle polo is a combination of polo (a hockey-like game that is played on horseback) and bicycle riding. There are two teams in bicycle polo. Each player has a mallet which is slightly shorter than the ones used in traditional polo. They use these mallets to hit the ball. The object of the game is to maneuver the ball down the field and hit it into the opponent's goal. Players are not allowed to hit each other with their mallets, and their feet must stay on the bike's pedals at all times. If a player's feet touch the ground, he or she has to ride out of bounds and back in before hitting the ball again.

WEB SITE *bicyclepolo.org*

UNDERWATER HOCKEY

Underwater hockey, also known as "octopush," was invented by four English scuba divers in 1954. The game is played at the bottom of a swimming pool between two teams of six. Players wear fins, a diving mask, and a snorkel to play. They use a short stick 10-12 inches long to slide a 3-pound puck into the opposing team's goal underwater. Everyone on a team has to work together to score, since no one can go too long without coming up for air! World championships are held every two years. The 2008 tournament took place in Durban, South Africa. The next tournament will be held in Medellin, Colombia in July, 2010.

WHO AM I?

I was born in 1978 in Oakland, California. In 1996 I was drafted by the Philadelphia Phillies in the second round. After working my way through the farm system, I started as a Phillies' shortstop in 2000, hitting a triple in my first major league at-bat, and I still play for the Phillies. Growing up in Oakland, I got a chance to meet rap artist MC Hammer, who is from my hometown, and I appeared in several of his videos in the late 1980s and early 1990s. But I am probably most proud of the fact that in 2007 I was voted the National League's Most Valuable Player with 212 hits and 139 runs. I have also played in three Major League All-Star Games.   Answer: Jimmy Rollins

PARALYMPICS

The Paralympic Games are the official Olympic Games for athletes with physical, mental, or sensory disabilities. The games got their start in 1948, when Sir Ludwig Guttman organized a competition for World War II veterans with spinal-cord injuries in England. When athletes from the Netherlands joined in 1952, the movement went international.

Olympic-style competition began in Rome in 1961, and the first Winter Paralympics were held in Sweden in 1976. Since 1991, the Paralympics have been held just after Winter and Summer Olympic competition. Following the 2006 Winter Olympics in Turin, Italy, about 590 athletes from more than 40 countries took part in the Paralympic Winter Games at the Turin Olympic venues. More than 200 U.S. athletes competed in the Paralympic Games in Beijing, China, in September 2008.

OFFICIAL PARALYMPIC SPORTS

Six Competitive Levels: wheelchair, intellectual disabilities, amputees, visual disabilities, cerebral palsy, and other mobility disabilities

Winter: alpine and nordic skiing, ice sledge hockey, wheelchair curling

Summer: archery, athletics, boccia, cycling, equestrian, football, goalball, judo, powerlifting, rowing, sailing, shooting, swimming, table tennis, volleyball, wheelchair basketball, wheelchair dance sport, wheelchair fencing, wheelchair rugby, wheelchair tennis

WEB SITE www.paralympic.org

SPECIAL OLYMPICS

The Special Olympics is the world's largest program of sports training and athletic competition for children and adults with intellectual disabilities. Founded in 1968, Special Olympics has offices in all 50 U.S. states and Washington, D.C., and throughout the world. The organization offers training and competition to more than 2.5 million athletes in more than 180 countries. In 2006, the U.S. held the first-ever National Special Olympics. The games took place in Ames, Iowa. More than 3,000 athletes from all 50 states competed.

The Special Olympics holds World Games every two years. These alternate between summer and winter sports. The next Special Olympic Winter Games will be held in Boise, Idaho, on February 6–13, 2009. The next World Summer Games are scheduled for June 2011 in Athens, Greece.

AUTO RACING

NASCAR®

Bill France founded the National Association for Stock Car Auto Racing in 1947.

The first NASCAR championship was staged in 1949. It was originally called Strictly Stock. Since 2007, the championship has been known as the Sprint Cup. Races in the Sprint Cup series include the Daytona 500, the Brickyard 400, and the Coca-Cola 600.

PAST NASCAR CHAMPIONS

1980	Dale Earnhardt	1987	Dale Earnhardt	1994	Dale Earnhardt	2001	Jeff Gordon
1981	Darrell Waltrip	1988	Bill Elliott	1995	Jeff Gordon	2002	Tony Stewart
1982	Darrell Waltrip	1989	Rusty Wallace	1996	Terry Labonte	2003	Matt Kenseth
1983	Bobby Allison	1990	Dale Earnhardt	1997	Jeff Gordon	2004	Kurt Busch
1984	Terry Labonte	1991	Dale Earnhardt	1998	Jeff Gordon	2005	Tony Stewart
1985	Darrell Waltrip	1992	Alan Kulwicki	1999	Dale Jarrett	2006	Jimmie Johnson
1986	Dale Earnhardt	1993	Dale Earnhardt	2000	Bobby Labonte	2007	Jimmie Johnson

INDIANAPOLIS 500

The first Indianapolis 500 was held in 1911. It was organized at the Indianapolis Motor Speedway, by a local car dealer named Carl Fisher. Ray Harroun won the first Indy with an average speed of only 74.602 mph.

Scott Dixon

PAST INDY WINNERS

1911	Ray Harroun	74.602 mph
1920	Gaston Chevrolet	88.618 mph
1930	Billy Arnold	100.448 mph
1940	Wilbur Shaw	114.277 mph
1950	Johnnie Parsons	124.002 mph
1960	Jim Rathmann	138.767 mph
1970	Al Unser	155.749 mph
1980	Johnny Rutherford	142.862 mph
1990	Arie Luyendyk	185.981 mph*
2000	Juan Montoya	167.607 mph
2001	Helio Castroneves	131.294 mph
2002	Helio Castroneves	166.499 mph
2003	Gil de Ferran	156.291 mph
2004	Buddy Rice	138.518 mph
2005	Dan Wheldon	157.603 mph
2006	Sam Hornish Jr.	157.085 mph
2007	Dario Franchitti	151.774 mph
2008	Scott Dixon	143.567 mph

* Race record for average lap speed.

237

BASEBALL

In the 2008 World Series, the Philadelphia Phillies beat the Tampa Bay Rays four games to one. It was a matchup that no one predicted before the season. The Phillies championship was just the second in their 126-year history. Tampa Bay had never won more than 70 games in a season. But young stars such as Evan Longoria and James Shields helped the Rays reach the postseason for the first time ever. In the World Series, Phillies pitchers shut down Tampa Bay's talented young lineup. Slugger Ryan Howard led the Philadelphia offense with three home runs. The deciding Game 5 was one of the strangest in history. With the teams tied 2–2 in the sixth inning, the umpires stopped the game due to heavy rain. The game did not resume until two nights later! The Phillies overcame near-freezing temperatures to finally win, 4–3. Philadelphia left-hander Cole Hamels was named most valuable player (MVP) of the series.

2008 MAJOR LEAGUE STANDOUTS

HITTERS

BATTING CHAMPS
NL: Chipper Jones, Atlanta Braves, .364
AL: Joe Mauer, Minnesota Twins, .328

HOME RUN CHAMPS
NL: Ryan Howard, Philadelphia Phillies, 48
AL: Miguel Cabrera, Detroit Tigers, 37

RUNS BATTED IN CHAMPS
NL: Ryan Howard, Philadelphia Phillies, 146
AL: Josh Hamilton, Texas Rangers, 130

PITCHERS

WINS LEADERS
NL: Brandon Webb, Arizona Diamondbacks, 22
AL: Cliff Lee, Cleveland Indians, 22

STRIKEOUTS LEADERS
NL: Tim Lincecum, San Francisco Giants, 265
AL: A.J. Burnett, Toronto Blue Jays, 231

EARNED RUN AVERAGE LEADERS
NL: Johan Santana, New York Mets, 2.53
AL: Cliff Lee, Cleveland Indians, 2.54

THE HOUSE THAT RUTH BUILT

Yankee Stadium in New York City was the home of the New York Yankees from 1923 through 2008. Located in the Bronx, the Yankees played 6,581 regular-season home games in the stadium.

The stadium is also known as "The House That Ruth Built." This nickname comes from the superstar player Babe Ruth, who was a Yankee during the beginning of the team's winning history.

The first game at the stadium was held on April 18, 1923, when the Yankees defeated the Boston Red Sox 4-1. The last game at the stadium was held on September 21, 2008, when the Yankees beat the Baltimore Orioles 7-3.

A new Yankee Stadium is being constructed across the street, west and north of the 1923 Yankee Stadium. The new stadium will open for the 2009 season.

SOME MAJOR LEAGUE RECORDS*

BATTERS

Most Home Runs

Career: 755, Hank Aaron (1954-76)
Season: 73, **Barry Bonds** (2001)
Game: 4, by 15 different players

Most Hits

Career: 4,256, Pete Rose (1963-86)
Season: 262, **Ichiro Suzuki** (2004)
Game: 7, Rennie Stennett (1975)

Most Stolen Bases

Career: 1,406, Rickey Henderson (1979-2003)
Season: 130, Rickey Henderson (1982)
Game: 6, Eddie Collins (1912)

PITCHERS

Most Strikeouts

Career: 5,714, Nolan Ryan (1966-93)
Season: 383, Nolan Ryan (1973)
Game: 20, **Roger Clemens** (1986, 1996); **Kerry Wood** (1998)

Most Wins

Career: 511, Cy Young (1890-1911)
Season: 41, Jack Chesbro (1904)

Most Saves

Career: 554, **Trevor Hoffman** (1993-2008)
Season: 62, **Francisco Rodrigues** (2008)

*Through the 2008 season. Players in bold played in 2008. Game stats are for nine-inning games only.

A CENTURY OF MEMORIES

It all began in 1903, when two major leagues—an established league known as the National League (NL) and an upstart league known as the American League (AL)—decided to hold a championship to determine which was best. The owners of the leagues' best teams—the NL's Pittsburgh and the AL's Boston—scheduled a series of nine games, the winner of which would be declared the best team in the nation. The famous Boston pitcher Cy Young threw the first pitch. Boston went on to upset the Pittsburgh team, 5 games to 3, and the "Fall Classic" was born.

The following year, the 1904 NL champion New York Giants refused to play Boston, so there was no series. But it resumed in 1905, when the Giants agreed to play Philadelphia in a best-of-seven game series. Since then, the World Series has followed the best-of-seven format (except from 1919–1921, when it was also best-of-nine).

Over the years, the Fall Classic has seen many amazing plays and players from pitchers Cy Young and Sandy Koufax to hitters Babe Ruth and Reggie Jackson. The New York Yankees hold the record for most championships, with 26 World Series wins to their name. They are followed by the St. Louis Cardinals with 10 championships, and the Boston Red Sox with 7.

BASEBALL Hall of Fame

The National Baseball Hall of Fame and Museum opened in 1939, in Cooperstown, New York. To be eligible for membership, players must be retired from baseball for five years. There are currently 286 members, including the six new inductees. In 2008, only one baseball player was inducted—pitcher Rich "Goose" Gossage, one of baseball's first closers. He played major league ball for 22 years, posting 124 wins and 310 saves. The other inductees included team owners Barney Dreyfuss and Walter O'Malley, managers Billy Southworth and Dick Williams, and Bowie Kuhn, baseball's commissioner from 1969 to 1984. **WEB SITE** *www.baseballhalloffame.org*

BASKETBALL

Basketball began in 1891 in Springfield, Massachusetts, when Dr. James Naismith invented it, using peach baskets as hoops. At first, each team had nine players instead of five. Big-time pro basketball started in 1949, when the National Basketball Association (NBA) was formed. The Women's National Basketball Association (WNBA) began play in 1997.

GOT BALL?

The Boston Celtics returned to the top of the basketball world by defeating the Los Angeles Lakers, four games to two, in the 2008 NBA Finals. On June 17, the Celtics won their 17th NBA title, and first since 1986, with a 131-92 victory over the Lakers in Game 6. Boston's 39-point win broke its own NBA record for the biggest margin of victory in a championship-clinching game.

The Game 6 victory for the Celtics ended a tough series. The margin of victory was 10 points or less in each of the first five games. Kevin Garnett, Ray Allen, and Paul Pierce played roles for the Celtics throughout the season and in the finals. Pierce averaged a team-high 21.8 points per game in the series and was voted NBA Finals MVP. The Lakers were led by regular-season MVP Kobe Bryant, who topped all players with a 25.7 scoring average during the finals.

Official leather NBA ball

Boston's title prevented Lakers' head coach Phil Jackson from winning his 10th NBA championship. He is tied at nine with legendary Celtics' coach Red Auerbach for the league record.

Television viewers returned to the NBA in large numbers for the Celtics-Lakers finals. The six games, which aired on ABC, were the six highest-rated and most-watched television programs for the month of June. The finals also set all-time traffic records on NBA.com, with nearly 70 million visits and more than 15.5 million video streams throughout the series.

Hall of Fame

The Naismith Memorial Hall of Fame in Springfield, Massachusetts, was founded to honor great basketball players, coaches, referees, and others important to the history of the game. The class, inducted in September 2008, included: NBA players Adrian Dantley, Patrick Ewing, and Hakeem Olajuwon; NBA coach Pat Riley; women's basketball pioneer and Immaculata University coach Cathy Rush; sportscaster Dick Vitale; and NBA team owner William Davidson.

WEB SITE *www.hoophall.com*

Some **All-Time** NBA Records*

POINTS

Career: 38,387, Kareem Abdul-Jabbar (1969-89)

Season: 4,029, Wilt Chamberlain (1961-62)

Game: 100, Wilt Chamberlain (1962)

ASSISTS

Career: 15,806, John Stockton (1984-2003)

Season: 1,164 John Stockton (1990-91)

Game: 30, Scott Skiles (1990)

REBOUNDS

Career: 23,924, Wilt Chamberlain (1959-73)

Season: 2,149, Wilt Chamberlain (1960-61)

Game: 55, Wilt Chamberlain (1960)

3-POINTERS

Career: 2,560, Reggie Miller (1987-2005)

Season: 269, Ray Allen (2005–2006)

Game: 12, Kobe Bryant (2003); Donyell Marshall (2005)

*Through the 2007–2008 season.

Highlights of the 2008 WNBA Season

The Detroit Shocks swept the San Antonio Silver Stars three-games-to-none in the WNBA best-of-five Finals. Detroit forward Katie Smith was named the series MVP. It was the Shock's third Championship in five years.

Scoring Leader
• Diana Taurasi, Phoenix Mercury
Points: 820
Average: 24.1

Rebounding Leader
• Candace Parker Los Angeles Sparks
Rebounds: 313
Average: 9.5

Assists Leader
• Lindsay Whalen Connecticut Sun
Assists: 166
Average: 5.4

COLLEGE BASKETBALL

The men's National Collegiate Athletic Association (NCAA) Tournament began in 1939. Today, it is a spectacular 65-team extravaganza. The Final Four weekend, when the semi-finals and finals are played, is one of the most-watched sports competitions in the U.S. The Women's NCAA Tournament began in 1982 and has soared in popularity.

THE 2008 NCAA TOURNAMENT RESULTS

MEN'S FINAL FOUR
Semi-Finals:
Kansas 84, North Carolina 66
Memphis 78, UCLA 63
Final:
Kansas 75, Memphis 68

Most Outstanding Player:
Mario Chalmers, Kansas

WOMEN'S FINAL FOUR
Semi-Finals:
Tennessee 47, LSU 46
Stanford 82, Connecticut 73
Final:
Tennessee 64, Stanford 48

Most Outstanding Player:
Candace Parker, Tennessee

FOOTBALL

Football began as a college sport. The first game that was like today's football took place between Yale and Harvard in New Haven, Connecticut, on November 13, 1875. The modern National Football League started in 1922. The rival American Football League began in 1960. The two leagues played the first Super Bowl in 1967. In 1970, the leagues merged to become the NFL as we know it today, with an American Football Conference (AFC) and a National Football Conference (NFC).

Super Bowl XLII, Giants Beat the Patriots

The New York Giants beat the New England Patriots, 17 to 14, in the most-watched Super Bowl ever, with 97.5 million viewers tuning in. The Patriots were attempting to make history as the NFL's first undefeated team since 1972, but the Giants squelched their hopes. Quarterback Eli Manning led New York to the game-winning touchdown with only 35 seconds left to play.

The Giants wide receiver Plaxico Burress snags the game-winning touchdown.

RUSHING YARDS: LaDainian Tomlinson, San Diego Chargers, 1,474
RUSHING TDS: LaDainian Tomlinson, San Diego Chargers, 15
RECEPTIONS: T. J. Houshmandzadeh, Cincinnati Bengals; Wes Welker, New England Patriots, 112
RECEIVING YARDS: Reggie Wayne, Indianapolis Colts, 1,510
RECEIVING TDS: Randy Moss, New England Patriots, 23
PASSING YARDS: Tom Brady, New England Patriots, 4,806
PASSER RATING: Tom Brady, New England Patriots, 117.2
PASSING TDS: Tom Brady, New England Patriots, 50
SCORING: Mason Crosby, Green Bay Packers, 141
INTERCEPTIONS: Antonio Cromartie, San Diego Chargers, 10
SACKS: Jared Allen, Kansas City Chiefs, 15.5

2007 NFL LEADERS

Pro Football Hall of Fame

Football's Hall of Fame in Canton, Ohio, was founded in 1963 by the National Football League to honor outstanding players, coaches, and contributors.

Defensive end Fred Dean, cornerback Darrell Green, wide receiver Art Monk, cornerback Emmitt Thomas, linebacker Andre Tippett, and tackle Gary Zimmerman were inducted on August 2, 2008.

WEB SITE *www.profootballhof.com*

Famous Pro Football Firsts

FIRST INDOOR GAME

December 28, 1902, World Series of Pro Football Tournament, Madison Square Garden, New York City, New York.
New York vs. Syracuse Athletic Club

Today, nine NFL teams have indoor stadiums. Many people think that indoor football is a relatively new development, but the first indoor pro football game was actually played in 1902. The team called "New York" was actually made up of players from two NFL teams in Philadelphia. They lost to Syracuse Athletic Club, 5-0, in front of a crowd of 3,500. Syracuse went on to win the tournament.

FIRST GAME PLAYED UNDER THE LIGHTS

November 6, 1929, Kinsley Park Stadium, Providence, Rhode Island. Providence Steam Roller vs. Chicago Cardinals

Providence used to have an NFL team from 1925 to 1931 called the Steam Roller. Their home stadium was called the Cyclodrome. In 1925, the Steam Roller played host to the visiting Chicago Cardinals (today's Arizona Cardinals). The teams were to play a four-game series over six days. Just before the second game, heavy rains made the Cyclodrome unplayable. So the game was moved to nearby Kinsley Park Stadium where floodlights had recently been installed. The night game was played in front of a crowd of 6,000. Chicago won, 16 to 0.

Old Madison Square Garden

THE FIRST FORWARD PASS

October 27, 1906, Massillon, Ohio.
Massillon Tigers vs. Benwood-Moundsville

In the old days of football, the forward pass was not allowed. Teams would only run the ball. This was fine in the beginning, but after a while running the ball became too difficult. To open up the game, the National Collegiate Athletic Association (NCAA) in 1906 voted to allow the forward pass. The same rule was adopted by the pros. The first forward pass in a college game took place in a game between St. Louis University and Carroll College on Sept. 5, 1906, when SLU's Bradbury Robinson threw a pass to Jack Schneider. The first known forward pass in a pro game took place in a game between the Massillon Tigers and Benwood-Moundsville. George Parratt of Massillon threw a pass to Dan "Bullet" Riley. Massillon won 61-0.

NFL All-Time Record Holders*

RUSHING YARDS
Career: 18,355, Emmitt Smith (1990-2004)
Season: 2,105, Eric Dickerson (1984)
Game: 296, Adrian Peterson (2007)

RECEIVING YARDS
Career: 22,895, Jerry Rice (1985-2004)
Season: 1,848, Jerry Rice (1995)
Game: 336, Willie Anderson (1989)

PASSING YARDS
Career: 61,657, Brett Favre (1991-2007)
Season: 5,084, Dan Marino (1984)
Game: 554, Norm Van Brocklin (1951)

POINTS SCORED
Career: 2,544, Morten Andersen (1982-2004, 2006-2007)
Season: 186, LaDainian Tomlinson (2006)
Game: 40, Ernie Nevers (1929)

*Through the 2007 season.

COLLEGE FOOTBALL

College football is one of America's most colorful and exciting sports. The National Collegiate Athletic Association (NCAA), founded in 1906, oversees the sport today. The second-ranked Louisiana Tigers upset the first-ranked Ohio Buckeyes, 38-24, at the Superdome in New Orleans on January 7, 2008. LSU quarterback Matt Flynn led the way, throwing four touchdown passes, and receiving the game ball for his efforts. The game started with the Buckeyes taking an early lead, 10-0, but LSU rallied and by halftime was winning by 24-10. After that, the Tigers never looked back. The win earned Louisiana a first-place standing in the college football poll, while Ohio State dropped to fifth.

HEISMAN TROPHY

Florida Gators' quarterback Tim Tebow was the first sophomore to win the Heisman Trophy. Tebow received 462 first-place votes, with a total of 1,957 votes. In his second season as a Gator, Tebow passed the ball for a total of 3,132 yards, with 29 touchdowns and 6 interceptions. He rushed for 838 yards and 22 touchdowns. He was the first college football player to both pass and rush for more than 20 touchdowns in a season. In addition to the Heisman Trophy, this amazing athlete also won several other national awards for 2007, including the Davey O'Brien Award as the nation's best quarterback and the James E. Sullivan Award as the nation's most outstanding amateur athlete in any sport.

ALL-TIME DIVISION I NCAA LEADERS

RUSHING YARDS

1. 6,397, Ron Dayne, Wisconsin
2. 6,279, Ricky Williams, Texas
3. 6,082, Tony Dorsett, Pittsburgh
4. 6,026, DeAngelo Williams, Memphis
5. 5,598, Charles White, USC

PASSING YARDS

1. 17,072, Timmy Chang, Hawaii
2. 15,031, Ty Detmer, Brigham Young
3. 14,193, Colt Brennan, Hawaii
4. 13,484, Philip Rivers, North Carolina State
5. 12,964, Kevin Kolb, Houston

Great Moment in *College Football*

JANUARY 2, 1984, ORANGE BOWL: MIAMI 31, NEBRASKA 30.
The underdog Miami Hurricanes led the top-ranked, undefeated Nebraska Cornhuskers, 17-0. But the "Huskers didn't give up—they even scored a TD on a trick play known as the "fumblerooski." The quarterback put the ball on the ground, where it was picked up by a lineman who ran it into the end zone. Miami still led, 31-17, in the fourth quarter, but Nebraska scored two more TDs to pull within a point of the 'Canes. After their final score, Nebraska tried a two-point conversion that would have given them the win. But quarterback Turner Gill's pass was blocked, and Miami earned the victory and a national championship.

GOLF

Golf began in Scotland as early as the 1400s. The first golf course in the U.S. opened in 1888 in Yonkers, NY. The sport has grown to include both men's and women's professional tours. And millions play just for fun.

The men's tour in the U.S. is run by the Professional Golf Association (PGA). The four major championships (with the year first played) are:
- British Open (1860)
- United States Open (1895)
- PGA Championship (1916)
- Masters Tournament (1934)

The women's tour in the U.S. is guided by the Ladies Professional Golf Association (LPGA). The four major championships are:
- United States Women's Open (1946)
- McDonald's LPGA Championship (1955)
- Kraft Nabisco Championship (1972)
- Women's British Open (1976)

The All-Time "Major" Players

These pro golfers have won the most major championships through August 2008. Tiger Woods won the 2008 U.S. Open.

MEN
1. Jack Nicklaus, 18
2. Tiger Woods, 14
3. Walter Hagan, 11
4. Ben Hogan, 9
   Gary Player, 9

WOMEN
1. Patty Berg, 15
2. Mickey Wright, 13
3. Louise Suggs, 11
4. Babe Didrikson Zaharias, 10
   Annika Sorenstam, 10

Tiger Woods

GYMNASTICS

Although the sport dates back to ancient Egypt, modern-day gymnastics began in Europe in the early 1800s. It has been part of the Olympics since 1896. The first World Gymnastic Championships were held in Antwerp, Belgium, in 1903.

Men today compete in the All-Around, High Bar, Parallel Bars, Rings, Vault, Pommel Horse, Floor Exercises, and Team Combined. The women's events are the All-Around, Uneven Parallel Bars, Vault, Balance Beam, Floor Exercises, and Team Combined. In rhythmic gymnastics, women compete in All-Around, Rope, Hoop, Ball, Clubs, and Ribbon.

U.S. gymnast Shawn Johnson led her team to a first-place finish at the 2007 World Championships. Johnson also won a gold medals on the balance beam in the 2008 Summer Olympics. This graceful teenager from Iowa won the 2008 Teen Choice Award for Female Athlete.

Shawn Johnson

ICE HOCKEY

Ice hockey began in Canada in the mid-1800s. The National Hockey League (NHL) was formed in 1916. Today the NHL has 30 teams—24 in the U.S. and 6 in Canada.

HIGHLIGHTS

In 2008, the Detroit Red Wings, after losing Game 5 in triple overtime, defeated the Pittsburgh Penguins, 3-2, in Game 6 to win the Stanley Cup title. It was the Wings' fourth Stanley Cup win. Henrik Zetterberg won the Conn Smythe Trophy as the MVP of the NHL post-season.

Washington Capitals left wing Alex Ovechkin, known as "AO" to fans, took home the Hart Trophy as NHL MVP. He scored a league-high 65 goals and 112 points.

In August, 2008, the four inductees for the U.S. Hockey Hall of Fame were announced. They were: U.S. Women's National Team captain Cammi Granato and NHL right wing Brett Hull, defenseman Brian Leetch and goalie Mike Richter.

SEASON	WINNER	RUNNER-UP
1990-91	Pittsburgh Penguins	Minnesota North Stars
1991-92	Pittsburgh Penguins	Chicago Black Hawks
1992-93	Montreal Canadiens	Los Angeles Kings
1993-94	New York Rangers	Vancouver Canucks
1994-95	New Jersey Devils	Detroit Red Wings
1995-96	Colorado Avalanche	Florida Panthers
1996-97	Detroit Red Wings	Philadelphia Flyers
1997-98	Detroit Red Wings	Washington Capitals
1998-99	Dallas Stars	Buffalo Sabres
1999-2000	New Jersey Devils	Dallas Stars
2000-01	Colorado Avalanche	New Jersey Devils
2001-02	Detroit Red Wings	Carolina Hurricanes
2002-03	New Jersey Devils	Anaheim Mighty Ducks
2003-04	Tampa Bay Lightning	Calgary Flames
2004-05	Season cancelled	
2005-06	Carolina Hurricanes	Edmonton Oilers
2006-07	Anaheim Ducks	Ottawa Senators
2007-08	Detroit Red Wings	Pittsburgh Penguins

Some All-Time NHL Records*

GOALS SCORED
Career: 894, Wayne Gretzky (1979-99)
Season: 92, Wayne Gretzky (1981-82)
Game: 7, Joe Malone (1920)

GOALIE WINS
Career: 551, Patrick Roy (1984-2003)
Season: 48, Martin Brodeur (2006-07)

*Through 2007-2008 season

POINTS
Career: 2,857, Wayne Gretzky (1979-99)
Season: 215, Wayne Gretzky (1985-86)
Game: 10, Darryl Sittler (1976)

GOALIE SHUTOUTS
Career: 103, Terry Sawchuk (1949-70)
Season: 22, George Hainsworth (1928-29)

WHO AM I?

I was born in Dartmouth, Nova Scotia, Canada, on August 7, 1987. I grew up in nearby Cole Harbour. My father played hockey for the Montreal Canadiens. I was the number one draft pick in 2005, taken by the Pittsburgh Penguins. The position I play is center. I'm the youngest player in the history of the NHL to score 100 points in a season.

Answer: Sydney Crosby

SOCCER
THE MLS CUP

The 2007 Major League Soccer season was the league's 12th season. Beginning on April 7, 2007, the season concluded with MLS Cup 2007 on November 18, 2007 at RFK Stadium in Washington, DC. The Houston Dynamo successfully defended their 2006 championship, winning their second MLS Cup in a row and defeating the New England Revolution (2-1). Dwayne De Rosario was named the MLS Cup's most valuable player.

In August, 2008, the league's best players competed in the Summer Olympics in Beijing.

The Beckham Rule
The Los Angeles Galaxy announced on January 11, 2007, that they had signed superstar English midfielder David Beckham. His five-year deal was worth $250 million. It was the richest yearly sports salary contract ever signed in the U.S. Both new and old fans came to MLS games to see the world famous player. But in his first season, Beckham's injuries cost him playing time. Still, he returned to practice in summer of 2008.

Beckham's deal was made possible by the so-called "Beckham Rule." The 2006 rule allows each MLS club to go over the league's salary limit for one designated player. The rule is called the Beckham Rule because it was made to lure a player of his caliber to the MLS.

Dwayne De Rosario

MLS ALL TIME LEADERS*

Most Goals, Game: 5, Clint Mathis, August 26, 2000

Most Goals, Season: 27, Roy Lassiter, 1996

Most Assists, Season: 26, Carlos Valderrama, 2000

Most Goals, Career: 122, Jaime Moreno

Most Shutouts, Season: 16, Tony Meola, 2000

Lowest Goals Against Average, Season: 0.82, Pat Onstad, 2007

*Through Aug. 2008. Players in bold played in 2008.

Clint Mathis, left, shoots for goal against Chris Albright

SOCCER IN CHINA 2008

The U.S. women's and the men's team from Argentina both struck gold at the 2008 Olympics.

After a disappointing showing at the FIFA 2007 World Cup, the U.S. women had something to prove. The Olympic gold medal game against Brazil was a hard-fought battle. Goalkeeper Hope Solo made several great saves to keep the game scoreless. Finally, Carli Lloyd scored in the sixth minute of extra time for the 1-0 win. The gold medal was the third for U.S. women's soccer in the last four Olympics.

On the men's side, Argentina won its second-straight Olympic soccer title. Forward Lionel Messi helped the Argentines beat Nigeria 1-0 to take home the gold. Nigeria had knocked the U.S. men out of the tournament with a 2-1 win in the opening round.

TENNIS

Modern tennis began in 1873. It was based on court tennis. In 1877 the first championships were held in Wimbledon, near London. In 1881 the first official U.S. men's championships were held at Newport, Rhode Island. Six years later, the first U.S. women's championships took place, in Philadelphia. The four most important ("grand slam") tournaments today are the Australian Open, the French Open, the All-England (Wimbledon) Championships, and the U.S. Open.

Grand Slam Tournaments

ALL-TIME GRAND SLAM SINGLES WIN

MEN	Australian	French	Wimbledon	U.S.	Total
Pete Sampras (b. 1971)	2	0	7	5	14
Roger Federer (b. 1981)**	3	0	5	4	12
Roy Emerson (b. 1936)	6	2	2	2	12
Bjorn Borg (b. 1956)	0	6	5	0	11
Rod Laver (b. 1938)	3	2	4	2	11
Bill Tilden (1893-1953)	*	0	3	7	10
WOMEN					
Margaret Smith-Court (b. 1942)	11	5	3	5	24
Steffi Graf (b. 1969)	4	6	7	5	22
Helen Wills Moody (1905-1998)	*	4	8	7	19
Chris Evert (b. 1954)	2	7	3	6	18
Martina Navratilova (b. 1956)	3	2	9	4	18

*Never played in tournament. **Player active in 2008. Wins as of August 2008.*

SPORTS SCRAMBLE

Unscramble the team name and match it with the athlete from that team.

X E T S A   N E A R S G R

Candace Parker

D O R N A L O   A M C I G

Randy Moss

N E S O N A T I M   G N I I K S V

Josh Hamilton

W E N   D A N G E L N   R O T S I P A T

Adrian Peterson

S O L   L E N G A S E   R A P S K S

Dwight Howard

The answer is:

X GAMES

The X Games were first held in June 1995 in Newport, Rhode Island. Considered the Olympics of action sports, star X Games athletes include skateboarders Ryan Sheckler and Danny Way, super motocross champion Jeremy McGrath, BMX freestyler Dave Mirra, and snowboarder Shaun White.

2008 Winter X Games

Athletes from all over the world competed in the 12th annual Winter X Games, held January 23-27, 2008 at Buttermilk Mountain in Colorado. Events included Snowboarding, Skiing, SnoCross (snowmobiling), and Mono-Skier X (a race for disabled sit-skiers). For the first time, snowmobilers showed their moves in the Snowmobile Speed & Style, a brand-new event. Snocross racer Levi LaVallee took home the gold, proving he can both win races and perform freestyle moves on his snowmobile. The 2009 Winter X Games will be held in January 2009.

▶ New Mono-Skier X

Summer X Games

The Summer X Games, held every year since 1995, feature competitions in events such as Skateboarding, Freestyle BMX, Moto X, and Rally Car Racing. Standout competitors in the 14th X Games held July 31-August 3, 2008 in Los Angeles included freestyle motorcross rider Kyle Loza, who won his second gold medal in the Men's Moto X Best Trick competition. Skateboarder Ryan Sheckler, the 2008 Teen Choice for "Action Sports Male," won a gold in the Skate Street finals. Although skateboarder Danny Way came in second in the Skate Big Air finals, he won "Athlete of the Games" for showing sheer grit by continuing to compete after a 40-foot fall on the Mega Ramp. The 2009 Summer X Games will be held in August 2009. **WEB SITE** *http://expn.go.com*

did you know?

Speedboarder Gary Hardwick holds the record for the fastest speed reached on a skateboard, standing up without the aid of other vehicles or engines. Hardwick was clocked at 62.55 mph during a competition in Fountain Hills, Arizona, on September 26, 1998.

◀ Travis Pastrana

X-FACT-ORS

✗ During the 2006 X Games, Travis Pastrana performed the first double back flip on a motorcycle in competition in the Men's Freestyle Motorcross. Pastrana won gold in the event.

✗ In 2008, skateboarder Andy Macdonald won his 17th X Games medal, passing Tony Hawk as the all-time leader in skateboarding medals. Macdonald has competed in fourteen X Games.

✗ Shaun White became the first athlete to medal in both Summer and Winter X Games competitions when he nabbed the Skateboard Vert silver medal at the 2005 X Games.

TECHNOLOGY & COMPUTERS

What is spyware? ➡ page 251

COMPUTER HIGHLIGHTS TIME LINE

1623 Wilhelm Schickard built the first machine that could automatically add, subtract, multiply, and divide. He called it a "calculating clock."

1946 The first electronic, programmable, general-purpose computer was invented. It was called ENIAC, for "Electronic Numerical Integrator and Computer."

1967 The Advanced Research Projects Agency (ARPA) allotted money toward creating a computer network. It became ARPAnet, which evolved into the Internet.

1968 The first hypertext system was built by Douglas Engelbart of Stanford Research Institute. Called NLS (oN Line System), the system's design allowed users to move text and data with a mouse (which Engelbart invented in 1963).

1971 The "floppy disk" was introduced by IBM as a means of affordable portable storage.

1975 The Altair 8800 entered the market. It was the first widely sold personal microcomputer.

1975 Bill Gates and Paul Allen founded Microsoft. Later came the first version of Windows.

1977 The Apple II, Apple's first fully packaged system with a keyboard, was introduced.

1990 The World Wide Web was first launched with one server by British physicist Tim Berners-Lee. He also created Uniform Resource Locators (URLs), the Hypertext Transfer Protocol (HTTP), and Hypertext Markup Language (HTML).

1996 Google, one of the Internet's most popular search engines, was founded.

2001 Apple introduced the iPod, a popular portable MP3/Media player.

2002 The 1 billionth personal computer was shipped to stores in April.

2003 MySpace, the popular online community that allows Internet users to connect and share interests and pictures, was founded.

2005 YouTube, the popular video sharing service, was founded.

2007 Apple released the Apple iPhone to the public.

🏠 ●**WA**for**Kids**.com ↪

Go to **www.WAforKids.com** and type 248 into the code box:
- Test your technological savvy with a chapter quiz
- Learn about mind-boggling inventions and famous scientists

COMPUTER TALK

BIT The smallest unit of data

BYTE An amount of data equal to 8 bits

COOKIE Some websites store information like your password on your computer's hard drive. When you go back to that site later, your browser sends the information (the "cookie") to the website.

DOWNLOAD To transfer information from a host computer to a personal computer through a network connection or modem

ENCRYPTION The process of changing information into a code to keep others from reading it

FLASH MEMORY Rewriteable ROM memory that saves information without power. Popular in handheld devices like memory cards or MP3 players.

HTTP Hypertext Transfer Protocol is the method of file exchange used on the World Wide Web.

MEGABYTE (MB) An amount of information equal to 1,048,516 bytes, or (in some situations) 1 million bytes

NETWORK A group of computers linked together so that they can share information

RAM OR RANDOM ACCESS MEMORY Memory your computer uses to open programs and store your work until you save it to a hard drive or disk. Information in RAM disappears when the computer is turned off.

ROM OR READ ONLY MEMORY Memory that contains permanent instructions for the computer and cannot be changed. The information in ROM stays after the computer is turned off.

SPYWARE Software that observes computer activity without the user's knowledge. May record key strokes or fill the screen with ads.

URL OR UNIFORM RESOURCE LOCATOR The technical name for a website address

VIRUS A program that damages other programs and data. It gets into a computer through the Internet or shared disks.

WI-FI OR WIRELESS FIDELITY Technology that allows people to link to other computers and the Internet from their computers without wires.

IM (INSTANT MESSAGE) DICTIONARY

ATM At the moment

B4N Bye for now

BBS Be back soon

BCNU Be seein' you

BRB Be right back

BTW By the way

CSL Can't stop laughing

EDM End of message

EZ easy

GTG Got to go

IDK I don't know

IMHO In my humble opinion

JK Just kidding

K or KK OK

LOL Laughing out loud

NM Nothing much or Nevermind

NP No problem

OMG Oh my God

OTP On the phone

PPL People

PWN To "own" (or beat someone in a game)

ROTFL Rolling on the floor laughing

SRY Sorry

THX Thanks

TLDR Too long, didn't read

TTFN Ta ta for now

TTYL Talk to you later

W0ot (expression of joy)

WTG Way to go

WU? What's up?

RESEARCH ON THE INTERNET

Using a Search Engine

A search engine is a tool that locates web pages according to keywords. Here are some of the most popular search engines and their addresses.

Google

http://www.google.com

Yahoo

http://www.yahoo.com

Ask (Ask Jeeves)

http://www.ask.com

AltaVista

http://www.altavista.com

AllTheWeb.com

http://www.alltheweb.com

HotBot

http://www.hotbot.com

Limit the Keyword Search

Before you start researching a topic, decide exactly what you need. Being as specific as possible makes it easier to find sites that have information about your topic. It can also help you evaluate the source.

As you search the internet, keep the following tips in mind.

> Be as specific as possible with the terms you use in your search. Suppose you have an assignment that asks you to describe three famous inventions of Thomas Edison. Search for: famous inventions Thomas Edison.

> Put words in quotes when you are searching for a specific phrase. Some search engines also have an "Advanced Search" tool that allows you to search for an exact wording or phrase.
To find out which president said, "I cannot live without books," type the exact phrase in quotation marks (as shown) to search.

> When you want two or more terms to appear in the search results, use the word AND (in caps) to connect the terms. You can also use the plus sign (+) to connect terms.
For example, to search for information on Davy Crockett and the Alamo, type: Davy Crockett AND Alamo, or Davy Crockett + Alamo.

> Try using a synonym if you are having trouble with your search. Suppose you are searching for the different ways in which moisture, or water, reaches the earth. Try searching for "forms of precipitation."

> Try different search engines if one isn't producing results. For example, if you are searching for information on popular culture, HotBot may be a better choice than Yahoo.

Identify the Web Site

Huge amounts of information are on the Internet. While this makes the Internet great for research, not all sources are reliable. Recognize that a wide variety of information is available, from facts and data to stories and opinions.

The url ending in web addresses may offer clues to the type of web page. Government sites end in **.gov**. These sites are reliable sources for data and objective reports. Non-profit organizations end in **.org**. Educational institutions end in **.edu**. Business sites usually end in **.com** or **.net**. Official U.S. sites end in **.us** (for example, official state sites).

Assessing the Web Site

Unlike published books, many web sources are not checked for accuracy. For this reason, it is very important to review the content and purpose of a web site. It can be difficult to distinguish informative sites from those that try to sell products or have a special interest.

Examine the site carefully to make sure it appears reliable. Check that data and sources have references. Look for links to other sites with additional information. Also look for the date of creation of the web page.

Try to select sources that offer the following:
> author's name,
> date of page creation or version,
> and a list of sources.

Citing a Website

To cite a website, include the **title of the web page**, the **name of the entire web site, the organization that posted it** (this may be the same as the name of the website). Also include the full **date the page was created or last updated** (day, month, year if available), the **date you looked at it**, and the URL address (in < > brackets).

Example for the web page that identifies Thomas Jefferson as the president who said, "I cannot live without books."

Jefferson Library: Famous Jefferson Quotations. Th. Jefferson Monticello. September 2, 2008. <www.monticello.org/library/reference/famquote.html>

TRANSPORTATION

Who built the first car with an internal combustion engine?
➡ **page 256**

Getting from There to Here:
A SHORT HISTORY OF TRANSPORTATION

5000 B.C. People harness animal-muscle power. Oxen and donkeys carry heavy loads.

3500 B.C. Egyptians create the first sailboat. Before this, people made rafts or canoes and paddled them with poles or their hands.

983 First locks to raise water level are built on China's Grand Canal. By 1400, a 1,500-mile water highway system was developed.

1450s Portuguese build fast ships with three masts. These plus the compass usher in an age of exploration.

1681 France's 150-mile Canal du Midi connects the Atlantic Ocean with the Mediterranean Sea.

5000 B.C.

3500 B.C.

800

Around 1000

1660s

In Mesopotamia (modern-day Iraq), vehicles with wheels are invented. But the first wheels are made of heavy wood, and the roads are terrible.

Fast, shallow-draft longships make Vikings a powerful force in Europe from 800 to 1100.

Using magnetic compasses, Chinese are able to sail long distances in flat-bottomed ships called junks.

Horse-drawn stagecoaches begin running in France. They stop at "stages" to switch horses and passengers—the first mass transit system.

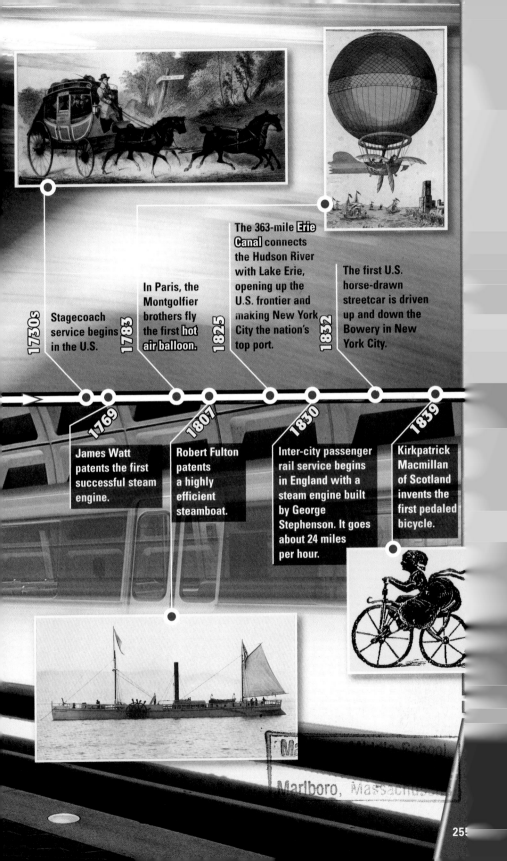

1730s Stagecoach service begins in the U.S.

1769 James Watt patents the first successful steam engine.

1783 In Paris, the Montgolfier brothers fly the first hot air balloon.

1807 Robert Fulton patents a highly efficient steamboat.

1825 The 363-mile Erie Canal connects the Hudson River with Lake Erie, opening up the U.S. frontier and making New York City the nation's top port.

1830 Inter-city passenger rail service begins in England with a steam engine built by George Stephenson. It goes about 24 miles per hour.

1832 The first U.S. horse-drawn streetcar is driven up and down the Bowery in New York City.

1839 Kirkpatrick Macmillan of Scotland invents the first pedaled bicycle.

Marlboro, Massachu

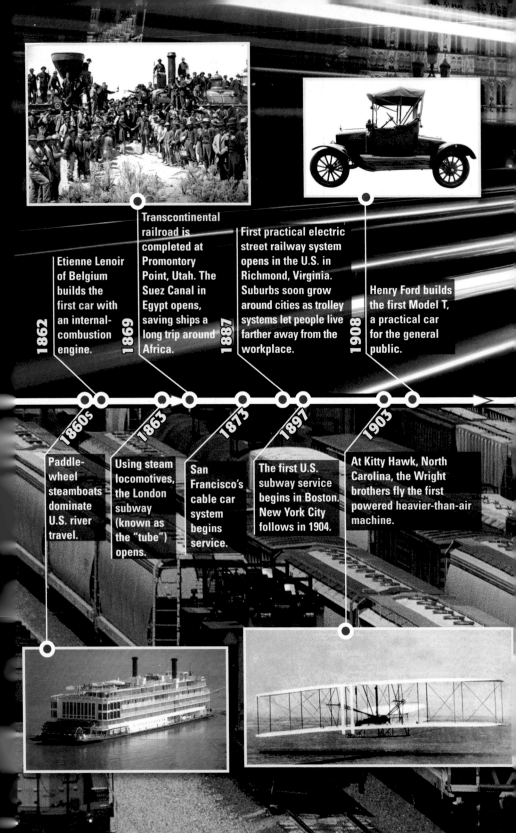

Transcontinental railroad is completed at Promontory Point, Utah. The Suez Canal in Egypt opens, saving ships a long trip around Africa.

Etienne Lenoir of Belgium builds the first car with an internal-combustion engine.

First practical electric street railway system opens in the U.S. in Richmond, Virginia. Suburbs soon grow around cities as trolley systems let people live farther away from the workplace.

Henry Ford builds the first Model T, a practical car for the general public.

1862

1869

1887

1908

1860s

1863

1873

1897

1903

Paddle-wheel steamboats dominate U.S. river travel.

Using steam locomotives, the London subway (known as the "tube") opens.

San Francisco's cable car system begins service.

The first U.S. subway service begins in Boston. New York City follows in 1904.

At Kitty Hawk, North Carolina, the Wright brothers fly the first powered heavier-than-air machine.

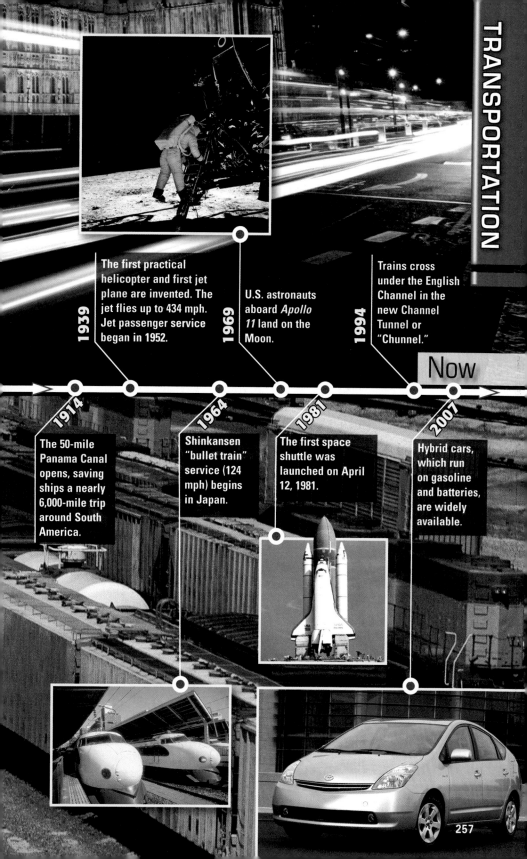

1939 The first practical helicopter and first jet plane are invented. The jet flies up to 434 mph. Jet passenger service began in 1952.

1969 U.S. astronauts aboard *Apollo 11* land on the Moon.

1994 Trains cross under the English Channel in the new Channel Tunnel or "Chunnel."

Now

1914 The 50-mile Panama Canal opens, saving ships a nearly 6,000-mile trip around South America.

1964 Shinkansen "bullet train" service (124 mph) begins in Japan.

1981 The first space shuttle was launched on April 12, 1981.

2007 Hybrid cars, which run on gasoline and batteries, are widely available.

257

TRAVEL

Where is the lunch box museum? ➡ page 260

In the late 13th century, famed Italian adventurer Marco Polo took a winding 5,600-mile journey overland from Venice, Italy, to Beijing, China. When he returned to Venice, Polo published a chronicle of his travels. The stories were so fantastic that many people didn't believe his tales.

You may not be taking a journey of thousands of miles on your next trip, but the excitement of traveling is the same. People travel for all kinds of reasons—business, fun, or to see distant friends and relatives. But whatever the reason, people have always had the desire to stretch their legs, explore new places, and have adventures that others may—or may not—believe.

▶ The World's 10 Most-Visited Countries*	▶ The 10 Most-Visited U.S. States*
1. France	1. California
2. Spain	2. Florida
3. U.S.	3. Texas
4. China	4. New York
5. Italy	5. Pennsylvania
6. United Kingdom	6. Illinois
7. Hong Kong	7. Ohio
8. Mexico	8. North Carolina
9. Germany	9. Georgia
10. Austria	10. Virginia
*2005	*2004

World's Five Most-Visited Amusement Parks*

1. Magic Kingdom (Lake Buena Vista, Florida), 16.6 million
2. Disneyland (Anaheim, California), 14.7 million
3. Tokyo Disneyland (Japan), 12.9 million
4. Disneyland Paris (Marne-La-Vallee, France), 10.2 million
5. Everland (Kyonggi, South Korea), 7.5 million

*2006

AMUSEMENT PARKS

The first amusement parks appeared in Europe more than 400 years ago. Attractions included flower gardens, bowling, music, and a few simple rides.

Today's amusement parks are much more impressive. With super-fast roller coasters, parades, shows, and other attractions, amusement parks now have something to amuse just about anyone. Here's a look at some of the most popular amusement parks in the U.S.

FABULOUS FACTS

Biggest Park: Walt Disney World, Lake Buena Vista, Florida, 28,000 acres

Most Rides: 74, Cedar Point, Sandusky, Ohio

Most Roller Coasters: 17, Cedar Point, Sandusky, Ohio

Fastest Roller Coaster: 128 mph, Kingda Ka, Six Flags Great Adventure, Jackson, New Jersey

Tallest Roller Coaster: 456 feet, Kingda Ka, Six Flags Great Adventure, Jackson, New Jersey

Maverick, new roller coaster at Cedar Point.

▶ **Cedar Point (Sandusky, Ohio)** One of the oldest amusement parks in the U.S., Cedar Point (on Lake Erie) opened in 1870. Its first roller coaster, the Switchback Railway, opened in 1892. It had a then-dizzying 25-foot-high hill, on which riders traveled at about 10 mph. Today at Cedar Point, the Top Thrill Dragster roller coaster reaches a height of 420 feet, and the cars zip along at a top speed of 120 mph! There are also plenty of other attractions, including Soak City, which features water rides and a wave pool.

▶ **Water World (Denver, Colorado)** One of the largest water parks in the United States, Water World opened in 1982. There are 42 rides on its 64 acres. Among a wide variety of attractions are more family tube rides than any other water park in the U.S. and Wally World for young children. Voyage to the Center of the Earth is an enclosed tube ride that spans more than $\frac{1}{4}$-mile. The park also includes some of the highest water slides in the world (Flatline, Redline, and Pipeline), where riders can reach speeds of up to 40 miles per hour.

▶ **Universal Studios Florida/Islands of Adventure (Orlando, Florida)** Universal Studios opened in 1990 and visitors have been "riding the movies" there ever since. Rides, shows, and other attractions feature favorite movie and TV characters, like Shrek, and take visitors behind the scenes. Islands of Adventure has been open since 1999. The rides and attractions there pay tribute to favorite characters from books and comic books, like Spiderman, the Incredible Hulk, and Dr. Doom.

ROAD TRIP

Wherever you are, there is likely to be a festival, amusement park, historic site, or national park just a short drive away. A road trip—short or long—can be lots of fun, with plenty of interesting sights along the way.

The first cross-country drive was made in 1903. H. Nelson Jackson and Sewall K. Crocker (and a bulldog named Bud) drove from San Francisco to New York City in an early car known as a Winton. There were few roads or bridges in the West, and lots of mud everywhere. The whole trip took 63 days and cost $8,000, including the price of the car. In 1909, Alice Huyler Ramsey became the first woman to drive across the U.S. Her trip from New York to San Francisco took 59 days.

By 1930, there were 23 million cars on the road. More than half of American families owned one. (Today in the U.S. there are more vehicles than licensed drivers.) People wanted to see things and go places—especially west. The first coast-to-coast highway was the Lincoln Highway, which was finished by 1930. The most famous highway was Route 66, completed in 1926, connecting Chicago to Los Angeles. Now called "Historic Route 66," it still has billboards and giant statues advertising its famous hotels, attractions, and restaurants.

H. Nelson Jackson

A ROADSIDE SAMPLER:

Lunch Box Museum Located in Columbus, Georgia, the Lunch Box Museum has more than 3,500 lunchboxes on display. Even though the boxes are old, you may recognize some of the cartoon and TV heroes on them. ▶

Corn Palace This huge concrete building in Mitchell, South Dakota, is covered with murals made of corn and other types of grains and grasses. No corny jokes please--they've heard them all here.

World's Largest Tire Located in Allen Park, Michigan, the Uniroyal Tire stands 80 feet tall. It was built for the 1964-65 World's Fair in New York. After the fair, it was moved to where it is now. In 1998, Uniroyal stabbed the tire with an 11-foot-long, 250-lb nail (the largest nail in the world) to show the toughness of Uniroyal tires. The nail was removed and sold. But the tire is as sturdy as ever.

World's Largest Solar System Scale Model This solar system model follows about 40 miles of highway U.S. 1 in northern Maine—from the sun, 50 feet in diameter, at the University of Maine at Presque Isle to tiny Pluto, 1 inch in diameter, mounted on a visitor center wall in Houlton. Area volunteers are planning to add the new dwarf planets, Ceres and Eris.

THE NEW 7 WONDERS OF THE WORLD

The New Seven Wonders of the World were announced on July 7, 2007 (07/07/07). The winners were based on an online poll with over 100 million people voting from 200 countries.

The New 7 Wonders, all equal in rank, are:

The Great Wall of China (220 B.C.. and 1368-1644 A.D.), China

Petra (9 B.C.- 40 A.D.), Jordan

The Roman Colosseum (70-82 A.D.), Rome, Italy

The Pyramid at Chichén Itzá (before 800 A.D.), Yucatan Peninsula, Mexico

Machu Picchu (1460-1470), Peru

Christ the Redeemer (1931), Rio de Janiero, Brazil

The Taj Mahal (1630 A.D.), Agra, India

Other popular sites that were considered include the Great Pyramid of Giza in Egypt (the only remaining wonder of the ancient world), the Acropolis in Athens, the Eiffel Tower in Paris, Ankor in Cambodia, and the Moai statues of Easter Island.

NATIONAL PARKS

The world's first national park was Yellowstone, established in 1872. Today in the U.S., there are 58 national parks, including parks in the Virgin Islands, Guam, Puerto Rico, and American Samoa. The National Park Service manages 390 units in all, including national monuments, memorials, battlefields, military parks, historic parks, historic sites, lakeshores, seashores, recreation areas, scenic rivers and trails, wilderness areas, and the White House—84.6 million acres in all! For more information, you can write the National Park Service, Department of the Interior, 1849 C Street NW, Washington, D.C. 20240.

WEB SITE *www.nps.gov/parks.html*

YOSEMITE NATIONAL PARK

This park, established in 1890, covers 761,266 acres in east-central California. It has the world's largest concentration of granite domes—mountain-like rocks that were created by glaciers millions of years ago. You can see many of them rising thousands of feet above the valley floor. Two of the most famous are Half Dome, which looks smooth and rounded, and El Capitan, which is the biggest single granite rock on Earth. Skilled climbers come from all over the world to scale this 3,000-foot-high wall of rock. Yosemite Falls, which drops 2,425 feet, is the highest waterfall in North America. It is actually two waterfalls, called the upper and lower falls, connected by a series of smaller waterfalls. Yosemite also features lakes, meadows, and giant sequoia trees, and is home to bighorn sheep and bears.

GRAND CANYON NATIONAL PARK

This national park, established in 1919, has one of the world's most spectacular landscapes, covering more than a million acres in northwestern Arizona. The canyon is 6,000 feet deep at its deepest point and 15 miles wide at its widest. Most of the 40 identified rock layers that form the canyon's 277-mile-long wall are exposed, offering a detailed look at the Earth's geologic history. The walls display a cross section of the Earth's crust from as far back as two billion years ago. The Colorado River—which carved out the giant canyon—still runs through the park, which is a valuable wildlife preserve with many rare, endangered animals. The pine and fir forests, painted deserts, plateaus, caves, and sandstone canyons offer a wide range of habitats.

DENALI NATIONAL PARK Located in the southern part of the Alaska Mountain Range in the south central part of Alaska, Denali is home to North America's highest mountain, 20,320-foot Mt. McKinley. The park was originally established in 1917 as Mount McKinley National Park, but it was expanded in 1980 and renamed Denali National Park and Preserve. Denali covers more than 6 million acres and is almost as big as the state of Massachusetts. The park is also teeming with wildlife. Among many other animals, it's possible to see what are known in Denali as the "Denali Big Five": caribou, Dall sheep, grizzly bears, moose, and wolves. Denali is the only national park that is patrolled mostly by staff riding on dog sleds.

OLYMPIC NATIONAL PARK This park was established in 1938 to preserve some of Washington's old growth forests. The park, located in the northwestern part of Washington state, covers 922,651 acres. Three distinctly different ecosystems lie within Olympic National Park. It includes coastal beaches, temperate rain forest valleys, and glacier capped mountains. There are 73 miles of wilderness coast along the Pacific Ocean. Less than 33 miles east of the ocean lies Mount Olympus, the highest peak in the Olympus range. With 60 named glaciers, Mount Olympus has the third largest glacial system in the lower 48 states. Forest communities include subalpine, montane, lowland, temperate rain forest, and coastal. The lush temperate rain forest, one of the few remaining in the world, has moderate temperatures and gets from 140 to 167 inches of rain each year.

YELLOWSTONE NATIONAL PARK Located mostly in northwestern Wyoming and partly in eastern Idaho and southwestern Montana, Yellowstone is known for its 10,000 hot springs and geysers—more than anyplace else in the world. Old Faithful, the most famous geyser, erupts for about four minutes every one to two hours, shooting 3,700-8,400 gallons of hot water as high as 185 feet. Other geysers include the Giant, which shoots a column of hot water 200 feet high, and the Giantess, which erupts for over four hours at a time, but only about two times per year. There are grizzly bears, wolves, elk, moose, buffalo, deer, beavers, coyotes, antelopes, and 300 species of birds. The use of snowmobiles in the park has been a big controversy. Some people want to ban them because of noise and air pollution; others disagree. They are allowed now, but their use is somewhat limited.

UNITED STATES

Which state's name means "snow-clad" in Spanish? ➡ page 293

FACTS & FIGURES

AREA	50 states and Washington, D.C.
LAND	3,537,437 square miles
WATER	181,272 square miles
TOTAL	3,718,709 square miles

POPULATION (MID-2008): 305,052,258

CAPITAL: WASHINGTON, D.C.

LARGEST, HIGHEST, and OTHER STATISTICS

Sears Tower

Largest state:	Alaska (663,267 square miles)
Smallest state:	Rhode Island (1,545 square miles)
Northernmost city:	Barrow, Alaska (71°17′ north latitude)
Southernmost city:	Hilo, Hawaii (19°44′ north latitude)
Easternmost city:	Eastport, Maine (66°59′ west longitude)
Westernmost city:	Atka, Alaska (174°12′ west longitude)
Highest settlement:	Climax, Colorado (11,360 feet)
Lowest settlement:	Calipatria, California (184 feet below sea level)
Oldest national park:	Yellowstone National Park (Idaho, Montana, Wyoming), 2,219,791 acres, established 1872
Largest national park:	Wrangell-St. Elias, Alaska (8,323,148 acres)
Longest river system:	Mississippi-Missouri-Red Rock (3,710 miles)
Deepest lake:	Crater Lake, Oregon (1,932 feet)
Highest mountain:	Mount McKinley, Alaska (20,320 feet)
Lowest point:	Death Valley, California (282 feet below sea level)
Tallest building:	Sears Tower, Chicago, Illinois (1,450 feet)
Tallest structure:	TV tower, Blanchard, North Dakota (2,063 feet)
Longest bridge span:	Verrazano-Narrows Bridge, New York (4,260 feet)
Highest bridge:	Royal Gorge, Colorado (1,053 feet above water)

WAforKids.com

Go to www.WAforKids.com and type 270 into the code box for more facts and fun:
- How much do you know about the United States? Take a chapter quiz to see how you rate.
- Supercharge your geography skills with a fun, interactive States and Cities map!
- Get even more homework help on U.S. symbols, history, and presidents.

SYMBOLS OF THE UNITED STATES

The Great Seal

The Great Seal of the United States shows an American bald eagle with a ribbon in its mouth bearing the Latin words *e pluribus unum* (out of many, one). In its talons are the arrows of war and an olive branch of peace. On the back of the Great Seal is an unfinished pyramid with an eye (the eye of Providence) above it. The seal was approved by Congress on June 20, 1782.

The Flag

1777

1795

1818

The flag of the United States has 50 stars (one for each state) and 13 stripes (one for each of the original 13 states). It is unofficially called the "Stars and Stripes."

The first U.S. flag was commissioned by the Second Continental Congress in 1777 but did not exist until 1783, after the American Revolution. Historians are not certain who designed the Stars and Stripes. Many different flags are believed to have been used during the American Revolution.

The flag of 1777 was used until 1795. In that year, Congress passed an act ordering that a new flag have 15 stripes, alternate red and white, and 15 stars on a blue field. In 1818, Congress directed that the flag have 13 stripes and that a new star be added for each new state of the Union. The last star was added in 1960 for the state of Hawaii.

There are many customs for flying the flag and treating it with respect. For example, it should not touch the floor and no other flag should be flown above it, except for the UN flag at UN headquarters. When the flag is raised or lowered, or passes in a parade, or during the Pledge of Allegiance, people should face it and stand at attention. Those in military uniform should salute. Others should put their right hand over their heart. The flag is flown at half-staff as a sign of mourning.

Pledge of Allegiance to the Flag

"I pledge allegiance to the flag of the United States of America and to the republic for which it stands, one nation under God, indivisible, with liberty and justice for all."

The National Anthem

"The Star-Spangled Banner" was a poem written in 1814 by Francis Scott Key as he watched British ships bombard Fort McHenry, Maryland, during the War of 1812. It became the National Anthem by an act of Congress in 1931. The music to "The Star-Spangled Banner" was originally a tune called "Anacreon in Heaven."

THE U.S. CONSTITUTION

The Foundation of American Government

The Constitution is the document that created the present government of the United States. It was written in 1787 and went into effect in 1789. It establishes the three branches of the U.S. government — the executive (headed by the president), the legislative (Congress), and the judicial (the Supreme Court and other federal courts). The first 10 amendments to the Constitution (the **Bill of Rights**) explain the basic rights of all American citizens.

You can find the constitution on-line at:

WEB SITE *www.house.gov/Constitution/Constitution.html*

THE PREAMBLE TO THE CONSTITUTION

The Constitution begins with a short statement called the Preamble. The Preamble states that the government of the United States was established by the people.

"We the people of the United States, in order to form a more perfect union, establish justice, insure domestic tranquility, provide for the common defense, promote the general welfare, and secure the blessings of liberty to ourselves and our posterity, do ordain and establish this Constitution for the United States of America."

THE ARTICLES

The original Constitution contained seven articles. The first three articles of the Constitution establish the three branches of the U.S. government.

Article 1, Legislative Branch Creates the Senate and House of Representatives and describes their functions and powers.

Article 2, Executive Branch Creates the office of the President and the Electoral College and lists their powers and responsibilities.

Article 3, Judicial Branch Creates the Supreme Court and gives Congress the power to create lower courts. The powers of the courts and certain crimes are defined.

Article 4, The States Discusses the relationship of the states to one another and to the citizens. Defines the states' powers.

Article 5, Amending the Constitution Describes how the Constitution can be amended (changed).

Article 6, Federal Law Makes the Constitution the supreme law of the land over state laws and constitutions.

Article 7, Ratifying the Constitution Establishes how to ratify (approve) the Constitution.

Amendments to the Constitution

The writers of the Constitution understood that it might need to be amended, or changed, in the future, but they wanted to be careful and made it hard to change. Article 5 describes how the Constitution can be amended.

In order to take effect, an amendment must be approved by a two-thirds majority in both the House of Representatives and the Senate. It must then be approved (ratified) by three-fourths of the states (38 states). So far, there have been 27 amendments. One of them (the 18th, ratified in 1919) banned the manufacture or sale of liquor. It was canceled by the 21st Amendment, in 1933.

The Bill of Rights: The First Ten Amendments

The first ten amendments were adopted in 1791 and contain the basic freedoms Americans enjoy as a people. These amendments are known as the Bill of Rights.

1. Guarantees freedom of religion, speech, and the press.
2. Guarantees the right to have firearms.
3. Guarantees that soldiers cannot be lodged in private homes unless the owner agrees.
4. Protects people from being searched or having property searched or taken away by the government without reason.
5. Protects rights of people on trial for crimes.
6. Guarantees people accused of crimes the right to a speedy public trial by jury.
7. Guarantees the right to a trial by jury for other kinds of cases.
8. Prohibits "cruel and unusual punishments."
9. Says specific rights listed in the Constitution do not take away rights that may not be listed.
10. Establishes that any powers not given specifically to the federal government belong to states or the people.

Other Important Amendments

13. (1865): Ends slavery in the United States.
14. (1868): Bars states from denying rights to citizens; guarantees equal protection under the law for all citizens.
15. (1870): Guarantees that a person cannot be denied the right to vote because of race or color.
19. (1920): Gives women the right to vote.
22. (1951): Limits the president to two four-year terms of office.
24. (1964): Outlaws the poll tax (a tax people had to pay before they could vote) in federal elections. (The poll tax had been used to keep African Americans in the South from voting.)
25. (1967): Specifies presidential succession; also gives the president the power to appoint a new vice president, if one dies or leaves office in the middle of a term.
26. (1971): Lowers the voting age to 18 from 21.

THE EXECUTIVE BRANCH

The **executive branch** of the federal government is headed by the president, who enforces the laws passed by Congress and is commander in chief of the U.S. armed forces. It also includes the vice president, people who work for the president or vice president, the major departments of the government, and special agencies. The **cabinet** is made up of the vice president, heads of major departments, and other officials. It meets when the president chooses. The chart at right shows cabinet departments in the order in which they were created. The Department of Homeland Security was created by a law signed in November 2002.

PRESIDENT

VICE PRESIDENT

CABINET DEPARTMENTS

1. State
2. Treasury
3. Defense
4. Justice
5. Interior
6. Agriculture
7. Commerce
8. Labor
9. Housing and Urban Development
10. Transportation
11. Energy
12. Education
13. Health and Human Services
14. Veterans Affairs
15. Homeland Security

How Long Does the President Serve?

The president serves a four-year term, starting on January 20. No president can be elected more than twice, or more than once if he or she had served two years as president filling out the term of a president who left office.

What Happens If the President Dies?

If the president dies in office or cannot complete the term, the vice president becomes president. If the president is unable to perform his or her duties, the vice president can become acting president. The next person to become president after the vice president would be the Speaker of the House of Representatives.

The White House has an address on the World Wide Web especially for kids. It is:

WEB SITE *www.whitehousekids.gov*

You can send e-mail to the president at:

EMAIL *president@whitehouse.gov*

The White House, home of the U.S. president

Voter Turnout in Presidential Elections, 1964-2004

(Percent of voting age, 18 and over in 1972 and afterwards, 21 and over in 1964 and 1968.)

Year	Turnout	Year	Turnout
1964	61.4%	1988	50.3%
1968	60.7%	1992	55.2%
1972	55.1%	1996	49.0 %
1976	53.6%	2000	50.3%
1980	52.8%	2004	55.5%
1984	53.3%		

Source: U.S. Census Bureau

THE LEGISLATIVE BRANCH

CONGRESS

The Congress of the United States is the legislative branch of the federal government. Congress's major responsibility is to pass the laws that govern the country and determine how money collected in taxes is spent. It is the president's responsibility to enforce the laws. Congress consists of two parts—the Senate and the House of Representatives. ▶

THE SENATE

The Senate has 100 members, two from each state. The Constitution says that the Senate will have equal representation (the same number of representatives) from each state. Thus, small states have the same number of senators as large states. Senators are elected for six-year terms. There is no limit on the number of terms a senator can serve.

The Senate also has the responsibility of approving people the president appoints for certain jobs: for example, cabinet members and Supreme Court justices. The Senate must approve all treaties by at least a two-thirds vote. It also has the responsibility under the Constitution of putting on trial high-ranking federal officials who have been impeached by the House of Representatives.

WEB SITE www.senate.gov

The Capitol, where Congress meets

THE HOUSE OF REPRESENTATIVES

The number of members of the House of Representatives for each state depends on its population according to a recent census. But each state has at least one representative, no matter how small its population. A term lasts two years.

The first House of Representatives in 1789 had 65 members. As the country's population grew, the number of representatives increased. Since 1911, however, the total membership has been kept at 435. After the results of Census 2000 were added up, 8 states gained seats and 10 states lost seats.

WEB SITE www.house.gov

The House of Representatives, by State

Here are the numbers of representatives each state had in 2009, compared with earlier times:

	2009	1995	1975		2009	1995	1975
Alabama	7	7	7	Montana	1	1	2
Alaska	1	1	1	Nebraska	3	3	3
Arizona	8	6	4	Nevada	3	2	1
Arkansas	4	4	4	New Hampshire	2	2	2
California	53	52	43	New Jersey	13	13	15
Colorado	7	6	5	New Mexico	3	3	2
Connecticut	5	6	6	New York	29	31	39
Delaware	1	1	1	North Carolina	13	12	11
Florida	25	23	15	North Dakota	1	1	1
Georgia	13	11	10	Ohio	18	19	23
Hawaii	2	2	2	Oklahoma	5	6	6
Idaho	2	2	2	Oregon	5	5	4
Illinois	19	20	24	Pennsylvania	19	21	25
Indiana	9	10	11	Rhode Island	2	2	2
Iowa	5	5	6	South Carolina	6	6	6
Kansas	4	4	5	South Dakota	1	1	2
Kentucky	6	6	7	Tennessee	9	9	9
Louisiana	7	7	8	Texas	32	30	24
Maine	2	2	2	Utah	3	3	2
Maryland	8	8	8	Vermont	1	1	1
Massachusetts	10	10	12	Virginia	11	11	10
Michigan	15	16	19	Washington	9	9	7
Minnesota	8	8	8	West Virginia	3	3	4
Mississippi	4	5	5	Wisconsin	8	9	9
Missouri	9	9	10	Wyoming	1	1	1

Washington, D.C., Puerto Rico, American Samoa, Guam, and the Virgin Islands each have one nonvoting member of the House of Representatives.

HOUSE COMMITTEES

The House creates committees for a variety of reasons. The members of a committee work together to study national problems and suggest solutions. They propose laws that are debated and then voted on by the whole House.

In committee hearings and meetings, members are presented with information about the issues related to the proposed law. They may question experts, review documents and exhibits, and discuss the material presented. Committees then draft a bill, rewrite a bill, or revise a bill. Next, the committee can vote to send the bill to the House Chamber for debate or to another committee. If not passed on, the bill usually "dies" in committee.

The U.S. House of Representatives has twenty standing (permanent) committees.

- Agriculture
- Appropriations
- Armed Services
- Budget
- Education and Labor
- Energy and Commerce
- Financial Services
- Foreign Affairs
- Homeland Security
- House Administration
- Judiciary
- Natural Resources
- Oversight and Government Reform
- Science and Technology
- Small Business
- Standards of Official Conduct
- Transportation and Infrastructure
- Veterans' Affairs

THE JUDICIAL BRANCH

The Supreme Court

The highest court in the United States is the Supreme Court. It has nine justices who are appointed for life by the president with the approval of the Senate. Eight of the nine members are called associate justices. The ninth is the Chief Justice, who presides over the Court's meetings.

What Does the Supreme Court Do?

The Supreme Court's major responsibilities are to judge cases that involve reviewing federal laws, actions of the president, treaties of the United States, and laws passed by state governments to be sure they do not conflict with the U.S. Constitution. If the Supreme Court finds that a law or action violates the Constitution, the law is struck down.

The Supreme Court's Decision Is Final.

Most cases must go through other state courts or federal courts before they reach the Supreme Court. The Supreme Court is the final court for a case, and the justices decide which cases they will review. After the Supreme Court hears a case, it may agree or disagree with the decision by a lower court. Each justice has one vote, and the majority rules. When the Supreme Court makes a ruling, its decision is final, so each of the justices has a very important job.

Below are the nine justices who were on the Supreme Court in May 2007. **Back row** (from left to right): Stephen Breyer, Clarence Thomas, Ruth Bader Ginsburg, Samuel Alito. **Front row** (from left to right): Anthony M. Kennedy, John Paul Stevens, Chief Justice John G. Roberts, Antonin Scalia, David H. Souter.

271

GEORGE WASHINGTON Federalist Party   1789–1797
Born: Feb. 22, 1732, at Wakefield, Westmoreland County, Virginia
Married: Martha Dandridge Custis (1731-1802); no children
Died: Dec. 14, 1799; buried at Mount Vernon, Fairfax County, Virginia
Vice President: John Adams (1789-1797)

JOHN ADAMS Federalist Party   1797–1801
Born: Oct. 30, 1735, in Braintree (now Quincy), Massachusetts
Married: Abigail Smith (1744-1818); 3 sons, 2 daughters
Died: July 4, 1826; buried in Quincy, Massachusetts
Vice President: Thomas Jefferson (1797-1801)

THOMAS JEFFERSON Democratic-Republican Party   1801–1809
Born: Apr. 13, 1743, at Shadwell, Albemarle County, Virginia
Married: Martha Wayles Skelton (1748-1782); 1 son, 5 daughters
Died: July 4, 1826; buried at Monticello, Albemarle County, Virginia
Vice President: Aaron Burr (1801-1805), George Clinton (1805-1809)

JAMES MADISON Democratic-Republican Party   1809-1817
Born: Mar. 16, 1751, at Port Conway, King George County, Virginia
Married: Dolley Payne Todd (1768-1849); no children
Died: June 28, 1836; buried at Montpelier Station, Virginia
Vice President: George Clinton (1809-1813), Elbridge Gerry (1813-1817)

JAMES MONROE Democratic-Republican Party   1817–1825
Born: Apr. 28, 1758, in Westmoreland County, Virginia
Married: Elizabeth Kortright (1768-1830); 1 son, 2 daughters
Died: July 4, 1831; buried in Richmond, Virginia
Vice President: Daniel D. Tompkins (1817-1825)

JOHN QUINCY ADAMS Democratic-Republican Party   1825–1829
Born: July 11, 1767, in Braintree (now Quincy), Massachusetts
Married: Louisa Catherine Johnson (1775-1852); 3 sons, 1 daughter
Died: Feb. 23, 1848; buried in Quincy, Massachusetts
Vice President: John C. Calhoun (1825-1829)

7 ANDREW JACKSON Democratic Party 1829–1837
Born: Mar. 15, 1767, in Waxhaw, South Carolina
Married: Rachel Donelson Robards (1767-1828); 1 son (adopted)
Died: June 8, 1845; buried in Nashville, Tennessee
Vice President: John C. Calhoun (1829-1833),
   Martin Van Buren (1833-1837)

8 MARTIN VAN BUREN Democratic Party 1837–1841
Born: Dec. 5, 1782, at Kinderhook, New York
Married: Hannah Hoes (1783-1819); 4 sons
Died: July 24, 1862; buried at Kinderhook, New York
Vice President: Richard M. Johnson (1837-1841)

9 WILLIAM HENRY HARRISON Whig Party 1841
Born: Feb. 9, 1773, at Berkeley, Charles City County, Virginia
Married: Anna Symmes (1775-1864); 6 sons, 4 daughters
Died: Apr. 4, 1841; buried in North Bend, Ohio
Vice President: John Tyler (1841-1845)

10 JOHN TYLER Whig Party 1841–1845
Born: Mar. 29, 1790, in Greenway, Charles City County, Virginia
Married: Letitia Christian (1790-1842); 3 sons, 5 daughters
   Julia Gardiner (1820-1889); 5 sons, 2 daughters
Died: Jan. 18, 1862; buried in Richmond, Virginia
Vice President: none

11 JAMES KNOX POLK Democratic Party 1845–1849
Born: Nov. 2, 1795, in Mecklenburg County, North Carolina
Married: Sarah Childress (1803-1891); no children
Died: June 15, 1849; buried in Nashville, Tennessee
Vice President: George M. Dallas (1845-1849)

12 ZACHARY TAYLOR Whig Party 1849–1850
Born: Nov. 24, 1784, in Orange County, Virginia
Married: Margaret Smith (1788-1852); 1 son, 5 daughters
Died: July 9, 1850; buried in Louisville, Kentucky
Vice President: Millard Fillmore (1849-1850)

13 MILLARD FILLMORE Whig Party 1850–1853
Born: Jan. 7, 1800, in Cayuga County, New York
Married: Abigail Powers (1798-1853); 1 son, 1 daughter
   Caroline Carmichael McIntosh (1813-1881); no children
Died: Mar. 8, 1874; buried in Buffalo, New York
Vice President: none

14 FRANKLIN PIERCE Democratic Party 1853–1857
Born: Nov. 23, 1804, in Hillsboro, New Hampshire
Married: Jane Means Appleton (1806-1863); 3 sons
Died: Oct. 8, 1869; buried in Concord, New Hampshire
Vice President: William R. King (1853-1857)

15 JAMES BUCHANAN Democratic Party 1857–1861
Born: Apr. 23, 1791, Cove Gap, near Mercersburg, Pennsylvania
Married: Never
Died: June 1, 1868, buried in Lancaster, Pennsylvania
Vice President: John C. Breckinridge (1857-1861)

16 ABRAHAM LINCOLN Republican Party 1861-1865
Born: Feb. 12, 1809, in Hardin County, Kentucky
Married: Mary Todd (1818-1882); 4 sons
Died: Apr. 15, 1865; buried in Springfield, Illinois
Vice President: Hannibal Hamlin (1861-1864),
                    Andrew Johnson (1865)

17 ANDREW JOHNSON Democratic Party 1865–1869
Born: Dec. 29, 1808, in Raleigh, North Carolina
Married: Eliza McCardle (1810-1876); 3 sons, 2 daughters
Died: July 31, 1875; buried in Greeneville, Tennessee
Vice President: none

18 ULYSSES S. GRANT Republican Party 1869–1877
Born: Apr. 27, 1822, in Point Pleasant, Ohio
Married: Julia Dent (1826-1902); 3 sons, 1 daughter
Died: July 23, 1885; buried in New York City
Vice President: Schuyler Colfax (1869-1873),

                    Henry Wilson (1873-1877)

19 RUTHERFORD B. HAYES Republican Party 1877–1881
Born: Oct. 4, 1822, in Delaware, Ohio
Married: Lucy Ware Webb (1831-1889); 7 sons, 1 daughter
Died: Jan. 17, 1893; buried in Fremont, Ohio
Vice President: William A. Wheeler (1877-1881)

20 JAMES A. GARFIELD Republican Party   1881
Born: Nov. 19, 1831, in Orange, Cuyahoga County, Ohio
Married: Lucretia Rudolph (1832-1918); 5 sons, 2 daughters
Died: Sept. 19, 1881; buried in Cleveland, Ohio
Vice President: Chester A. Arthur (1881-1881)

21 CHESTER A. ARTHUR Republican Party   1881–1885
Born: Oct. 5, 1829, in Fairfield, Vermont
Married: Ellen Lewis Herndon (1837-1880); 2 sons, 1 daughter
Died: Nov. 18, 1886; buried in Albany, New York
Vice President: none

22 GROVER CLEVELAND Democratic Party   1885–1889
Born: Mar. 18, 1837, in Caldwell, New Jersey
Married: Frances Folsom (1864-1947); 2 sons, 3 daughters
Died: June 24, 1908; buried in Princeton, New Jersey
Vice President: Thomas A. Hendricks (1885-1889)

23 BENJAMIN HARRISON Republican Party   1889-1893
Born: Aug. 20, 1833, in North Bend, Ohio
Married: Caroline Lavinia Scott (1832-1892); 1 son, 1 daughter
        Mary Scott Lord Dimmick (1858-1948); 1 daughter
Died: Mar. 13, 1901; buried in Indianapolis, Indiana
Vice President: Levi Morton (1889-1893)

24 GROVER CLEVELAND   1893–1897
See 22, above
Vice President: Adlai E. Stevenson (1893-1897)

25 WILLIAM MCKINLEY Republican Party   1897–1901
Born: Jan. 29, 1843, in Niles, Ohio
Married: Ida Saxton (1847-1907); 2 daughters
Died: Sept. 14, 1901; buried in Canton, Ohio
Vice President: Garret A. Hobart (1897-1901),
               Theodore Roosevelt (1901-1901)

26 THEODORE ROOSEVELT Republican Party   1901–1909
Born: Oct. 27, 1858, in New York City
Married: Alice Hathaway Lee (1861-1884); 1 daughter
        Edith Kermit Carow (1861-1948); 4 sons, 1 daughter
Died: Jan. 6, 1919; buried in Oyster Bay, New York
Vice President: none from 1901-1905, Charles W. Fairbanks (1905-1909)

27 WILLIAM HOWARD TAFT Republican Party 1909–1913
Born: Sept. 15, 1857, in Cincinnati, Ohio
Married: Helen Herron (1861-1943); 2 sons, 1 daughter
Died: Mar. 8, 1930; buried in Arlington National Cemetery, Virginia
Vice President: James S. Sherman (1909-1913)

28 WOODROW WILSON Democratic Party 1913–1921
Born: Dec. 28, 1856, in Staunton, Virginia
Married: Ellen Louise Axson (1860-1914); 3 daughters
    Edith Bolling Galt (1872-1961); no children
Died: Feb. 3, 1924; buried in Washington, D.C.
Vice President: Thomas R. Marshall (1913-1921)

29 WARREN G. HARDING Republican Party 1921–1923
Born: Nov. 2, 1865, near Corsica (now Blooming Grove), Ohio
Married: Florence Kling De Wolfe (1860-1924)
Died: Aug. 2, 1923; buried in Marion, Ohio
Vice President: Calvin Coolidge (1921-1923)

30 CALVIN COOLIDGE Republican Party 1923–1929
Born: July 4, 1872, in Plymouth, Vermont
Married: Grace Anna Goodhue (1879-1957); 2 sons
Died: Jan. 5, 1933; buried in Plymouth, Vermont
Vice President: none from 1923-1925, Charles G. Dawes (1925-1929)

31 HERBERT C. HOOVER Republican Party 1929-1933
Born: Aug. 10, 1874, in West Branch, Iowa
Married: Lou Henry (1875-1944); 2 sons
Died: Oct. 20, 1964; buried in West Branch, Iowa
Vice President: Charles Curtis (1929-1933)

32 FRANKLIN DELANO ROOSEVELT Democratic Party 1933–1945
Born: Jan. 30, 1882, in Hyde Park, New York
Married: Anna Eleanor Roosevelt (1884-1962); 4 sons, 1 daughter
Died: Apr. 12, 1945; buried in Hyde Park, New York
Vice President: John N. Garner (1933-1941),
             Henry A. Wallace (1941-1945),
             Harry S. Truman (1945)

33 HARRY S. TRUMAN Democratic Party   1945–1953
Born: May 8, 1884, in Lamar, Missouri
Married: Elizabeth Virginia "Bess" Wallace (1885-1982); 1 daughter
Died: Dec. 26, 1972; buried in Independence, Missouri
Vice President: none from 1945-1949, Alben W. Barkley (1949-1953)

34 DWIGHT D. EISENHOWER Republican Party   1953–1961
Born: Oct. 14, 1890, in Denison, Texas
Married: Mary "Mamie" Geneva Doud (1896-1979); 2 sons
Died: Mar. 28, 1969; buried in Abilene, Kansas
Vice President: RichardM. Nixon (1953-1961)

35 JOHN FITZGERALD KENNEDY Democratic Party   1961–1963
Born: May 29, 1917, in Brookline, Massachusetts
Married: Jacqueline Lee Bouvier (1929-1994); 2 sons, 1 daughter
Died: Nov. 22, 1963; buried in Arlington National Cemetery, Virginia
Vice President: Lyndon B. Johnson (1961-1963)

36 LYNDON BAINES JOHNSON Democratic Party   1963–1969
Born: Aug. 27, 1908, near Stonewall, Texas
Married: Claudia "Lady Bird" Alta Taylor (b. 1912); 2 daughters
Died: Jan. 22, 1973; buried in Johnson City, Texas
Vice President: none from 1963-1965, Hubert H. Humphrey (1965-1969)

37 RICHARD MILHOUS NIXON Republican Party   1969–1974
Born: Jan. 9, 1913, in Yorba Linda, California
Married: Thelma "Pat" Ryan (1912-1993); 2 daughters
Died: Apr. 22, 1994; buried in Yorba Linda, California
Vice President: Spiro T. Agnew (1969-1973),
                Gerald R. Ford (1973-1974)

38 GERALD R. FORD Republican Party   1974-1977
Born: July 14, 1913, in Omaha, Nebraska
Married: Elizabeth "Betty" Bloomer (b. 1918); 3 sons, 1 daughter
Died: Dec. 26, 2006; buried in Grand Rapids, Michigan
Vice President: Nelson A. Rockefeller (1974-1977)

39 JIMMY (JAMES EARL) CARTER Democratic Party   1977-1981
Born: Oct. 1, 1924, in Plains, Georgia
Married: Rosalynn Smith (b. 1927); 3 sons, 1 daughter
Vice President: Walter F. Mondale (1977-1981)

RONALD REAGAN Republican Party   1981–1989
Born: Feb. 6, 1911, in Tampico, Illinois
Married: Jane Wyman (b. 1914); 1 son, 1 daughter
Nancy Davis (b. 1923); 1 son, 1 daughter
Died: June 5, 2004; buried in Simi Valley, California
Vice President: George H. Bush (1981-1989)

GEORGE H.W. BUSH Republican Party   1989–1993
Born: June 12, 1924, in Milton, Massachusetts
Married: Barbara Pierce (b. 1925); 4 sons, 2 daughters
Vice President: Dan Quayle (1989-1993)

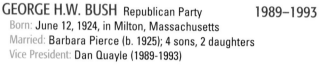

BILL (WILLIAM JEFFERSON) CLINTON   1993–2001
Democratic Party
Born: Aug. 19, 1946, in Hope, Arkansas
Married: Hillary Rodham (b. 1947); 1 daughter
Vice President: Al Gore (1993-2001)

GEORGE W. BUSH Republican Party   2001-2008
Born: July 6, 1946, in New Haven, Connecticut
Married: Laura Welch (b. 1946); 2 daughters
Vice President: Dick Cheney (2001-2008)

BARACK OBAMA Democratic Party   2009–
Born: August 4, 1961, in Honolulu, Hawaii
Married: Michelle LaVaughn Robinson (b. 1964); 2 daughters
Vice President: Joe Biden

★ ★ *The New* ★ ★ ★ ★ ★
First Lady

In the early days of the United States, there was no title for the wife of the president. Many early first ladies expressed their own preference for how they were addressed, including the use of such titles as "Lady," "Mrs. President," "Mrs. Presidentress," and "Queen." The term "First Lady" is used to refer to the wife of an elected male head of state. Creation of the title is credited to the United States, where it was first used in 1849. U. S. President Zachary Taylor called Dolley Madison "First Lady" at her state funeral while reciting a eulogy.

Michelle Obama, wife of Barack Obama, is the new first lady. She was born Michelle LaVaughn Robinson on January 17, 1964 in Chicago, Illinois. She graduated from Princeton University and Harvard Law School. For three years after law school, Michelle worked as an associate in the area of marketing and intellectual property at the Chicago law firm Sidley and Austin, where she met Barack Obama.

She left the corporate law world in 1991 to pursue a career in public service, serving as an assistant to the mayor and then as the assistant commissioner of planning and development for the city of Chicago.

In May 2007, three months after her husband declared his presidential candidacy, she reduced her professional responsibilities by eighty percent to support his presidential campaign.

Michelle married Barack Obama on October 18, 1992. They have two daughters, Malia Ann born in 1998 and Natasha (known as Sasha) born in 2001.

Meet the First Ladies

DOLLEY MADISON, wife of James Madison, was famous as a hostess and for saving a portrait of George Washington during the War of 1812, when the British were about to burn the White House.

MARY TODD LINCOLN, wife of Abraham Lincoln, was a well-educated Southerner who strongly opposed slavery. Sadly, her husband was assassinated and three of her four children died young.

LOU HENRY HOOVER, wife of Herbert Hoover, spoke several languages, including Chinese, and had a degree in geology. As First Lady she worked to involve all children in sports.

Eleanor Roosevelt, wife of Franklin D. Roosevelt was First Lady from 1933 to 1945. She supported the New Deal policies of her husband, and assumed a role as an advocate for civil right. After her husband's death in 1945, she continued to be an internationally prominent author and speaker and was active in politics for the rest of her life.

JACQUELINE KENNEDY, wife of John Kennedy, met her husband while she was working as a photographer and reporter. As First Lady, she redecorated the White House, filling it with historic furnishings and artwork. "Jackie" was also a fashion icon whose clothes and hairstyles were copied by millions of women.

BETTY FORD, wife of Gerald Ford, studied modern dance as a young woman and was part of the Martha Graham troupe. As First Lady, she fought for women's rights and supported the Equal Rights Amendment. In 1982 she established the Betty Ford Center for the treatment of drug and alcohol dependency.

LAURA BUSH, wife of George W. Bush, was a librarian and teacher. She is interested in books, history, art, and the well-being of children. She and her husband have twin daughters, Jenna and Barbara. Both girls graduated from college in 2004.

United States History

14,000 B.C.– 11,000 B.C.
Paleo-Indians use stone points attached to spears to hunt big **mammoths** in northern parts of North America.

11,000 B.C.
Big mammoths disappear and Paleo-Indians begin to gather **plants** for food.

After A.D. 500
Anasazi peoples in the Southwestern United States live in homes on cliffs, called **cliff dwellings**. Anasazi pottery and dishes are well known for their beautiful patterns.

After A.D. 700
Mississippian Indian people in the Southeastern United States **develop farms** and build burial mounds.

30,000 B.C. – 11,000 B.C.
First people (called **Paleo-Indians**) cross from Siberia to Alaska and begin to move into North America.

9500 B.C. – 1000 B.C.
North American Indians begin using **stone** to grind food and to hunt bison and smaller animals.

1000 B.C.– A.D. 500
Woodland Indians, who lived east of the Mississippi River, bury their dead under large **mounds** of earth (which can still be seen today).

700-1492
Many **different Indian cultures** develop throughout North America.

Colonial America
and the American Revolution:
1492-1783

1492
Christopher **Columbus** sails across the Atlantic Ocean and reaches an island in the Bahamas in the Caribbean Sea.

1513
Juan **Ponce de León** explores the Florida coast.

1524
Giovanni da **Verrazano** explores the coast from Carolina north to Nova Scotia, enters New York harbor.

1540
Francisco Vásquez de **Coronado** explores the Southwest.

1565
St. Augustine, Florida, the *first town* established by Europeans in the United States, is founded by the Spanish. Later burned by the English in 1586.

BENJAMIN FRANKLIN (1706-1790)
was a great American leader, printer, scientist, and writer. In 1732, he began publishing a magazine called *Poor Richard's Almanack*. Poor Richard was a make-believe person who gave advice about common sense and honesty. Many of Poor Richard's sayings are still known today. Among the most famous are "God helps them that help themselves" and "Early to bed, early to rise, makes a man healthy, wealthy, and wise."

1634
Maryland is founded as a Catholic colony, with religious freedom for all granted in 1649.

1664
The English seize **New Amsterdam** from the Dutch. The city is renamed New York.

1699
French settlers move into Mississippi and Louisiana.

1732
Benjamin Franklin begins publishing *Poor Richard's Almanack*.

1754-1763
French and Indian War between England and France, The French are defeated and lose their lands in Canada and the American Midwest.

1764-1766
England places taxes on sugar that comes from their North American colonies. England also requires colonists to buy stamps to help pay for royal troops. Colonists protest, and the **Stamp Act** is repealed in 1766.

1607
Jamestown, Virginia, the first permanent English settlement in North America, is founded by Captain John Smith.

1609
Henry Hudson sails into **New York Harbor,** explores the Hudson River. Spaniards settle Santa Fe, New Mexico.

1619
The first African **slaves** are brought to Jamestown. (Slavery is made legal in 1650.)

1620
Pilgrims from England arrive at Plymouth, Massachusetts, on the *Mayflower.*

1626
Peter Minuit buys **Manhattan** island for the Dutch from Manahata Indians for goods worth $24. The island is renamed New Amsterdam.

1630
Boston is founded by Massachusetts colonists led by John Winthrop.

FAMOUS WORDS FROM THE DECLARATION OF INDEPENDENCE, JULY 4, 1776

"We hold these truths to be self-evident, that all men are created equal, that they are endowed by their Creator with certain unalienable rights, that among these are life, liberty, and the pursuit of happiness."

1770
Boston Massacre: During a demonstration against English taxes, protestors began throwing rocks at English troops. The troops opened fire, killing 7 .

1773
Boston Tea Party: English tea is thrown into the harbor to protest a tax on tea.

1775
Fighting at **Lexington and Concord,** Massachusetts, marks the beginning of the American Revolution.

1776
The Declaration of Independence is approved July 4 by the Continental Congress (made up of representatives from the American colonies).

1781
British General **Charles Cornwallis** surrenders to the Americans at Yorktown, Virginia, ending the fighting in the Revolutionary War.

283

The New Nation
1784-1900

1784
The first successful daily **newspaper** in the U.S., the *Pennsylvania Packet & General Advertiser*, is published.

1787
The **Constitutional Convention** meets to write a Constitution for the U.S.

1789
The new **Constitution** is approved by the states. George Washington is chosen as the first president.

1800
The federal government moves from Philadelphia to a new capital, **Washington, D.C.**

1803
The U.S. makes the **Louisiana Purchase** from France. The Purchase doubles the area of the U.S.

THE LOUISIANA PURCHASE (1803)

WHO ATTENDED THE CONVENTION?
The **Constitutional Convention** met in Philadelphia in the hot summer of 1787. Most of the great founders of America attended. Among those present were George Washington, James Madison, and John Adams. They met to form a new government that would be strong and, at the same time, protect the liberties that were fought for in the American Revolution. The Constitution they created is still the law of the United States.

1836
Texans fighting for independence from Mexico are defeated at the **Alamo**.

1838
Cherokee Indians are forced to move to Oklahoma, along "The **Trail of Tears**." On the long march, thousands die because of disease and the cold weather.

1844
The **first telegraph** line connects Washington, D.C., and Baltimore.

1846–1848
U.S. war with Mexico: Mexico is defeated, and the United States takes control of the Republic of Texas and of Mexican territories in the West.

1848
The discovery of **gold** in California leads to a "rush" of 80,000 people to the West in search of gold.

1852
Uncle Tom's Cabin Harriet Beecher Stowe's novel about the suffering of slaves, is published.

1804

Lewis and Clark, with their guide Sacagawea, explore what is now the northwestern United States.

1812-1814

War of 1812 with Great Britain: British forces burn the Capitol and White House. Francis Scott Key writes the words to "The Star-Spangled Banner."

1820

The **Missouri Compromise** bans slavery west of the Mississippi River and north of 36°30' latitude, except in Missouri.

1823

The **Monroe Doctrine** warns European countries not to interfere in the Americas.

1825

The **Erie Canal** opens, linking New York City with the Great Lakes.

1831

The Liberator, a newspaper opposing slavery, is published in Boston.

1869

The **first railroad** connecting the East and West coasts is completed.

1898

Spanish-American War: The U.S. defeats Spain, gains control of the Philippines, Puerto Rico, and Guam.

1858

Abraham Lincoln and Stephen Douglas **debate about slavery** during their Senate campaign in Illinois.

1860

Abraham **Lincoln** is elected president.

1861

The **Civil War** begins.

1863

President Lincoln issues the **Emancipation Proclamation**, freeing most slaves.

1865

The **Civil War** ends as the South surrenders. President Lincoln is assassinated.

1890

Battle of Wounded Knee is fought in South Dakota—the last major battle between Indians and U.S. troops.

CIVIL WAR DEAD AND WOUNDED

The U.S. **Civil War** between the North and South lasted four years (1861-1865) and resulted in the death or wounding of more than 600,000 people. Little was known at the time about the spread of diseases. As a result, many casualties were also the result of illnesses such as influenza, measles, and infections from battle wounds.

United States Since 1900

WORLD WAR I
In **World War I** the United States fought with Great Britain, France, and Russia (the Allies) against Germany and Austria-Hungary. The Allies won the war in 1918.

1903
The United States begins digging the **Panama Canal**. The canal opens in 1914, connecting the Atlantic and Pacific oceans.

1908
Henry Ford introduces the **Model T** car, priced at $850.

1916
Jeannette Rankin of Montana becomes the first woman elected to Congress.

1917-1918
The United States joins **World War I** on the side of the Allies against Germany.

1927
Charles A. **Lindbergh** becomes the first person to fly alone nonstop across the Atlantic Ocean.

1929
A stock market crash marks the beginning of the **Great Depression**.

1954
The U.S. Supreme Court **forbids racial segregation** in public schools.

SCHOOL SEGREGATION
The U.S. Supreme Court ruled that **separate schools** for black students and white students were **not equal**. The Court said such schools were against the U.S. Constitution. The ruling also applied to other forms of segregation (separation of the races supported by some states.)

1963
President John **Kennedy** is assassinated.

1964
Congress passes the **Civil Rights Act**, which outlaws discrimination in voting and jobs.

1965
The United States sends first soldiers to fight in the **Vietnam War**.

1968
Civil rights leader **Martin Luther King Jr.** is assassinated in Memphis. Senator **Robert F. Kennedy** is assassinated in Los Angeles.

1969
U.S. Astronaut Neil Armstrong becomes the **first person** to walk **on the moon**.

1973
U.S. participation in the **Vietnam War ends**.

THE GREAT DEPRESSION

The stock market crash of October 1929 led to a period of severe hardship for the American people—the **Great Depression**. As many as 25 percent of all workers could not find jobs. The Depression lasted until the early 1940s. The Depression also led to a great change in politics. In 1932, Franklin D. Roosevelt, a Democrat, was elected president. He served as president for 12 years, longer than any other president.

1933

President Franklin D. Roosevelt's **New Deal** increases government help to people hurt by the Depression.

1941

Japan attacks **Pearl Harbor**, Hawaii. The United States enters World War II.

1945

Germany and Japan surrender, **ending World War II**. Japan surrenders after the U.S. drops atomic bombs on Hiroshima and Nagasaki.

1947

Jackie Robinson becomes the **first black baseball player** in the major leagues when he joins the Brooklyn Dodgers.

1950-1953

U.S. armed forces fight in the **Korean War**.

WATERGATE

In June 1972, five men were arrested in the **Watergate** building in Washington, D.C., for trying to bug telephones in the offices of the Democratic National Committee. Some of those arrested worked for the committee to re-elect President Richard Nixon. Later it was discovered that Nixon was helping to hide information about the break-in.

1991

The Persian Gulf War: The United States and its allies defeat Iraq.

2000

George W. Bush narrowly defeats Al Gore in a closely fought presidential race.

2008

2008 Senators **Barack Obama** and **John McCain** vie for the presidency, with tk winning.

1974

President Richard **Nixon resigns** because of the Watergate scandal.

1979

U.S. **hostages** are taken **in Iran**, beginning a 444-day crisis that ends with their release in 1981.

1981

Sandra Day O'Connor becomes the **first woman** on the U.S. Supreme Court.

1985

U.S. President Ronald Reagan and Soviet leader Mikhail Gorbachev begin working together to **improve relations** between their countries.

1999

After an **impeachment** trial, the Senate finds President Bill Clinton not guilty.

2001

Hijacked jets crash into the World Trade Center and the **Pentagon**, September 11, killing about 3,000 people.

2003

U.S.-led forces invade Iraq and remove dictator **Saddam Hussein**.

African Americans:
A Time Line

Would you like to learn more about the history of African Americans from the era of slavery to the present? These events and personalities can be a starting point. Can you add some more?

Barack Obama ▶

1619	●	First Africans are brought to Virginia as slaves.
1831	●	Nat Turner starts a **slave revolt** in Virginia that is unsuccessful.
1856-57	○	**Dred Scott**, a slave, sues to be freed because he had left slave territory, but the Supreme Court denies his claim.
1861-65	●	The North defeats the South in the brutal Civil War; the **13th Amendment** ends nearly 250 years of slavery. The Ku Klux Klan is founded.
1865-77	○	Southern blacks play leadership roles in government under **Reconstruction**; the 15th Amendment (1870) gives black men the right to vote.
1896	●	Supreme Court rules in a case called *Plessy versus Ferguson* that segregation is legal when facilities are "**separate but equal**." Discrimination and violence against blacks increase.
1910	○	W. E. B. Du Bois (1868–1963) founds National Association for the Advancement of Colored People (NAACP), fighting for equality for blacks.
1920s	●	African American culture (jazz music, dance, literature) flourishes during the **Harlem Renaissance**.
1954	○	Supreme Court rules in a case called ***Brown versus Board of Education*** of *Topeka* that school segregation is unconstitutional.
1957	●	Black students, backed by federal troops, enter recently desegregated Central High School in **Little Rock**, Arkansas.
1955-65	○	**Malcolm X** (1925–65) emerges as key spokesman for black nationalism.
1963	●	**Rev. Dr. Martin Luther King Jr.** (1929–68) gives his "I Have a Dream" speech at a march that inspired more than 200,000 people in Washington, D.C.—and many others throughout the nation.
1964	○	Sweeping **civil rights bill** banning racial discrimination is signed by President Lyndon Johnson.
1965	●	King leads protest march in **Selma**, Alabama; blacks riot in **Watts** section of Los Angeles.
1967	○	Gary, Indiana, and Cleveland, Ohio, are first major U.S. cities to elect black mayors; Thurgood Marshall (1908–93) becomes first African American on the Supreme Court.
2001	○	Colin Powell becomes first African American secretary of state.
2005	○	**Condoleezza Rice** becomes first African American woman secretary of state.
2008	●	Barack Obama claims the Democratic presidential nomination, the first African American candidate to head a major party ticket.

These people of color made big contributions to the growth of the United States as a free country.

HARRIET TUBMAN (1821-1913) escaped slavery when she was in her twenties. Before the Civil War, she repeatedly risked her life to lead hundreds of slaves to freedom by way of a network of homes and churches called the "Underground Railroad."

LEWIS LATIMER (1848-1928), American inventor and son of runaway slaves who patented a more durable version of Thomas Edison's light bulb by using a carbon filament instead of paper. He worked on the patent for the telephone and oversaw the installation of public lights throughout New York, Philadelphia, London, and Montreal. He also invented the first railroad-car toilet.

DALIP SINGH SAUND (1899–1973) was the first Asian elected to Congress. Born in India, Saund immigrated to the U.S., where he became a mathematician, farmer, and judge. In 1956 he was elected to the House of Representatives, opening the door for Asian Americans to enter U.S. politics.

THURGOOD MARSHALL (1908–1993) was one of the key lawyers in the fight to end legal segregation in the United States, winning many important cases. In 1967 he became the first African American to serve on the U.S. Supreme Court, the highest court in the nation.

ROSA PARKS (1913–2005) is called the mother of America's civil rights movement. When she refused to give up her bus seat to a white man in 1955, blacks in Montgomery, Alabama, started a boycott of the bus system, which led to desegregation of the city's buses. After her death she became the first woman (and 31st person) in history to lie in honor in the Capitol Rotunda in Washington, D.C.

CESAR CHAVEZ (1927-1993), a Mexican American who was raised in migrant worker camps, started a national farm workers union, the United Farm Workers of America, in 1966. Along with UFW cofounder **DOLORES HUERTA** (1930), he organized boycotts that eventually made growers agree to better conditions for field workers.

REV. DR. MARTIN LUTHER KING JR. (1929–1968) was the most influential leader of the U.S. civil rights movement from the mid-1950s to his assassination in 1968. In 1964 he received the Nobel Peace Prize. His wife, **CORETTA SCOTT KING** (1927-2006), helped carry on his work.

ELLISON S. ONIZUKA (1946-1986) was the first Asian American astronaut. He flew as a mission specialist in 1985. Sadly, he died in 1986 during another mission when the *Challenger* exploded just after launch.

ANTONIO VILLARAIGOSA (born 1953), a Mexican American, in 2005 became the first Latino mayor of Los Angeles since the 1870s. He is a former labor leader and speaker of the California State Assembly.

ELAINE CHAO (born 1954) moved with her family to the U.S. from Taiwan when she was eight years old and did not speak any English. After years of public service, including a term as director of the Peace Corps, Chao in 2001 became the 24th secretary of labor and the first Asian-American woman in U.S. history to be appointed to a president's cabinet.

BARACK OBAMA (born 1961) is the son of an American mother and Kenyan father. After serving in the Illinois Senate for eight years, he was elected to the U.S. Senate in 2004. From there he launched a campaign to be President of the United States, and was the Democratic nominee in 2008.

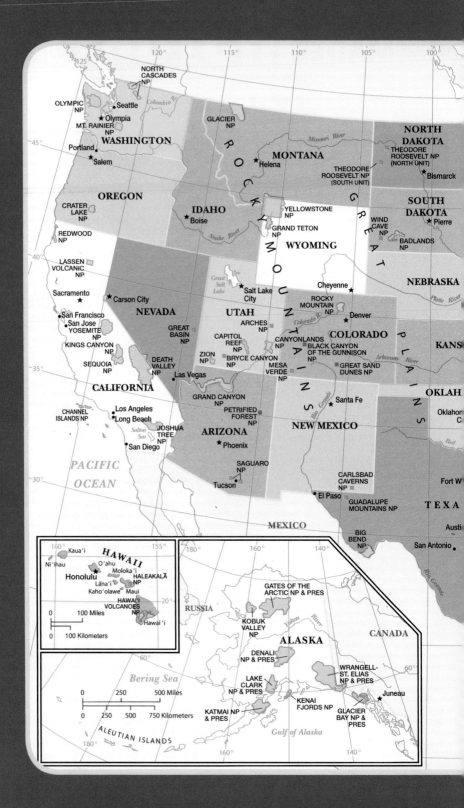

THE UNITED STATES

CANADA

Lake of the Woods

Lake Superior

Lake Huron

Lake Michigan

Lake Ontario

Lake Erie

SEURS NP

NESOTA

ISLE ROYALE NP

WISCONSIN

MICHIGAN

IOWA

ILLINOIS

INDIANA

OHIO

MISSOURI

KENTUCKY

ARKANSAS

TENNESSEE

MISSISSIPPI

ALABAMA

GEORGIA

LOUISIANA

MAINE

NEW YORK

VT. N.H.

MASS.

CONN. R.I.

PENNSYLVANIA

N.J.

DEL.

MD

WEST VIRGINIA

VIRGINIA

NORTH CAROLINA

SOUTH CAROLINA

FLORIDA

APPALACHIAN MTNS.

St. Paul

apolis

Madison

Milwaukee

Lansing

Detroit

Chicago

Cleveland

CUYAHOGA VALLEY NP

Columbus

Indianapolis

Springfield

Des Moines

Kansas City

Jefferson City

St. Louis

Frankfort

MAMMOTH CAVE NP

Nashville

Memphis

Little Rock

HOT SPRINGS NP

Jackson

Montgomery

Atlanta

Baton Rouge

New Orleans

ouston

Tallahassee

Jacksonville

Orlando

Tampa

St. Petersburg

Miami

BISCAYNE NP

EVERGLADES NP

DRY TORTUGAS NP

Charleston

Richmond

SHENANDOAH NP

Raleigh

GREAT SMOKY MTNS. NP

Columbia

CONGAREE NP

Augusta

ACADIA NP

Montpelier

Concord

Albany

Boston

Hartford

Providence

New York City

Trenton

Philadelphia

Harrisburg

Baltimore

Annapolis

Washington, D.C.

Dover

Tennessee

Mississippi River

Ohio River

ATLANTIC OCEAN

THE BAHAMAS

CUBA

THE UNITED STATES

⊛ National Capital
★ State Capital
• Other City
■ National Park

0   200   400 Miles

0   200   400   600 Kilometers

© GeoNova

ALABAMA comes from an Indian word for "tribal town."

Alaska

ALASKA comes from *alakshak*, the Aleutian (Eskimo) word meaning "peninsula" or "land that is not an island."

ARIZONA comes from a Pima Indian word meaning "little spring place" or the Aztec word *arizuma*, meaning "silver-bearing."

ARKANSAS is a variation of Quapaw, the name of an Indian tribe. Quapaw means "south wind."

CALIFORNIA is the name of an imaginary island in a Spanish story. It was named by Spanish explorers of Baja California, a part of Mexico.

COLORADO comes from a Spanish word meaning "red." It was first given to the Colorado River because of its reddish color.

CONNECTICUT comes from an Algonquin Indian word meaning "long river place."

DELAWARE is named after Lord De La Warr, the English governor of Virginia in colonial times.

FLORIDA, which means "flowery" in Spanish, was named by the explorer Ponce de León, who landed there during Easter.

GEORGIA was named after King George II of England, who granted the right to create a colony there in 1732.

HAWAII probably comes from *Hawaiki*, or *Owhyhee*, the native Polynesian word for "homeland."

IDAHO's name is of uncertain origin, but it may come from a Kiowa Apache name for the Comanche Indians.

Hawaii

ILLINOIS is the French version of *Illini*, an Algonquin Indian word meaning "men" or "warriors."

INDIANA means "land of the Indians."

IOWA comes from the name of an American Indian tribe that lived on the land that is now the state.

KANSAS comes from a Sioux Indian word that possibly meant "people of the south wind."

KENTUCKY comes from an Iroquois Indian word, possibly meaning "meadowland."

LOUISIANA, which was first settled by French explorers, was named after King Louis XIV of France.

MAINE means "the mainland." English explorers called it that to distinguish it from islands nearby.

Maine

MARYLAND was named after Queen Henrietta Maria, wife of King Charles I of England, who granted the right to establish an English colony there.

MASSACHUSETTS comes from an Indian word meaning "large hill place."

MICHIGAN comes from the Chippewa Indian words *mici gama*, meaning "great water" (referring to Lake Michigan).

MINNESOTA got its name from a Dakota Sioux Indian word meaning "cloudy water" or "sky-tinted water."

MISSISSIPPI is probably from Chippewa Indian words meaning "great river" or "gathering of all the waters," or from an Algonquin word, *messipi*.

MISSOURI comes from an Algonquin Indian term meaning "river of the big canoes."

Got Their Names

MONTANA comes from a Latin or Spanish word meaning "mountainous."

NEBRASKA comes from "flat river" or "broad water," an Omaha or Otos Indian name for the Platte River.

NEVADA means "snow-clad" in Spanish. Spanish explorers gave the name to the Sierra Nevada Mountains.

NEW HAMPSHIRE was named by an early settler after his home county of Hampshire, in England.

NEW JERSEY was named for the English Channel island of Jersey.

New Mexico

NEW MEXICO was given its name by 16th-century Spaniards in Mexico.

NEW YORK, first called New Netherland, was renamed for the Duke of York and Albany after the English took it from Dutch settlers.

NORTH CAROLINA, the northern part of the English colony of Carolana, was named for King Charles I.

NORTH DAKOTA comes from a Sioux Indian word meaning "friend" or "ally."

OHIO is the Iroquois Indian word for "good river."

OKLAHOMA comes from a Choctaw Indian word meaning "red man."

OREGON may have come from *Ouaricon-sint,* a name on an old French map that was once given to what is now called the Columbia River. That river runs between Oregon and Washington.

PENNSYLVANIA meaning "Penn's woods," was the name given to the colony founded by William Penn.

RHODE ISLAND may have come from the Dutch "Roode Eylandt" (red island) or may have been named after the Greek island of Rhodes.

Pennsylvania

SOUTH CAROLINA, the southern part of the English colony of Carolana, was named for King Charles I.

SOUTH DAKOTA comes from a Sioux Indian word meaning "friend" or "ally."

TENNESSEE comes from "Tanasi," the name of Cherokee Indian villages on what is now the Little Tennessee River.

TEXAS comes from a word meaning "friends" or "allies," used by the Spanish to describe some of the American Indians living there.

Texas

UTAH comes from a Navajo word meaning "upper" or "higher up."

VERMONT comes from two French words, *vert* meaning "green" and *mont* meaning "mountain."

VIRGINIA was named in honor of Queen Elizabeth I of England, who was known as the Virgin Queen because she was never married.

WASHINGTON was named after George Washington, the first president of the United States. It is the only state named after a president.

WEST VIRGINIA got its name from the people of western Virginia, who formed their own government during the Civil War.

WISCONSIN comes from a Chippewa name that is believed to mean "grassy place." It was once spelled *Ouisconsin* and *Mesconsing.*

WYOMING comes from Algonquin Indian words that are said to mean "at the big plains," "large prairie place," or "on the great plain."

FACTS About the STATES

After every state name is the postal abbreviation. The Area includes both land and water; it is given in square miles (sq mi) and square kilometers (sq km). Numbers in parentheses after Population, Area, and Entered Union show the state's rank compared with other states. City populations are for mid-2005.

ALABAMA
(AL) Heart of Dixie, Camellia State

POPULATION (2007): 4,627,851 (23rd) **AREA:** 52,419 sq mi (30th) (135,765 sq km) 🌼 Camellia 🐦 Yellowhammer 🌲 Southern longleaf pine 🎵 "Alabama" **ENTERED UNION:** December 14, 1819 (22nd) ⭐ Montgomery **LARGEST CITIES (WITH POP.):** Birmingham, 229,800; Montgomery, 204,086; Mobile, 191,411; Huntsville, 171,327

⚙ clothing and textiles, metal products, transportation equipment, paper, industrial machinery, food products, lumber, coal, oil, natural gas, livestock, peanuts, cotton

Birmingham •

⭐ Montgomery

Montgomery was the capital of the Confederacy during the early months of the Civil War between February 18 and May 21, 1861. The Confederate capital then moved to Richmond, Virginia.

ALASKA
(AK) The Last Frontier

POPULATION (2007): 683,478 (47th) **AREA:** 663,267 sq mi (1st) (1,717,854 sq km) 🌼 Forget-me-not 🐦 Willow ptarmigan 🌲 Sitka spruce 🎵 "Alaska's Flag" **ENTERED UNION:** January 3, 1959 (49th) ⭐ Juneau **LARGEST CITIES (WITH POP.):** Anchorage, 279,671; Fairbanks, 34,540; Juneau, 30,690; Sitka, 8,874

⚙ oil, natural gas, fish, food products, lumber and wood products, fur

Anchorage •

Juneau ⭐

Travelers can use a plane, a boat, maybe even try a catapult, but Juneau is the only state capital that can not be reached by road.

ARIZONA
(AZ) Grand Canyon State

POPULATION (2007): 6,338,755 (16th) **AREA:** 113,998 sq mi (6th) (295,253 sq km) 🌼 Blossom of the Saguaro cactus 🐦 Cactus wren 🌲 Paloverde 🎵 "Arizona" **ENTERED UNION:** February 14, 1912 (48th) ⭐ Phoenix **LARGEST CITIES (WITH POP.):** Phoenix, 1,552,259; Tucson, 525,529; Mesa, 452,933; Glendale, 253,152; Chandler, 246,399; Scottsdale, 235,677

⚙ electronic equipment, transportation and industrial equipment, instruments, printing and publishing, copper and other metals

Phoenix ⭐

Tucson •

You can find London Bridge in Lake Havasu City, AZ. Built in London, England, in the 1830s, the bridge was taken down and sold to Robert P. McCulloch in 1968. He re-assembled it on Lake Havasu in 1971.

WAforKids.com Go to *www.WAforKids.com* for even more U.S. facts.

294

ARKANSAS (AR) Natural State, Razorback State

POPULATION (2007): 2,834,797 (32nd) **AREA:** 53,179 sq mi (29th) (137,733 sq km) 🌸Apple blossom 🐦Mockingbird 🌲Pine 🎵"Arkansas" **ENTERED UNION:** June 15, 1836 (25th) ⭐Little Rock **LARGEST CITIES (WITH POP.):** Little Rock, 187,452; Fort Smith, 84,375; Fayetteville, 72,208; Springdale, 66,881

⚙ food products, paper, electronic equipment, industrial machinery, metal products, lumber and wood products, livestock, soybeans, rice, cotton, natural gas

Little Rock ⭐

The only working diamond mine in the U.S. is located in Murfreesboro, AR, at Crater of Diamonds State Park. It is also the only diamond-producing site in the world that is open to the public. Visitors can keep whatever diamonds they find.

CALIFORNIA (CA) Golden State

POPULATION (2007): 36,553,215 (1st) **AREA:** 163,696 sq mi (3rd) (423,971 sq km) 🌸Golden poppy 🐦California valley quail 🌲California redwood 🎵"I Love You, California" **ENTERED UNION:** September 9, 1850 (31st) ⭐Sacramento **LARGEST CITIES (WITH POP.):** Los Angeles, 3,834,340; San Diego, 1,266,731; San Jose, 939,899; San Francisco, 764,976; Long Beach, 466,520; Fresno, 470,508; Sacramento, 460,242; Oakland, 401,489

⚙ transportation and industrial equipment, electronic equipment, oil, natural gas, motion pictures, milk, cattle, fruit, vegetables

Sacramento ⭐

San Francisco

Los Angeles •

San Diego •

The iconic "Hollywood" hillside sign in Los Angeles was built as an advertisement for an upscale real estate development in 1923. It originally said "Hollywoodland" and was lit by 4,000 light bulbs. The "land" was removed by the city in 1949.

COLORADO (CO) Centennial State

POPULATION (2007): 4,861,515 (22nd) **AREA:** 104,094 sq mi (8th) (269,602 sq km) 🌸Rocky Mountain columbine 🐦Lark bunting 🌲Colorado blue spruce 🎵"Where the Columbines Grow" **ENTERED UNION:** August 1, 1876 (38th) ⭐Denver **LARGEST CITIES (WITH POP.):** Denver, 588,349; Colorado Springs, 376,427; Aurora, 311,794; Lakewood, 140,305; Fort Collins, 133,899

⚙ instruments and industrial machinery, food products, printing and publishing, metal products, electronic equipment, oil, coal, cattle

Denver ⭐

Colorado Springs •

The Anasazi Indians built entire cities into cliffsides across the American southwest. The settlements built between 1100 and 1300 at Mesa Verde in southwestern Colorado are the largest and best preserved.

Key: 🌸Flower 🐦Bird 🌲Tree 🎵Song ⭐Capital ⚙Important Products

CONNECTICUT (CT) Constitution State, Nutmeg State

Hartford

POPULATION (2007): 3,502,309 (29th) **AREA:** 5,543 sq mi (48th) (14,356 sq km) ✿Mountain laurel 🐦American robin 🌳White oak 🎵"Yankee Doodle" **ENTERED UNION:** January 9, 1788 (5th) ⭐ Hartford **LARGEST CITIES (WITH POP.):** Bridgeport, 136,695; New Haven, 123,932; Hartford, 124,563; Stamford, 118,475; Waterbury, 107,174

⚙ aircraft parts, helicopters, industrial machinery, metals and metal products, electronic equipment, printing and publishing, medical instruments, chemicals, dairy products, stone

did you know? The Hartford Courant *is the country's oldest newspaper in continuous publication. It started as a weekly in 1764. George Washington once placed an ad in the paper to rent out some of his land in Mount Vernon, VA.*

DELAWARE (DE) First State, Diamond State

Dover

POPULATION (2007): 864,764 (45th) **AREA:** 2,489 sq mi (49th) (6,446 sq km) ✿Peach blossom 🐦Blue hen chicken 🌳American holly 🎵"Our Delaware" **ENTERED UNION:** December 7, 1787 (1st) ⭐Dover **LARGEST CITIES (WITH POP.):** Wilmington, 72,868; Dover, 35,811; Newark, 29,992

⚙ chemicals, transportation equipment, food products, chickens

did you know? *The Mason-Dixon line is an L-shaped border that separates Delaware, Pennsylvania, and Maryland. Charles Mason and Jeremiah Dixon drew it in the 1760s to settle a dispute between the colonies. The border is marked to this day with stones about every 1,000 feet.*

FLORIDA (FL) Sunshine State

Tallahassee

Jacksonville

Miami •

POPULATION (2007): 18,251,243 (4th) **AREA:** 65,755 sq mi (22nd) (170,305 sq km) ✿Orange blossom 🐦Mockingbird 🌳Sabal palmetto palm 🎵"Old Folks at Home" **ENTERED UNION:** March 3, 1845 (27th) ⭐Tallahassee **LARGEST CITIES (WITH POP.):** Jacksonville, 805,605; Miami, 409,719; Tampa, 336,823; St. Petersburg, 246,407; Hialeah, 212,217; Orlando, 227,907; Ft. Lauderdale, 183,606

⚙ electronic and transportation equipment, industrial machinery, printing and publishing, food products, citrus fruits, vegetables, livestock, phosphates, fish

did you know? *The Daytona 500, NASCAR's most prestigious race, was first run in 1959. The race is run each February at Daytona International Speedway.*

●WAforKids.com Go to *www.WAforKids.com* for even more U.S. facts.

296

GEORGIA (GA) Empire State of the South, Peach State

POPULATION (2007): 9,544,750 (9th) **AREA:** 59,425 sq mi (24th) (153,910 sq km) 🌸Cherokee rose 🐦Brown thrasher 🌳Live oak 🎵"Georgia on My Mind" **ENTERED UNION:** January 2, 1788 (4th) ⭐Atlanta **LARGEST CITIES (WITH POP.):** Atlanta, 519,145; Augusta, 192,142; Columbus, 187,046; Savannah, 130,331; Athens, 114,063

⚙ clothing and textiles, transportation equipment, food products, paper, chickens, peanuts, peaches, clay

★ Atlanta

did you know? *Hartsfield-Jackson Atlanta International Airport is the busiest in the world. Nearly a million planes land or depart from it every year. It is the largest single employer in the state providing some 56,000 jobs.*

HAWAII (HI) Aloha State

POPULATION (2007): 1,283,388 (42nd) **AREA:** 10,931 sq mi (43rd) (28,311 sq km) 🌸Yellow hibiscus 🐦Hawaiian goose 🌳Kukui 🎵"Hawaii Ponoi" **ENTERED UNION:** August 21, 1959 (50th) ⭐Honolulu **LARGEST CITIES (WITH POP.):** Honolulu, 375,571; Hilo, 40,759; Kailua, 36,513; Kaneohe, 34,970

⚙ food products, pineapples, sugar, printing and publishing, fish, flowers

★ Honolulu

did you know? *The most massive volcano in the world, Mauna Loa ("Long Mountain"), is located on the island of Hawaii, the "Big" island. About four-fifths of the volcano lies underwater, but its peak reaches 13,681 feet above sea level.*

IDAHO (ID) Gem State

POPULATION (2007): 1,499,402 (39th) **AREA:** 83,570 sq mi (14th) (216,445 sq km) 🌸Syringa 🐦Mountain bluebird 🌳White pine 🎵"Here We Have Idaho" **ENTERED UNION:** July 3, 1890 (43rd) ⭐Boise **LARGEST CITIES (WITH POP.):** Boise, 202,832; Nampa, 79,249; Meridian, 64,642; Pocatello, 54,572; Idaho Falls, 53,279

⚙ potatoes, hay, wheat, cattle, milk, lumber and wood products, food products

★ Boise

did you know? *In 1951, an experimental nuclear reactor built near Arco, ID became the first to produce electricity that was usable in homes and buildings. In 1955, Arco became the world's first town to have all of its power generated by a nuclear reactor.*

Key: 🌸Flower 🐦Bird 🌳Tree 🎵Song ⭐Capital ⚙Important Products

ILLINOIS
(IL) Prairie State

POPULATION (2007): 12,852,548 (5th) **AREA:** 57,914 sq mi (25th) (149,997 sq km) 🌼Native violet 🐦Cardinal 🌳White oak 🎵"Illinois" **ENTERED UNION:** December 3, 1818 (21st) ⭐Springfield **LARGEST CITIES (WITH POP.):** Chicago, 2,836,658; Aurora, 170,855; Rockford, 156,596; Joliet, 144,316; Naperville, 142,479; Springfield, 117,090; Peoria, 113,546

⚙ industrial machinery, metals and metal products, printing and publishing, electronic equipment, food products, corn, soybeans, hogs

did you know? The Chicago River, which today flows away from Lake Michigan, used to flow in the opposite direction. Between 1898 and 1900, engineers dug what became known as the Sanitary and Ship Canal, or Main Canal, connecting the Chicago River to the Mississippi River. This caused the water to reverse its flow.

Chicago
Springfield ⭐

INDIANA
(IN) Hoosier State

POPULATION (2007): 6,345,289 (15th) **AREA:** 36,418 sq mi (38th) (94,322 sq km) 🌸Peony 🐦Cardinal 🌳Tulip poplar 🎵"On the Banks of the Wabash, Far Away" **ENTERED UNION:** December 11, 1816 (19th) ⭐Indianapolis **LARGEST CITIES (WITH POP.):** Indianapolis, 805,489; Fort Wayne, 251,247; Evansville, 116,253; South Bend, 104,069; Gary, 96,429

⚙ transportation equipment, electronic equipment, industrial machinery, iron and steel, metal products, corn, soybeans, livestock, coal

Indianapolis ⭐

did you know? Two main routes of the Underground Railroad, a movement that helped free black slaves, went through Indiana. From 1827 to 1847, the Coffins ran a stop, in Newport (now Fountain City). They helped more than 2,000 runaway slaves escape.

IOWA
(IA) Hawkeye State

POPULATION (2007): 2,988,046 (30th) **AREA:** 56,272 sq mi (26th) (145,744 sq km) 🌼Wild rose 🐦Eastern goldfinch 🌳Oak 🎵"The Song of Iowa" **ENTERED UNION:** December 28, 1846 (29th) ⭐Des Moines **LARGEST CITIES (WITH POP.):** Des Moines, 196,998; Cedar Rapids, 126,396; Davenport, 98,975; Sioux City, 82,684

⚙ corn, soybeans, hogs, cattle, industrial machinery, food products

Des Moines ⭐

did you know? The only member of the Lewis and Clark expedition to die was Sgt. Charles Floyd. He died from peritonitis near present-day Sioux City, IA. A monument stands where he was buried.

 WAforKids.com Go to *www.WAforKids.com* for even more U.S. facts.

298

KANSAS (KS) Sunflower State

POPULATION (2007): 2,775,997 (33rd) **AREA:** 82,277 sq mi (15th) (213,096 sq km) 🌼Native sunflower 🐦Western meadowlark 🌲Cottonwood 🎵"Home on the Range" **ENTERED UNION:** January 29, 1861 (34th) ⭐Topeka **LARGEST CITIES (WITH POP.):** Wichita, 361,420; Overland Park, 169,403; Kansas City, 142,320; Topeka, 122,642

🔧 cattle, aircraft and other transportation equipment, industrial machinery, food products, wheat, corn, hay, oil, natural gas

did you know? The pioneers of flight Amelia Earhart and Clyde Cessna were both from Kansas. The state is still one of the world's major airplane builders.

KENTUCKY (KY) Bluegrass State

POPULATION (2007): 4,241,474 (26th) **AREA:** 40,409 sq mi (37th) (104,659 sq km) 🌼Goldenrod 🐦Cardinal 🌲Tulip poplar 🎵"My Old Kentucky Home" **ENTERED UNION:** June 1, 1792 (15th) ⭐Frankfort (population, 27,098) **LARGEST CITIES (WITH POP.):** Louisville, 557,789; Lexington, 279,044; Owensboro, 55,398; Bowling Green, 54,244

🔧 coal, industrial machinery, electronic equipment, transportation equipment, metals, tobacco, cattle

did you know? More than 360 miles of natural caves and underground passageways have been mapped under Mammoth Cave National Park. It's the largest network of natural tunnels in the world and extends up to 1,000 miles.

LOUISIANA (LA) Pelican State

POPULATION (2007): 4,293,204 (25th) **AREA:** 51,840 sq mi (31st) (134,265 sq km) 🌼Magnolia 🐦Eastern brown pelican 🌲Cypress 🎵"Give Me Louisiana" **ENTERED UNION:** April 30, 1812 (18th) ⭐Baton Rouge **LARGEST CITIES (WITH POP.):** New Orleans, 239,124; Baton Rouge, 227,071; Shreveport, 199,569; Lafayette, 113,544

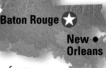

🔧 natural gas, oil, chemicals, transportation equipment, paper, food products, cotton, fish

did you know? Louisiana is the only state whose legal system comes from Napoleonic Code, the system put into place in France by Napoleon Bonaparte. This is because Louisiana used to belong to France. The law codes of the other 49 states are based on English common law, which was practiced in England. The differences are minor.

Key: 🌼Flower 🐦Bird 🌲Tree 🎵Song ⭐Capital 🔧Important Products

MAINE (ME) Pine Tree State

Augusta

POPULATION (2007): 1,317,207 (40th) **AREA:** 35,385 sq mi (39th) (91,647 sq km) 🌲White pine cone and tassel 🐦Chickadee 🌳Eastern white pine 🎵"State of Maine Song" **ENTERED UNION:** March 15, 1820 (23rd) ⭐Augusta **LARGEST CITIES (WITH POP.):** Portland, 62,825; Lewiston, 35,234; Bangor, 31,853

⚙ paper, transportation equipment, wood and wood products, electronic equipment, footwear, clothing, potatoes, milk, eggs, fish, seafood

Georgeana, now the town of York, was the first city in America to be chartered by England in 1641.

MARYLAND (MD) Old Line State, Free State

Baltimore •
Annapolis ⭐
⭐
Washington, D.C.

POPULATION (2007): 5,618,344 (19th) **AREA:** 12,407 sq mi (42nd) (32,134 sq km) 🌼Black-eyed susan 🐦Baltimore oriole 🌳White oak 🎵"Maryland, My Maryland" **ENTERED UNION:** April 28, 1788 (7th) ⭐Annapolis (**LARGEST CITIES (WITH POP.):** Baltimore, 637,455; Frederick, 59,220; Rockville, 58,706; Gaithersburg, 57,670; Bowie, 53,193

⚙ printing and publishing, food products, transportation equipment, electronic equipment, chickens, soybeans, corn, stone

Maryland's official state sport is jousting. Competitors on horseback ride through a course and use their lances to collect rings. Competitors are called either "knights" or "maids."

MASSACHUSETTS (MA) Bay State, Old Colony

Boston ⭐

POPULATION (2007): 6,449,755 (14th) **AREA:** 10,555 sq mi (44th) (27,337 sq km) 🌸Mayflower 🐦Chickadee 🌳American elm 🎵"All Hail to Massachusetts" **ENTERED UNION:** February 6, 1788 (6th) ⭐Boston **LARGEST CITIES (WITH POP.):** Boston, 599,351; Worcester, 173,966; Springfield, 149,938; Lowell, 103,512; Cambridge, 101,388

⚙ industrial machinery, electronic equipment, fish, instruments, printing, publishing, metal products, flowers, shrubs, cranberries

Pink flamingos, the tacky plastic lawn ornaments, were first made by a young sculptor named Don Featherstone in 1957. Every "authentic" pink flamingo was made by Union Products, of Leominster from 1957 until the factory closed in 2006.

WAforKids.com Go to *www.WAforKids.com* for even more U.S. facts.

300

MICHIGAN (MI) — Great Lakes State, Wolverine State

POPULATION (2007): 10,071,822 (8th) **AREA:** 96,716 sq mi (11th) (250,493 sq km) 🌸Apple blossom 🐦Robin 🌲White pine 🎵"Michigan, My Michigan" **ENTERED UNION:** January 26, 1837 (26th) ⭐Lansing **LARGEST CITIES (WITH POP.):** Detroit, 916,952; Grand Rapids, 193,627; Warren, 134,223; Sterling Heights, 127,349; Ann Arbor, 115,092; Lansing, 114,947; Flint, 114,662

⚙️ automobiles, industrial machinery, metal products, office furniture, plastic products, chemicals, food products, milk, corn, natural gas, iron ore, blueberries

did you know? Battle Creek, the headquarters for Kellogg's, Ralston Foods, and the Post Cereal division of Kraft Foods, is known as the Cereal Capital of the World.

Lansing ⭐ Detroit ●

MINNESOTA (MN) — North Star State, Gopher State

POPULATION (2007): 5,197,621 (21st) **AREA:** 86,939 sq mi (12th) (225,171 sq km) 🌸Pink and white lady slipper 🐦Common loon 🌲Red pine 🎵"Hail! Minnesota" **ENTERED UNION:** May 11, 1858 (32nd) ⭐St. Paul **LARGEST CITIES (WITH POP.):** Minneapolis, 377,392; St. Paul, 277,251; Rochester, 99,121; Duluth, 84,397; Bloomington, 81,446

⚙️ industrial machinery, printing and publishing, computers, food products, scientific and medical instruments, milk, hogs, cattle, corn, soybeans, iron ore

did you know? The "Land of 10,000 Lakes" has 11,842 lakes bigger than 10 acres within its borders. One out of every six Minnesotans owns a boat, the highest rate of any state.

Minneapolis St. Paul ⭐

MISSISSIPPI (MS) Magnolia State

POPULATION (2007): 2,918,785 (31st) **AREA:** 48,430 sq mi (32nd) (125,433 sq km) 🌸Magnolia 🐦Mockingbird 🌲Magnolia 🎵"Go, Mississippi!" **ENTERED UNION:** December 10, 1817 (20th) ⭐Jackson **LARGEST CITIES (WITH POP.):** Jackson, 175,710; Gulfport, 66,271; Hattiesburg, 50,233; Biloxi, 44,292

⚙️ transportation equipment, furniture, electrical machinery, lumber and wood products, cotton, rice, chickens, cattle

did you know? In 1902, President Theodore "Teddy" Roosevelt went bear hunting in Mississippi. He refused to shoot a bear that had been tied to a tree by his companions. The story inspired some toy makers to create a stuffed toy bear, which they called "Teddy's Bear." That's how the teddy bear was born.

⭐ Jackson

Key: 🌸Flower 🐦Bird 🌲Tree 🎵Song ⭐Capital ⚙️Important Products

MISSOURI (MO) Show Me State

POPULATION (2007): 5,878,415 (18th) **AREA:** 69,704 sq mi (21st) (180,533 sq km) 🌺Hawthorn 🐦Bluebird 🌳Dogwood 🎵"Missouri Waltz" **ENTERED UNION:** August 10, 1821 (24th) ⭐Jefferson City **LARGEST CITIES (WITH POP.):** Kansas City, 450,375; St. Louis, 350,759; Springfield, 154,777; Independence, 110,704

⚙ transportation equipment, electrical and electronic equipment, printing and publishing, food products, cattle, hogs, milk, soybeans, corn, hay, lead

did you know? *The waffle cone for ice cream was first sold at the 1904 World's Fair in St. Louis.*

MONTANA (MT) Treasure State

POPULATION (2007): 957,861 (44th) **AREA:** 147,042 sq mi (4th) (380,837 sq km) 🌺Bitterroot 🐦Western meadowlark 🌲Ponderosa pine 🎵"Montana" **ENTERED UNION:** November 8, 1889 (41st) ⭐Helena **LARGEST CITIES (WITH POP.):** Billings, 101,876; Missoula, 67,165; Great Falls, 58,827; Bozeman, 37,981

⚙ cattle, copper, gold, wheat, barley, wood and paper products

did you know? *The capital, Helena, was started by miners who found gold in a creek, or gulch, in 1864. It was first called Crabtown after one of the miners, John Crab. The city's main street, last Chance Gulch, covers the length of the gulch.*

NEBRASKA (NE) Cornhusker State

POPULATION (2007): 1,774,571 (38th) **AREA:** 77,354 sq mi (16th) (200,346 sq km) 🌺Goldenrod 🐦Western meadowlark 🌳Cottonwood 🎵"Beautiful Nebraska" **ENTERED UNION:** March 1, 1867 (37th) ⭐Lincoln **LARGEST CITIES (WITH POP.):** Omaha, 424,482; Lincoln, 248,744; Bellevue, 48,391; Grand Island, 44,802

⚙ cattle, hogs, milk, corn, soybeans, hay, wheat, sorghum, food products, industrial machinery

did you know? *Nebraska has the only unicameral (one house) state legislature in the U.S. Called the Nebraska Unicameral, its members are called Senators and they serve four-year terms. The head of their legislature is called the Speaker.*

●WAforKids.com Go to *www.WAforKids.com* for even more U.S. facts.

302

NEVADA (NV) Sagebrush State, Battle Born State, Silver State

POPULATION (2007): 2,565,382 (35th) **AREA:** 110,561 sq mi (7th) (286,352 sq km) ✿Sagebrush 🐦Mountain bluebird 🌲Single-leaf piñon, bristlecone pine 🎵"Home Means Nevada" **ENTERED UNION:** October 31, 1864 (36th) ★Carson City **LARGEST CITIES (WITH POP.):** Las Vegas, 558,880; Henderson, 249,386; Reno, 214,853; North Las Vegas, 212,114

⚙ gold, silver, cattle, hay, food products, plastics, chemicals

did you know? Extending for about 110 miles, Lake Mead is the largest artificial lake in the U.S. It provides water for Nevada, Arizona, California, and northern Mexico. It was formed on the Colorado River when the Hoover Dam was built in 1936.

★ Carson City

Las Vegas •

NEW HAMPSHIRE (NH) Granite State

POPULATION (2007): 1,315,828 (41st) **AREA:** 9,350 sq mi (46th) (24,216 sq km) ✿Purple lilac 🐦Purple finch 🌲White birch 🎵"Old New Hampshire" **ENTERED UNION:** June 21, 1788 (9th) ★Concord **LARGEST CITIES (WITH POP.):** Manchester, 108,874; Nashua, 86,837; Concord, 42,392

⚙ industrial machinery, electric and electronic equipment, metal products, plastic products, dairy products, maple syrup and maple sugar

did you know? New Hampshire was the first colony to declare its independence from England and start its own government in 1776—six months before the Declaration of Independence was signed.

Concord ★

NEW JERSEY (NJ) Garden State

POPULATION (2007): 8,685,920 (11th) **AREA:** 8,721 sq mi (47th) (22,587 sq km) ✿Purple violet 🐦Eastern goldfinch 🌲Red oak 🎵none **ENTERED UNION:** December 18, 1787 (3rd) ★Trenton **LARGEST CITIES (WITH POP.):** Newark, 280,135; Jersey City, 242,389; Paterson, 146,545; Elizabeth, 124,862; Trenton, 82,804

⚙ chemicals, pharmaceuticals/drugs, electronic equipment, nursery and greenhouse products, food products, tomatoes, blueberries, and peaches

did you know? The city of Paterson is one of the birthplaces of the Industrial Revolution in America. In the 1790s, the Society for Establishing Useful Manufacturers built a factory on the Passaic River. Until the early 20th century, Paterson produced many types of goods, including large amounts of silk fabric, inspiring the nickname "Silk City."

Newark •

★

Trenton

Key: ✿Flower 🐦Bird 🌲Tree 🎵Song ★Capital ⚙Important Products

NEW MEXICO (NM) Land of Enchantment

POPULATION (2007): 1,969,915 (36th) **AREA:** 121,589 sq mi (5th) (314,914 sq km) 🌼Yucca 🐦Roadrunner 🌳Piñon 🎵"O, Fair New Mexico" **ENTERED UNION:** January 6, 1912 (47th) ⭐Santa Fe **LARGEST CITIES (WITH POP.):** Albuquerque, 518,271; Las Cruces, 89,722; Santa Fe, 73,199; Rio Rancho, 75,978

⚙ electronic equipment, foods, machinery, clothing, lumber, transportation equipment, hay, onions, chiles

 In 1950, the town of hot Springs renamed itself Truth or Consequences, NM, after a popular game show of the time.

NEW YORK (NY) Empire State

POPULATION (2007): 19,297,729 (3rd) **AREA:** 54,556 sq mi (27th) (141,299 sq km) 🌼Rose 🐦Bluebird 🌳Sugar maple 🎵"I Love New York" **ENTERED UNION:** July 26, 1788 (11th) ⭐Albany **LARGEST CITIES (WITH POP.):** New York, 8,272,527; Buffalo, 272,632; Rochester, 206,759; Yonkers, 199,244; Syracuse, 139,079

⚙ books and magazines, automobile and aircraft parts, toys and sporting goods, electronic equipment, machinery, clothing and textiles, metal products, milk, cattle, hay, apples

 New York City is the largest city in the U.S. and was the nation's first capital. It was also the home of another major first in American history— the first pizza restaurant in the U.S. opened there in 1895.

NORTH CAROLINA (NC) Tar Heel State, Old North State

POPULATION (2007): 9,061,032 (10th) **AREA:** 53,819 sq mi (28th) (139,391 sq km) 🌼Dogwood 🐦Cardinal 🌳Pine 🎵"The Old North State" **ENTERED UNION:** November 21, 1789 (12th) ⭐Raleigh **LARGEST CITIES (WITH POP.):** Charlotte, 671,588; Raleigh, 375,806; Greensboro, 247,847; Durham, 217,847; Winston-Salem, 215,348; Fayetteville 171,853

⚙clothing and textiles, tobacco and tobacco products, industrial machinery, electronic equipment, furniture, cotton, soybeans, peanuts

The Outer Banks, a line of offshore sandy islands, were full of pirates and smugglers in the early 1700s. The most notorious, Blackbeard, terrorized sailors along the coast before the crews of two British ships sent him to his watery grave there in 1718.

●WAforKids.com Go to *www.WAforKids.com* for even more U.S. facts.

304

NORTH DAKOTA (ND) Peace Garden State

POPULATION (2007): 639,715 (48th) **AREA:** 70,700 sq mi (19th) (183,112 sq km) Wild prairie rose Western meadowlark American elm "North Dakota Hymn" **ENTERED UNION:** November 2, 1889 (39th) Bismarck **LARGEST CITIES (WITH POP.):** Fargo, 92,660; Bismarck, 59,503; Grand Forks, 51,740; Minot, 35,281

★ Bismarck

wheat, barley, hay, sunflowers, sugar beets, cattle, sand and gravel, food products, farm equipment, high-tech electronics

did you know? *During their expedition, Lewis and Clark spent, 1804-05, in North Dakota. They named their fort after the Mandan tribe that lived nearby. They met Sacagawea, who gave birth to her son at Fort Mandan.*

OHIO (OH) Buckeye State

POPULATION (2007): 11,466,917 (7th) **AREA:** 44,825 sq mi (34th) (116,096 sq km) Scarlet carnation Cardinal Buckeye "Beautiful Ohio" **ENTERED UNION:** March 1, 1803 (17th) Columbus **LARGEST CITIES (WITH POP.):** Columbus, 747,755; Cleveland, 438,042; Cincinnati, 332,458; Toledo, 295,029; Akron, 207,934; Dayton, 155,461

Cleveland
Columbus ★
Cincinnati

metal and metal products, transportation equipment, industrial machinery, rubber and plastic products, electronic equipment, printing and publishing, chemicals, food products, corn, soybeans, livestock, milk

did you know? *Though it was admitted to the Union in 1803, Ohio didn't technically become a state until 1953. Because of an oversight, Congress didn't formally vote on the resolution to admit Ohio as a state until August 7, 1953, when it made Ohio's statehood official, retroactive to 1803.*

OKLAHOMA (OK) Sooner State

Tulsa
★ Oklahoma City

POPULATION (2007): 3,617,316 (28th) **AREA:** 69,898 sq mi (20th) (181,035 sq km) Mistletoe Scissor-tailed flycatcher Redbud "Oklahoma!" **ENTERED UNION:** November 16, 1907 (46th) Oklahoma City **LARGEST CITIES (WITH POP.):** Oklahoma City, 547,274; Tulsa, 384,037; Norman, 106,707; Lawton, 91,568; Broken Arrow, 90,714

natural gas, oil, cattle, nonelectrical machinery, transportation equipment, metal products, wheat, hay

did you know? *The American Indian nations called the Five Civilized Tribes (Cherokee, Chickasaw, Choctaw, Creek, and Seminole) were resettled in eastern Oklahoma by the federal government between 1817 and 1842.*

Key: 🌼Flower 🐦Bird 🌲Tree 🎵Song ★Capital ⚙Important Products

OREGON (OR) Beaver State

POPULATION (2007): 3,747,455 (27th) **AREA:** 98,381 sq mi (9th) (254,806 sq km) 🌸Oregon grape 🐦Western meadowlark 🌲Douglas fir 🎵"Oregon, My Oregon" **ENTERED UNION:** February 14, 1859 (33rd) ⭐Salem **LARGEST CITIES (WITH POP.):** Portland, 550,396; Salem, 151,913; Eugene, 149,004; Gresham, 99,721

⚙️lumber and wood products, electronics and semiconductors, food products, paper, cattle, hay, vegetables, Christmas trees

did you know? The name Portland was settled by a coin toss between two founders, Asa Lovejoy and Francis Pettygrove, who both wanted to name the city after their home towns. Pettygrove, from Portland, Maine, won the toss. Lovejoy, from Boston, Massachusetts, lost.

PENNSYLVANIA (PA) Keystone State

POPULATION (2007): 12,432,792 (6th) **AREA:** 46,055 sq mi (33rd) (119,282 sq km) 🌸Mountain laurel 🐦Ruffed grouse 🌲Hemlock 🎵"Pennsylvania" **ENTERED UNION:** December 12, 1787 (2nd) ⭐Harrisburg (population, 47,196) **LARGEST CITIES (WITH POP.):** Philadelphia, 1,449,634; Pittsburgh, 311,218; Allentown, 107,117; Erie, 103,650

⚙️ iron and steel, coal, industrial machinery, printing and publishing, food products, electronic equipment, transportation equipment, stone, clay and glass products

did you know? An enormous fire has been burning since 1962 in the coal mines below the town of Centralia. Fewer than 20 people remain in the town. Surface temperatures have been measured at over 700°F.

RHODE ISLAND (RI) Little Rhody, Ocean State

POPULATION (2007): 1,057,832 (43rd) **AREA:** 1,545 sq mi (50th) (4,002 sq km) 🌸Violet 🐦Rhode Island red 🌲Red maple 🎵"Rhode Island" **ENTERED UNION:** May 29, 1790 (13th) ⭐ Providence **LARGEST CITIES (WITH POP.):** Providence, 172,459; Warwick, 85,097; Cranston, 80,463; Pawtucket, 72,342

⚙️ costume jewelry, toys, textiles, machinery, electronic equipment, fish

did you know? A third of Rhode Island's area is water. Narragansett Bay is the largest in New England and contains about 35 islands. More than 20 million tourists visit the tiny state each year to boat, fish, and bask along its 384 miles of sandy coast. The smallest state also has the 11th biggest fishing industry.

SOUTH CAROLINA (SC) Palmetto State

POPULATION (2007): 4,407,709 (24th) **AREA:** 32,020 sq mi (40th) (82,931 sq km) ✿Yellow jessamine ☻Carolina wren ☙Palmetto ♪"Carolina" **ENTERED UNION:** May 23, 1788 (8th) ✪Columbia **LARGEST CITIES (WITH POP.):** Columbia, 124,818; Charleston, 110,015; North Charleston, 91,421; Rock Hill, 64,858

✿ clothing and textiles, chemicals, industrial machinery, metal products, livestock, tobacco, Portland cement

Columbia

did you know?

Gullahs are descendants of West African slaves who have chosen to live a traditional African life along the coast and islands of South Carolina, Georgia, and Florida. They have their own language, arts, crafts, religious beliefs, and foods that have been passed down for generations.

SOUTH DAKOTA (SD) Mt. Rushmore State, Coyote State

POPULATION (2007): 796,214 (46th) **AREA:** 77,116 sq mi (17th) (199,730 sq km) ✿Pasqueflower ☻Chinese ring-necked pheasant ☙Black Hills spruce ♪"Hail, South Dakota" **ENTERED UNION:** November 2, 1889 (40th) ✪Pierre **LARGEST CITIES (WITH POP.):** Sioux Falls, 151,505; Rapid City, 63,997; Aberdeen, 24,410

✿ food and food products, machinery, electric and electronic equipment, corn, soybeans

✪ Pierre

did you know?

The Corn Palace in Mitchell is redecorated every year with themed murals made from corn, grains, and grasses by local artisans. When winter comes, birds and squirrels munch away the exterior.

TENNESSEE (TN) Volunteer State

POPULATION (2007): 6,156,719 (17th) **AREA:** 42,143 sq mi (36th) (109,150 sq km) ✿Iris ☻Mockingbird ☙Tulip poplar ♪"My Homeland, Tennessee"; "When It's Iris Time in Tennessee"; "My Tennessee"; "Tennessee Waltz"; "Rocky Top" **ENTERED UNION:** June 1, 1796 (16th) ✪Nashville **LARGEST CITIES (WITH POP.):** Memphis, 674,028; Nashville, 590,807; Knoxville, 183,546; Chattanooga, 169,884

✿ chemicals, machinery, vehicles, food products, metal products, publishing, electronic equipment, paper products, rubber and plastic products, tobacco

✪ Nashville

Memphis

did you know?

The Grand Ole Opry, the world's longest-running live radio program, was first broadcast from Nashville in 1925. It was originally called the WSM Barn Dance, but the name changed to the Grand Ole Opry in 1927.

Key: ✿Flower ☻Bird ☙Tree ♪Song ✪Capital ✿Important Products

TEXAS (TX) Lone Star State

POPULATION (2007): 23,904,380 (2nd) **AREA:** 268,581 sq mi (2nd) (695,622 sq km) ❀Bluebonnet 🐦Mockingbird 🌳Pecan 🎵"Texas, Our Texas" **ENTERED UNION:** December 29, 1845 (28th) ⭐Austin **LARGEST CITIES (WITH POP.):** Houston, 2,208,180; San Antonio, 1,328,984; Dallas, 1,240,499; Austin, 743,074; Fort Worth, 681,818; El Paso, 606,913; Arlington, 371,038; Corpus Christi, 285,507; Plano, 260,796

⚙ oil, natural gas, cattle, milk, eggs, transportation equipment, chemicals, clothing, industrial machinery, electrical and electronic equipment, cotton, grains

Dallas •
• El Paso
Austin ⭐ Houston •
San Antonio •

did you know? *Texas is the only state that is allowed by law to split into smaller states if its people want it to.*

UTAH (UT) Beehive State

POPULATION (2007): 2,645,330 (34th) **AREA:** 84,899 sq mi (13th) (219,887 sq km) ❀Sego lily 🐦Seagull 🌳Blue spruce 🎵"Utah, This is the Place" **ENTERED UNION:** January 4, 1896 (45th) ⭐Salt Lake City **LARGEST CITIES (WITH POP.):** Salt Lake City, 180,651; West Valley City, 122,374; Provo, 117,592; West Jordan, 102,445

⚙ transportation equipment, medical instruments, electronic parts, food products, steel, copper, cattle, corn, hay, wheat, barley

Salt Lake City

did you know? *Early white settlers in Utah were saved from starvation by seagulls, the state bird. In 1848, hordes of locusts came into the Salt Lake Valley and began devouring the settlers' crops. All seemed lost before a flock of seagulls flew in and ate the locusts, saving the crops.*

VERMONT (VT) Green Mountain State

POPULATION (2007): 621,254 (49th) **AREA:** 9,614 sq mi (45th) (24,900 sq km) ❀Red clover 🐦Hermit thrush 🌳Sugar maple 🎵"These Green Mountains" **ENTERED UNION:** March 4, 1791 (14th) ⭐Montpelier **LARGEST CITIES (WITH POP.):** Burlington, 38,531; Essex Junction, 19,465; South Burlington, 17,445; Colchester, 17,207; Rutland, 16,826

⚙ machine tools, furniture, scales, books, computer parts, foods, dairy products, apples, maple syrup

Montpelier
⭐

did you know? *The Green Mountain Boys who famously fought against the British during the American Revolution were originally formed in 1770 to fight off New York settlers. When the revolution broke out, the Vermonters and New Yorkers set aside their differences and united against the British.*

●WAforKids.com Go to *www.WAforKids.com* for even more U.S. facts.

308

VIRGINIA (VA) Old Dominion

POPULATION (2007): 7,712,091 (12th) **AREA:** 42,774 sq mi (35th) (110,784 sq km) 🌸Dogwood 🐦Cardinal 🌳Dogwood 🎵"Carry Me Back to Old Virginia" **ENTERED UNION:** June 25, 1788 (10th) ⭐Richmond **LARGEST CITIES (WITH POP.):** Virginia Beach, 434,743; Norfolk, 235,747; Chesapeake, 219,154; Arlington, 204,568; Richmond, 200,123; Newport News, 179,153

⚙ transportation equipment, textiles, chemicals, printing, machinery, electronic equipment, food products, coal, livestock, tobacco, wood products, furniture

 Nancy Langhorne Astor in 1919 became the first woman to serve in the British House of Commons. She was born and raised in Virginia.

Alexandria
Richmond
Norfolk

WASHINGTON (WA) Evergreen State

POPULATION (2007): 6,468,424 (13th) **AREA:** 71,300 sq mi (18th) (184,666 sq km) 🌸Western rhododendron 🐦Willow goldfinch 🌳Western hemlock 🎵"Washington, My Home" **ENTERED UNION:** November 11, 1889 (42nd) ⭐Olympia **LARGEST CITIES (WITH POP.):** Seattle, 594,210; Spokane, 200,975; Tacoma, 196,520; Vancouver, 161,436; Bellevue, 121,347

⚙ aircraft, lumber, pulp and paper, machinery, electronics, computer software, aluminum, processed fruits and vegetables

 Mount Rainier is the tallest volcano in the lower 48 states. It hasn't erupted in centuries. However, another volcano in Washington, Mount St. Helens, had a huge eruption on May 18, 1980. It lasted 9 hours and destroyed 230 square miles of woods. It is still active today.

Seattle
Olympia

WEST VIRGINIA (WV) Mountain State

POPULATION (2007): 1,812,035 (37th) **AREA:** 24,230 sq mi (41st) (62,755 sq km) 🌸Big rhododendron 🐦Cardinal 🌳Sugar maple 🎵"The West Virginia Hills"; "This Is My West Virginia"; "West Virginia, My Home Sweet Home" **ENTERED UNION:** June 20, 1863 (35th) ⭐Charleston **LARGEST CITIES (WITH POP.):** Charleston, 50,478; Huntington, 48,982; Parkersburg, 31,617; Morgantown, 29,361; Wheeling, 29,101

⚙ coal, natural gas, fabricated metal products, chemicals, automobile parts, aluminum, steel, machinery, cattle, hay, apples, peaches, tobacco

 Charleston

did you know? The Golden Delicious variety of apple is the state fruit. It grew by chance on a family farm about 1900. It is now one of the most popular types of apples.

Key: 🌸Flower 🐦Bird 🌳Tree 🎵Song ⭐Capital ⚙Important Products

WISCONSIN (WI) Badger State

POPULATION (2007): 5,601,640 (20th) **AREA:** 65,498 sq mi (23rd) (169,639 sq km) 🌸Wood violet 🐦Robin 🌲Sugar maple 🎵"On, Wisconsin!" **ENTERED UNION:** May 29, 1848 (30th) ⭐Madison **LARGEST CITIES (WITH POP.):** Milwaukee, 602,191; Madison, 228,775; Green Bay, 100,781; Kenosha, 96,265; Racine, 70,017

⚙ paper products, printing, milk, butter, cheese, foods, food products, motor vehicles and equipment, medical instruments and supplies, plastics, corn, hay, vegetables

Madison ⭐ • **Milwaukee**

The first ever ice cream sundaes were served in the towns of Manitowoe and Two Rivers in 1851.

WYOMING (WY) Cowboy State

POPULATION (2007): 522,830 (50th) **AREA:** 97,814 sq mi (10th) (253,337 sq km) 🌸Indian paintbrush 🐦Western meadowlark 🌲Plains cottonwood 🎵"Wyoming" **ENTERED UNION:** July 10, 1890 (44th) ⭐Cheyenne **LARGEST CITIES (WITH POP.):** Cheyenne, 55,641; Casper, 53,003; Laramie, 27,241

⚙ oil, natural gas, petroleum (oil) products, cattle, wheat, beans

Cheyenne ⭐

Dude Ranches offer "tenderfeet" the opportunity to live the ropin' and ridin' way of the cowboy. Three brothers, Howard, Willis, and Alden Eaton received so many guests at their ranch (including Pres. Theodore Roosevelt) that they opened the first dude ranch near Sheridan in 1904.

COMMONWEALTH OF PUERTO RICO (PR)

⭐ **San Juan**

HISTORY: Christopher Columbus landed in Puerto Rico in 1493. Puerto Rico was a Spanish colony for centuries, then was ceded (given) to the United States in 1898 after the Spanish-American War. In 1952, still associated with the United States, Puerto Rico became a commonwealth with its own constitution. **POPULATION (2007):** 3,942,375 **AREA:** 5,324 sq mi (13,789 sq km) 🌸Maga 🐦Reinita 🌲Ceiba **NATIONAL ANTHEM:** "La Borinqueña" ⭐San Juan **LARGEST CITIES (WITH POP.):** San Juan, 424,951; Bayamón, 220,629; Carolina, 187,607; Ponce, 180,376; Caguas, 142,984

⚙ chemicals, food products, electronic equipment, clothing and textiles, industrial machinery, coffee, sugarcane, fruit, hogs

Puerto Ricans have most of the same rights as other Americans, but they cannot vote in U.S. presidential elections and they have no voting representatives in the federal government. They don't have to pay federal taxes.

●WAforKids.com Go to *www.WAforKids.com* for even more U.S. facts.

310

WASHINGTON, D.C.
The Capital of the
UNITED STATES

LAND AREA: 61 square miles **POPULATION (2007):** 588,292
FLOWER: American beauty rose **BIRD:** Wood thrush

WEB SITE *www.dc.gov* • *www.washington.org*

HISTORY The District of Columbia, or Washington, D.C., became the capital of the United States in 1800, when the federal government moved there from Philadelphia. The city of Washington was designed and built to be the capital. It was named after George Washington. Many of its major sights are on the Mall, an open grassy area that runs from the Capitol to the Potomac River.

CAPITOL, which houses the U.S. Congress, is at the east end of the Mall on Capitol Hill. Its dome can be seen from far away.

JEFFERSON MEMORIAL, a circular marble building located near the Potomac River, is partly based on a design by Thomas Jefferson for the University of Virginia.

LIBRARY OF CONGRESS, research library for Congress and the largest library in the world, is on Independence Avenue across the street from the Capitol.

LINCOLN MEMORIAL, at the west end of the Mall, is built of white marble and styled like a Greek temple. Inside is a large, seated statue of Abraham Lincoln. His Gettysburg Address is carved on a nearby wall.

NATIONAL ARCHIVES, on Constitution Avenue, holds the Declaration of Independence, Constitution, and Bill of Rights.

NATIONAL WORLD WAR II MEMORIAL, located between the Lincoln Memorial and the Washington Monument at the Mall, honors the 16 million Americans who served during the war.

SMITHSONIAN INSTITUTION has 18 museums (2 of them are in New York City), including the new National Museum of the American Indian, the National Air and Space Museum and the Museum of Natural History. The National Zoo is part of the Smithsonian.

U.S. HOLOCAUST MEMORIAL MUSEUM presents the history of the Nazis' murder of more than six million Jews and millions of other people from 1933 to 1945. The exhibit *Daniel's Story* tells the story of the Holocaust from a child's point of view.

WASHINGTON MONUMENT is a white marble pillar, or obelisk, standing on the Mall and rising to more than 555 feet. From the top there are wonderful views of the city.

WHITE HOUSE, at 1600 Pennsylvania Avenue, has been the home of every U.S. president except George Washington.

WOMEN IN MILITARY SERVICE FOR AMERICA MEMORIAL, stands near the entrance to Arlington National Cemetery in Virginia. It honors the 2 million women who have served in the U.S. armed forces.

VIETNAM VETERANS MEMORIAL, located near the Lincoln Memorial, includes a wall with all the names of those killed or missing in action during the conflict.

◀ Jefferson Memorial

WEATHER

What is a sundog? ➡ **see page 312**

How to Read a Weather Map

Meteorologists around the world basically use the same set of symbols to show weather conditions. This allows them to quickly and easily communicate with one another. The symbols in a newspaper or TV weather map might vary somewhat from the ones shown below.

By examining this map, meteorologists can predict what the weather might be like in the future. They are able to do this because they know how the weather usually changes. For example, dry, calm weather typically occurs in high-pressure areas while precipitation is seen in low-pressure areas. Storms usually come before a cold front. As a cold front passes through an area, its temperature drops. Light rain might herald a warm front. As a warm front moves through an area, it gets warmer.

Because so many things—big and small—can influence the weather, only forecasts of up to five days tend to be accurate.

Selected Weather Symbols		
Sky Cover	**Fronts**	**Weather**
○ Clear	▲▲ Cold front	▪ Rain ═ Fog
◖ Scattered	●●● Warm front	✳ Snow ∞ Haze
● Overcast	∿ Stationary front	⚡ Thunderstorm
Wind: ◎ Calm	—— 1-2 knots (1-2 mph)	⌐ 3-7 knots (3-8 mph)
L Low Pressure Center		**H** High Pressure Center

WEIRD WEATHER FACTS

Winds are known by specific names in certain parts of the world. Here is a sample:

Föhn, or foehn—Warm, dry wind that travels down a mountain's leeward side, or the side of the mountain facing away from the wind. This occurs after a cool, moist wind travels up and over the side of the mountain facing the wind. Originally used to refer to a wind in the Alps.

Chinook—A föhn wind common in the Rocky Mountains. Named after a Native American tribe.

Mistral—Strong, cold, dry wind that blows from the northwest across the southern coast of France. It can reach speeds of up to about 85 miles per hour.

Sirocco—Warm, humid wind that originates as a hot, dry wind in North Africa. It picks up moisture as it crosses the Mediterranean and brings rain to Europe.

A **sundog**, or parhelia, is a phenomenon caused by light passing through or reflecting off of ice crystals in the atmosphere. Sundogs appear as bright spots of light on either side of the Sun. If you drew a line through sundogs and the Sun, the line would be parallel to the horizon.

RECORD TEMPERATURES BY STATE

(Through 2007)

Coldest Temperature →

Hottest Temperature →

STATE	Lowest °F	Lowest Latest date	Highest °F	Highest Latest date
Alabama	−27	Jan. 30, 1966	112	Sept. 5, 1925
Alaska	−80	Jan. 23, 1971	100	June 27, 1915
Arizona	−40	Jan. 7, 1971	128	June 29, 1994
Arkansas	−29	Feb. 13, 1905	120	Aug. 10, 1936
California	−45	Jan. 20, 1937	134	July 10, 1913
Colorado	−61	Feb. 1, 1985	118	July 11, 1888
Connecticut	−32	Jan. 22, 1961	106	July 15, 1995
Delaware	−17	Jan. 17, 1893	110	July 21, 1930
Florida	−2	Feb. 13, 1899	109	June 29, 1931
Georgia	−17	Jan. 27, 1940	112	Aug. 20, 1983
Hawaii	12	May 17, 1979	100	Apr. 27, 1931
Idaho	−60	Jan. 18, 1943	118	July 28, 1934
Illinois	−36	Jan. 5, 1999	117	July 14, 1954
Indiana	−36	Jan. 19, 1994	116	July 14, 1936
Iowa	−47	Feb. 3, 1996	118	July 20, 1934
Kansas	−40	Feb. 13, 1905	121	July 24, 1936
Kentucky	−37	Jan. 19, 1994	114	July 28, 1930
Louisiana	−16	Feb. 13, 1899	114	Aug. 10, 1936
Maine	−48	Jan. 19, 1925	105	July 10, 1911
Maryland	−40	Jan. 13, 1912	109	July 10, 1936
Massachusetts	−35	Jan. 12, 1981	107	Aug. 2, 1975
Michigan	−51	Feb. 9, 1934	112	July 13, 1936
Minnesota	−60	Feb. 2, 1996	114	July 6, 1936
Mississippi	−19	Jan. 30, 1966	115	July 29, 1930
Missouri	−40	Feb. 13, 1905	118	July 14, 1954
Montana	−70	Jan. 20, 1954	117	July 5, 1937
Nebraska	−47	Dec. 22, 1989	118	July 24, 1936
Nevada	−50	Jan. 8, 1937	125	June 29, 1994
New Hampshire	−47	Jan. 29, 1934	106	July 4, 1911
New Jersey	−34	Jan. 5, 1904	110	July 10, 1936
New Mexico	−50	Feb. 1, 1951	122	June 27, 1994
New York	−52	Feb. 18, 1979	108	July 22, 1926
North Carolina	−34	Jan. 21, 1985	110	Aug. 21, 1983
North Dakota	−60	Feb. 15, 1936	121	July 6, 1936
Ohio	−39	Feb. 10, 1899	113	July 21, 1934
Oklahoma	−27	Jan. 18, 1930	120	June 27, 1994
Oregon	−54	Feb. 10, 1933	119	Aug. 10, 1898
Pennsylvania	−42	Jan. 5, 1904	111	July 10, 1936
Rhode Island	−25	Feb. 5, 1996	104	Aug. 2, 1975
South Carolina	−19	Jan. 21, 1985	111	June 28, 1954
South Dakota	−58	Feb. 17, 1936	120	July 15, 2006
Tennessee	−32	Dec. 30, 1917	113	Aug. 9, 1930
Texas	−23	Feb. 8, 1933	120	June 28, 1994
Utah	−69	Feb. 1, 1985	117	July 5, 1985
Vermont	−50	Dec. 30, 1933	105	July 4, 1911
Virginia	−30	Jan. 22, 1985	110	July 15, 1954
Washington	−48	Dec. 30, 1968	118	Aug. 5, 1961
West Virginia	−37	Dec. 30, 1917	112	July 10, 1936
Wisconsin	−55	Feb. 4, 1996	114	July 13, 1936
Wyoming	−66	Feb. 9, 1933	115	Aug. 8, 1983

Record temperatures may have occurred on earlier dates. Dates listed here are for most recent occurrence of a record temperature.

WEIGHTS & MEASURES

How many feet in a mile? ➡ **page 316**

Metrology isn't the study of weather. (That's meteorology.) It is the science of measurement. Almost everything you use every day is measured—either when it is made or when it's sold. Materials for buildings and parts for machines must be measured carefully so they will fit together. Clothes have sizes so you'll know which to choose. Many items sold in a supermarket are priced by weight or by volume.

EARLIEST MEASUREMENTS

The human body was the first "ruler." An "inch" was the width of a thumb; a "hand" was five fingers wide; a "foot" was—you guessed it—the length of a foot! A "cubit" ran from the elbow to the tip of the middle finger (about 20 inches), and a "yard" was the length of a whole arm.

Later, measurements came from daily activities, like plowing. A "furlong" was the distance an ox team could plow before stopping to rest (now we say it is about 220 yards). The trouble with these units was that they were different from person to person, place to place, and ox to ox.

MEASUREMENTS WE USE TODAY

The official system in the U.S. is the customary system (sometimes called the imperial or English system). Scientists and most other countries use the International System of Units (metric system). The Weights and Measures Division of the U.S. National Institute of Standards and Technology (NIST) makes sure that a gallon of milk in California is the same as one in New York. When the NIST was founded in 1901, there were as many as eight different "standard" gallons in the U.S. and four different legal measures of a "foot" in Brooklyn, New York, alone.

ANCIENT MEASURE

1 foot =
length of a person's foot

12 inches

1 yard =
from nose to fingertip

3 feet or 36 inches

1 acre =
land an ox could plow in a day

4,840 square yards

MODERN MEASURE

TAKING TEMPERATURES

There are two main systems for measuring temperature. One is **Fahrenheit** (abbreviated F). The other is **Celsius** (abbreviated C). Another word for Celsius is Centigrade.

Zero degrees (0°) Celsius is equal to 32 degrees (32°) Fahrenheit.

To convert from Celsius to Fahrenheit:

Multiply by 1.8 and add 32.
($°F = 1.8 \times °C + 32$)

Example: $20°C \times 1.8 = 36$; $36 + 32 = 68°F$

To convert from Fahrenheit to Celsius, reverse the process:

Subtract 32 and divide by 1.8.

Example: $68°F - 32 = 36$; $36 \div 1.8 = 20°C$

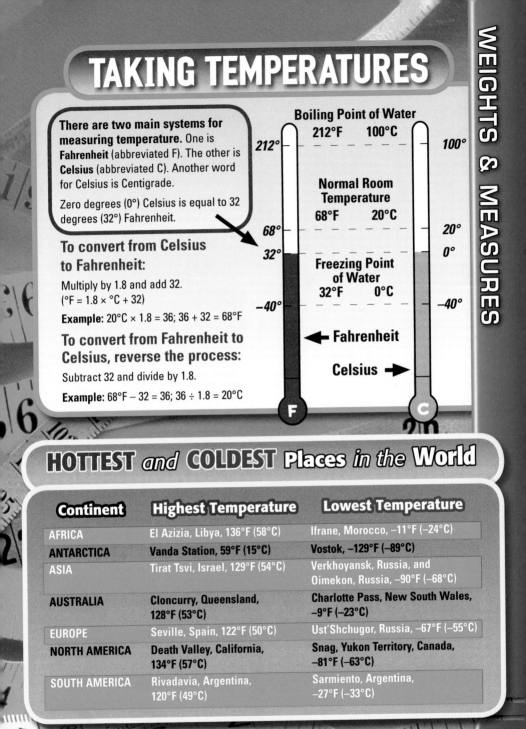

Boiling Point of Water
212°F   100°C

Normal Room Temperature
68°F   20°C

Freezing Point of Water
32°F   0°C

◄ **Fahrenheit**

Celsius ►

212°   100°
68°   20°
32°   0°
−40°   −40°

F   C

HOTTEST and COLDEST Places in the World

Continent	Highest Temperature	Lowest Temperature
AFRICA	El Azizia, Libya, 136°F (58°C)	Ifrane, Morocco, −11°F (−24°C)
ANTARCTICA	Vanda Station, 59°F (15°C)	Vostok, −129°F (−89°C)
ASIA	Tirat Tsvi, Israel, 129°F (54°C)	Verkhoyansk, Russia, and Oimekon, Russia, −90°F (−68°C)
AUSTRALIA	Cloncurry, Queensland, 128°F (53°C)	Charlotte Pass, New South Wales, −9°F (−23°C)
EUROPE	Seville, Spain, 122°F (50°C)	Ust'Shchugor, Russia, −67°F (−55°C)
NORTH AMERICA	Death Valley, California, 134°F (57°C)	Snag, Yukon Territory, Canada, −81°F (−63°C)
SOUTH AMERICA	Rivadavia, Argentina, 120°F (49°C)	Sarmiento, Argentina, −27°F (−33°C)

did you know?

Six of the ten warmest years on record for the contiguous U.S. have occurred since 1998, according to the National Climatic Data Center Annual Report for the Climate of 2007. Annual temperature records date back to 1895.

315

LENGTH

The basic unit of **length** in the U.S. system is the **inch**. Length, width, and thickness all use the inch or larger related units.

1 foot (ft) = 12 inches (in.)

1 yard (yd) = 3 feet = 36 inches

1 rod (rd) = 5½ yards

1 furlong (fur) = 40 rods = 220 yards
= 660 feet

1 mile (mi) (also called statute mile) =
8 furlongs = 1,760 yards = 5,280 feet

1 nautical mile = 6,076.1 feet = 1.15 statute miles

1 league = 3 miles

AREA

Area is used to measure a section of a two-dimensional surface like the floor or a piece of paper. Most area measurements are given in **square units**. Land is measured in **acres**.

1 square foot (sq ft) = 144 square inches
(sq in.)

1 square yard (sq yd) = 9 square feet =
1,296 square inches

1 square rod (sq rd) = 30¼ square yards

1 acre = 160 square rods = 4,840 square yards
= 43,560 square feet

1 square mile (sq mi) = 640 acres

CAPACITY

Units of **capacity** are used to measure how much of something will fit into a container. **Liquid measure** is used to measure liquids, such as water or gasoline. **Dry measure** is used with large amounts of solid materials, like grain or fruit. Although both liquid and dry measures use the terms "pint" and "quart," they mean different amounts and should not be confused.

Dry Measure

1 quart (qt) = 2 pints (pt)
1 peck (pk) = 8 quarts
1 bushel (bu) = 4 pecks

Liquid Measure

1 gill = 4 fluid ounces (fl oz)
1 pint (pt) = 4 gills = 16 ounces (oz)
1 quart (qt) = 2 pints = 32 ounces
1 gallon (gal) = 4 quarts = 128 ounces

For measuring most U.S. liquids,
1 barrel (bbl) = 31½ gallons

For measuring oil, 1 barrel = 42 gallons

Cooking Measurements

The measurements used in cooking are based on the **fluid ounce**.

1 teaspoon (tsp) = ⅙ fluid ounce (fl oz)
1 tablespoon (tbsp) = 3 teaspoons
= ½ fluid ounce
1 cup = 16 tablespoons = 8 fluid ounces
1 pint = 2 cups
1 quart (qt) = 2 pints (pt)
1 gallon (gal) = 4 quarts

VOLUME

The amount of space taken up by a three-dimensional object (or the amount of space available within an object) is measured in **volume**. Volume is usually expressed in **cubic units**. If you wanted to buy a room air conditioner and needed to know how much space there was to be cooled, you could measure the room in cubic feet.

1 cubic foot (cu ft) = 12 inches x 12 inches
x 12 inches = 1,728
cubic inches (cu in.)
1 cubic yard (cu yd) = 27 cubic feet

DEPTH

Some measurements of length are used to measure ocean depth and distance.

1 fathom = 6 feet (ft)
1 cable = 120 fathoms = 720 feet

WEIGHT

Although 1 cubic foot of popcorn and 1 cubic foot of rock take up the same amount of space, it wouldn't feel the same if you tried to lift them. We measure heaviness as **weight**. Most objects are measured in **avoirdupois weight** (pronounced a-ver-de-POIZ):

1 dram (dr) = 27.344 grains (gr)
1 ounce (oz) = 16 drams = 437.5 grains
1 pound (lb) = 16 ounces
1 hundredweight (cwt) = 100 pounds
1 ton = 2,000 pounds (also called short ton)

THE **METRIC** SYSTEM

The metric system was created in France in 1795. Standardized in 1960 and given the name International System of Units, it is now used in most countries and in scientific works. The system is based on 10, like the decimal counting system. The basic unit for length is the **meter**. The **liter** is a basic unit of volume or capacity, and the **gram** is a basic unit of mass. Related units are made by adding a prefix to the basic unit. The prefixes and their meanings are:

milli-   = $\dfrac{1}{1,000}$

centi- = $\dfrac{1}{100}$

deci-   = $\dfrac{1}{10}$

deka-   = **10**

hecto- = **100**

kilo-   = **1,000**

For Example

millimeter (mm) = $\dfrac{1}{1,000}$ of a meter

kilometer (km) = **1,000** meters

milligram (mg) = $\dfrac{1}{1,000}$ of a gram

kilogram (kg) = **1,000** grams

To get a rough idea of measurements in the metric system, it helps to know that a **liter** is a little more than a quart. A **meter** is a little over a yard. A **kilogram** is a little over 2 pounds. And a **kilometer** is just over half a mile.

Homework Tip Converting Measurements

From:	Multiply by:	To get:	From:	Multiply by:	To get:
inches	2.5400	centimeters	centimeters	0.3937	inches
inches	0.0254	meters	centimeters	0.0328	feet
feet	30.4800	centimeters	meters	39.3701	inches
feet	0.3048	meters	meters	3.2808	feet
yards	0.9144	meters	meters	1.0936	yards
miles	1.6093	kilometers	kilometers	0.6210	miles
square inches	6.4516	square centimeters	square centimeters	0.1550	square inches
square feet	0.0929	square meters	square meters	10.7639	square feet
square yards	0.8361	square meters	square meters	1.1960	square yards
acres	0.4047	hectares	hectares	2.4710	acres
cubic inches	16.3871	cubic centimeters	cubic centimeters	0.0610	cubic inches
cubic feet	0.0283	cubic meters	cubic meters	35.3147	cubic feet
cubic yards	0.7646	cubic meters	cubic meters	1.3080	cubic yards
quarts (liquid)	0.9464	liters	liters	1.0567	quarts (liquid)
ounces	28.3495	grams	grams	0.0353	ounces
pounds	0.4536	kilograms	kilograms	2.2046	pounds

Each of the five sections in this chapter tells the history of a major region of the world: the Middle East, Africa, Asia, Europe, or the Americas. Major events from ancient times to the present are described under the headings for each region.

THE ANCIENT MIDDLE EAST

4000–3000 B.C. The world's first cities are built by the Sumerian peoples in Mesopotamia, now southern Iraq. Sumerians develop a kind of writing called **cuneiform**. Egyptians develop a kind of writing called **hieroglyphics**.

▲ *hieroglyphics*

2700 B.C. Egyptians begin building the great pyramids in the desert.

1792 B.C. Some of the first written laws are created in Babylonia. They are called the Code of Hammurabi.

1200 B.C. Hebrew people settle in Canaan in Palestine after escaping from slavery in Egypt. They are led by the prophet Moses.

1000 B.C. King David unites the Hebrews in one strong kingdom. ▶

ANCIENT PALESTINE

Palestine was invaded by many different peoples after 1000 B.C., including the Babylonians, Egyptians, Persians, and Romans.

336 B.C. Alexander the Great, King of Macedonia, builds an empire from Egypt to India.

ISLAM: A RELIGION GROWS IN THE MIDDLE EAST A.D. 610–632

Around 610, the prophet Muhammad starts to proclaim and teach Islam. This religion spreads from Arabia to all the neighboring regions in the Middle East and North Africa. Its followers are called Muslims.

THE KORAN

The holy book of Islam is the Koran. It was related by Muhammad beginning in 611.

▲ *The Koran*

THE SPREAD OF ISLAM

The Arab armies that went across North Africa brought great change:

• The people who lived there were converted to Islam.

• The Arabic language replaced many local languages as an official language. North Africa is still an Arabic-speaking region today, and Islam is the major faith.

63 B.C. Romans conquer Palestine and make it part of their empire.

Around 4 B.C. Jesus Christ, the founder of the Christian religion, is born in Bethlehem. He is crucified about A.D. 29.

A.D. 632 Muhammad dies. By now, Islam is accepted in Arabia as a religion.

641 Arab Muslims conquer the Persians.

Late 600s Islam begins to spread to the west into Africa and Spain.

▼ *The pyramids at Giza*

THE MIDDLE EAST

THE UMAYYAD AND ABBASID DYNASTIES The Umayyads (661-750) and the Abbasids (750-1256) are the first two Muslim-led dynasties. Both empires stretch across northern Africa and the Middle East into Asia.

711–732 Umayyads invade Europe but are defeated by Frankish leader Charles Martel in France. This defeat halts the spread of Islam into Western Europe.

1071 Muslim Turks conquer Jerusalem.

1095–1291 Europeans try to take back Jerusalem and other parts of the Middle East for Christians during the Crusades.

1300-1900s The Ottoman Turks, who are Muslims, create a huge empire, covering the Middle East, North Africa, and part of Eastern Europe. European countries take over portions of it beginning in the 1800s.

1914-1918 World War I begins in 1914. Most of the Middle East falls under British or French control.

1921 Two new Arab kingdoms are created: Transjordan and Iraq. The French take control of Syria and Lebanon.

1922 Egypt becomes independent from Britain.

JEWS MIGRATE TO PALESTINE Jews began migrating to Palestine in the 1880s. In 1945, after World War II, many Jews who survived the Holocaust migrated to Palestine.

1948 The state of Israel is created.

THE ARAB-ISRAELI WARS Arab countries near Israel (Egypt, Iraq, Jordan, Lebanon, and Syria) attack the new country in 1948 but fail to destroy it. Israel and its neighbors fight wars again in 1956, 1967, and 1973. Israel wins each war. In the 1967 war, Israel captures the Sinai Desert from Egypt, the Golan Heights from Syria, and the West Bank from Jordan.

1979 Egypt and Israel sign a peace treaty. Israel returns the Sinai to Egypt.

◀ *Anwar al-Sadat, Jimmy Carter, Menachem Begin celebrate signing of peace treaty.*

THE MIDDLE EAST AND OIL About 20% of the oil we use to drive cars, heat homes, and run machines comes from the Middle East. Many countries rely on oil imports from the region, which has more than half the world's crude oil reserves.

The 1990s and 2000s

• In 1991, the U.S. and its allies go to war with Iraq after Iraq invades Kuwait. Iraq is defeated and signs a peace agreement but is accused of violating it. In 2003, the U.S., Britain, and other allies invade Iraq and remove the regime of Saddam Hussein. Free elections are held and a democratic government is formed, but violence there continues.

• Tensions between Israel and the Palestinians increase. In 2005, Israel pulls out from Gaza. In 2006, Palestinian elections in the West Bank and Gaza bring Hamas, an organization that has historically been dedicated to eliminating the state of Israel, to power.

Dome of the Rock and the Western Wall, Jerusalem ▼

319

ANCIENT AFRICA

ANCIENT AFRICA In ancient times, northern Africa was dominated by the Egyptians, Greeks, and Romans. However, we know very little about the lives of ancient Africans south of the Sahara Desert. They did not have written languages. What we learn about them comes from weapons, tools, and other items from their civilization.

2000 B.C. The Nubian Kingdom of Kush, rich with gold, ivory, and jewels, arises south of Egypt. It is a major center of art, learning, and trade until around A.D. 350.

1000 B.C. Bantu-speaking people around Cameroon begin an 1,800-year expansion into much of eastern and southern Africa.

500 B.C. Carthage, an empire centered in Tunisia, becomes rich and powerful through trading. Its ports span the African coast of the Mediterranean Sea. Rome defeats Carthage and its most famous leader, ◄Hannibal, during the second Punic War (218-201 B.C.).

• The Nok in Nigeria are the earliest users of iron for tools and weapons south of the Sahara Desert. They are also known for their terracotta sculptures.

• The Christian Kingdom of Aksum in northern Ethiopia becomes a wealthy trading center on the Red Sea for treasures like ivory. It makes its own coins and monuments, many of which survive today.

By A.D. 700 Ghana, the first known empire south of the Sahara Desert, takes power through trade around the upper Senegal and Niger Rivers. Its Mande people control the trade in gold from nearby mines to Arabs in the north.

By 900 Arab Muslim merchants bring Islam to the Bantu speakers along the east coast of Africa, creating the Swahili language and culture. Traders in Kenya and Tanzania export ivory, slaves, perfumes, and gold to Asia.

1054-1145 Islamic Berbers unite into the Almoravid Kingdom centered at Marrakech, Morocco. They spread into Ghana and southern Spain.

1230-1400s A Mande prince named Sundiata (the "Lion King") forms the Mali Kingdom where Ghana once stood. Timbuktu becomes its main city.

1250-1400s Great Zimbabwe becomes the largest settlement (12,000-20,000 Bantu-speaking people) in southern Africa.

1464-1591 As Mali loses power, Songhai rises to become the third and final great empire of western Africa.

1481 Portugal sets up the first permanent European trading post south of the Sahara Desert at Elmina, Ghana. Slaves, in addition to gold and ivory, are soon exported.

1483-1665 Kongo, the most powerful kingdom on central Africa's west coast, provides thousands of slaves each year for Portugal. Portugal's colony Angola overtakes the Kongo in 1665.

Camel train moving across the Sahara

AFRICA

1650-1810 Slave trading peaks across the "Slave Coast" from eastern Ghana to western Nigeria as competing African states sell tens of thousands of captured foes each year to competing European traders.

THE AFRICAN SLAVE TRADE

African slaves were taken to the Caribbean to harvest sugar on European plantations. Later, slaves were taken to South America and the United States. The ships from Africa were overcrowded and diseased. About 20% of the slaves died during the long journey.

1652 The Dutch East India Company sets up a supply camp in southern Africa at the Cape of Good Hope (later Cape Town). Dutch settlers and French Protestants called Huguenots establish Cape Colony. Their descendants are known as the Boers or Afrikaners and develop a distinct language and culture.

1792 Freed slaves, mostly from Britain and the Americas, found Freetown in Sierra Leone.

1803 Denmark is the first European country to ban slave trading. Britain follows in 1807, the U.S. in 1808. Most European nations ban the trade by 1820, but illegal trading continues for decades.

1814 Britain purchases the Dutch South African colony at Cape Town. British colonists arrive after 1820.

1816-28 The Zulus, ruled by the chieftain Shaka, dominate eastern South Africa.

1835-43 The "Great Trek" (march) of the Boers away from British Cape Town.

1884-85 European nations meet in Berlin and agree to divide control of Africa. No African states are invited to the agreements. The "Scramble for Africa" lasts until World War I. Only Ethiopia and Liberia remain independent.

1899-1902 Great Britain and the Boers fight in South Africa in the Boer War. The Boers accept British rule but are allowed a role in government.

1948 The white Afrikaner-dominated South African government creates the policy of apartheid ("apartness"), the total separation of races. Blacks are banned from many restaurants, theaters, schools, and jobs. Apartheid sparks protests, many of which end in bloodshed.

1957 Ghana gains independence from Britain, becoming the first territory in Africa below the Sahara to regain freedom from European rule. Over the next 20 years, the rest of Africa gains independence.

1990-94 South Africa abolishes its policy of apartheid. In 1994, Nelson Mandela becomes South Africa's first black president. ▶

1994 Fighting between Hutu and Tutsi ethnic groups in Rwanda leads to the massacre of more than 800,000 civilians.

1998-2004 Fighting in the Democratic Republic of the Congo involves 9 nations. About 4 million die, mostly from starvation and disease. While the war is officially over by 2003, fighting continues.

▼ **2006** Ellen Johnson-Sirleaf becomes president of Liberia, and Africa's first elected female leader.

2008 Conflict that began in 2003 continues in the Darfur region of Sudan.

A savanna in Kenya

3500 B.C. People settle in the Indus River Valley of India and Pakistan and the Yellow River Valley of China.

2500 B.C. Cities of Mohenjo-Daro and Harappa in Pakistan become centers of trade and farming.

Around 1523 B.C. Shang peoples in China build walled towns and use a kind of writing based on pictures. This writing develops into the writing Chinese people use today.

Around 1050 B.C. Chou peoples in China overthrow the Shang and control large territories.

563 B.C. Siddhartha Gautama is born in India. He becomes known as the Buddha—the "Enlightened One"—and is the founder of the Buddhist religion (Buddhism).

551 B.C. The Chinese philosopher Confucius is born. His teachings—especially rules about how people should treat each other— spread throughout China and are still followed today.

320–232 B.C.

• Northern India is united under the emperor Chandragupta Maurya.

• Asoka, emperor of India, sends Buddhist missionaries throughout southern Asia to spread the Buddhist religion.

221 B.C. The Chinese begin building the Great Wall. Its main section is more than 2,000 miles long and is meant to keep invading peoples out.

202 B.C. The Han people of China win control of all of China.

A.D. 320 The Gupta Empire controls northern India. The Guptas, who are Hindus, drive the Buddhist religion out of India. They are well known for their many advances in mathematics and medicine.

618 The Tang dynasty begins in China. The Tang dynasty is well known for music, poetry, and painting. They export silk and porcelains as far away as Africa.

THE SILK ROAD Around 100 B.C., only the Chinese knew how to make silk. To get this light, comfortable material, Europeans sent fortunes in glass, gold, jade, and other items to China. The exchanges between Europeans and Chinese created one of the greatest trading routes in history—the Silk Road. Chinese inventions such as paper and gunpowder were also spread via the Silk Road. Europeans found out how to make silk around A.D. 500, but trade continued until about 1400.

960 The Northern Sung dynasty in China makes advances in banking and paper money. China's population of 50 million doubles over 200 years, thanks to improved ways of farming that lead to greater food production.

The Forbidden City

ASIA

1000 The Samurai, a warrior people, become powerful in Japan. They live by a code of honor known as *Bushido*. ▶

1180 The Khmer Empire in Cambodia becomes widely known for its beautiful temples.

1206 The Mongol leader Genghis Khan creates an empire that stretches from China to India, Russia, and Eastern Europe.

1264 Kublai Khan, grandson of Genghis Khan, rules China as emperor from his new capital at Beijing.

1368 The Ming dynasty comes to power in China. The Ming drive the Mongols out of the country.

1526 The Mughal Empire in India begins under Babur. The Mughals are Muslims who invade and conquer India.

1644 The Ming dynasty in China is overthrown by the Manchu peoples.

1839 The Opium War takes place in China between the Chinese and the British. The British and other Western powers want to control trade in Asia. The Chinese want the British to stop selling opium to the Chinese. Britain wins the war in 1842.

1858 The French begin to take control of Indochina (Southeast Asia).

1868 In Japan, Emperor Meiji comes to power. Western ideas begin to influence the Japanese.

THE JAPANESE IN ASIA Japan became a powerful country during the early 20th century. In the 1930s, Japan began to invade some of its neighbors. In 1941, the United States and Japan went to war after Japan attacked the U.S. Navy at Pearl Harbor, Hawaii.

▼ *Statues from Angkor Wat temple, Cambodia*

1945 Japan is defeated in World War II after the U.S. drops atomic bombs on the Japanese cities of Hiroshima and Nagasaki.

1947 India and Pakistan become independent from Great Britain.

1949 China comes under the rule of the Communists led by Mao Zedong. The Communist government abolishes private property and takes over all businesses. ▶

1950–1953 THE KOREAN WAR North Korea, a Communist country, invades South Korea. The U.S. and other nations join to fight the invasion. China joins North Korea. The fighting ends in 1953. Neither side wins.

1954–1975 THE VIETNAM WAR The French are defeated in Indochina in 1954 by Vietnamese nationalists. The U.S. sends troops in 1965 to fight on the side of South Vietnam against the Communists in the North. The U.S. withdraws in 1973. In 1975, South Vietnam is taken over by North Vietnam.

1989 Chinese students protest for democracy, but the protests are crushed by the army in Beijing's Tiananmen Square.

The 1990s Britain returns Hong Kong to China (1997). China builds its economy, but does not allow democracy.

The 2000s U.S.-led military action overthrows the Taliban regime in Afghanistan (2001) and seeks to root out terrorists there. North Korea admits it has been developing nuclear weapons, and Iran is believed to be developing them.

A powerful earthquake in the Indian Ocean in December 2004 sets off huge waves (tsunamis) that kill more than 226,000 people in Indonesia, Sri Lanka, and other countries.

An earthquake in central China kills more than 8,500 people in May 2008.

In August 2008, for the first time China hosts the Summer Olympic Games in Beijing.

4000 B.C. People in Europe start building monuments out of large stones called megaliths, such as Stonehenge in England.

2500 B.C.–1200 B.C.
The Minoans and the Mycenaeans
- People on the island of Crete (Minoans) in the Mediterranean Sea build great palaces and become sailors and traders.
- People from Mycenae invade Crete and destroy the power of the Minoans.

THE TROJAN WAR The Trojan War was a conflict between invading Greeks and the people of Troas (Troy) in Southwestern Turkey around 1200 B.C. Although little is known today about the real war, it has become a part of Greek mythology (pages 144-145). According to legend, a group of Greek soldiers hid inside a huge wooden horse. The horse was pulled into the city of Troy. Then the soldiers jumped out of the horse and conquered Troy.

900-600 B.C. Celtic peoples in Northern Europe settle on farms and in villages and learn to mine for iron ore.

600 B.C. Etruscan peoples take over most of Italy. They build many cities and become traders.

SOME ACHIEVEMENTS OF THE GREEKS
The early Greeks were responsible for
- the first governments that were elected by people,
- great poets such as Homer, who composed the *Iliad* and the *Odyssey*,
- great thinkers such as Socrates, Plato, and Aristotle,
- great architecture, like the Parthenon and the Temple of Athena Nike on the Acropolis in Athens.

▲ *Socrates*

431 B.C. The Peloponnesian Wars begin between the Greek cities of Athens and Sparta. The wars end in 404 B.C. when Sparta wins.

338 B.C. King Philip II of Macedonia in northern Greece conquers all of Greece.

336 B.C. Philip's son Alexander the Great becomes king. He makes an empire from the Mediterranean Sea to India. For the next 300 years, Greek culture dominates this vast area.

264 B.C.– A.D. 476
THE ROMAN EMPIRE
The city of Rome in Italy begins to expand and capture surrounding lands. The Romans gradually build a great empire and control all of the Mediterranean region. At its height, the Roman Empire includes Western Europe, Greece, Egypt, and much of the Middle East. It lasts until A.D. 476.

Stonehenge

ROMAN ACHIEVEMENTS

- Roman law; Many of our laws are based on Roman law.
- Great roads to connect their huge empire; The Appian Way, south of Rome, is a Roman road that is still in use today.
- Aqueducts to bring water to the people in large cities;
- Great sculpture; Roman statues can still be seen in Europe
- Great architecture; The Colosseum, which still stands in Rome today, is an example.
- Great writers, such as the poet Virgil, who wrote the *Aeneid*.

49 B.C. A civil war breaks out that destroys Rome's republican form of government.

45 B.C. Julius Caesar becomes the sole ruler of Rome but is murdered one year later by rivals.

27 B.C. Octavian becomes the first emperor of Rome. He takes the name Augustus. A peaceful period of almost 200 years begins.

THE CHRISTIAN FAITH

Christians believe that Jesus Christ is the Son of God. The history and beliefs of Christianity are found in the New Testament of the Bible. Christianity spread slowly throughout the Roman Empire. The Romans tried to stop the new religion and persecuted the Christians. They were forced to hold their services in hiding, and some were crucified. Eventually, more and more Romans became Christian.

▲ *A painting of Jesus Christ*

THE BYZANTINE EMPIRE, centered in modern-day Turkey, was the eastern half of the old Roman Empire. Byzantine rulers extended their power into western Europe; the Byzantine Emperor Justinian ruled parts of Spain, North Africa, and Italy. Constantinople (now Istanbul, Turkey) became the capital of the Byzantine Empire in A.D. 330.

A.D. 313 The Roman Emperor Constantine gives full rights to Christians. He eventually becomes a Christian himself.

410 The Visigoths and other barbarian tribes from northern Europe invade the Roman Empire and begin to take over its lands.

▲ *Constantine*

476 The last Roman emperor, Romulus Augustus, is overthrown.

768 Charlemagne becomes king of the Franks in northern Europe. He rules a kingdom that includes parts of France, Germany, and northern Italy.

800 Feudalism becomes important in Europe. Feudalism means that poor farmers are allowed to farm a lord's land in return for certain services to the lord.

896 Magyar peoples found Hungary.

800s–900s Viking warriors and traders from Scandinavia begin to move into the British Isles, France, and parts of the Mediterranean.

989 The Russian state of Kiev becomes Christian.

▼ *The Colosseum, Rome*

1066 William of Normandy, a Frenchman, successfully invades England and makes himself king. He is known as William the Conqueror.

1096–1291 THE CRUSADES In 1096, Christian leaders send a series of armies to try to capture Jerusalem from the Muslims. In the end, the Christians do not succeed. However, trade increases greatly between the Middle East and Europe.

1215 The Magna Carta is a document agreed to by King John of England and the English nobility. The English king agrees that he does not have absolute power and has to obey the laws of the land. The Magna Carta is an important step toward democracy.

▲ *King John*

1290 The Ottoman Empire begins. It is controlled by Turkish Muslims who conquer lands in the eastern Mediterranean and the Middle East.

1337 The Hundred Years' War begins in Europe between France and England. The war lasts until 1453 when France wins.

1348 The bubonic plague (Black Death) begins in Europe. As much as one-third of the whole population of Europe dies from this disease, caused by the bite of infected fleas.

1453 The Ottoman Turks capture the city of Constantinople and rename it Istanbul.

1517 THE REFORMATION The Protestant Reformation splits European Christians apart. It starts when German priest Martin Luther breaks away from the Roman Catholic pope.

▲ *Martin Luther*

1534 King Henry VIII of England breaks away from the Roman Catholic church. He names himself head of the English (Anglican) church.

1558 The reign of King Henry's daughter Elizabeth I begins in England.

1588 The Spanish Armada (fleet of warships) is defeated by the English Navy as Spain tries to invade England.

1600s The Ottoman Turks expand their empire through most of eastern and central Europe.

1618 Much of Europe is destroyed in the Thirty Years' War, which ends in 1648.

1642 The English Civil War begins. King Charles I fights against the forces of the Parliament. The king is defeated, and executed in 1649. His son, Charles II, returns as king in 1660.

1789 THE FRENCH REVOLUTION The French Revolution ends the rule of kings in France and leads to democracy there. At first, however, there are wars and times when dictators take control. Many people are executed. King Louis XVI and Queen Marie Antoinette are overthrown in the Revolution, and both are executed in 1793.

◀ *Arc de Triomphe, Paris*

1762 Catherine the Great becomes Empress of Russia. She extends the Russian Empire.

1799 Napoleon Bonaparte, an army officer, becomes dictator of France. Under his rule, France conquers most of Europe by 1812.

1815 Napoleon's forces are defeated by the British and German armies at Waterloo (in Belgium). Napoleon is exiled to a remote island and dies there in 1821.

1848 Revolutions break out in countries of Europe. People force their rulers to make more democratic changes.

1914–1918 WORLD WAR I IN EUROPE
At the start of World War I in Europe, Germany, Austria-Hungary, and the Ottoman Empire oppose England, France, Russia, and, later, the U.S. (the Allies). The Allies win in 1918.

▼ *Tsar Nicholas II*

1917 The czar is overthrown in the Russian Revolution. The Bolsheviks (Communists) under Vladimir Lenin take control. Millions are starved, sent to labor camps, or executed under Joseph Stalin (1929-1953).

THE RISE OF HITLER Adolf Hitler became dictator of Germany in 1933. He joined forces with rulers in Italy and Japan to form the Axis powers. In World War II (1939-1945), the Axis powers were defeated by the Allies—Great Britain, the Soviet Union, and the U.S. During his rule, Hitler's Nazis killed millions of Jews and other people in the Holocaust.

▲ *Italy's Benito Mussolini and Adolf Hitler*

The 1990s Communist governments in Eastern Europe are replaced by democratic ones. Divided Germany becomes one nation, and the Soviet Union breaks up. The European Union (EU) forms. The North Atlantic Treaty Organization (NATO) bombs Yugoslavia in an effort to protect Albanians driven out of the Kosovo region.

2005 Riots in Paris suburbs express the discontent of France's large minority Muslim population, which numbers 5-6 million.

2007 Bulgaria and Romania join the EU, bringing the number of EU nations to 27.

All About >> AUSTRALIA

Australian aborigines (native peoples) have lived there for more than 60,000 years. In the 17th century, Portuguese, Dutch, and Spanish expeditions explored Australian coasts. In the 1770s, Capt. James Cook of Britain made three voyages to the continent, cementing Britain's claims of ownership. On May 13, 1787, Capt. Arthur Phillip brought 11 ships from Britain, carrying convicts and guards. Although the first communities were prison colonies, regular immigrants settled around the continent over the 19th century. Wool and mining were major industries. Australia was established as a commonwealth of Great Britain on January 1, 1901. Today, Australia is a country of more than 20 million people. It is famous for exotic animals like kangaroos and koalas. It is also the home of actors Russell Crowe and Nicole Kidman. The Sydney Opera House is a world-famous landmark.

Sydney Opera House ▶

THE AMERICAS

10,000-8000 B.C. People in North and South America gather plants for food and hunt animals using stone-pointed spears.

Around 3000 B.C. People in Central America begin farming, growing corn and beans for food.

1500 B.C. Mayan people in Central America begin to live in small villages.

500 B.C. People in North America begin to hunt buffalo to use for meat and for clothing.

100 B.C. The city of Teotihuacán is founded in Mexico. It becomes the center of a huge empire extending from central Mexico to Guatemala. Teotihuacán contains many large pyramids and temples.

A.D. 150 Mayan people in Guatemala build many centers for religious ceremonies. They create a calendar and learn mathematics and astronomy.

900 Toltec warriors in Mexico begin to invade lands of Mayan people. Mayans leave their old cities and move to the Yucatan Peninsula of Mexico.

1000 Native Americans in the southwestern United States begin to live in settlements called pueblos. They learn to farm.

1325 Mexican Indians known as Aztecs create the huge city of Tenochtitlán and rule a large empire in Mexico. They are warriors who practice human sacrifice.

1492 Christopher Columbus sails from Europe across the Atlantic Ocean and lands in the Bahamas, in the Caribbean Sea. This marked the first step toward the founding of European settlements in the Americas.

Christopher ▲
Columbus

1500 Portuguese explorers reach Brazil and claim it for Portugal.

1519 Spanish conqueror Hernán Cortés travels into the Aztec Empire in search of gold. The Aztecs are defeated in 1521 by Cortés. The Spanish take control of Mexico. ▶

WHY DID THE SPANISH WIN? How did the Spanish defeat the powerful Aztec Empire in such a short time? One reason is that the Spanish had better weapons. Another is that many Aztecs died from diseases brought to the New World by the Spanish. The Aztecs had never had these illnesses before, and so did not have immunity to them. Also, many neighboring Indians hated the Aztecs as conquerors and helped the Spanish to defeat them.

1534 Jacques Cartier of France explores Canada.

1583 The first English colony in Canada is set up in Newfoundland.

1607 English colonists led by Captain John Smith settle in Jamestown, Virginia. Virginia was the oldest of the Thirteen Colonies that turned into the United States.

1619 First African slaves arrive in English-controlled America.

1682 The French explorer René Robert Cavelier, sieur de La Salle, sails down the Mississippi River. The area is named Louisiana after the French King Louis XIV.

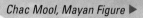

Chac Mool, Mayan Figure ▶

THE AMERICAS

EUROPEAN COLONIES By 1700, most of the Americas are under the control of Europeans.

Spain: Florida, southwestern United States, Mexico, Central America, western South America

Portugal: eastern South America

France: central United States, parts of Canada

England: eastern U.S., parts of Canada

Holland: eastern U.S., West Indies, eastern South America

1700s European colonies in North and South America grow in population and wealth.

1775-1783 AMERICAN REVOLUTION The American Revolution begins in 1775 when the first shot is fired in Lexington, Massachusetts. The thirteen original British colonies in North America become independent under the Treaty of Paris, signed in 1783.

SIMÓN BOLÍVAR: LIBERATOR OF SOUTH AMERICA In 1810, Simón Bolívar began a revolt against Spain. He fought against the Spanish and in 1924 became president of the independent country of Greater Colombia. As a result of his leadership, ten South American countries became independent from Spain by 1830.

1810-1910 MEXICO'S REVOLUTION In 1846, Mexico and the United States go to war. Mexico loses parts of the Southwest and California to the U.S. A revolution in 1910 overthrows Porfirio Díaz.

Porfirio Diaz ▶

Becoming Independent

Most countries of Latin America gained independence from Spain in the early 1800s. Others weren't liberated until much later.

COUNTRY	YEAR OF INDEPENDENCE
Argentina	1816
Bolivia	1825
Brazil	1822[1]
Chile	1818
Colombia	1819
Ecuador	1822
Guyana	1966[2]
Mexico	1821
Paraguay	1811
Peru	1824
Suriname	1975[3]
Uruguay	1825
Venezuela	1821

[1] from Portugal [2] from Britain [3] from the Netherlands

1867 The Canadian provinces are united as the Dominion of Canada.

1898 THE SPANISH-AMERICAN WAR Spain and the U.S. fight a brief war in 1898. Spain loses its colonies Cuba, Puerto Rico, and the Philippines.

U.S. POWER IN THE 1900s During the 1900s, the U.S. sent troops to various countries, including Mexico (1914; 1916–1917), Nicaragua (1912–1933), Haiti (1915–1934; 1994–1995), and Panama (1989). In 1962, the U.S. went on alert when the Soviet Union put missiles on Cuba.

1994 The North American Free Trade Agreement (NAFTA) increases trade between the U.S., Canada, and Mexico.

2001 Radical Muslim terrorists crash planes into U.S. targets, killing about 3,000 people; the U.S. launches a "war on terrorism."

2003 U.S.-led forces invade Iraq and overthrow the regime of Saddam Hussein.

2007 With a population of about 12 million unauthorized migrants, the U.S. debates immigration reform.

THEN & NOW

10 Years Ago–1998

Then: The House impeaches President Bill Clinton for lying under oath and concealing information. He is acquitted by the Senate in 1999.

Now: After leaving office in 2001, President Clinton writes a best-selling book and works hard to promote aid for humanitarian issues around the world. His wife, Hillary Rodham Clinton, is a U.S. senator.

Then: For the first time ever, scientists in Britain and the U.S. map the genome of a polycellular organism, a worm.

Now: Scientists map the entire human genome. Now, they can study genes for information about disease.

50 Years Ago–1958

Then: The first successful American satellite, *Explorer 1*, is launched. Congress approves creation of the National Aeronautics and Space Administration (NASA) in October.

Now: Americans land on the moon in 1969 and send many different satellites and rockets into space to explore our solar system. Today, new ships are being built to take more people to the moon, and more probes will be sent to the surface of Mars.

Then: National Airlines operates the first domestic jet passenger service in the U.S., between New York and Miami.

Now: U.S. airlines carry more than 600 million passengers on domestic flights each year.

100 Years Ago–1908

▲Then: Wilbur and Orville Wright fulfill a contract with the U.S. Army Signal Corps to produce a plane that can fly for 10 minutes at a speed of 40 miles per hour.

Now: NASA's X-43A scramjet is the fastest unmanned, jet-powered aircraft, flying at about Mach 9.6, or nearly 7,000 mph.

Then: Henry Ford produces the first Model T, a low-cost car that will later be made on a factory assembly line. Ford sells 15 million Model Ts.

Now: More than 136 million cars are registered in America. In 2007, Ford had two models of hybrid (gasoline-electric) cars on the market and three more in development.

Then: U.S. President Theodore Roosevelt creates the U.S. Army Reserve.

Now: The U.S. Army Reserve is made up of more than 189,000 troops and is playing a major role in the war in Iraq.

500 Years Ago–1508

In 1508, Roman Catholic Pope Julius II asks Michelangelo to paint the ceiling of the Sistine Chapel in Rome. It takes Michelangelo four years to finish it, but today the ceiling is still a masterpiece. In 1989, a 10-year restoration of the painting is completed.

THEN & NOW FROM 2009

10 Years Ago–1999

Then: After overcoming cancer, Lance Armstrong wins his first Tour de France, the world's best-known bicycle race. He goes on to win the race a record seven times, from 1999 to 2005.

Now: In September 2008, Armstrong announces he will come out of retirement in an attempt to compete in the 2009 Tour de France.

Then: On December 31, the US turns over the administration of the Panama Canal to the Panamanian Government. Completed by the United States in 1914, the Panama Canal is 48 miles long and joins the Pacific and Atlantic Oceans.

Now: In 2007, Panama breaks ground to expand the Canal with a third set of locks. The project should be complete between 2014 and 2015.

50 Years Ago–1959

Then: Alaska and Hawaii are admitted as the 49th and 50th states in the United States.

Now: Both states have their first women governors: Sarah Palin, Governor of Alaska, and Linda Lingle, Governor of Hawaii. Governor Sarah Palin runs as the Vice-Presidential candidate for the Republican Party.

Then: Fidel Castro comes to power in Cuba.

Now: Castro is the leader of Cuba until February 2008. His brother Raul Castro is chosen as his successor as President of Cuba.

100 Years Ago–1909

Then: The National Association for the Advancement of Colored People (NAACP) is founded on February 12, Lincoln's birthday. Led by W. E. B. Du Bois, the NAACP includes both prominent black and white intellectuals.

Now: As one of its guiding mission objectives, the NAACP continues to work "to ensure the political, educational, social, and economic equality of all citizens."

Then: Einar Dessau of Denmark becomes the first ham radio operator to broadcast using a short-wave radio transmitter.

Now: Amateur radio, or "ham radio," continues to be a popular hobby throughout the world. Radio amateurs have access to a range of wave bands that allow them to transmit and communicate with each other.

Then: Karl Landsteiner discoveres that all blood is not alike. He classifies blood into four main groups, or types: A, B, AB, and O. Landsteiner wins the Nobel Prize in Medicine for this discovery in 1930.

Now: Blood tests are used to test for a wide variety of conditions, including infection, cholesterol levels, and disease.

500 Years Ago–1509

In 1509, at the age of 17, Henry VIII became the King of England. He is one of England's most famous kings. Henry's divorce from his first wife led to the formation of his own church, the Church of England. He eventually had six wives, two of whom he had executed. His daughter with Anne Boleyn (his second wife), Elizabeth I, eventually succeeded her father and became one of the most powerful monarchs in England.

Henry VIII remains a popular figure in film and television. He is portrayed in *The Other Boleyn Girl*, a film from 2008, and the TV series *Tudors* from 2007.

331

WOMEN IN HISTORY

The following women played important roles in shaping some of history's biggest events.

CLEOPATRA
(69-30 B.C.), queen of Egypt famous for her association with Roman leaders Julius Caesar and Mark Antony. After her father's death, Cleopatra, at the age of about 17, and her 12-year-old brother Ptolemy jointly ruled. By custom, they were forced to marry each other. A few years later, she was sent away, but came back to rule when Caesar defeated her enemies. For a time, she lived with Caesar in Rome until his assassination in 44 B.C. She later went back to Egypt, where she met and married Antony.

JOAN OF ARC
(1412-1431), heroine and patron saint of France, known as the Maid of Orléans. She led French troops to a big victory over the English in the Battle of Orléans (1429), a turning point in the Hundred Years' War. Joan believed she was guided by voices from God, and she dressed like a male soldier. In 1431, she was burned at the stake as a heretic. The Catholic Church later declared her innocent, and she was made a saint in 1920. She is the subject of many monuments, paintings, and works of literature.

CATHERINE THE GREAT
(1729-1796), empress of Russia (1762-1796). Catherine made Russia a European power and greatly expanded the territory of the Russian Empire. She raised the status of the nobles by granting them privileges such as freedom from military service and legal control over their serfs. She promoted culture as well as the education of women and religious tolerance.

SOJOURNER TRUTH
(c. 1797-1883), abolitionist and women's rights activist (born Isabella Baumfree). She was raised as a slave on an estate in upstate New York. She escaped in 1826. In 1843, she became a traveling preacher and took the name Sojourner Truth. She traveled widely, speaking out against slavery and for women's rights. Her famous speech, "Ain't I a Woman?" was about how women were as smart and strong as men.

FLORENCE NIGHTINGALE
(1820-1910), British nurse and founder of modern nursing. She was a superintendent of female nurses during the Crimean War in Turkey, where she trained nurses and helped set up field hospitals, saving many lives. In 1860 she founded the first professional nursing school, at Saint Thomas's Hospital in London. In 1907, she became the first woman to receive the British Order of Merit.

HARRIET TUBMAN
(1821-1913), born Arminta Ross, escaped slavery when she was in her twenties. Before the Civil War, she repeatedly risked her life to lead hundreds of slaves to freedom by way of a network of homes and churches called the "Underground Railroad." During her nineteen trips back into the south, none of the fugitive slaves she guided was ever captured. She became known as the "Moses of her people" for her courage. During the Civil War, Tubman acted as a scout, spy, and nurse for the Union troops in South Carolina.

MARIE CURIE (1867-1934), Polish-French physical chemist known for discovering the radioactive element radium, which is used to treat some diseases. She also discovered the rare element polonium (named after Poland, her country of birth). She won the Nobel Prize for chemistry in 1911. She and her husband, Pierre Curie, also won the Nobel Prize for physics in 1903 for their work on radiation. Sadly, her work led to her death—she died from radiation poisoning.

BILLIE JEAN KING (born 1943), American tennis player who became a symbol for women's equality. King won 12 Grand Slam singles titles. But her most famous victory may have been in

the 1973 "Battle of the Sexes" match, when she beat male player Bobby Riggs in three straight sets. King helped start the first women's pro tennis tour in 1970. In 1971, she became the first woman athlete to win more than $100,000 in one season.

ANNE FRANK (1929-1945), young German born Jewish girl whose diary of her family's two years in hiding--in the back rooms of an Amersterdam office

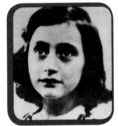

building--during the German occupation of The Netherlands, became a worldwide classic in literature. The Gestapo arrested the occupants of the secret annex after acting on a tip. Frank died in the Bergen-Belsen concentration camp in 1945. Her diary was saved by office worker Miep Gies and presented to Frank's father Otto when he was the only family member to return from the camps. Published in 1947 as Het Achterhuis (The House Behind), it appearred in the U.S. in 1952 as Anne Frank: The Diary of a Young Girl.

JODY WILLIAMS (born 1950) Activist who helped found the International Campaign to Ban Landmines. A landmine is a weapon which is placed in the ground and explodes when triggered by a vehicle or person. More than 15,000 people are injured or killed by landmines each year. Williams travels the world, speaking about how landmines kill and injure innocent civilians and working with governments to create a worldwide ban. Williams and her organization won the 1997 Nobel Peace Prize for their work.

VALENTINA TERESHKOVA (born 1937), Russian cosmonaut and the first woman in space. During her 3-day spaceflight in June 1963 aboard the *Vostok 6,* she orbited Earth 48 times. Five months later, she married cosmonaut Andrian Nikolayev. In 1964, she gave birth to a daughter, the first child born to parents who had both flown in space.

▲ **DR. MAE JEMISON** (born 1956) The first African American woman to go into space. She flew on the 1992 space shuttle *Endeavour* as a science mission specialist. She was born in Decatur, Alabama, and grew up in Chicago, Illinois. Dr. Jemison is a medical doctor who also has degrees in chemical engineering and African and African-American studies.

ANSWERS

Buildings Quiz, p. 64

1. Eiffel Tower
2. The Great Sphinx
3. Transamerica Pyramid Building
4. Stonehenge
5. Space Needle

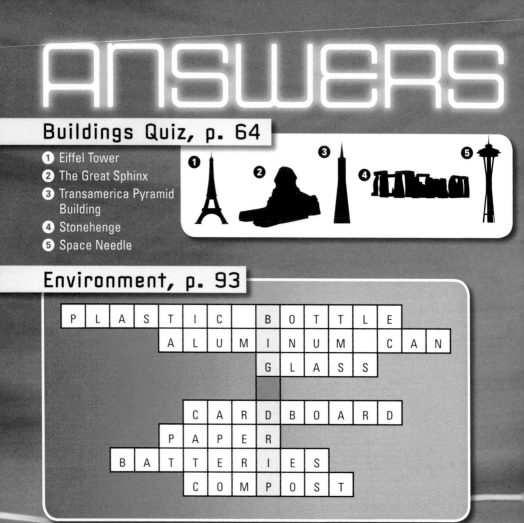

Environment, p. 93

	P	L	A	S	T	I	C		B	O	T	T	L	E		
			A	L	U	M	I	N	U	M		C	A	N	
						G	L	A	S	S					
				C	A	R	D	B	O	A	R	D			
			P	A	P	E	R								
	B	A	T	T	E	R	I	E	S						
			C	O	M	P	O	S	T						

Matching Game, p. 97

Lederhosen (short pants with suspenders): **Germany**

Pien-fu (2-piece robe): **China**

Kikoi (sarong-type skirt): **Uganda**

Chamanto (knee-length poncho): **Chile**

Kamiks (watertight boots): **Arctic Inuit people**

Kaftan (belted shirt-dress): **Morocco**

Jokes and Riddles, p. 124-125

1 The President **2** One combined bale **3** Your eardrum **4** Add a g and it's gone. **5** Your lap **6** You take your feet off the floor. **7** For beating the eggs **8** They're both the capital of England. **9** It gets wet. **10** It's too far to walk. **11** Language **12** Don't look, I'm changing. **13** The shoppers are a woman, her daughter, and her granddaughter. **14** Grow older **15** A hole **16** With an asteroid belt **17** Your word **18** A newspaper **19** A garbage truck **20** Any dog—skyscrapers can't jump. **21** The letter M **22** To measure how long he slept. **23** Your breath **24** I'm telling motherboard on you. **25** Because if they flew over a bay, they would be bagels! **26** One **27** All of them **28** His breath **29** Nine **30** Because he's living. **31** Mississippi **32** Umbrellas **33** A bird that gets up at the quack of dawn! **34** Nightmares **35** Time to get a new fence. **36** When it turns into a driveway. **37** A chair **38** You're the bus driver, how old are you? **39** There are no stairs, it's a one-story house. **40** A Whale of a Tale

Roman Numerals, p. 191

2009 = MMIX

50,000 = MMMMMMMMMMMMMMMMMMMMMMMMMMMMMMMMMMMMMMMMMMMMM
MMMMMMMMMMMMMMMM

Word Connect, p. 125

Movies & TV Match-Up, p. 137

Mac & Blooregard: *Foster's Home for Imaginary Friends*

Katara & Sokka: *Avatar: The Last Airbender*

Will & Elizabeth: *Pirates of the Caribbean*

Tony and Pepper: *Ironman*

Susan & Reed: *Fantastic Four*

Sophie & Calcifer: *Howl's Moving Castle*

Alex & Justin: *Wizards of Waverly Place*

Quinn & Lola: *Zoey 101*

Sudoku, p. 193

9	2	7	8	5	1	3	6	4
6	8	1	4	7	3	5	9	2
5	4	3	2	9	6	7	8	1
7	9	5	6	3	2	4	1	8
1	6	8	7	4	5	2	3	9
2	3	4	9	1	8	6	5	7
8	1	2	3	6	7	9	4	5
3	5	9	1	2	4	8	7	6
4	7	6	5	8	9	1	2	3

Sports Scramble, p. 248

Texas Rangers: **Josh Hamilton**

Orlando Magic: **Dwight Howard**

Minnesota Vikings: **Adrian Peterson**

New England Patriots: **Tedy Bruschi**

Los Angeles Sparks: **Candace Parker**

INDEX

Photo Credits

This product/publication includes images from Artville, Comstock, Corbis Royalty-Free, Corel Stock Photo Library, Digital Stock, Digital Vision, EyeWire Images, IndexOpen.com, Ingram Publishing, One Mile Up Inc., PhotoDisc, Rubberball Productions, which are protected by the copyright laws of the U.S., Canada, and elsewhere. Used under license.

FRONT COVER: (l) ©2008 Kathy Hutchins/Hutchins/drr.net; (c) © Frans Lanting/Minden Pictures; (r) AP Images. **BACK COVER**: (tl) Olaru Radian-Alexandru/Shutterstock.com; (l) reggieworld.com/Jupiter Images; (r) Superstock; (bl) Jeff Hinds/Shutterstock.com. **03**: Wii Wheel: Norman Chan/Shutterstock;Tyra Banks: AP Images; Calendar: MalDix/Shutterstock.com. **04**: Sheet Music: atanasija1/Shutterstock.com. **05**: Manuel Fernandes/Shutterstock.com. **06**: (t) AP Images; (b) Steve Broer/Shutterstock.com; (t) AP Images;(b) Frontpage/Shutterstock.com. **07**: AP Images. **09**: (r) AP Images; (l) AP Images. **10**: (t) AP Images; (b) Joe Raedle/Getty Images. **12**: Mark Wilson/Getty Images. **13**: (tl) AP Images; (br) David McNew/Getty Images. **12-13**: Alex Wong/Getty Images. **14**: (t) AP Images; (br) LWA/Dann Tardif/Getty Images. **15**: AP Photo/Douglas C. Pizac. **14-15**: Alex Wong/Getty Images. **18**: (bkgd) AP Images. **20**: (t) AP Photo/Litboy; (b)Mark Sullivan/WireImage. **21**: (l) AP Photo/Dan Steinberg (b) Heidi Gutman/NBC NewsWire via AP Images; (t) Business Wire via Getty Images; (bkgd) Supplied by FilmStills.net. **22**: (b) Supplied by FilmStills.net. **23**: (t) Supplied by Capital Pictures. **24**: (b) Supplied by Capital Pictures. **25**: (b) Supplied by Capital Pictures. **24-25**: (bkgd) Supplied by Capital Pictures. **26**: (tl) AP Photo/Bill Kostroun; (b) AP Photo/Evan Agostini. **27**: George Napolitano/FilmMagic/Getty Images. **28**: (bl) AP Photo/Nati Harnik; (r) Evan Pinkus/Getty Images. **29**: (t) AP Photo/Steve Holland; (b) AP Photo/Denis Poroy. **30**: (b) Stephanie Himango/NBC NewsWire via AP Images; (bkgd) Eric Gay/Pool/Getty Images. **31**: (t) George Pimentel/WireImage/Getty Images; (b) Kristian Dowling/Getty Images. **32**: (t) Norbert Wu; (br) Michael Pettigrew/Shutterstock; (bl) © 2008 Jupiterimages Corporation. **36**: © 2008 Jupiterimages Corporation; **37**: (t) Jurie Maree/Shutterstock; (cl) susan flashman/Shutterstock; (cr) Pichugin Dmitry/Shutterstock; **39**: (t) Angelina Dimitrova/Shutterstock; (b) nialat/Shutterstock; (c) Jason Kasumovic/Shutterstock; (bkgd) Yellowj/Shutterstock; **40**: Donald Gargano/Shutterstock. **41**: Darren Green/Shutterstock. **42**: © 2008 Jupiterimages Corporation. **43**: (tl) iofoto/Shutterstock. **45**: (tc) © SuperStock, Inc./SuperStock ; (bc) "Poppy",Georgia O'Keefe, 1927. Courtesy of the Museum Of Fine Arts, St. Petersburg. **48**: (tl) Consolidated News Pictures/Hulton Archive/Getty Images; (b) AP Photo/Carlo Allegri; (r) Department of Labor. **48-51**: Hallgerd/Shutterstock.com. **49**: (tc) Alan C. Heison/Shutterstock; (bl) Courtesy of the Library of Congress,LC-USZ62-49568; (br) AP Photo/Bill Kostroun. **50**: (tr) Chad Buchanan/Getty Images; (tl) PHIL MCCARTEN/UPI /Landov; (b) Courtesy of the Library of Congress, LC-USZ62-53017. **51**: (bl) AP Photo/ Jackie Johnston; (t) Department of State; (br) Courtesy of the Library of Congress, LC-USZ62-108565. **52**: (bkgd) Heiko Rothe/Shutterstock.com; (br) Courtesy of Edward A.Thomas. **54**: (bl) Courtesy of Hachette Book Group USA. **55**: (tl) John Chillingworth/Picture Post/Getty Images; (bl) AP Photo/Al Grillo. **56**: (br) Jacket Cover from TALES OF A FOURTH GRADE NOTHING by Judy Blume. Used by permission of Random House Children's Books, a division of Random House Inc.; (bl) Cover Illustration Copyright © 1989 by Daniel Maffia. Used by Permission of HarperCollins Publishers; (tl) The House with the Clock in Its Walls by John Bellairs, illustrated by Edward Gorey. Used courtesy of Penguin Books for Young Readers; (tr) Book Cover from THE LITTLE PRINCE by Antoine de Saint-Exupery, copyright 1943 by Harcourt, Inc. and renewed 1971 by Consuelo de Saint-Exupery, English translation copyright © 2000 by Richard Howard, reproduced by permission of Houghton Mifflin Harcourt Publishing Company. **57**: (tr) "Diary of a Wimpy Kid" by Jeff Kiney; (cr) Cover from LINCOLN: A PHOTOBIOGRAPHY by Russell Freedman. Jacket copyright © 1987 by Houghton Mifflin Company. Reprinted by permission Calrion Books, an imprint of Houghton Mifflin Harcourt Publishing Company. All rights reserved. **58**: Library of Congress, LC-USZ62-10610. **60**: (tl) Shawn Kashou/Shutterstock.com. **61**: (bl) Courtesy of the Library of Congress, LC-USZ62-69629; (bl) Danilo Tee/Shutterstock. **58-61**: (bkgd) © 2008 Jupiterimages Corporation. **62**: (b) Neale Cousland/Shutterstock; (tl) 2008 Jupiterimages Corporation; (cr) Ron Blunt Photography. **63**: (tr) tamir niv/Shutterstock; (bl) Photodisc. **64**: (tl) Near and Far Photography/ Shutterstock; (bl) Stas Volik/Shutterstock; (tr,cr) © 2008 Jupiterimages Corporation. **66-67**: (bkgd) © 2008 Jupiterimages Corporation. **67**: (cr) Sergei Bachlakov/Shutterstock.com; (bl) © 2008 Jupiterimages Corporation. **68**: (t) Jun Xiao/Shutterstock.com; (b) Konstantin Sutyagin/Shutterstock. **69**: (tr) ©iStockphoto.com/Jill Fromer; (bl) Monkey Business Images/Shutterstock.com. **70**: (t) Peter Kirillov/ Shutterstock; (b) Monkey Business Images/Shutterstock.com. **71**: (tr) © 2008 Jupiterimages Corporation; (b) Tischenko Irina/Shutterstock.com. **72**: (tl) © 2008 Jupiterimages Corporation; (br) Norman Pogson/ Shutterstock.com. **73**: (tr) David Lee/Shutterstock.com; (cr) Kelpfish/Shutterstock. **74**: (bc) AP Photo; (tl) Courtesy of the Library of Congress, LC-USZ62-25166; (tr) AP Photo; (bkgd) © 2008 Jupiterimages Corporation. **74-75**: (bkgd) © 2008 Jupiterimages Corporation. **77**: (c) iStockphoto.com/Sean Martin. **80**: Naval Air Engineering Station (NAES) Lakehurst. **81**: (t) Library of Congress, LC-USZC4-10986; (br) National Oceanic and Atmospheric Administration/Department of Commerce. **83**: (t) ©iStockphoto.com/